Perspectives on Development

The political transformation of the Brazilian Catholic Church

)M

Perspectives on Development is organized by and edited from the Centre for Developing-Area Studies, McGill University, Montreal, Canada. The primary focus of the series is on economic, social and political development in third world countries. The series includes works of a broad, comparative and interpretive character as well as specific institutional and empirical studies which stem from research activities of the Centre. However, the series also includes other works judged by the Editors to be valuable contributions to our understanding of the development process.

Series Editors

R. Cranford Pratt, Professor of Political Science, University of
    Toronto, Chairman
John A. Barnes, Professor of Sociology, University of Cambridge
Irving Brecher, Professor of Economics, McGill University
B. Higgins, Professor of Economics, Université de Montréal
Peter C. W. Gutkind, Professor of Anthropology, McGill
    University
Kari Levitt, Associate Professor of Economics, McGill University
Richard F. Salisbury, Professor of Anthropology, McGill
    University

THE POLITICAL TRANSFORMATION OF THE BRAZILIAN CATHOLIC CHURCH

Thomas C. Bruneau
Associate Professor of Political Science, McGill University

Cambridge University Press

Published by the Syndics of the Cambridge University Press
Bentley House, 200 Euston Road, London NW1 2DB
American Branch: 32 East 57th Street, New York, N.Y.10022

© Cambridge University Press 1974

Library of Congress Catalogue Card Number: 73–79319

First published 1974

ISBN:
0 521 20256 6 hardcovers
0 521 09848 3 paperback

Text set in 10/11½ pt. Monotype Times New Roman,
printed by letterpress, and bound in Great Britain
at The Pitman Press, Bath

TO MY MOTHER AND FATHER

Contents

Tables

Preface and Acknowledgements

This book is a political study of a religious institution. As the study of religious institutions is infrequently a topic for political scientists, I think it proper to indicate in a few words why I have undertaken this task. I originally became interested in studying the Roman Catholic Church as the Second Vatican Council was nearing completion in 1965. Pope John XXIII was then dead but the forces unleashed within the Church were obvious and had become a subject for intense discussion. As a student of institutions I was sceptical about the degree to which the ferment of change within the Church would be reflected in structural modifications and new programs once the Council ended.

The ferment within the Latin American Churches, which was widely recognized for the first time in North America with the death of Pe. Camilo Torres in February 1966, has increased of late and it has become common for observers of the Latin American scene to refer to the Church as the fastest changing institution in the continent and to dramatic aspects of the religious drama currently being enacted there. Most commonly, the observers note the political as opposed to the exclusively religious nature of the changes and events. Indeed, it is almost impossible to find any point of change in the Latin American Churches which does not have obvious implications for politics. These religious institutions were founded with the societies and politics and have evolved equally haphazardly during the ensuing four and a half centuries. The Churches are so intricately linked with all features of these countries – from overall legitimation to education, to charity, to political pressure groups – that a change in any aspect is immediately recognized as a political fact. This book does describe the high and low points of the Brazilian religious drama with its political content, but I hope to accomplish far more. I am concerned with explaining why change is taking place in this historic institution, its direction and importance not only for the Church but also for the society and polity. In short, I present here a historical analysis of the Church as an institution, in which my main focus will be the Church in its political relations and the political importance of change.

The Catholic Churches in Latin America remained stable for so long that they were regarded as a constant and thus uninteresting for study. The historical and sociological studies available on these institutions in the twenty republics, not to mention comparative material, are minimal. Today, when the institutions are becoming more interesting, there is a spurt of largely journalistic accounts of events and personalities but still very few serious studies. Few hypotheses have been tested and even less material is available for establishing a pattern of study. My approach here is both by necessity and choice *sui generis*. By necessity because there is nothing else, and by choice because I want to approach the Church as a political scientist. I have no theological training, cannot claim to be a competent historian and am not at this point worried about generating broad theoretical propositions. This book is a study of change in one Latin American religious institution, yet with obvious theoretical implications. Since I have picked the religious institution of one country, Brazil, a few words are necessary on this choice.

Brazil is the most important country in Latin America. Today, after more than two decades of fits and starts, an industrial and capital infrastructure has been created which produced growth increases of some 9% for three consecutive years, 1969–71. As the government is fond of pointing out and as all the business reports indicate, Brazil is indeed on the move. In terms of size, the Catholic Church in Brazil is the largest in the world, with some 94% of the ninety million population formally declared of the faith. Historically, the Church in Brazil is similar to that in the other Latin American countries; if anything, it could serve as a prototype. Brazil is the world center of Spiritism, which is ironic for the world's largest Catholic country, and is also a fertile plot for Protestant conversion. Several Brazilian Church personalities are of continent-wide importance and in some cases of world renown. Innovation in the Church occurred first in Brazil and Chile on a number of important levels, and the Brazilian institution has played a significant role in socio-political change programs for almost two decades. However, the innovations in the Church have brought it into very serious conflict with the military dictatorship that has ruled the country since 1964 and, in the heat of this conflict, the Church has increasingly adopted a progressive political position. The Church is the only institutional opponent of the government and the number of bishops, priests, nuns and laymen who have suffered for their beliefs and actions are legion. The Church in Brazil is probably the most interesting example of change in a religious institution today, and politically the implications of this change are extremely important. While I doubt that the Churches in the other Latin American countries will follow the exact path of Brazil, I suspect that they will follow one of the various options that this Church has adopted during the century.

It would be impossible for me to give fair recognition to all those who have helped me since I began working on this study some six years ago. Originally I presented the work as a PhD thesis in the Department of Political Science at the University of California, Berkeley. The chairman of the committee, Warren Ilchman, gave many valuable criticisms of the various drafts and at all times offered encouragement, whether it was deserved or not. Ivan Vallier first introduced me to the fascination and importance of studying religious institutions and all but directed me in making this study more than a descriptive story. His work on the Church in Latin America is the best being carried out today and I suspect that more than a little of the 'discovery' I have achieved here really belongs to him. Thomas Sanders of the American Universities Field Staff (AUFS) offered not only initial information and encouragement but a continuing flow of material, as well as the stimulus of a long series of often excellent studies on politics and the Churches in Latin America.

Denis Goulet gave accurate criticisms on a cumbersome manuscript which enabled me to recreate the work for a wider audience. It was Rosalind E. Boyd who further refined the text through her valuable editorial skills. Zeno Santiago helped me in the translation of the Portuguese originals. Lana Coviensky typed the final manuscript with excellent speed and accuracy.

I originally visited Brazil for fourteen months in 1967–8, with a National Defense Foreign Language grant administered by the University of California. The Institute of International Studies provided the funds and the conditions for writing the thesis and the Center for Latin American Studies, along with Hilgard O'Reilly Sternberg, provided the stimulus for making the thesis into a book by awarding me a recognition grant. I was enabled by the Canada Council to visit Brazil again in the Summer of 1970, so that the material contained herein is not only current but is also offered with some degree of confidence, as I found that my conclusions of two years before were fairly accurate.

Undoubtedly my greatest debt in this work is to the approximately two hundred Brazilians – bishops, priests, nuns, laymen, men of affairs, workers – who were willing to spend their often valuable time with an inquisitive foreigner. Due to their cooperation and kindness, I collected a great deal of material and enjoyed doing so. Initially, Pe. Affonso Gregory of Centro de Estatística Religiosa e Investigações Sociais (CERIS) and Frei Francisco Rolim provided sociological orientation, research information and contacts which proved to be most valuable. Frequent reference to their works in this book will reiterate my appreciation to them. Beyond these two men it is very unfortunate that I can offer only partial recognition. Given the present political situation in Brazil, anyone mentioned in this Acknowledgement might attract the attention of the police. Of the forty people I formally interviewed in the Summer of 1970 at least twenty had been in jail one or more times or had a relative in jail at that moment. If anyone doubts the political relevance of the Brazilian Catholic Church, he need only talk with some of those churchmen now suffering in prison for their understanding of the Gospel message. To those who assisted me so generously I can only say that I hope this book will indicate that their time was not in vain and that they may profit from the analysis of an outsider. I will be pleased if the book at least provides a foil against which they can sharpen their own analyses of the Church's responsibilities and options.

My family accepted more than any family should in the writing of this book. They made life in Brazil both richer and more pleasant, and during the writing in Berkeley and Montreal they tolerated my frequent periods of intolerance. To the little ones goes a reluctant admission that children do in fact make life far more interesting although chaotic. My wife Celia helped at various points in this work and typed the draft that was presented as a thesis. That I could maintain my momentum through several writings is due to her emotional support.

La Prairie, Quebec, Summer of 1972

Abbreviations

ACB	Ação Católica Brasileira
ACO	Ação Católica Operária
AEC	Associação de Educação Católica
AP	Ação Popular
ARENA	Aliança Nacional Renovadora
AUFS	American Universities Field Staff
CC	Comissão Central
CDN	Conselho Diretor Nacional
CEI	Centro Ecumênico de Informação
CELAM	Conselho do Episcopado Latino-Americano
CENFI	Centro de Formação Intercultural
CERIS	Centro de Estatística Religiosa e Investigações Sociais
CICOP	Catholic Inter-American Cooperation Program
CIDA	Comitê Interamericano de Desenvolvimento Agrícola
CNBB	Conferência Nacional dos Bispos do Brasil
CONTAG	Confederação Nacional dos Trabalhadores na Agricultura
CRB	Conferência dos Religiosos do Brasil
DOPS	Departamento de Ordem Política e Social
FNT	Frente Nacional do Trabalho
IBGE	Instituto Brasileiro de Geografia e Estatística
IBRA	Instituto Brasileira de Reforma Agrária
IBRADES	Instituto Brasileiro de Desenvolvimento
IDOC	*International Documentation on the Contemporary Church*
IFT	Instituto de Filosofia e Teologia
INDA	Instituto Nacional de Desenvolvimento Agrário
ISPAC	Instituto Superior Para Pastoral de Catequese
ISPAL	Instituto Superior Para Pastoral de Liturgia
ITER	Instituto de Teologia do Recife
JAC	Juventude Agrária Católica
JEC	Juventude Estudantil Católica
JIC	Juventude Independente Católica
JOC	Juventude Operária Católica
JUC	Juventude Universitária Católica
LADOC	Latin American Documentation
LEC	Liga Eleitoral Católica
MDB	Movimento Democrático Brasileiro
MEB	Movimento de Educação de Base
MFC	Movimento Familiar Cristão
MG	Minas Gerais
Msgr.	Monsignor
NIU	*Notícias da Igreja Universal*
O.F.M.	Franciscan
O.P.	Dominican (religious order)
OPENO	Operação Nordeste
PDC	Partido Democrata Cristão
Pe.	Padre
PMV	*Pro Mundi Vita*

PPC	Plano de Pastoral de Conjunto
PSD	Partido Social Democrático
PSP	Partido Social Progressista
PTB	Partido Trabalhista Brasileiro
REB	*Revista Eclesiástica Brasileira*
RN	Rio Grande do Norte
RS	Rio Grande do Sul
SAR	Serviço de Assistência Rural
SCAI	Serviço de Colaboração Apostólica Internacional
SEC	Serviço de Extensão Cultural
SEDOC	*Serviço de Documentação*
SJ	Jesuit-Society of Jesus
SNI	Serviço Nacional de Informação
SORPE	Serviço de Orientação Rural de Pernambuco
SPESE	Sociedade de Pesquisas e Estudos Sócio-Eclesiais
SUDENE	Superintendência do Desenvolvimento do Nordeste
TFP	Tradição, Família e Propriedade
UDN	União Democrática Nacional
UNE	União Nacional dos Estudantes

A Political Map of Brazil (Based on a map from *Politics in Brazil, 1930–64* by Thomas E. Skidmore. Copyright © 1967 by Oxford University Press, Inc.)

Introduction

My goals in this book are threefold: to describe change in the Church and give a case study of the process in Brazil; to explain why change came about and present a hypothesis based on this analysis; and to speculate on the political implications of change in the Church. Once the goals are stated the question of how I am going to achieve them is immediately raised. The work of Ivan Vallier is most relevant and useful in this regard, for he focuses on the institutional level and relations between the Churches and other social orders.[1] In opting for this approach, which I selected when beginning my field research, I am intentionally leaving other approaches aside. For example, I am not particularly concerned here with the 'Catholic ethic' and its role in economic underdevelopment. Nor am I going to focus exclusively on the Church's programs of social change, although I do devote the better part of a chapter to them and their importance. Nor will I focus directly on 'Church and state' in the traditional sense of studying concordats and the nuncios' machinations with political leaders.

This book brings together much of the institutional character and process of the Church and links it to the society and politics. I have opted for this larger and more complex approach because it is quite impossible to analyze change in this institution independent of others. To clarify the changing nature of the interrelationships between the Church and other groups, and to show the political dimension of the problem of change, I analyze the Church from a historical perspective.[2]

By 'the Church' I mean four distinct but closely interrelated components: a message, an institution and its relationships with the Universal Church and the state. The message is that of Christ, which seeks to lead all men to salvation. The Church is inseparable from this message: it is holy because it was created by God to bring his message to man. This message is, of course, transcendental as it relates man to an ultimate end in a Creator. Thus the Church has a very special 'product', and one which gives it a distinctive identity far beyond secular institutions. The total message in doctrine and theology has been systematized and is constantly being updated to relate the message to different times and places. Thus the religion, as a system of symbols, beliefs, and acts, shows tremendous continuity over the past two thousand years as well as considerable variations with relation to particular questions. In some cases, an apparently minor reinterpretation in a concrete situation can have tremendous importance.

[1] Ivan Vallier, *Catholicism, Social Control, and Modernization in Latin America* (Englewood Cliffs, N.J.: Prentice-Hall Inc., 1970).

[2] My approach is informed by Selznick's. 'The study of institutions is in some ways comparable to the clinical study of personality. It requires a genetic and developmental approach, an emphasis on historical origins and growth stages. There is a need to see the enterprise as a whole and to see how it is transformed as new ways of dealing with a changing environment evolve.' Philip Selznick, *Leadership in Administration* (Evanston, Ill.: Row, Peterson and Co., 1957), p. 141.

In Brazil, for example, the theological linking of man as soul with man as body, during the grave social situation of the 1950s, was instrumental in the move toward religion as a stimulant rather than an opiate. At times, also, the message is out of the control of the institution. Beyond the official doctrine, there are often pockets of 'folk' or 'cultural' Catholicism which have become captured or bounded in a particular time and place.

While the endowment of Christ's message makes the Church a very special institution, it is basically just that – an institution. There have been varying stresses upon the Church as institution at different times. Today, after the Second Vatican Council, the emphasis is tending toward the idea of the Church as a community, but this community is still an institution and if one doubts it he need but review one of the thousands of texts on Canon Law which set forth the institutional rules to regulate its operations.[3] While there are competing interpretations of the institutional content of the Church, it is worth noting that the CERIS study entitled *A Igreja no Brasil* (The Church in Brazil) deals exclusively with structures and personnel.[4]

In Brazil, this institution is divided into 190 ecclesiastical units, such as archdioceses, and dioceses, under approximately 241 archbishops, bishops, and other ecclesiastical dignitaries. These units are further divided into 4,947 parishes under the supervision of some 12,000 priests. Then there are 40,000 nuns and a few thousand brothers who teach in the Church's 2,000 secondary schools and 12 universities or who minister to the sick and needy in 865 hospitals and 2,334 social institutes. Personnel are trained in 77 major seminaries, 283 minor seminaries and 85 novitiates. The faithful are reached not only through services in the parishes, but also through some 50 lay movements or organizations.[5] Although Canon Law sets forth explicitly the relations between all units, in actual fact there are enormous complications in administering the institution and it bears little resemblance to the monolithic image critics often present.

The two relationships of a national Church are with the Holy See and with the state within whose boundaries it is located. These relationships are integral aspects of the Church, not being in any way tangential or secondary to its nature, yet they are often ignored in discussions or dealt with as matters of secondary importance.

A Roman Catholic Church located in any part of the world has as its primary referent, in terms of controls and doctrine, the Universal Church with its center in the Vatican. Bishops are finally selected by the Pope; they must visit Rome

---

[3] See e.g., René Metz, *What Is Canon Law?* trans. Michael Derrick (New York: Hawthorn Books, 1960). One can also note that, in a recent excellent book, John L. McKenzie gives particular emphasis to the structural features as they define for him what is particularly Roman about the Roman Catholic Church. John L. McKenzie, *The Roman Catholic Church* (Garden City: Image Books, 1969).

[4] Winifredo Plagge, *A Igreja no Brasil* (Rio de Janeiro: CERIS, 1965).

[5] Centro de Estatística Religiosa e Investigações Sociais (CERIS), *Anuário Católico do Brasil* 3rd. ed. (Rio de Janeiro: CERIS, 1965). See Appendix for further selected statistics on the institution. CERIS is in part a research center for the Church. Much of their material is in mimeographed form, which makes it difficult to give full and consistent citations.

every five years and remain in constant communication with the various sectors of the Holy See. Since the Second Vatican Council, the National Bishops' Conferences have increasingly gained in jurisdiction, but their standing is minimal in comparison with the Pope and his ambassador – the nuncio, legate, etc. Seminary training is closely regulated by Rome; liturgy and catechism changes must be approved there and all recourse must ultimately be directed to this level.

After having stated that a national Church is only part of the Universal, I must turn around and point out that it shares the same territory, constituency and aspiration for men's allegiance as that other all-inclusive institution, the state. For reasons of power as well as the impact of belief, the relations between Church and state have been historically dynamic and often intense. In those countries of the world (Latin America, Latin Europe, Holland and even Germany) where the Church has been established, and thus linked with government, and where a majority of the population are members of the faith, the state must pay considerable attention to its relationship with the Church. The latter, for reasons of survival if nothing more, pays equal heed to this relationship.

The Church is the combination of these four components. In order to bring them together and to discuss change, I have adopted as an analytical focus the setting and implementation of goals. The goals of any institution are definitions of its relationship with its environment. Goals inform us where the institution fits into society and what it is expected to accomplish for society. The Church's goal is to influence individuals and whole societies.[6] Influence means that the Church gives a specific and direct orientation to individuals and societies. It is 'marking' the object of influence with the message of Christ. Influence, in this sense, is the capacity whereby one actor has another act in a way he ordinarily would not. For the Church, this meant at times forced conversion or religious wars; occasionally, it refers to spontaneous conversion on the basis of beliefs; and sometimes it just means assuming that a Catholic culture will gently guide the individual towards salvation. Optimally, the bases of influence lie in belief, faith, or reliance upon written and spoken authority. It implies a commitment which leads the believer to move more or less spontaneously in the direction of salvation, as defined by the institution.[7]

The use here of the Church's goal of influence is very broad. The goal is the stated end in salvation, as well as the particular formulation of this goal in

---

[6] 'It [the goal] consists in two points: 1. to convert men to make them disciples; therefore, evangelization; 2. to guide the world towards God; therefore, action in the temporal sphere, or civilization.' Yves Congar, O.P., *Priest and Layman*, trans. P. J. Hepburne-Scott (London: Darton, Longman and Todd Ltd, 1967), p. 307.

[7] Vallier's definition of influence is appropriate here. 'In my judgment, influence should be equated with the capacity of a unit (whether an individual, a group, an association, or a state) to generate commitments – loyalties, resources, behavioral support, etc. – in amounts sufficient to allow the agency of influence to impose a direction of its own choosing on the structure, and thereby to change a situation. An influential is thus a person or corporate unit that is able to place a distinct stamp on a valued sphere of interest or activity.' Vallier, p. 12. See also Robert H. Dahl, *Modern Political Analysis* (Englewood Cliffs, N.J.: Prentice-Hall, Inc., 1963), pp. 14–35 for a formulation of influence similar to the one used above.

concrete situations, and the mechanisms or instruments whereby the goal is achieved. I am thus combining both the message and the institution when I refer to the goal of influence. Change for the purposes of this work is change in both the goal and the instruments or mechanisms whereby it is implemented. Some categories which can be useful in constructing a model or ideal type are: 1. the dominant organizational principle which describes the Church's perception of the environment and the obstacles to implementing the general goal of influence. 2. the groups or sectors of society to which the Church directs its particular attention, the favored strata, so to speak. 3. Church–society relationship or the manner in which the organization seeks to link itself with the larger environment. 4. the instruments or mechanisms whereby the Church exercises influence and generates commitments.[8]

I should emphasize that I am talking about the goal of influence and the manner in which it is implemented *vis-à-vis* the institution. This approach could be distinguished from another, which takes the individual as its primary focus and studies the functional, therapeutic, etc. role of influence on him. Probably the main difficulty in describing influence is that it is almost impossible to measure. Social scientists have devoted a great deal of time to the conceptualization and quantification of influence and still have not made much progress. If there are difficulties with political influence, how can one expect to measure religious influence, where the goal is salvation? I have completely ignored quantification of saved souls and have relied instead on intermediate data of importance to the Church itself, such as mass attendence, ability to stimulate vocations, number of schools, money received and percentage of the population formally declared members of the religion.

Descriptively, therefore, we now have the categories to be used in discussing Church change in influence and its implementation. The analytical part of the work seeks more – namely to explain how change takes place. My approach to this subject is both a conceptual scheme and a hypothesis to be explored throughout the book. Initially it can be observed that goals are not defined in a vacuum but by an institution in relation to its environment. Environments change and if the institution is to maintain influence, it must adapt.[9] However, what will be argued here is more than the generalized control of environments over goals and implementation. I propose that the Church's goal of influence and its implementation is determined by the institution in interaction with the state and the Holy See. In other words, the Church is not a free actor, is neither autonomous nor independent and cannot set its own goals. It falls prey to its relationship with the other actors and is in fact dependent upon them for its survival as the environment changes and influence wanes.

[8] Vallier's work was again helpful in the formulation of these categories, although I have selected only four of his ten and am using each one in a slightly broader sense. I have found that the empirical material fits these four very well. Cf. Vallier, p. 72.
[9] For a very provocative analysis of these issues, see Shirley Terreberry, 'The Evolution of Organizational Environments', *Administrative Science Quarterly* 12 (March 1968), pp. 590–613. See also J. Thompson and W. McEwen, 'Organizational Goals and Environment', *American Sociological Review* 23 (February 1958), pp. 23–31.

It is well to recall that any national Church is but part of the Universal Church. However, the character of the relationship fluctuates according to various factors, including the political position of the papacy, the intermediate goals of the papacy, the nature of communications, the strength of a national hierarchy and particular religious and political issues. The fluctuations may be so drastic in fact that a brief outline of some conceptual indices for describing the relationship may be useful. I want to discuss them by levels of autonomy in order to capture a dimension of the control involving not only the setting of goals, but also the structures that implement them. From the level of least autonomy to that of the greatest, four relationships can be stipulated: coalition – the virtual identity of goals and structures; cooperation – at times identical goals pursued through separate structures; competition – similar goals pursued through separate structures utilizing different strategies; and conflict – mutually ex-clusive or antagonistic goals pursued through distinct structures.

It can be presumed that even though the structural relationships between the Universal Church and a national Church vary, the goal of influence – salvation – remains the same and changes only at some intermediate points. When one considers the relationship with the state, however, the situation becomes more complex. To put it quite simply, when they were first set up, the Latin American Churches had closer relationships with the Iberian states than they did with the papacy and this situation continued up to the turn of this century. The Churches have been more dependent upon the states than on the Vatican in many import-ant respects, with the result that change in the Church's goal of influence is of political concern and is in essence a political problem. The formulation of the proposition that I will argue in the work is that from the start, and continu-ing until the present, the Church's goal of influence was defined primarily through the mechanism of power. What is special about power is that it is linked with positive and negative coercion and is thus by definition linked to the state, as this body regulates physical coercion and the distribution of societal values and resources.[10] Power is but one mechanism or basis for influence, but for these Churches it was always the central one and is still crucial to the way they define influence. There are built-in problems when defining influence by means of power; with this basis, there was no need to develop other bases of influence such as personal commitments, beliefs, faith and mobilization of the layman. Thus change, adaptation to a changing environment, involves not only an autonomy relationship with the Vatican and the state, but also the generating of new bases for influence.

Despite what one might imagine from the transitory nature of political events – of changes in government, military coups, congresses being opened and closed – there is in fact a tremendous degree of institutional stability both in Brazil and Latin America as a whole. I find the initial observation of Claudio Veliz much to the point.

[10] See Dahl, *Modern Political Analysis*, pp. 14–35, and also the difficult but valuable essay by Talcott Parsons, 'On the Concept of Political Power', *Proceedings of the American Philo-sophical Society* 107 (June 1963), pp. 232–62.

6 Introduction

There exists in the region a resilient traditional structure of institutions, hierarchical arrangements, and attitudes which conditions every aspect of political behavior and which has survived centuries of colonial governments, movements for independence, foreign wars and invasions, domestic revolutions, and a confusingly large number of lesser palace revolts. More recently it has not only successfully resisted the impact of technological innovation and industrialization, but appears to have been strengthened by it.[11]

With specific reference to Brazil a broad and sophisticated sociological and historical literature exists on the stability of institutions. For example, José Honório Rodrigues argues that 'The socio-economic institutions remain the same, independent of the transitory names they are given. The granite stability of the institutions corresponds to a mere governmental instability.'[12]

In Brazil, at least, there is a form of consensus on the stability of institutions. I agree with this consensus but will show that the Church as an institution has indeed changed and is now changing. I feel that certain lessons can be drawn from my study about the conditions of change which are applicable to other Brazilian institutions.

At the risk of anticipating the conclusions, I would go one step further and argue that change in the Church will probably make for substantial change in other institutions and social orders. The Church has always been linked with the state; it was never autonomous. Today, however, it is defining its autonomy through an intense process of conflict. In the development of this process, the Church has increasingly adopted a role of promoting social change and is presently taking on a role of prophecy. This is at the intentional level. Further, because the institution has always been linked with all other orders, this change has direct implications for the whole society. The Church in Brazil is indeed coming to play a 'transformative role' in society, because as it changes there will of necessity be greater secularization, increased pluralism and further structural differentiation. A number of sociologists have developed hypotheses on the role of religion in transformation of societies and from my data I can make a strong case for this role in Brazil. In the simplest terms, the Church is moving from a position as unifying force in the creation and support of a cultural synthesis to a revolutionary and disruptive force in the present political situation.[13]

---

[11] Claudio Veliz, ed., *Obstacles to Change in Latin America* (London: Oxford University Press, 1965), p. 1.

[12] José Honório Rodrigues, *Conciliação e Reforma no Brasil* (Rio de Janeiro: Editôra Civilização Brasileira, 1965), p. 13. See also: Raymundo Faoro, *Os Donos do Poder* (Rio de Janeiro: Editôra Globo, 1958), p. 271; Francisco de Oliveira Vianna, *Populações Meridionaisdo Brasil* (Rio de Janeiro: Livraria José Olympio Editôra, 1952) 1:222; Nestor Duarte, *Ordem Privada e A Organização Política Nacional* (São Paulo: Companhia Editôra Nacional, 1966). Unless otherwise stated, all Portuguese originals have been translated by the author.

[13] See on the 'transformative role', Vallier, p. 6. For key parts of this argument see also: S. M. Eisenstadt, 'Transformation of Social, Political, and Cultural Orders in Modernization', *American Sociological Review* 30 (October 1965), p. 670; Robert Bellah, 'Religious Evolution', *American Sociological Review* 29 (June 1964), p. 368; Christopher Dawson, *Religion and Culture* (New York: Meridian Books, 1959), p. 202.

The historical scope of this study is rather broad. The range of description and analysis is also comprehensive, in that I move from the realm of institutional interrelations to internal political tactics, to political opposition and to prophecy. I have divided my discussion into four main sections. The first two chapters cover historical ground from 1500 to 1950; here I show how the Church was linked with political power and remained so tied until at least the middle of this century. Section II begins with an analysis of the threats to Church influence presented by the social and political changes which took place in Brazil after World War II. The Church responded to the threats as perceived in two rather contradictory ways; on the one hand, it acted through a political pressure group to ensure traditional influence, and on the other, it innovated and assisted the 'Brazilian revolution' prior to 1964. The innovation will be analyzed with particular emphasis on the autonomy relationship. Section III begins with a discussion of the problems inherent in a changing society for the Church's traditional influence and goes on to show the impediments to innovation. This section is mainly concerned with internal Church problems and strategies but concludes with case studies which indicate that the problem of change does not lie exclusively within the Church's competence. Section IV describes a long series of Church–state conflicts and analyzes the results of the conflict process for the Church, its relations with the state and the likelihood of change.

Section I:

The Political and Religious Bases of Catholicism in Brazil

1. Establishment, decay and separation from the state

Brazil was founded by the Portuguese in 1500, and the type of Church established in the colony was an extension of the one current in the mother country. Even after the Protestant Reformation, the model of Church then prevalent in the rest of Europe remained intact in both Spain and Portugal, the two countries promoting the Counter-Reformation and then engaged in founding and colonizing the New World. This Church model is best characterized by the term 'Christendom' and was dominant in Europe from approximately the fourth century until the Reformation. Until the latter part of the period, no conception of the state *per se* existed, so the Church was the overriding institution in most realms of society. As it possessed a monopoly on the means of salvation and as all matters can somehow be related to salvation, the Church then had authority over both spiritual and temporal affairs.[1]

However, the papacy was threatened immediately from within by the Conciliar Movement and even more severely from without by the Turks, and as the states developed, the lack of distinction between Church and state created a situation in which the authority was reversed. The state became dominant in place of the Church. The initial Portuguese Church model was elaborated in Brazil by an extensive system of patronage grants, given to the Crown by the papacy to further what had begun as a crusade against the Turks and continued as a mission for souls in the New World. Before describing the details of patronage, a brief overview of the 'Christendom' model is necessary.[2]

First, the organizational principle was total coverage of all territories; where people could be found, a Christian ruler had to ensure conversion, even if this meant the imposition of religion through force. The whole world was to be Christian: the message of Christ was universal. Secondly, the groups and sectors focused upon were all-inclusive, as the form was based on a monopoly of the faith. Everyone in the geographical entity was fair game for the religion. In Brazil, for example, Indians were baptized *en masse* as were the slaves from Africa before they landed in their new homeland.

A third factor of this model was the comprehensive relationship of the Church and society. As all matters were related to salvation, the Church was bound up with every phase of man's existence. Society itself was constructed from within the Church, on the Church's terms, and received from it express and direct regulation. Finally, the instruments used in exercising and generating influence were the webs of structures and groups which constituted society. Through a

---

[1] For a description of the Church in Europe during this period and the outline of the Christendom model, see Ernst Troeltsch, *The Social Teaching of the Christian Churches*, 2 vols., trans. Olive Wyon (New York: Harper Torchbooks, 1931, repr. 1960), 1, Chapter 2.

[2] For a comprehensive treatment of the patronage and an analysis of its causes and evolution, see W. Eugene Shiels, SJ, *King and Church: The Rise and Fall of the Patronato Real* (Chicago: Loyola University Press, 1961). For particular discussion of the crusade basis of the patronage, see pp. 44–50.

Christian ruler, the influence of the Church filtered down to all people. Structures made men Christian rather than the other way around.

What is manifest in the description of these four categories is the comprehensiveness of the model; it sought to permeate everything, through any means, by all mechanisms of state and society. This model contrasts significantly with the form of Church established in the United States, where the minority status of the Church meant that total coverage was impossible. A monopoly was also not feasible, especially in the strongly anti-Catholic areas, and the Church focused mainly on ethnic minorities. Fusion of Church–society in a Protestant society was impossible and even the U.S. Constitution forbade the integration of Church and state. Men were made Catholic through the sacraments and evangelization; they then made the structures Christian. The Reformation spelled the passing of the Christendom form in Europe, but it was implemented in Latin America at about the same period. From their beginnings, therefore, the Churches in Latin America were in important ways different from those in other areas, although all were part of the same Universal Church.

A key premise of the Christendom model is the integration of Church and state. The state must assist the Church if all people in the area are to be influenced through all the structures. The discovery and settlement of Brazil was a joint venture of the Portuguese state and the Catholic Church. With the sword went the cross, and in fact the colony was originally called the land of the true cross, Vera Cruz. Expansion in the colonial period by the Iberian powers was based on a combination of economic, political and religious motives. Gilberto Freyre makes a widely-accepted point in stating: 'It is impossible to deny that the economic imperialism of Spain and Portugal was bound up in the most intimate fashion with the Church and the religious. The conquest of markets, lands, and slaves – the conquest of souls.'[3]

The Crown of Portugal had been historically on very good terms with the Church. Because of Portugal's efforts in the Reconquest from the Moors and in the propagation of 'the true faith', in 1179 the Pope accorded the King of Portugal divine right and in effect guaranteed the country's statehood. Portuguese expansion in Africa, Asia and finally America was always carried out with strong religious overtones, and is seen by many as simply a continuation of the Reconquest (completed in Portugal in 1249; Spain in 1492). The expansion and conquests were appreciated by the Popes and duly recognized. Von Pastor's comments on Pope Leo X and the King of Portugal are indicative of the good will between them. Leo X sent the sword and hat blessed by him at Christmas in 1515, and von Pastor observed: 'In this way did the Supreme Head of the Church proclaim before the whole world the value he set on the war which the King of Portugal alone among Christian princes had been found to carry on against the infidel by which such brilliant prospects were opened to Christendom.'[4]

---

[3] Gilberto Freyre, *The Masters and the Slaves*, trans. Samuel Putnam (New York: Knopf and Co., 1946), p. 249.

[4] Ludwig Freiherr von Pastor, *The History of the Popes*, 40 vols., trans. E. F. Peeler (St Louis, Mo.: Herder and Herder, 1898, repr. 1953), 7:78.

Due to the inherent limitations of the Christendom model, supported by the affinity of the papacy for Portugal, and further stimulated by the nature of the colonial venture, the Church in the colony became totally subservient to the state. In the movement from East to West, from Portugal to Brazil, the Christendom form took on the features of Caesaropapism. Most of the papal bulls, and most certainly those forming the basis of the patronage for Brazil, were granted well before discovery of the colony in 1500. Portugal received them primarily for wars against the infidel or for discoveries in Africa. For example, the first bull granted to Portugal in this regard, 'Romanus Pontifex' of 1455, was issued by Pope Nicholas V, just two years after he had seen the Turks overrun Constantinople. Because of this event he, as well as subsequent Popes, felt that an aggressive crusade was necessary to save Christianity, and it was in this context that Alfonso V of Portugal waged an African crusade and received broad powers over the Church.[5]

Beyond the initial crusading character of the discoveries, it must be remembered that the state supplied the ships and financed the ventures. As a consequence, the Popes granted to the Crown of Portugal what amounted to virtual control over the new Church. The control extended from the most basic issues of building the first churches to such matters as paying the clergy, nominating bishops, approving documents, selecting sites for convents and to almost all areas of Church concern.[6]

The legal basis for state control over the Church was a series of papal bulls which gave patronage concessions to the Kings of Portugal. Patronage is a grant by the Church in Rome of some degree of control over a local or national Church to a civil ruler in appreciation for his efforts in spreading the religion, his zeal and dedication, and as a stimulus for future 'good works'. It can be illustrated by the expression: what the ruler builds he can control. The system of patronage in Brazil was formed by the bulls issued by four Popes between 1455 and 1515.[7]

The first relevant bull was 'Romanus Pontifex' issued by Pope Nicholas V on 8 January 1455, to Alfonso, King of Portugal, granting him the right to found the first churches in the new territories and to staff them as he saw fit. King Alfonso was also the recipient of the next bull, which was entitled 'Inter Caetera' and was granted by Pope Calixtus III on 13 March 1456. This bull gave the

---

[5] Shiels, *King and Church*, p. 49.
[6] As Mecham observes about the whole of Latin America: 'Never before or since did a sovereign with the consent of the Pope so completely control the Catholic Church within his dominions.' J. Lloyd Mecham, *Church and State in Latin America*, rev. ed., (Chapel Hill, N.C.: University of North Carolina Press, 1966), p. 36. Brazil was certainly a case in point. Shiels refers to the 'outright grants', p. 17.
[7] All the bulls are in Frances Davenport, ed., *European Treaties Bearing on the History of the United States and its Dependencies to 1648* (Washington, D.C.: The Carnegie Institution, 1917). The Latin originals of the first two bulls are found in Shiels and his analysis of the reasons for the grants and their relationship to Spanish grants is worth reading. See especially pp. 44–60.

Great Prior of the Order of Christ responsibility for filling all the ordinary episcopal jurisdictions in the overseas lands conquered and to be conquered.[8]

Leo X was thoroughly impressed by the vigor with which King Emanuel of Portugal spread the faith throughout the world and he was granted important rights in two bulls issued in June 1514. In 'Dum Fidei Constantiam' of 7 June while still granting to the Order of Christ the patronage of benefices in all new lands discovered or not, Leo allotted to Emanuel as Grand Master the patronage of all minor benefices, which until then had been exercised by the Great Prior of the Order.[9] In 'Pro Excellenti' of 12 June Leo created the diocese of Funchal in Madeira and included within its jurisdiction the territory of Brazil. With the creation of a diocese the jurisdiction of the Order of Christ, which was 'nullius Dioecesis', should have lapsed. Strictly, only one form of patronage should have covered the new colony. The Pope, however, expressly intended that both forms of patronage should be continued, both under the Crown of Portugal.[10] Thus to the King of Portugal and his successors fell a double patronage: the secular patronage of the episcopal benefice of Funchal which was granted to the king as king; and the spiritual patronage of the minor benefices granted to the king as Grand Master of the Order of Christ.

With this series of papal bulls, the Crown of Portugal was handsomely rewarded for its vigor in vanquishing the Moors, discovering new lands and bringing many new souls into the realm of Christendom. Apart from the formal grants included in the bulls, there were informal privileges which evolved from the exercise of the patronage. One of these was the right of recourse to the Crown in cases of ecclesiastical discipline. If a member of the Church was disciplined by a superior of an order or a bishop, he could call upon his right of recourse to the crown. This meant that the Church could not effectively enforce discipline. Another informal privilege was the placet, or right of the Crown to censor all ecclesiastical bulls, letters and other documents prior to their publication in the colony. Church communications had to go through Lisbon before they could be received in Brazil. In fact, it was 1830 before the papal legate in Brazil could relay information directly to Rome; it was some time later before Rome could communicate directly with Brazil.[11]

The combination of the double patronage and the informal privileges arising

---

[8] The Order of Christ was the most important of three religious-military orders in Portugal at the time. The Order had been founded by King Diniz in 1317 to replace the Templars so as to inherit their great wealth and holdings. Diniz wanted to keep the wealth and holdings in Portugal rather than allow a claim by Rome with the passing of the Templars. The Order had been very important in fighting the infidel and reconquering territories for Christianity in Portugal and other places so that the Popes had granted it extensive control over various Church matters. 'Inter Cætera' extended this control to further territories.

[9] Originally the Grand Mastership had been an elective post. The future King Emanuel was elected to the position in 1483 and from then on the Popes affixed the position to the Portuguese Crown. The bull 'Præclara Charissimi' of 30 December 1551, reaffirmed this.

[10] Dom Oscar de Oliveira, *Os Dízimos Eclesiásticos do Brasil: Nos Períodos da Colônia e do Império* (Belo Horizonte: Universidade de Minas Gerais, 1964), p. 61.

[11] William J. Coleman, *The First Apostolic Delegation in Rio de Janeiro and Its Influence in Spanish America* (Washington, D.C.: Catholic University of America Press, 1950), p. 58.

from it, the power of the Portuguese state and relative weakness of the papacy during this period, the Christendom model itself and the nature of colonization meant that the Church in Brazil was more closely linked with the state than with the papacy. Because of the patronage, communication blocks, concessions to the state and the placet, Rome was unable to exercise authority. The state was in an ideal position to control, but at this time its goals were more or less identical to those of the Church. The Crown may have been more interested in gold than souls, but both Church and state were concerned with the spread of the true faith. Even though the state's goals were largely identical with the Church's, the relationship itself had certain implications for influence which were serious and of long duration. An examination of Church–state finances will illustrate this point.

The Christendom model includes all orders of society within it. All are thus expected to support the institution, and the usual form in this period was by means of the tithe, which was a 10 % levy on everything produced in the society.[12] As with much else concerning Church–state arrangements at this time, the concession of the tithes was apparently based on tradition and de facto power relations between Rome and the various monarchs. Dom Oscar de Oliveira concludes that a formal concession was really unnecessary since the spiritual patronage implied the right. At first the Order and later the Crown, as patron of the Church in new territories, was expected to promote the establishment of the structures; it was only right that resources be made available to encourage this task.

In the early days of the colony, the tithes were evidently insufficient and the King made up the deficits from his personal revenue. With time, and especially with the discovery of gold and precious gems, the tithes amounted to a very considerable sum and the Crown became accustomed to setting aside for state use what remained after providing what the *king* considered sufficient for the progress of the Church. The mixing of the tithes with the royal treasury and the discretion over how much to use for the Church easily led to considerable abuse. Caio Prado notes that even as early as the eighteenth century the tithe was known as the *dízimo real* (royal tithe), indicating that it belonged to the state. It became, in fact, the principal form of colonial tribute.[13]

The state's jurisdiction and subsequent abuse in the administration of the tithes produced several serious results. One specialist in comparative Church history has observed that 'Spanish America arrived at the status of a Church very quickly. . .while Brazil kept for a longer time the character of a mission, or of something that was in preparation for something else, of something that still

---

[12] In Brazil, the tithe was called the *dízimo*, or tenth. '*Dízimos* are the tenth part of all movable goods legally acquired and owed to God and his ministers by Divine institution and human law. Just as there are three sources of movable goods and fruits – buildings, personal and mixed – so there are three types of *dízimos*.' Dom Oscar de Oliveira, *Os Dízimos Eclesiásticos do Brasil*, p. 26.

[13] Caio Prado, Jr, *The Colonial Background of Modern Brazil*, trans. Suzette Macedo (Berkeley: University of California Press, 1967), p. 375.

remained fragile and weak.'[14] The state was to found new dioceses and support them. The first was founded in 1551 in Bahia, the second not until 1676, and by 1750 (250 years after the discovery of Brazil) there were only eight dioceses in the immense colony. Even in so few, the financial problems were apparently very serious indeed. Because of the scarcity of episcopal units and the control by the state, there was very little which one might call a colonial Church institution. The Dioceses of Pará and Maranhão were under the See of Lisbon until 1827, whereas the others were responsible to the Archbishop of Bahia. Communications were extremely difficult and permission of the Crown was required even before a synod could be convened. The first synod was called in 1707 to update Church regulations in accord with the Council of Trent (which ended in 1563); of the four episcopal units in Brazil, only the host could attend.[15]

Units below the level of dioceses were also scarce. Since the state was responsible for the support of new parishes, it simply did not found new ones. The clergy were to be trained in seminaries, but these also had to be supported by the state. Despite repeated attempts, no seminary for the secular clergy was set up until 1739. The training of priests was thus rather *sui generis*, as Camargo notes.[16] Once priests had their own parishes they were regarded as civil servants inasmuch as they were paid by the state. As civil servants, the laity did not feel obliged to support the priests, so in the face of underpayment by the state the clergy found other means of survival and as a consequence were considered rapacious.

The matter of finances is illustrative and the same lessons could be drawn from the areas of nominations of the clergy and coordination in general. While it is true that under the Christendom form the Church does not need the centralized and close-linked organization that is necessary in an hostile environment such as the United States (or even Europe at particular periods), Brazil's almost total lack of institutions and correlate dependence upon the state for resources created an initial weakness. There were few dioceses; parishes were few and far between; communications were impossible; priests were underpaid; and the Church itself was regarded by everyone as a sector of the civil bureaucracy. In fact, during the whole colonial period (1500–1822) it is probably misleading to talk about a Church. There were a few bishops in their dioceses; some secular priests looked after the cult; several religious orders such as the Franciscans and Jesuits taught school and preached throughout the country; and there were church buildings. With these characteristics, it is only logical that the Church 'drifted'; that is, it related to sectors of society in a search for resources and support. In order to see how the Church was inserted and the implications of

---

[14] Robert Ricard, 'Comparison of Evangelization in Portuguese and Spanish America', *The Americas* 14 (April 1958), p. 446.

[15] The Brazilian Church had its origins before the Council of Trent, but the bishops did not attend this conclave as the Kings of Portugal requested from the Pope their dispensation. Pe. Arlindo Rubert, 'Os Bispos do Brasil no Concílio Vaticano I (1869–1870)', *Revista Eclesiástica Brasileira* 29 (March 1969), p. 104.

[16] Msgr. Paulo Florêncio da Silveira Camargo, *História Eclesiástica do Brasil* (Petrópolis, R. J.: Editôra Vozes, 1955), p. 284.

this as a process, a few observations on the nature of colonial society are necessary.

The colony was a patrimonial system. At the center, in Portugal, was the Crown, which represented in this system the focus of personal and arbitrary power limited only by tradition and the truths of the faith. The bureaucratic control to make this patrimonial system effective was lacking, however, everywhere but in administrative centers. Implementation of the patrimonial state system was on a par with the implementation of the Christendom model, i.e. it was low. The colonization of Brazil was rural in character; much more so than in Spanish America. There were no great centers like Mexico, Puebla, Lima, etc. '. . .the whole life of the country gravitated completely around the country estate: the city was practically, if not totally, a mere appendage of the latter'.[17] In view of the low state control over Brazil during the colonial period, the rural family with its sugar mills and extensive dependencies became the dominant institution of society. Most observers of this period in Brazil agree on the importance of the rural family and would concur with Freyre's evaluation:

The family and not the individual, much less the State or any commercial company, was from the sixteenth century the great colonizing factor in Brazil, the productive unit, the capital that cleared the land, founded plantations, purchased slaves, oxen, implements; and in politics it was the social force that set itself up as the most powerful colonial aristocracy in the Americas. Over it the King of Portugal may be said, practically, to have reigned without ruling.[18]

The Church, and obviously this term is a misnomer because it simply means here many members of the clergy, became a part of the rural family. As often as not the second son was expected to be a priest; the Church was really the domestic chapel; the priest received his wages from the family and he often received his values from them as well. The one characteristic which seems to have most fascinated foreign observers of colonial Brazil was the immorality of the clergy.[19] The clergy lived with the family, accepted its values, and these values did not deny the priest some form of female companionship.

The nature of society in the few important cities (Salvador da Bahia, Rio de Janeiro, Ouro Prêto, etc.) did not weaken the influence of the rural family nor help develop a central Church authority. The dominant colonial institutions which joined the Church and society in the cities were the *irmandades* or brotherhoods.[20] They were voluntary associations with diverse aims and activities.

[17] Sérgio Buarque de Hollanda, *Raízes do Brasil* (Rio de Janeiro: Livraria José Olympio Editôra, 1936), p. 44.
[18] Freyre, *The Masters and the Slaves*, pp. 26–7. See also the extensive works of Oliveira Vianna on the rural clan's role in the formation of Brazilian society. While approaching the topic from a different perspective than Freyre, he formulates an analysis which has exactly the same implications for the Church. Francisco de Oliveira Vianna, *Populações Meridionais do Brasil*, 2 vols. (Rio de Janeiro: Livraria José Olympio Editôra, 1952).
[19] This may be due only in part to the fact that a high proportion of these observers were Protestant missionaries looking for converts and quick to criticize the Catholic clergy.
[20] 'These brotherhoods of colonial Brazil. . .were among the most important institutions in Portuguese America. Much of the work that was done by the government or by the Church

Some existed for purely religious purposes; in Bahia alone there were no fewer than thirty-one approved *irmandades* dedicated to the Blessed Virgin.[21] Others were of a guild and professional nature; others were racial in tone in that they were only for blacks. Some existed primarily to construct churches and others for social work. The main hospitals in the colony, the Santa Casas de Misericórdia, were built and administered by *irmandades*.

In the rural areas, the family either built the churches or used the house's chapel. In the cities, families and *irmandades* built the churches. Dom Oscar states, 'Our old churches owe themselves, in general, to the *irmandades* of the Most Holy Sacrament and to the Third Orders, particularly of Carmo and Penitência'.[22] And Boxer observes in regard to a church in Minas Gerais,

The entire cost was defrayed by the local brotherhoods and a levy on the townspeople. It was a similar story elsewhere in Minas Gerais, the Crown only contributing tardily and occasionally, although it carefully collected the tithes which it was in theory supposed to spend on the stipends of the clergy and the construction and upkeep of churches.[23]

The priest was paid by the *irmandade* to serve in their church.

The *irmandades* gave a content and style to the practice of religion in Brazil, as did the rural family. The main public activity of a majority of the *irmandades* was the celebration of its patron saint's feast day. The *irmandades* competed with each other for the most impressive gala celebration and the focus of religion was on these manifestations with their great festivities, noise and fireworks. Boxer observes that, 'Popular amusements were few, and the gaily dressed and richly decorated religious processions, with their masquerades, musicians, and dancers, served social needs which are nowadays supplied by the dance-hall, the theater, and the cinema.'[24] Just as the Church was integrated into the family in the rural areas and affected with its values so it developed in the cities through the *irmandades*.

A striking contrast to the picture I have drawn of the Church and religion is provided by the experience of the Society of Jesus. Many observers of the colonial Church have noted that the regular (order) clergy were far better than the seculars. The regulars included the Benedictines, Franciscans, Carmelites, Capuchins, Oratorians and Jesuits. The most impressive of all were the Jesuits. Founded in 1540, this order was the main arm in Europe of the Counter-Reformation. In Brazil, the Jesuits were consistently the ones who accomplished the tasks that made the Church somehow important in the early society. All the

---

authorities in Spanish America was done in Brazil by these religious brotherhoods; that is, by private enterprise and not by bishops nor by the clergy.' Gilberto Freyre, 'Some Aspects of the Social Development of Portuguese America', in Manoel S. Cardozo, 'The Lay Brotherhoods of Colonial Bahia', *Catholic Historical Review* 33 (April 1947), p. 19.

[21] *Ibid.*, p. 22.
[22] Dom Oscar de Oliveira, p. 152.
[23] C. R. Boxer, *The Golden Age of Brazil: 1695–1750* (Berkeley: University of California Press, 1964), p. 179.
[24] *Ibid.*, p. 134.

heroes – Pe. José de Anchieta, Pe. Manuel da Nóbrega, Pe. Alexandre de Gusmão – were Jesuits; they founded schools, catechized the Indians, developed new methods of teaching and reformed other members of the clergy. Boxer observes, in discussing the moral laxity of the clergy, that:

The Jesuits, as we have more than once had occasion to observe, should be entirely exempted from these strictures; and their labors in both the missionary and educational fields can fairly be described as herculean. If they did not achieve more – and they did achieve a great deal – it was through lack of numbers, and not through lack of high standards or of self-sacrificing efforts.[25]

The local groups were unable to integrate the Jesuits as they had most of the Church. They were an anomaly in the society and were disliked for this.

What made the Jesuits more effective was their greater degree of organization, independence and discipline. The Jesuits were formed on a military model, committed to the Pope, steeped in discipline and obedience, imbued with doctrinal purity that was lacking in most of the seculars, and thus did not fall within the structures of the Christendom model (which they superseded). Sérgio Buarque de Hollanda went so far as to argue that, 'In Brazil, during the first centuries, it was also only the Jesuits who brought an organization guided by a positively constructive spirit.'[26] It seems clear that their organization and independence made the Jesuits a very effective instrument of Church influence. They could bring influence to bear when the rest of the Church could not. They had their own lines of control, generated resources beyond the state's and were not caught up in the local society.

The success of the Jesuits was also their undoing. To generate religious influence, they had to rely upon political power, just as the larger Church, but more directly. In the colony, they alienated a great many people, including other members of the Church. The order survived in Brazil because of the efforts of a few extremely capable Jesuits in the court at Lisbon. However, in the face of increasing opposition to the order in Brazil and with decreasing political support, they were restricted. The restriction took place even while the Crown was interested in establishing the Church, and this suggests a lesson as to the tolerable limits of religion which is still relevant today. In 1759, the Jesuits were eliminated from Brazil and Portugal as the goals of the Crown changed and brought it into opposition to the Church institution centered in Rome. The Jesuits were linked to Rome and therefore were suppressed. The Jesuits were not only the most effective clergy in Brazil, but they were also the largest single order.[27] Not only did the Brazilian Church lose the largest and best contingent of personnel and programs, but they were not replaced by other clergy. In short, a weak Church with little influence became even weaker.

---

[25] *Ibid.*, p. 322. See also Caio Prado, Jr, p. 102 for a similar view.

[26] Sérgio Buarque de Hollanda, p. 65.

[27] Ricard, 'Comparison of Evangelization,' p. 449. Serafim Leite, SJ., in *Summa Histórica da Companhia de Jesus no Brasil 1549–1760* (Lisbon: Junta de Investigações do Ultramar, 1965), p. 237, states that there were 670 Jesuits in 1760.

The example of the Jesuits was soon generalized to the whole institution. During the colonization of Brazil, the Church in Portugal – and particularly the Society of Jesus – was powerful. Power rested not only on a basis of religious influence that could be mobilized and turned into political power, but also on the political competence of several Church leaders. The Church in Brazil at this point could rely only on the carry-over effects from Portugal. No solid basis for influence had yet been built in Brazil. Given this situation the attacks on Church power in Portugal had very serious results for the Church in Brazil.

Sebastião de Carvalho e Mello, the Marquis of Pombal, was minister to King Joseph I of Portugal from 1750 to 1777.[28] Following his impressive performance in rebuilding Lisbon after the devastating earthquake of 1755, Pombal obtained such power over the King that he became 'de facto' ruler of Portugal and the colonies. The Marquis was a modern statesman, in that he created an absolute monarchy in Portugal along the lines of Spain or France. To achieve absolutism, Pombal seized for the state the control held by the nobles, the papacy, the national Church and especially the Society of Jesus. Under Pombal, the Church at all levels was brought fully under control and dominated by the state.

Pombal began his war on the Church by attacking the Jesuits. He dealt severely with them through suppression, death and expulsion, not only from Portugal but also from Brazil in 1759. After 1760, Pombal severed relations with the Vatican and evicted the Nuncio. From then until the re-establishment of relations in 1770, the Church in Portugal was entirely national in character, so that the bishops exercised their functions independent of Rome. Relations were resumed in 1770 under Pope Clement XIV, one of the lesser lights in the history of the papacy. Pombal obtained from the Pope acknowledgement of his control over the national Church, a cardinal's hat for his brother and, some say, the world-wide suppression of the Jesuits in 1773.[29] In attacking the power of the Church in Portugal, Pombal almost completely obliterated what there was of the Church in Brazil.

With the break between Lisbon and Rome, episcopal sees in Brazil were left vacant for years. Rome was unable to appoint bishops without a nomination from the state, and the latter did not go so far as to make a national Church in Brazil with civilly-appointed bishops. Lacking bishops, priests could not be ordained, but vocations were few anyway since the state guaranteed only clerical penury. In general, Pombal's policies were devastating for the Church. The basic influence model was still present and still required state implementation. However, instead of receiving support for implementation, it was rather intentionally being weakened and in some aspects destroyed.

[28] There is a great deal of material on Pombal in both Portuguese and English. See e.g., Visconde de Carnaxide, *O Brasil na Administração Pombalina* (São Paulo: Companhia Editôra Nacional, 1940), and John Smith, *Memoires of the Marquis of Pombal* (London: Longman, Brown and Green, 1843).

[29] Leopold von Ranke, *The History of the Popes During the Last Four Centuries*, 3 vols., trans. George R. Dennis (London: G. Bell and Sons, Ltd, 1939), 2:493.

Pombal's impact on the Brazilian Church was long lasting. The fact that its chances for political power were destroyed before influence was created resulted in an extremely weak basis for future development. Further, the Church was so linked with the state that Rome, even had it so desired, could not have assisted the colonial Church.[30] Moreover, the clergy was socialized in a way which often caused them to act against their institutions' best interests. Only in the light of these attitudes can some of the clergy's often bizarre activities be understood.

In 1772, Pombal reorganized the University of Coimbra to break away from the traditional curriculum of Jesuitical scholasticism and introduced in its place (among other things) courses in theology and canon law which were heavily influenced by regalism and Jansenism.[31] As the most important center of learning in Portugal, Coimbra became a focal point in disseminating these doctrines.

Coimbra was important for Brazil since it was the only Portuguese center of education for Brazilian students, both lay and clerical. Through his reorganization of Coimbra, Pombal initiated 'the Pombalization of the clergy, a systematic indoctrination of clerical students with libertine ideas and false doctrines which made some priests ready accomplices in the Pombaline scheme of establishing in Portugal and her colonies a Liberal Catholicism, inimical to the papacy'.[32] The influence of the new doctrines reached Brazil directly as the bishops in Brazil were appointed from the clergy who had studied in Coimbra. In 1800, one of these bishops, Dom José Joaquim da Cunha de Azeredo Coutinho, founded a seminary in Olinda which was the third seminary in Brazil and served the whole North and Northeast of the country. Regalism ensured state control over the Church with subordination of the latter's interests; Jansenism denied the supremacy of the Pope even in Church affairs; and now Liberalism was included (following the Revolution in France in 1789), which in the Portuguese context meant anticlericalism and confiscation of Church property. Judging from comments by some observers at the time, these doctrines were accepted by a majority of Church members.[33]

---

[30] 'Indeed, the Papacy, already considerably weakened and preoccupied with more important matters, made no attempt to assert its rights in the kingdom and Brazil, and the colony's religious affairs were left entirely to the "Most Faithful" king.' Caio Prado, Jr, p. 389.

[31] Regalism is a theory which holds the state to be all-powerful over a church, so that state interests dominate those of the church. As a theory it had existed in Portugal since Antônio de Gouvea had expounded the doctrine in the early sixteenth century, when the country was building its colonial empire. In the eighteenth century it was common in much of Europe, being termed Gallicanism in France, Josephism in Austria, Febronianism in Germany and simply Regalism in Spain and Portugal. Jansenism takes many variations, but its importance here is that the theories of Jansenism expounded in Portugal attacked the primacy of the Pope. Pombal assisted in the publication of Jansenist tracts in Portugal thereby giving them broad circulation.

[32] Sister Mary Crescentia Thornton, *The Church and Freemasonry in Brazil, 1872–1875* (Washington, D.C.: The Catholic University of America Press, 1948), pp. 36–7.

[33] F. Badaró, *L'Eglise au Brésil pendant l'Empire et pendant la République* (Rome, 1895), p. 29. Cited in Thornton, p. 65. See also Gustavo Pérez, Affonso Gregory, and François Lepargneur, *O Problema Sacerdotal no Brasil* (Rio de Janeiro: CERIS, 1965), p. 32.

By the early nineteenth century, the influence of the Church in Brazil was virtually non-existent. Its bases had never really been established, its political power from the time of Pombal was nil and the priests were educated in doctrines which made them oppose attempts to increase political power. This did not mean, however, that priests were inactive politically. Because they were better educated than most of the population and as this education included large elements of Liberalism, many priests were revolutionaries seeking independence from Portugal, but they functioned individually and often not in the Church's institutional interests. Interestingly enough, many priests, and even three bishops, became Masons, because the lodges were foci of opposition to Portugal. The abortive republican revolt in Pernambuco of 1817 included so many clerics that it has been called 'the Revolution of the Padres'. After independence was declared by Emperor Pedro I in 1822, the National Constituent Assembly operated under the Presidency of the bishop of Rio de Janeiro and included fifteen members of the clergy.

Although Brazil became independent in 1822, the Church–state relationship did not change. The political charter of the Empire (1822–89) was the Constitution of 1824, which declared in Article 5 that 'the Roman Catholic, apostolic religion will continue to be the religion of the Empire'. The writers of the Constitution wanted to ensure that the 'uniqueness' of Brazil would continue to be reflected in its Church. As the important statesman Joaquim Nabuco suggested, the Church would have to conform to the 'customs of our country'.[34] 'For this the legislator constituted the Emperor as the first ecclesiastical authority of the country in the sense that to him belonged not only the choice of personnel – the formation of the Church hierarchy – but also the supreme judgment of all the laws and decrees of the Popes and councils.'[35]

For a few years after independence, Rome tried to negotiate with Brazil to change the Church relationship, while at the same time waiting for Portugal to recognize the independent empire. Essentially, full recognition was given and after another four months the patronage of the Order of Christ was also granted. However, a concordat was not signed, so that the relationship was more or less temporary. In short, it was a *modus vivendi* in which the patronage was only tolerated. But although Rome only tolerated the patronage, it was taken very much for granted by statesmen during the First Empire and even more so by Emperor Pedro II (1840–89).

Pedro II was not particularly interested in the Church and religion, although he officially and effectively controlled them. He was known as a 'limited Catholic', although some argue that he was not Catholic at all but was obliged to play a role because of his position.[36] He was a Voltairean, a rationalist and very

---

[34] Joaquim Nabuco, 'O Partido ultramontano: suas invasões, seus órgãos, e Seu futuro', artigos publicados na *Reforma* (Rio de Janeiro, 1873), p. 9. Cited in Thornton, p. 225.
[35] *Ibid.*
[36] Basílio de Magalhães, *Estudos de História do Brasil* (Rio de Janeiro: Companhia Editôra Nacional, 1940), p. 152.

interested in science, Sanskrit and exotic matters. Joaquim Nabuco characterized his attitudes toward the Church and clergy in the following way:

Dom Pedro II was raised in anti-clerical prejudice. He was not exactly anti-clerical – he
saw no real danger in the existence of the clergy. Instead, he found the religous vocation
unattractive. To him, a tireless student of the sciences, the soldier and the priest were
two social phenomena with no future, two temporary necessities which he would like
to put to better use.[37]

Pedro utilized his legal powers of patronage and the accrued powers of
recourse and placet fully, for he was extremely concerned with the threat of
ultramontanism and suspected that the Holy See might try to interfere in internal
state matters; these matters, of course, concerned Church policy as well. He
turned down the prestigious offer of a cardinalate in Brazil, the first in Latin
America, in 1847, so as 'To avoid subtleties which constantly prevail in the
Roman Curia.'[38] During his fifty year reign, he founded only three dioceses,
all within the first fifteen years. Again Pedro was worried about involvement
with Rome. In referring to the creation of more dioceses, the Emperor was
reported to have exclaimed, 'Create another bishopric! Augment the number of
these combatants in favor of the ambitions of the Roman Curia!'[39]

During Pedro's long reign the Church was nothing more than an ordinary
bureau of government. Through the patronage, he nominated bishops and
other important members, interpreting the extent of his jurisdiction as he wished.
Also through the patronage, he collected the tithes and paid the clergy; they
were treated no differently from any other group of public functionaries. The
lack of regulations from the Holy See on Church affairs combined with placet
meant that the Emperor could decide what to allow through; the state passed
legislation and did this in a very thorough manner indeed.

A few examples will illustrate the extent and bothersome nature of these
laws. Bishops were forbidden to leave their dioceses without governmental
permission, on penalty of having their see declared vacant and a successor
nominated; military chaplains were removed from the supervision of the bishops
and given permission to use the ring; the necessity or not of candles in the
churches was regulated; and the government decided on the eligibility of
nominations for mace carriers in the cathedrals.[40]

Regulations and petty directives of this nature discouraged Church influence
and merely maintained the organization at the whim of the government. In

---

[37] Joaquim Nabuco, *Um Estadista do império: Nabuco de Araujo*, sua vida, suas opiniões, sua
época, 3 vols. (Rio de Janeiro: [1897–1899] repr. 1936 in São Paulo), 2:260.
[38] Basílio de Magalhães, p. 107.
[39] Dom Antônio de Macedo Costa, *Lutas e Victorias*, p. 81. Quoted in manuscript by Sister
Mary Crescentia Thornton on 'The Church in the Old Republic'. Rubert offers another
view on the low organizational development, pointing out that Pedro denied the request for
more dioceses in 1867 because of lack of finances to support them. This view shows less
of a political concern and more of a total lack of any concern. Rubert, p. 108.
[40] Basílio de Magalhães notes that these regulations covered some 150 pages in the *Manual
Eclesiástico*, p. 104.

some cases, the legislation seemed to be directed against an increase in influence, particularly if it somehow involved a closer Church connection with Rome. The case of the religious orders illustrates this point.

The orders had members coming in from Europe as nearly all had their centers abroad; discipline was enforced internationally, the turnover brought in new people and ideas; and they were usually better off financially and thus less likely to compromise. Following the example of Pombal and of post-Revolutionary French Liberalism, the Empire had from the beginning tried to increase state control over the orders or eliminate them completely. From 1827 on, numerous laws and regulations were issued which restricted, limited or in some way lessened the independence of the orders. Some were suppressed, others 'reformed' and the property of a few confiscated. The legislation culminated in the circular of 1855 by José Nabuco de Araujo, which prohibited the orders from receiving novices until a proposed concordat with Rome had been approved. The concordat was never negotiated and the orders thus could not legally receive more novices. The circular was clearly intended to eliminate the orders by a policy of gradual attrition. Apparently the policy worked; one piece of relevant information is that in 1868 there were eleven Benedictine monasteries in Brazil with a total of only forty-one monks. As far as one can judge, a similar predicament existed in all the orders.

Without an increase in or even a constant number of order priests, the Church in Brazil had to rely upon the secular clergy. By and large, this was not the sort of group that might be expected to increase Church influence. One or two descriptions might be appropriate here. The village priest of Paracatu in Minas Gerais was described as, 'characteristic of the Brazil of his time – valiant, a politician, conscientious, living with his woman, and tenderly rearing his children'.[41] When Dom Pedro Maria de Lacerda became bishop of Rio de Janeiro in 1868, he selected as his Vicar General a monsignor who was notorious for his lack of chastity. 'Despite his reputation the bishop chose him because the whole chapter led similar lives, and there was no one else to whom the priests could turn.'[42] Most of the descriptions provide a similar view of the clergy as being more politicians than priests, weak in clerical discipline and more in favor of the Empire than the suspected pretensions of the Holy See. What is more, their numbers were decreasing; by the end of the Empire there were only 700 mainly secular priests for 14 million people in the immense country.

The primary reason given by the government for suppressing the religious orders was that the members were immoral, especially regarding the vow of chastity. The policies regarding education in the seminaries for secular priests give some indication of how the government proposed to improve the quality of at least the secular priests. Of the twelve dioceses which existed in 1889, nine had seminaries. In these, the government regulated priestly education through

[41] George Boehrer, 'The Church and the Overthrow of the Brazilian Monarchy', *Hispanic American Historical Review* 48 (August 1968), p. 384.
[42] *Ibid.*

control over finances, texts, instructors and diplomas.[43] The government made no efforts to change the type or standards of education in the seminaries and even prevented certain reform-minded bishops from doing so. The decrees of the Holy See regarding the seminaries were not implemented in Brazil. In short, where the government had clear authority to act in the seminaries, it failed to do so, thereby lowering the standards of the future secular clergy.

Given the great control the state exercised over the Church (often abetted by an uncommitted clergy), the latter's influence did not increase during the period of the Empire. How can levels of influence be indicated specifically? This is not really feasible on an historical basis, but some material can be cited which supports this widely accepted conclusion. By 1889, there were only twelve dioceses and thirteen bishops in all Brazil and only about 700 priests. At the same time in the United States, which was smaller than Brazil and had a much smaller Catholic population, there were eighty-four bishops and some 8,000 priests.[44] The Brazilian secular clergy were trained in only nine seminaries and their education was more influenced by the state than the Church. Reliance upon state structures did not apparently call forth any particular action on the part of the government, and in general things religious were ignored. Religion per se was not attacked; the elite considered it useful as an aid to national unity and as a way to keep the people content. However, they simply were not very interested in the Church and were definitely opposed to further links with Rome. A very astute commentator on the Brazilian Church has observed 'during the monarchical era, Catholicism showed no signs of development or activity except for individual acts of the Faith and religious ceremonies which, incidentally were. . .greatly distorted in the life of the parishes'.[45] This sad predicament was to improve, but first the relationships between the state and Rome had to change.

The Religious conflict of 1874

In 1874, a conflict erupted between two bishops and the state which was instrumental in the later separation of Church and state after the fall of Pedro II in 1889. This event alone did not lead to the fall of the Empire, but it was one important factor of many which eroded the government's support and culminated in a military coup, leading to the founding of the First Republic. Its main importance here is its role in bringing about a different relationship between Rome and the state.

The main source of the conflict was Rome's increasing efforts to gain control over the Brazilian Church. As noted earlier, by about 1820 the Vatican was

---

[43] An imperial decree of 1863 declared the government competent to appoint seminary professors and select texts to be used in courses. See Dom Oscar de Oliveira, p. 159 and Gustavo Pérez et al., p. 37.

[44] Pe. Júlio Maria, O Catolicismo no Brasil (Rio de Janeiro: Livraria Agir Editôra [1st ed. 1900] repr. 1950), p. 175.

[45] Ibid., p. 211.

attempting to improve the very unfavorable relationship, but progress was slow. The main factors that catalyzed the conflict were: the increase of ultramontanism in Rome; its reverberations among some members of the hierarchy in Brazil; and the overreactions on the part of the Imperial government.

Rome's most energetic attempts to bring the Brazilian Church under control were during the reign of Pope Pius IX (1846–78). Pius IX began as a liberal Pope but finished with a reputation as the most reactionary and ultramontane pontif of recent times. He was especially concerned with the condition of the Church in predominantly Catholic countries, where he tried to secure special protection for the Church in the most advantageous terms possible.[46] Pius IX is considered ultramontane because he demanded Church centralization in matters of doctrine and ecclesiastical government. The 'Syllabus of Errors' codified his view of the Church, the world and the errors of the time. Liberals all over the world responded with amazement and scorn to its publication in 1864. Hales argues convincingly that the syllabus was not written with reference to countries such as England and the United States, but rather with Italy primarily in mind, where the Church had serious and particular problems. It is also clear that the syllabus was extremely relevant to the situation of the Church in Brazil and in fact, Pedro II did not give the placet to 'Quanta Cura', the papal encyclical to which the syllabus was an addenda. For all intents and purposes, the syllabus did not exist in Brazil; if it had, the contradictions between the Church situation in that country and Pius' ideas would have been obvious. Of the eighty theses which made up the syllabus, it is worth noting that: No. 28 declares the placet illegal; No. 37 comes out against national Churches; and No. 42 states that the dominance of civil law over canon law in conflicts is wrong. The syllabus spoke violently against Masonry; at this time in Brazil the most important ministers and the Emperor himself were associated with Masonic lodges. The significance of the syllabus was increased when Pius had the First Vatican Council declare papal infallibility in 1870; that is institutional centralization of the Universal Church in the papacy. The combination of the syllabus, papal infallibility and Pius' whole orientation and attitudes had two main results in Brazil.

On the one hand, it alerted government officials in Brazil to interpret any weak glimmering of Church independence as the evil face of ultramontanism and thus a threat to sovereignty.[47] On the other hand, the combination gave support to a few members of the hierarchy who adopted a course of action in accord with the Pope but in opposition to the Emperor. Pre-eminent in the galvanization of the situation was the First Vatican Council, which terminated in 1870. Seven of the

---

[46] E. E. Y. Hales, *Pio Nono* (Garden City, NY: Image Books, 1962), p. 277. It is worth mentioning that before he became Pope, he visited Latin America and was aware of Church problems on the continent. A response to this awareness was his founding of Collegio Pio Latino Americano Pontifico, especially for Latin American priests, in Rome in 1858.

[47] Thornton notes that in order to counteract the centralization of the papacy, the officials implemented further the right of recourse to the Crown, initiated measures which required civil registration of births and deaths, etc. 'A form of exalted nationalism spurred imperial statesmen to defend uncompromisingly the authority of the State against what it imputed to be the fanaticism of the Roman curia.' *The Church and Freemasonry in Brazil*, p. 110.

eleven Brazilian bishops attended the Council, were motivated to some degree, depending on each individual's commitment to ultramontanism, and became more unified. On the other side, the Council was followed with interest by Empire statesmen, who spoke and wrote against Council decisions and expected the worst from the returning bishops.

Pe. Rubert, in his article on the Brazilian bishops at the Council, observes that in the second half of the nineteenth century the hierarchy was intellectually and morally superior to that of any previous period.[48] The reason for the improvement is fairly simple: Pedro II ran the Church as a bureau of government and given his penchant for rationality, scholarship and other relatively positive matters, he preferred bureaucrats with reputable moral standings. By roughly 1850, the Emperor was nominating bishops whose private lives were not marked by party politics or immoral behavior. However, in doing so he unwittingly began selecting men who would likely be more amenable to the ultramontanism of Pius IX. That is, Pedro was distinguishing between priests who were flexible on morals and in tune with the situation of the Church in Brazil and those who were more moral but also more likely to be somewhat badly disposed towards the weak and fully dominated Church.[49] By 1872, there were at least five bishops who tended toward Roman ideas and had in fact studied in Europe.

The bishop who touched off the conflict was a young (27-year-old) Capuchin, Dom Vital Maria Gonçalves de Oliveira, who had studied in France and had become imbued with the ultramontane spirit. Dom Vital may have acted on his own, but he was certainly acting in the spirit of Rome, with a sense of mission according to this spirit and quite possibly with the direct encouragement of the Pope. The letters which the Pope sent to Dom Vital indicate that at least he had his full support. For example: 'You have acted wisely, continue. We cannot refrain from commending the zeal with which you have striven and are striving to resist so great an evil. We commit full power to you. . .'[50] Or, again in a letter of February 1875: 'The bishops. . .conducted themselves perfectly well, in conformity with canon law; yet inasmuch as civil law is not in accord with Canon law, *a conflict was bound to arise.*'[51] With this encouragement, Dom Vital confronted the Church–state relationship and made it a sort of crusade. As he pleaded in a letter addressed to an imperial minister: 'Your Excellency understands that this question is one of life or death for the Brazilian Church; it behooves me to support [it] with the greatest sacrifices rather than to relax.'[52]

---

[48] Rubert, pp. 108–10.

[49] Boehrer comments on the bishops' nominations: 'If a candidate's philosophy was acceptable, his morals generally were not. Often, therefore, the Emperor had to turn to ultramontane clergy whose private lives he could tolerate.' Boehrer, *Hispanic American Historical Review*, 48:386.

[50] *Relatório do Ministério dos Negocios do Império* (Rio de Janeiro, 1874), p. 75, quoted in Thornton, *The Church and Freemasonry in Brazil*, p. 162.

[51] Félix de Olivola, *Um Grande Brasileiro: D. Frei Vital Maria Gonçalves Oliveira*, 2nd ed. (Recife, 1936), p. 194, quoted in Thornton, *The Church and Freemasonry in Brazil*, p. 243. Emphasis added.

[52] Letter of 27 February 1873, reproduced in Thornton, *Ibid.*, pp. 259–62.

Dom Vital was willing to give up establishment and certain privileges if these meant, as they did in Brazil, subservience to the interests of the state: 'we renounce all the civil honors that the Government of His Majesty gives us, on the condition that it restore to us the liberty of being able to direct and govern in conformity with the teaching of Holy Mother Church and the dictates of our conscience the portion of the flock of Our Lord Jesus Christ which the Holy Spirit confined to our care and solicitude'.[53] The particular issue that gave rise to this support from the Pope and crusading spirit from the Bishop was relatively simple and in itself not particularly important.

By the mid-nineteenth century, the *irmandades* had become centers of Masonic activity. Since many priests and important government officials were Masons, there was nothing strange in having Masonic *irmandades*. There has been some debate as to whether the Brazilian form of Masonry was anti-Catholic or anti-clerical, but with the syllabus of errors and anathematization of Masonry, it became antagonistic to anybody who opposed it. Even before Dom Vital was invested in Olinda in May 1872, he was denounced by the Masons as ultra-montane. To test the new Bishop, the Masons in Olinda announced that a mass would be celebrated to commemorate the anniversary of a lodge. Dom Vital ordered the clergy not to participate; they did as he directed. To draw him out, the Masons then published a list of laymen and clergy who were members of *irmandades* and Masons at the same time. Dom Vital ordered the clergy to abjure and the *irmandades* to expel members who refused to abjure. When the *irmandade* of the Most Holy Trinity refused to comply, the Bishop laid down an interdict on it and the *irmandade* promptly appealed to the government for recourse. Despite the fact that Dom Vital made it clear the interdict applied only to the spiritual aspect of the *irmandade*, the National Council of State accepted the recourse. Pedro II then accepted the recommendation of the Council and ordered his minister to force Dom Vital to back down. Dom Vital was joined in precisely the same issue by another Bishop, Dom Macedo Costa, and they both refused to lift the interdicts on the *irmandades*.[54]

Dom Vital's position was intransigent, as already indicated by his acceptance of the mission to do battle for the papacy. The state was also determined, as they perceived that Dom Vital was simply doing the work of Rome. The petition of recourse from the *irmandade* stated, 'the bishop showed excessive zeal for the doctrines of the Holy Roman Curia and a lack of concern for the prerogatives of the state'.[55] Obviously, the matter was not simply one of two bishops arguing within their own dioceses; much larger issues of sovereignty and control were involved. When the bishops refused to lift the interdicts they were imprisoned, tried and sentenced to four years' hard labor. The Emperor later commuted their

---

[53] *Relatório do Ministério dos Negocios do Império*, p. 73, quoted in Thornton, *Ibid.*, p. 160.
[54] Dom Macedo Costa, Bishop of Pará, was a Sulpician and also trained in France.
[55] 'Dom Vital's independence of action appeared especially threatening to Brazilian statesmen because it was judged to be part of a universal movement inaugurated by Pius IX to enforce his illiberal doctrines throughout the world, and especially among nations where a union of Church and State existed.' Thornton, *The Church and Freemasonry in Brazil*, pp. 225–6.

sentences to simple imprisonment and with a change in ministries in 1875 they were granted amnesty. The conflict and subsequent imprisonment were really quite dramatic. The Church, after all, had always been established as a state institution; thus, the Brazilian government convicted two of its highest ranking officials. The matter came to this point, it seems, because it was basically a test case of who controlled the Church. The decision appears to demonstrate that the state controlled the Church, for it could intervene in the dioceses, order the bishops to act and imprison them if they did not. Further, the Church's influence was so weak at this time that there was little reaction in society against the government for its actions. Only two members of the assembly spoke out in favor of the bishops and these were not among the five priests who were members. Within the Church itself, especially around the other three more or less ultra-montane bishops, there was some activity on behalf of the two criminal bishops, but nothing very significant.

There are two ways of interpreting the importance of the Religious Question for the Church; they are not contradictory but rather reveal different timings and emphases. One could argue that the conflict itself led to the separation of Church and state some fifteen years later, insofar as this event prompted both bishops and politicians to assess the situation objectively and to recognize that things had to be changed. To do so, however, would be to ignore Rome's increasing efforts to control the Church since the early part of the century, the diffusion of the legitimacy of this attempt among the Brazilian hierarchy and the state's reaction to the Church's assertion. Rather than arguing that the events of 1874 led to the separation, it seems more sensible to view them both as a signal that separation was imminent and as a high point in this process. The Religious Question demonstrated to all the bishops the liabilities of the Church's close relationship with the state, reinforcing an awareness which had already been generated at an abstract level by Pius IX's statements on precisely this point, and through this combination the bishops came to perceive that something was amiss. In their Pastoral letter of March 1890 they referred to the patronage as, 'a protection that smothered us... Among us, the oppression exercised by the State in the name of a pretended patronage was a main cause of weakness in our Church and almost led to its destruction.'[56] To the government, the conflict indicated the extent of the diffusion of ultramontane ideas among sectors of the Church. From rather different viewpoints, therefore, a nebulous agreement emerged that the Church–state relationship should change and the opportunity presented itself in the founding of the Republic.

The Empire which had been founded in 1822 was overthrown in 1889 and replaced by the First Republic (1889–1930). A good deal has been written on the role of the 1874 conflict in contributing to the fall of the Empire.[57] Although

[56] Quoted in João Dornas Filho, *O Padroado e A Igreja Brasileira* (Rio de Janeiro: Companhia Editôra Nacional, 1937), p. 289.
[57] See e.g., Percy A. Martin, 'Causes of the Collapse of the Brazilian Empire', *Hispanic American Historical Review* 4 (February 1921), pp. 4–48, which argues an important role for the conflict; others have taken a similar view. The opposition may be seen in Boehrer, *Hispanic American Historical Review* 48.

some sectors of the Church increased their opposition to the government of the Emperor, and thus withdrew a degree of legitimacy, it is obvious that the Church did not have enough influence to make much of an impact by itself. There were several other reasons for the end of the Empire: abolition of slavery in 1888 without compensation made many plantation owners unhappy with the government; an increase in militarism after the Paraguayan War of 1870 resulted in a military coup and a military man as the first Republican president; the Republican idea and Republican movements expanded in the latter half of the century; a monarchy in the New World was an anomaly which became less attractive as Pedro II aged and the succession of his daughter was undesirable; and, of course, the Religious Questions of 1874 also contributed. At the least, the conflict tended to unify the Church, so that it did not divide during the change of regimes as had been the case in Spanish America at an earlier period. The greater part of the Church came out in favor of the republic.[58]

The provisional government which ruled from November 1889 until March 1891 decreed the separation of Church and state. In fact, the provisional government and the subsequent Constitution of February 1891 went considerably further and enacted laws which reflected a studied disregard for the Church and religion. The provisional government guaranteed freedom of worship and recognized the rights of all religions to hold property; the Catholic clergy was to be supported by the state for one more year, after which state and national authorities were prohibited from subsidizing any religion. In this way the Catholic religion was put on a par with all others, despite the fact that the vast majority of the population were nominally Catholics. The Republican Constitution was not declared in the name of God, thus proclaiming the essentially non-religious character of the new regime. The measures of the provisional government on separation and on non-support were ratified. Members of religious orders, congregations and communities that obeyed a vow of obedience were disenfranchised. Only civil, and not religious, marriages were officially recognized. The cemeteries were secularized and put under the administration of municipal authorities. The clergy did not enjoy political immunity. And finally, education was made secular, religion being omitted from the curriculum, and the government was prohibited from subsidizing religious schools.[59] After 400 years of establishment, the Church was suddenly excluded from the public realm and state support of religious influence. The Church and state were to have little or no contact and were legally directed to ignore each other.

There are three main reasons why the government so totally excluded the Church from the public realm. First, the conflict of 1874 convinced the statesmen that they did not want a continued union of Church and state, as it

---

[58] On the fall of the Empire, see Francisco de Oliveira Vianna, *O Ocaso do Império* (Rio de Janeiro: Livraria José Olympio Editôra, 1959), and C. H. Haring, *Empire in Brazil* (Cambridge: Harvard University Press, 1958). For the situations in the Spanish American countries, see Mecham, Chaps. 2 and 3.

[59] Pe. Geraldo Fernandes, 'A Religião nas Constituições Republicanas do Brasil', *Revista Eclesiástica Brasileira* 25 (December 1948), pp. 832–44.

obviously was not functioning very well. But beyond this, it must be remembered that the coup which removed the Emperor and initiated the Republic brought to an end the previous regime. The Church had always been an integral part of of this regime and had to be disposed of as well.[60] Secondly, the Church lacked political influence with the new leaders at both ideological and organizational levels. Ideologically, as the Church was so weak in influence and unable to innovate during the Empire period, it simply did not appeal to the new leaders. The number of committed Catholic laymen in the elite of this period could be counted on the fingers of two hands. All the others were adherents of one or more of the various ideological formulations then current in Brazil. Two of these – Positivism and Liberalism – were most important in the new regime and for systemic as well as historical reasons had little use for Catholicism and the Church. Organizationally, the Church lacked political power in the new government; this was always the case. The bishops attempted to influence the Assembly and the provisional president by means of letters, appeals and personal visits, but they accomplished little. Thirdly, the new regime and its constitution were artificial and alien to the reality of Brazil at this time, including its religious character. Religion has been established and protected at different times in many different places, including Brazil, partly because it makes governing easier. The statesmen under the Empire, which had tightly controlled the Church, were careful not to attack the religion as such: religion was good for the people. Now, however, they went out of their way to alienate the Church and legalized their lack of concern for religion. They did not think they needed the legitimacy of religion – even a weak one – because the Constitution they drafted was an imitation of the clauses and ideas of other countries, especially the United States and France. In the former, separation and neutrality in religious matters was a political tenet; in the latter, the Radicals were presently in power and attempting to vanquish a Church which represented the *Ancien Régime*. The new Constitution, and thus institutions, of the Republic did not reflect the reality of the situation in Brazil in 1891, but rather a projected illusion of what alienated intellectuals thought the situation should be. Or, as Oliveira Vianna concluded, there was 'no relationship between the idealism of the Constitution and the national reality'.[61]

The hierarchical reaction to the Republic and its treatment of the Church are contradictory if one does not keep in mind the historic manner of defining and exercising influence. The views of the episcopacy can be seen in their pastoral letter of March 1890 where they welcomed the Republic for 'assuring to the

---

[60] For precisely the same point, see the brilliant account of the Church's position in the French Revolution in Alexis de Tocqueville, *The Old Regime and the French Revolution* (New York: Doubleday Anchor Books, 1955).

[61] Francisco de Oliveira Vianna, *O Idealismo da Constituição* (São Paulo: Companhia Editôra Nacional, 1939), p. 93. Also see his *Instituições Políticas Brasileiras* (Rio de Janeiro: Livraria José Olympio Editôra, 1955), p. 413. An instance of reaction to the exclusion of religion was the Canudos Rebellion of 1896–7 in which the leader, Antônio Conselheiro, villified the 'Godless Republic'. See the fascinating account of this movement, Euclides da Cunha, *Rebellion in the Backlands*, trans. by Samuel Putnam (Chicago: Phoenix Books, 1957).

Brazilian Catholic Church certain liberties which she never enjoyed in the time of the monarchy'.[62] In analyzing the initial decree of the provisional government, they pointed to the improvements over the past system, in which the Church was but a bureau of government. The pastoral showed clearly that the bishops appreciated increased independence from the state.

But then the bishops seemed to contradict themselves when they stated: 'In the name of social order, of public peace, of harmony among the citizenry, in the name of the right of conscience, we Catholics repudiate the separation of Church and State. We demand the union of the two powers...'[63] The explanation is simple: Church influence had always been defined through state power and state structures were used to generate and exercise it. Without this support, there was no influence. Thus, while the bishops wanted more independence from the government, they still believed in the necessity of state support, and this meant a form of establishment. Their perception of other alternatives was probably inhibited by the fact that they were unwillingly excluded from the public realm. They did not overcome their initial reaction and indeed a rallying cry of the Church from then on would be re-entry into government. As the bishops stated in their pastoral of 1900:

We loudly proclaim that we shall not enter into a pact which includes this wicked innovation...Let us use the liberty, which we shall enjoy, and before our representatives, before those who have been entrusted with supreme power, let us present our respectful but firm and unwavering petition: We do not wish to be a Nation without religion and without God; we do not wish to be governed by an atheistic government.[64]

Until 1930, the Church sought to regain political power as an integral part of its approach to influence. As the 1900 pastoral suggests, it attempted to persuade the political representatives to grant what it considered to be its proper public position.

Because of the separation of Church and state, with the associated elimination of the patronage, recourse, placet and informal means of state control, the Holy See entered into a 'normal' autonomy relationship with the Brazilian Church for the first time. Through the creation of dioceses, appointment of bishops, direct communications, reforms in the seminaries and all the other features of institutional control characteristic of the post-Vatican I era, the goals and structures of the Universal Church superseded those of the Empire in directing and building the Church. The relationship was one of coalition, in that the goals and structure of the larger body became those of the national body as the latter became integrated into the former. The Holy See was aware of the great problems of the Brazilian Church and took steps such as national and regional synods, a Latin American Plenary Council in 1899, a full nuncio in 1901, a cardinalate in 1905 and the general channeling of ideas and resources into Brazil, to orient and strengthen the institution. The relationship between the

[62] Dornas Filho, p. 290.
[63] Ibid.
[64] Gustavo Pérez et al., p. 40.

Church and the Republic was one of competition. They had similar goals of building up influence over the country; they used separate structures; and their strategies as political and religious bodies differed. Relations between the two institutions were generally friendly although officially very formal. Pope Leo XIII encouraged the people to be loyal to the government, and the state allowed the creation of the nunciature and the cardinalate. The significant relationship at this period was with Rome, however; with the changed ties, a different influence model was formulated.

The most obvious change in the influence model concerned the instruments or mechanisms for generating and exercising influence. Basic to this was simple organizational development; the Brazilian Church had never really evolved as an institution, both because it could presumably rely on state structures and because the state was never willing to put resources into development or allow its expansion. After 1891, the Church built up its organization starting from almost nothing. In 1889, there were only eleven dioceses and one archdiocese, an increase of three from 1840 when Pedro II had become Emperor. In 1893, Pope Leo XIII created another ecclesiastical province in addition to the one already existing and made four new dioceses. From then on the increase in ecclesiastical divisions was rapid. In 1900 there were 17; in 1910 there were 30; in 1920 there were 58; and by 1964 a total of 178 ecclesiastical divisions existed. In other words, in the relatively brief period of 70 years there was a 1,500% increase in the number of dioceses, archdioceses, etc.[65] It is also worth emphasizing that the bishops now selected for the sees were the choice of Rome and not of the government, although there was usually some prior consultation before nomination.

Another indication of organizational development is in the founding of seminaries. In 1890, there were nine major and eleven minor seminaries. The Holy See encouraged the founding of new diocesan seminaries and stimulated the Vicentians, Jesuits and Lazarists to staff them. By 1927 there were fifteen major seminaries and around thirty minor ones. The seminaries did not increase more rapidly because of a lack of vocations. To overcome the shortage of clergy, the Holy See directly encouraged religious orders to send priests, nuns and brothers to Brazil. They reopened convents and monasteries closed in the middle of the nineteenth century and established new centers for orders and congregations, with some orders moving into education. Indicative of the results of this policy is the fact that in 1946 there were 6,383 priests in Brazil: 2,964 were secular; 3,419 were members of the orders; and two-thirds of the latter were foreign-born.[66] The same sort of indicators can be cited for all sectors and levels of the Brazilian Church to demonstrate the rapid organizational development after 1891. While coordination and other characteristics of efficient organizations, such as communication, cohesion and leadership were slower in

[65] See the appendix for rates of growth and population per division.
[66] In 1964 of a total of 12,181 priests, 4,872 were secular, of which about 16% were foreign-born; there were 7,309 order priests and of these nearly 53% were foreign-born. Data from CERIS.

coming, by 1930 the Church in Brazil resembled in many ways the large bureau-cratic organization that most people visualize when reading about the Church.

On the basis of this organizational development, the mechanisms of influence became similar to those of Europe in the period, simply because the Church was now linked to the Universal Church from which it received orientation and a large part of its personnel. There were, therefore, the following types of mech-anisms or activities: the usual administration of sacraments, Church schools for the middle classes, and various pious groups, associations and works, which were also aimed at a bourgeois society that was more relevant for Europe than for Brazil. The Church in the urban areas was modeled on the European pattern; the clergy as well as the political elite were alienated from Brazilian reality. More than one student of Brazilian Church history has noted the resemblance to Europe, 'but with one fundamental difference: the institutions were not established out of necessity, but because of a desire to imitate'.[67]

The original organizational principle of full territorial coverage became dor-mant with the separation of Church and state, because it was not feasible in the existing situation and because Rome's emphasis differed. It did not disappear, however, and would re-emerge when the political conditions changed after 1930. There were now two dominant organizational principles: one due exclusively to Rome's orientation and the other caused by the manner of Church exclusion from the public realm and the latent principle of territorial coverage. In the first instance, the Church 'denationalized' itself, in the sense that by adopting Rome's goals the institution related more to a non-Brazilian situation than to local conditions. Probably the main orientation of the Church in the post-Vatican I era was opposition to modern threats to the faith such as Modernism, Socialism and secularism. In Brazil, a fortress mentality against Socialism, Protestantism, Masonry and the like became the organizational principle. This predisposition was not very rational in Brazil as the Socialists, Protestants and other groups were insignificant. For example, Pope Pius X denounced Modernism in 1907. Despite the fact that Modernism was the very least of the problems facing the Brazilian Church, the hierarchy took the condemnation to heart and sealed off the seminaries and a good part of the Church from this threat, in fact from much of the outside world. In the process, other significant problems such as Spiritism, a lack of a laity and autonomous resources were ignored, as they were not the priorities of Rome. In its goals, therefore, the Brazilian Church was somewhat alienated from the Brazilian reality.

One set of enemies with which the Church did contend was the political elite that had excluded the institution from the public domain. The second organiza-tional principle was, therefore, the use of political strategies to enter into a closer relationship with the state. Since influence had historically been defined largely through power, the political facts of the Constitution not being in the

[67] Pe. José Comblin, 'Situação Histórica do Catolicismo no Brasil', *Revista Eclesiástica Brasileira* 26 (September 1966), pp. 574–601. 'In becoming Romanized, the Church denation-alized itself.' Roger Bastide, 'Religion and the Church in Brazil', in T. Lynn Smith and A. Marchant, eds, *Brazil: Portrait of Half a Continent* (New York: Druden Press, 1951), p. 343.

name of God, the lack of resources for Church education, and its absence in public activities, were completely unacceptable. The clergy wanted state support and thus wrote about it, tried to convince government officials and generally protested. The rationale was the fact that the Church should be recognized in public as the institution which represented the vast majority of Brazilians in their religious belief. The clergy wanted the state structures that would result from such a recognition in order to expand influence.

The groups or sectors of society influenced by the Church were in theory still comprehensive. However, lacking state structures and with only a few thousand priests by the 1930s, such a scope was obviously ridiculous. Some priests, mainly from Europe, were engaged in evangelizing work in the interior, but the Church's main focus was the middle class in urban areas. They were influenced by a school system staffed largely by foreign personnel, through pious groups and associations, and in fact by the whole orientation of the Church as seen in sermons, devotions, and programs. The selection of this stratum was logical in that the Church needed resources and the middle class had them; priests, despite their lower-class backgrounds, adopted middle-class attitudes in the seminaries and in effect received middle-class recognition; and the Church in Europe had developed strategies for focusing on the bourgeoisie which were adopted without much question in Brazil. Thus while the institution claimed to be concerned with all the people, it did in fact concentrate almost exclusively on the middle classes.

The Church–society relationship was also supposedly still comprehensive. The clergy wanted to penetrate and influence all levels of society but, with separation and the subsequent lack of state resources and structures, this was not possible. What in effect happened when the Church was forced from the national and central structures was a protracted decentralization and a continued fusion with local and regional political and social groupings. Probably the best way to visualize the Church at this time is on the basis of two Churches, at least, with one becoming more centralized and dogmatic in the cities and another operating pretty much as always in close relationship with local social and political groups.[68]

There is no doubt that a different model of influence resulted from Church separation in 1889. With separation, the Church associated with Rome in a coalition relationship and had to change some parts of the model, both because of this association and because state structures were no longer available. From the change in relationship, another approach to influence emerged and it is clear that at least potential influence increased. The institution was larger and better organized; it could draw ideas and personnel from abroad, and it was able to make almost autonomous decisions. However, the link with Rome was not totally without liabilities as the European orientation was frequently not relevant

---

[68] On the decentralized nature of society in this era see Juarez Rubens Brandão Lopes, *Desenvolvimento e Mudança Social* (São Paulo: Companhia Editôra Nacional, 1968), Chapter 5. For an excellent study on the relationships between the local Church, local power groups, and the national Church and politics, see Ralph della Cava, *Miracle at Joaseiro* (New York: Columbia University Press, 1970).

to the situation in Brazil. Was the Church influential? This question cannot be answered with assurance, because the statements available from observers of that time, or on observers of that time, are contradictory. It is easier to start from the point of influence and show how perception of the question led to a particular line of political action.[69]

Sebastião Leme da Silveira Cintra (1882–1942) did more than any other cleric in the first half of the twentieth century to orient and mobilize the Brazilian Church. As Archbishop of Olinda-Recife (1916–21), coadjutor in Rio de Janeiro (1921–30) and Cardinal Archbishop in Rio until 1942, Dom Leme was crucial in determining the direction taken by the whole institution. He was extremely concerned with the lack of Church influence, and because of his actions to remedy the situation he was considered an innovator.[70]

Don Leme put forth his ideas on the Church and influence in his famous 1916 pastoral letter addressed to the people of Olinda-Recife.[71] The fundamental fact for Leme was that Brazil was essentially a Catholic country – traditionally, historically and in the beliefs of the people. Yet a paradoxical situation existed, in that the Church had little influence. Indications of low influence could be found in the lack of religion in most fields of social action including politics, arts and letters; in the lack of vocations, finances and organizations; and in the lack of Catholics among the intellectual elites. That is, the Church which represented the religion of the great majority of Brazilians had little impact. What was the reason behind this paradox of a Church with no influence in a Catholic country? According to Dom Leme, it was the lack of religious education.

[69] Gustavo Pérez *et al.* were in favor of the autonomy relationship and saw it giving stimulus for a more dynamic Church; Camargo was also in favor. Pe. Desiderio Deschand, *A Situação Actual da Religião no Brasil* (Rio de Janeiro: H. Garnier, Libreiro-Editor, 1910), was against Church autonomy as it lessened influence, because of the lack of state structures at its 'disposal'. It is interesting to note, however, that Deschand seems to confuse Brazil with France and is thus an example of an alientated Churchman who cannot perceive what is relevant to Brazil.

[70] It is necessary to mention that the lack of Church influence was recognized by at least one other important Churchman of this period, although his solutions were rather different from Leme's. Pe. Júlio Maria, 1850–1916, was extremely active from about 1890 until his death, in preaching, evangelizing and writing – all with the intention of mobilizing the Church. He welcomed the Republic for the freedom it offered the Church to prosper and develop. 'What we cannot forget is that the Republic, right from the beginning, freed the Brazilian Church from the slavery in which she was buried; and despite the omissions in the Constitution, the Brazilian Church, in this system of common law inaugurated by the decree which abolished the patronage, is prospering and the Catholic conscience is developing'. *O Católicismo no Brasil*, p. 226. Pe. Maria had two main lines of approach: to make Brazil Catholic and unite the Church with the people. What he meant was that there was really no basis yet for a Catholic Brazil and that the Church had to focus on the individual. In his works it is clear that the analysis of influence was more critical than Leme's and his solution, by active evangelization, was a far cry from Leme's of using state power. See also his *Apostrophes* (Nicteroy, [Niterói] R.J.: Escola Typographica Salesiana, 1898).

[71] On Leme, see Irmã Maria Regina do Santo Rosário, O.C.D. (Laurita Pessôa Gabaglia) *O Cardeal Leme* (Rio de Janeiro: Livraria José Olympio Editôra, 1962), and Alceu Amoroso Lima, *O Cardeal Leme: Um Depoimento* (Rio de Janeiro: Livraria José Olympio Editôra, 1943). This pastoral letter is his *Carta Pastoral a Olinda* (Petrópolis, R. J.: Editôra Vozes, 1916).

The people were not instructed in the faith; they were ignorant of the teachings; and consequently religion had no impact on them. The solution? To organize, unify, and then pressure the government for a rightful position in public affairs. From this position, which is of course a matter of Catholic leaders and a privileged Church, it would be easy to promote religious education, abolish religious ignorance and consequently increase Church influence. In short, the solution for Leme lay in a pressure group strategy, to re-enter public life and from this position use power to promote influence. What Leme showed was a continued adherence to the comprehensive and monopolistic goals of the Christendom model, and the realization that these could be attained only with the support of the state. That is, power was still a necessity for influence if goals of this scope and range were adopted.

From his beginning as a member of the hierarchy, Leme organized and mobilized sectors of the Church with the intention of regaining a rightful position for the Church in public life. What is extraordinary is that he succeeded. If one looks to other countries where the Church was forced out of the public domain (Mexico, Chile, Cuba, France, etc.), one finds that the institution never re-entered on its own terms. Usually after protracted periods of recrimination the Church innovated, developed new strategies and promoted a different model of influence. In Brazil, however, Leme's strategy worked and the Church again entered the public domain on a privileged basis.

2. The revolution of 1930: Church–state reintegration

The best analyses of the politics of the First or Old Republic are those that emphasize its decentralized and malleable character. The advantage of this system was its short-run capacity to juggle various groups and in the process maintain the *status quo*. However, by the early 1920s, with low levels of industrialization, urbanization and social differentiation forcing political centralization, the system became less able to cope and civil disturbances became manifest.[1] In these times of unrest, the civil authorities looked to the Church as a means of increasing their legitimacy in the eyes of the people.

When the government of President Epitácio Pessôa (1918–22) was threatened with revolutionary activity he went to Leme for help. The President asked Leme to ride with him in a public procession in order 'to show. . .that the ecclesiastical authority in Rio supported the civil authority [which] was so detested'.[2] Leme agreed to support the civil authority and in the process promoted his cause of bringing the Church and state closer together.[3] During the more difficult tenure of President Artur Bernardes (1922–6), a Republican president made the first official visit of a head of state to the head of the Brazilian Church. In his visit the President emphasized, '. . .the importance of constant collaboration of our ecclesiastical authorities with the government in maintaining order and promoting national progress'.[4] An observer demonstrates her political acumen in commenting on the importance of a similar later meeting between Church and state officials: 'The meeting showed very well how our statesmen. . .were beginning to realize the dangerous mistakes of state secularization and the necessity of appealing to the religiosity of the people.'[5]

Apparently, however, Church support was not yet valued as a negotiable commodity, for the government was unwilling to put the *rapprochement* into law. In 1925, the Constitution of 1891 was slightly modified, and Leme took this opportunity to offer an amendment which would give official recognition to the Catholic religion as the faith of the people and permit religious education in public schools. Primarily on account of President Bernardes' opposition, the amendment was not accepted.[6] Political instability increased and the First Republic eventually fell in 1930 before the revolutionary movement of Getúlio Vargas.

[1] Juarez Rubens Brandão Lopes, *Desenvolvimento e Mudança Social* (São Paulo: Companhia Editôra Nacional, 1968), pp. 83–6 for description of the system.
[2] Regina do Santo Rosário, p. 134. She is the daughter of President Pessôa and was very much an insider in politics.
[3] 'Pleased to accept the mission for a double motive: to give a service for the cause of order personified in a good man, and, at the same time, his presence next to the President would be valued as a public testimony of the so desirable approximation between the Church and the government of the lay Republic of 1889.' *Ibid.*
[4] *Ibid.*, p. 167.
[5] *Ibid.*, p. 169.
[6] *Ibid.*, p. 172.

Getúlio Vargas is the most impressive and important Brazilian statesman of this century. He ruled in a provisional government from the time of the revolution in 1930 until the 1934 Constitution (which replaced that of 1891) was completed. He was President under this Constitution until 1937, when he declared the Estado Nôvo and ruled as dictator until the military coup of 1945 removed him from office. He was elected to office again in 1950 and committed suicide while still president four years later. The system he formulated remained operative in Brazil at least until April 1964 when Vargas' understudy, President João Goulart, was forced from power by a military coup. The Vargas system of government may best be described as an authoritarian regime.[7]

In this system, Vargas was able to buy off all politically and economically important groups through complex compromises. Most traditional groups, such as the coffee planters, were not harmed and the emerging middle classes found jobs in the state bureaucracies. The rural system of land-holding and political power remained largely unchanged and Vargas continued to rely on the support of these traditional elements. A small urban proletariat existed along with some union movements, which Vargas formed into an organized body under his Ministry of Labor, giving it privileges and thus creating a new political resource. But the fifteen years of Vargas' regime were mainly characterized by stability, order and general lack of social change. The initially low mobilization of the population and Vargas' lack of ideology seem crucial in its low pressure character.

Many writers on Brazil have been unable to characterize the Estado Nôvo, because it was neither democratic nor totalitarian. While it partly resembled the Fascist systems then in vogue, close observers recognized its differences. Very simply, the Estado Nôvo was an authoritarian regime; rather than an ideology, Vargas used a mentality that had its basis in Catholicism. For Linz, mentalities are 'ways of thinking and feeling, more emotional than rational, that provide non-codified ways of reacting to situations'.[8] It was difficult to distinguish Vargas' manipulation of symbols, concepts and myths, because the mentality conformed to the basic culture of the country and its predominant religion.

Whereas Vargas worked with a mentality which was not obvious because of its continuity, there was a Fascist movement in Brazil – the *Integralistas* of Plínio Salgado – which had a distinctive ideology. Many in the Church were attracted to the *Integralistas* because of their agreement with Catholic beliefs on some points and because of their opposition to 'atheistic Communism'. The Church was not taken in by the *Integralistas*, however, and Vargas crushed them during the Estado Nôvo. He used the symbols and beliefs of Catholicism to give his

---

[7] 'Authoritarian regimes are political systems with limited, not responsible, political pluralism: without elaborate and guiding ideology (but with distinctive mentalities); without intensive nor extensive political mobilization (except some points in their development); and in which a leader (or occasionally a small group) exercises power within formally ill-defined limits but actually quite predictable ones.' Juan J. Linz, 'An Authoritarian Regime: Spain', in Erik Allardt and Yrjo Littunen, eds., *Cleavages, Ideologies and Party Systems* (Helsinki: Transactions of the Westermarck Society, 1964), p. 297.

[8] Linz, p. 301.

rule legitimacy and therefore placed great value on Church support, as the institution presumably controlled and interpreted the religion. Vargas' daughter explained to me that her father placed the backing of the Church on an equal basis with that of the military. Whereas the latter had the instruments of force, the former provided a means of support that made force less necessary.[9]

Vargas himself was an avowed agnostic and quite uninterested in religion, as were all those in his immediate entourage. However, Dom Leme was his great personal friend. This friendship began as the revolutionary movement of Vargas moved north from Rio Grande do Sul towards Rio de Janeiro and the President, Washington Luís, refused to abdicate. In an attempt to avoid the violence and bloodshed that would inevitably result from a clash between Luís' loyal guard and the revolutionary movement, the military junta representing Vargas asked Leme to speak to the President. Leme agreed and succeeded in convincing Luís to step down. Vargas was extremely grateful to him for his role in making the assumption of power largely non-violent.

One of the reasons the Church was excluded from public life in 1889 was its lack of organizational impact on the new elites. It was a weak and disorganized body that not only lacked a compelling message but could not even bring any political influence to bear. By 1930, after forty years of separation and the importation of foreign resources, the Church had become a large and organized body with Cardinal Leme at its head. In his 1916 pastoral letter Leme had argued that the Church had to organize, unify and then pressure the government. Since 1921 in Rio de Janeiro, he had been active in organizing and unifying; now he had the opportunity with the fall of the First Republic to pressure the next regime. The Church message might still not appeal to the political elites, but if the institution proved itself an organized and mobilized body at least the leaders would have to pay attention to it.

To make it clear to the new rulers that Church support was a desirable commodity, Leme organized two massive demonstrations in Rio de Janeiro in 1931. The first was a week-long celebration in honor of the country's patron saint, Our Lady of Aparecida, and the second was another week-long celebration for Christ the Redeemer. These popular religious events attracted thousands of people and showed that some form of religious spirit was still very much alive among the Brazilians. Oswaldo Aranha, one of Vargas' most important aides, indicated the impact of the events on the provisional government: 'When we arrived from the south [Rio Grande do Sul] we tended to the Left! But after we saw the popular religious movements, in honor of Our Lady of Aparecida and of Christ the Redeemer, we understood we could not go against the sentiments of the people!'[10] To make the pressure more specific, Leme took advantage of the

[9] Interview with Dona Alzira Vargas do Amaral Peixoto on 8 March 1968 in Rio de Janeiro. On Vargas see: Karl Lowenstein, *Brazil Under Vargas* (New York: Macmillan, 1942); Thomas Skidmore, *Politics in Brazil* (New York, Oxford University Press, 1968); and Robert Levine, *The Vargas Regime* (New York: Columbia University Press, 1970).
[10] Regina do Santo Rosário, p. 289.

presence of fifty bishops in Rio for the latter celebration to present to Vargas jointly with them a list of Catholic requests for consideration by the new regime.

In order to have a voice in deciding precisely what sort of public position or role the Church would have in the new regime, Leme promoted various pressure group strategies. Initially, when the provisional government formed a council to study proposals for reformulation of the basic laws, Leme created a group to follow the council's work and to present suggestions. In this way, he kept himself informed about the changes in the law and could offer modifications. The various strategies of personal influence with Vargas, demonstrations of mass support and internal operations in committees resulted in the formation of the Liga Eleitoral Católica (LEC) in 1932. When elections for a constituent assembly were announced, many of Leme's assistants wanted to create a Catholic political party so as to express their demands better. Leme, however, followed a strategy based on the idea that the Church represented all Brazilians, that the Catholic religion was an integral part of the country and that a party would indicate faction: something less than the whole to which the Church aspired. The LEC was a pressure group separate from or above political parties and claimed to represent the whole of Brazil. The group's goals were twofold: to enlist, organize and instruct the Catholic electorate; and to guarantee the Catholic vote to those candidates who accepted the Church's program and agreed to defend it in the forthcoming constituent assembly. The LEC aspired to be a national body, since Leme contacted the hierarchy all over Brazil and had them promote it in their dioceses. On the national level, Leme was the leader, but laymen such as Alceu Amoroso Lima and Sobral Pinto worked closely with him.

In the elections to the constituent assembly of May 1933, most of those supported by the LEC were elected. Leme then maintained pressure on the delegates in the constitutional convention itself. He was aided by Vargas, and 'the political situation was so much under the control of Vargas that the majority of the deputies elected were inclined to follow his directions even without the cruder methods of electoral coercion of which there was still enough'.[11] The Constitution was tailored to the needs and priorities of Vargas.

The 1934 Constitution included all the demands of the LEC. The Constitution was prefaced with the phrase, 'putting our confidence in God'. Separation of Church and state continued, but now the government could assist the Church financially 'in the collective interest'. Members of the religious orders could now vote. Religious associations were granted much more legal recognition. Spiritual assistance was permitted in the military and official establishments. Religious marriage was fully recognized in civil terms and divorce was prohibited. Probably most important, religious education was provided for within school hours and the state could provide subventions for Catholic schools. The Constitution

---

[11] Lowenstein, pp. 20–1. Even before the convention, the Vargas provisional government decreed religious education in the public schools. In 1933 they gave women the vote for the first time, and women tend, more than men, to vote along the lines suggested by the Church.

of 1934 was a great victory for the Church in obtaining public recognition of what it considered its proper role in society.[12]

In 1937, Vargas abolished the 1934 Constitution and ruled as dictator for the next eight years. The Constitution of the Estado Nôvo was much less specific on matters of importance to the Church, because religious matters 'were not constitutional material'. The documents were not the important factors: President Vargas was the key agent and he continued to formalize and deepen his close relationships with the Church. 'In fact the Church continued in the same juridical situation as before, enjoying the same guarantees and liberties.'[13] As the bishop of Pôrto Alegre commented after reviewing several sections of the 1937 Constitution including labor, education, marriage and foreign affairs: 'it cannot be denied that the new Constitution [has] a certain spiritual and Christian character; it is impossible to say this about the Constitution of 1891 which was based on concepts of agnosticism and Comtism'.[14]

There are two illustrative examples of the intimate Church–state relations under Leme and Vargas. Just before the publication of the 1937 Constitution, Leme heard that it recognized divorce. He immediately contacted Dona Luisinha Aranha and asked her to meet with Vargas on this matter. 'Getúlio Vargas, laughing comfortingly said: "Tell Dom Sebastião, Dona Luisinha, that I will decree divorce only on the day when I receive a petition to this effect signed by Cardinal Leme and Dona Luisinha Aranha".'[15] And, when Vargas was considering establishing trade relations with the Soviet Union, Leme wrote a brief arguing against the policy because it might give the Communists an entry into Brazil. Shortly thereafter, Vargas announced that relations would not be established and to show his reasons published Leme's brief verbatim.[16]

In conclusion, the revolution of 1930 provided the Church under the able and astute Cardinal Leme with the opportunity to re-enter the public realm, to regain a hold in state structures in order to establish and exercise influence. President Vargas brought the Church into the public domain in order to obtain the support it could and indeed did offer; by this time the Church had built up its institutional structure and could serve as a valuable ally in ruling the country. The Church and state cooperated very well during the Vargas era and this situation did not change with the coup of 1945. The framers of the 1946 Constitution had no reason to alter the Church–state arrangement developed during the previous sixteen years and the relationship was merely formalized. As one

---

[12] 'We succeeded in incorporating into the constitutional legislation of 1934 the essential political aspirations of national Catholicism. We succeeded in introducing a new principle in the relations between Church and state. We succeeded finally in adjusting the juridical order to agree, in its fundamental lines, with the Brazilian social order, that is, the law would henceforth respect the fact.' Alceu Amoroso Lima, *Indicações Políticas: Da Revolução à Constituição* (Rio de Janeiro: Editôra Civilização Brasileira, S.A., 1936), p. 131. For all constitutions affecting the Church see Fernandes, pp. 830–58.

[13] Fernandes, p. 853.

[14] Dom João Becker, *A Religião e a Pátria em Face das Ideologias Modernas* (Pôrto Alegre: Typographia do Centro, 1939), p. 34.

[15] Regina do Santo Rosário, pp. 371–2.

[16] *Ibid.*

observer noted in 1955, 'The relations between the Church and state have in fact improved extraordinarily over the past decades and seem more intimate in recent years.'[17]

The combination of extensive formal arrangements in the constitutional documents and the even more important informal arrangements of 'understandings' in political practice constituted a substantial return to a relationship of autonomy, which was closer to that of the Empire than the First Republic. The coalition relationship with the Holy See naturally continued, but at the same time the Church moved much closer to the state and continued to use its structures and resources. The Church–state relationship was one of cooperation – at times identical goals being pursued through separate structures – although after 1934 the structures were in fact often identical. The goal at the most general level was to establish a stable Christian order in Brazil. The Church emphasized 'Christianity and order' and the state 'stability and order', but they were almost indistinguishable. As one writer observed of the post-1930 period: 'The Church came to be considered as the institution working in society for objectives identical to those of the state, that is, for the common good of the nation.'[18] The structures varied, depending on the issue at hand. In some cases, the Church used state structures, such as religious education in public schools, religious preparation in the military and the general idea of declaring the Constitution in the name of God. In other cases, the state supplied funds for the maintenance of Church structures, such as schools, seminaries, churches and even hospitals.[19] Once again, the Church could say 'to be Brazilian is to be Catholic', for it enjoyed government approval and support.

The implications of the Church's return to the public domain are tremendous. After a period of innovation and a change in the influence approach, a reintegration became possible. One result was the subsequent elimination of a need for innovation, which can best be illustrated by the case of lay mobilization. While it is true that Vargas' Estado Nôvo discouraged innovation and experimentation in general, this was not necessarily true for the Church. On the whole, the Church approved of the Vargas system, because of its order, anti-Communism and stability; and further, the clergy found Vargas a vast improvement over the elite of the First Republic. Innovation was discouraged within the Church not because of political repression against activist priests, but because it

[17] Thales de Azevedo, *O Catolicismo no Brasil* (Rio de Janeiro: Government of Brazil, Ministério de Educação e Cultura, 1955), p. 21.

[18] Msgr. Paulo Florêncio da Silveira Camargo, *História Eclesiástica do Brasil* (Petrópolis, R.J.: Editôra Vozes, 1955), p. 385.

[19] As one observer noted in the mid-1950s: 'It cannot be denied, however, that as a result of assistance received and continually solicited from the Government for establishing and maintaining her charitable works, for building seminaries and reconstructing churches, the Church is becoming financially dependent on the state.' Thales de Azevedo, p. 24. In 1968, a member of the Congress wrote: 'The dependency of Brazilian Christianity vis-à-vis the state can easily be proven by reading the budgets of the union and the states. In these budgets considerable sums are allocated for the Catholic universities, for the myriad religious *colégios*, for the asylums and hospitals which are run by priests and nuns all over the country.' Márcio Moreira Alves, *O Cristo do Povo* (Rio: Editôra Sabiá, 1968), p. 43.

was not considered necessary as power for influence in the state was readily available.

The solution to many of the problems of influence posed by Leme in his 1916 pastoral letter was a mobilized and organized lay movement. Leme felt that a mobilized laity could bring pressure to bear so as to improve the Church's public position, and, moreover, influence could be increased through the impression made by these laymen – especially the intellectuals – on other laymen.

When Leme became coadjutor of Rio de Janeiro in 1921, he immediately began to organize a lay movement. He followed two paths in his efforts. On the one hand, he tried to unify the various dispersed and often insignificant religious groups, which had either been around for some time or had been created more recently by foreign priests following European examples. On the other hand, he stimulated a movement around the Centro Dom Vital to attract intellectuals. The movements converged at a number of points: the personnel was similar and in many cases identical; the movements were devoted to general mobilization on religious and indirectly political bases which fitted into Leme's pressure group strategy; and both movements ultimately tied in with Catholic Action.

The first of Leme's lay movements centered on the Confederation of Catholic Associations of Rio de Janeiro (Confederação das Associações Católicas), which he founded in December 1922. The purpose of the Confederation was 'to bring together, as in a net, the multiplicity of Catholic initiatives, not to uniformize them, but in order to obtain of them, by an intelligent union of views and forces, a greater productive capacity'.[20] The groups included: The Saint Vincent de Paul Society, the League of Jesus, Mary, and Joseph, the Foundations of the Redemptorists, the Brazilian Catholic Union, the Congregation of Mary, the Apostolate of Prayer, and other associations of this sort. Leme consolidated the groups, organized and disciplined them, and thus created a manpower resource which he could use when necessary.

The second movement, which was based on the Centro Dom Vital, was important in that it initiated what is referred to as the 'Catholic Revival' in Brazil: a revival which culminated in political success. The Centro was founded in 1922 by the layman Jackson de Figueiredo, at Leme's instigation. Jackson had been an atheist, a free-thinker and was anti-Church. On reading Leme's 1916 pastoral, he experienced some sort of 'calling' and from 1921 until his early death in 1928 was the promoter of the Centro, the head of the Catholic intellectual movement and Leme's right-hand man. Through the Centro, and its organ, *A Ordem* Leme and Jackson sought to stimulate, mobilize and increase the influence of the Church by focusing primarily on the country's intellectual elite.

The Centro attracted a number of the brighter intellectual lights of Brazil in this period. Some of these were Perilo Gomes, Hamilton Nogueira, Sobral Pinto, Jonatas Serrano, Allindo Vieira and Alceu Amoroso Lima, after Jackson's death the most important layman of this century in Brazil, who took over the direction of the Centro. The group around the Centro never became very numerous, but its members were first-rate thinkers, and it did expand to the

[20] Regina do Santo Rosário, p. 145.

other cities of São Paulo, Salvador and Recife. From its inception in 1922 until about 1933 the Centro coordinated, in conjunction with Leme, all the lay movements of the 'new type' which arose as a result of its stimulus. These included: University Catholic Action, The Catholic Institute of Higher Studies (which became the Catholic University of Rio), the National Confederation of Catholic Workers, the Confederation of Catholic Press and so forth. Because of the activity in and around the Centro, the Church obtained much prestige and some influence among the intellectual elite in Brazil. Through the Centro, the thinking of Jacques Maritain and Georges Bernanos was introduced to Brazil and related to the social situation in a convincing way, so that more active elements were drawn to the Church. Another characteristic of the Centro's orientation was an emphasis on liturgical piety, a deepening of theological thought and instruction and a channel for lay participation in dynamic Church activities.[21]

In 1933, the greater part of the movement around the Centro was reorganized into the Brazilian Catholic Alliance (Coligação Católica Brasileira) and finally into Brazilian Catholic Action, which was offiically founded in 1935. Catholic Action was an international movement and was intended to be something unique in the Church. It was, according to Rome, 'an organization of laymen participating in the hierarchical apostolate of the Church, outside of any party affiliation in order to establish the universal reign of Jesus Christ'.[22]

Leme officially declared the foundation of Catholic Action at the urging of Pius XI; it was adopted throughout the country by seventy bishops, and by 1937 had formally superseded all other lay movements.[23] Brazil adopted the Italian model, which was centralized, corporate and authoritarian; based on the diocese, it included the parishes and was divided into four groups according to age and sex.

Leme's goal of mobilizing the laity on a long-term basis as a means to increase influence was never achieved. The failure may be attributed to the success of short-term mobilization and other strategies whereby the Church achieved state support and a central public position. The nature of the first mobilization process also had serious consequences on later efforts to organize the laity in a Christian Democratic movement.

Catholic Action was Leme's great hope for mobilizing the layman in the service of the Church; however, he died in distress over the fate of the movement.[24] He was disillusioned because the movement never caught on: it suffered from an 'early sclerosis of the organism'.[25] The early success of lay mobilization

[21] On the philosophical and political themes of the Centro, see Thomas G. Sanders, 'The Evolution of a Catholic Intellectual', Field Letter to Richard H. Nolte, Institute of Current World Affairs, New York, October 1967. The intellectual is Alceu Amoroso Lima. For the early stages under Jackson, see *In Memoriam: Jackson de Figueiredo (1891–1928)* (Rio de Janeiro: Centro Dom Vital, 1929).
[22] Regina do Santo Rosário, p. 300.
[23] Sister M. Ancilla O'Neill, *Tristão de Athayde and the Catholic Social Movement in Brazil* (Washington, D.C.: The Catholic University of America Press, 1939), p. 11.
[24] Amoroso Lima, *O Cardeal Leme*, p. 147.
[25] Regina do Santo Rosário, p. 342.

was reversed in the mid-1930s and resulted in failure for two reasons: the movement was Leme's and its *raison d'être* was early achieved. Leme created the movement and directed it under both Jackson and Amoroso Lima. The choice of leadership was Leme's and it was his instrument in the various political strategies. Even so, the movement might have prospered if its goal had not been achieved so early. In the first stages, Catholic Action was very dynamic, as it had enemies which included not only the Communists but particularly the Godless state run by a group of unbelievers. The movement was most vigorous when all its energies were focused in the LEC as a diffuse pressure group with very specific goals.[26] But then it succeeded and there was nothing else to do. There was no longer a need for a mobilized lay body because Vargas took care of the Communists and he also took good care of the Church. The movement simply withered away.[27]

The experience of lay mobilization could be generalized to other sectors, such as the Church in labor, in communications or in the social field. In all cases, the important factor was the combination of the orderly and stable Vargas politics and the use of power to define influence. In such a situation, there was simply no need for innovation.[28]

The particular political strategy chosen by Leme had important long-term implications. Leme preferred a pressure group instead of a political party, because the latter would indicate the existence of factions and the Church claimed to be all-inclusive. The LEC strategy was successful and was used again in the late 1940s for the 1946 Constitution and yet again in the 1950s. Each time, however, it was an *ad hoc* organization, under the direction of the Cardinal of Rio and the local bishops. There were no membership criteria and it had no explicit ideology, except the promotion of Church interests. The initial success of the LEC, and its tight control under the hierarchy, made it most attractive to the Church and discouraged attempts to form a Christian Democratic party, such as had been started in many European countries and in some countries of Latin America (most notably in Chile). One result of following this strategy, instead of setting up a party, was that the Church as an institution entered into overt politics at each election, a situation that could have been largely avoided by the use of a

[26] See e.g. Amoroso Lima, *Indicações Políticas* on dynamic.

[27] A reading of *A Ordem* for the period 1928–50 will support my argument. The articles were polemical and relevant to Brazil until roughly 1935. In the issue of July 1935, Alceu Amoroso Lima noted that the Centro and the Church were well satisfied with the government because it adopted the LEC programs. By the end of the 1930s, the articles were no longer related to Brazil and might as well have been published as the 'Catholic Review of the World Press'. That is, the movement lost its raison d'être just when Catholic Action was being formed. See also Alceu Amoroso Lima, *João XXIII* (Rio de Janeiro: Livraria José Olympio Editôra, 1966), which contains comments on how Catholic Action died and the clergy took over all activities in the Church.

[28] See the extremely interesting study on the Círculos Operários, which were very active from their founding in 1932 but slowed down as a result of complacency in the Vargas era. My reading of the Círculos leads me to believe that they are almost a microcosm of the whole Church in this period. See Howard J. Wiarda, 'The Brazilian Catholic Labor Movement' (Amherst, Mass.: University of Massachusetts Labor Relations & Research Center, 1969).

party. However, the hierarchy naively failed to perceive this fact, as they considered the Church the personification of all that was good in Brazil. The combination of the close relationship with the state and periodic involvement in elections gave the Church a high degree of political involvement. Another result of this strategy was to leave no room for the Catholic militants. The LEC was periodic and *ad hoc*, and the Centro Dom Vital lost intellectual appeal. Without a party to join, the Catholic militants had no choice but to desist, which further increased the tendency for the Church as an institution to assume a direct role in politics. The Church thus increasingly became involved in intricate political maneuvers which might have been better left to the layman.

The model of influence resulting from the much closer autonomy relationship with the state is best termed neo-Christendom. The relationship with Rome remained extremely close and the Brazilian Church continued to oppose Protestants, Socialists, and other European enemies, but now the organizational principles were much more attuned to the bishops' perception of the Brazilian situation. Most obviously, there was a return to the principle of total coverage of the country by the religion. It was continually pointed out that Brazil was the largest Catholic country in the world, with some 95 % of Catholics among its population of 60 million; of course, this figure included various types of Catholics, from 'nominal' to 'marginal' to 'popular,' and it is not clear just how the Church exercised its influence over this number of people spread out over such a large area. Interestingly enough, when the Church tried to exert influence it was often seen in a bad light.[29] The whole territory might be covered, but it is not clear just what this 'coverage' meant and influence in this sense had little or no meaning.

A secondary organizational principle was the continued vigilance against political threats to influence and power. In this way the influence was protected politically by the LEC, by bishops enlisting their politician friends, by the Catholic press and by priests in their sermons. Power was defended as an integral part of influence, so that the Church's predicament during the First Republic would not recur. More directly on influence, the Church operated to guarantee through the laws Christian morality, the sanctity of marriage, the sanctity of life, and so forth. The political level, therefore, was split into both an intermediate level and a tertiary level; in the former, it was to guarantee points of influence and in the latter, it was to ensure continued power.

The groups or sectors focused upon were still claimed to be all-inclusive: the religion was nearly a complete monopoly. In reality, the primary strata were the middle classes. This had been the case after 1891, and despite the influx of resources from abroad and the support of the state, it largely remained so. There

---

[29] Willems points out in regard to the important religious festivals: 'The people defend the tradition against the Church itself and its representatives. The priest who tries to change the tradition of the feasts is seen in a poor light and his intentions are considered meddling.' Emilio Willems, *Uma Vila Brasileira* (São Paulo: Difusão Européia do Livro, 1961), p. 85. See also Frei José M. Audrin, O.P., *Os Sertanejos que Eu Conheci* (Rio de Janeiro: Livraria José Olympio Editôra, 1963), and Frei Bernardino Leers, O.F.M., *Religiosidade Rural* (Petrópolis, R.J.: Editôra Vozes, 1967).

are several reasons for this. As before, the middle classes were the only ones who could afford to assist the Church financially. By assist, I do not mean a few cents at mass, but sizable sums for aiding in construction and maintenance; or in supporting, along with the state, private schools. Again, the clergy were educated in the seminaries in middle-class values. Regardless of their personal backgrounds, they emerged with middle-class preconceptions and tastes. In a society as class-stratified as Brazil, it was extremely difficult for a priest to deal with the lower classes. And third, there was little or no innovation in relating to the apostolate. They still used methods from Europe and these were most appropriate for the middle classes. These included not only the schools and religious groups, but even the level of sermons and the type of attire one was expected to wear in Church or in a school.

The more recent data indicate that the focus is indeed middle class. Assuming that this is likely to be reflected in the level of attendance at mass, the following figures are suggestive. In Maceió, Alagoas, where the city average of Sunday mass attendance was 16.5%, the middle-class areas showed 31% and the poorer areas from 2% to 6.3%. In Natal, Rio Grande do Norte, where the city average was 12.1%, the middle-class area again showed 31%, and the poorer ones 5.5% to 7.1%. In Estância, Bahia, the attendance of literates was 28.5% and of illiterates (naturally lower class) 5.5%. In Ribeirão Prêto, São Paulo, 50% of those attending are literate and 12% illiterate. The general conclusions are always the same in these surveys.[30]

Brazil is often divided into poor and middle-class areas. The Northeast is poor and the South is middle class. If the priest–population ratios in these areas are compared, a stunning discrepancy emerges between the attention given to the people in various parts of the country. Certain historical factors have caused a higher vocation ratio in parts of the South, but even so the Church is a national institution and has imported a good 40% of its clergy from abroad. That is, the Church could provide for equal coverage throughout the country if this were a priority. With a national average of 7,272 Catholics per priest in Brazil the following breakdown by states is suggestive:

	people per priest
South – Rio Grande do Sul and Santa Catarina	4,377
São Paulo	5,984
Guanabara and Estado do Rio	7,376
Minas Gerais and Espírito Santo	6,236
Northeast – Maranhão, Piauí, and Ceará	11,450
Rio Grande do Norte, Paraíba, Pernambuco and Alagoas	10,573
Bahia and Sergipe	14,933[31]

[30] See Godofredo J. Deelen, *A Sociologia a Serviço da Pastoral* (Petrópolis, R.J.: Editôra Vozes, 1966), pp. 69–84, on class and mass attendance; and Frei Francisco Rolim, 'Quelques Aspects de la Pratique Dominicale au Brésil', *Social Compass* 14 (May–June 1967), pp. 457–68 as well.

[31] Source is *Convergência* 6 (July 1968) from CERIS.

Education is another area in which the middle-class emphasis is obvious. In Brazil, the literacy rate is about 50%. It is thus interesting to note that the Church's involvement in primary education, where illiteracy could be fought, is very low, with 2,184 schools out of a total of 105,525 in 1968. On the other hand, secondary education is only for a small part of the population and is almost exclusively middle class. Here, the Church has between one-third and one-half of the total schools.[32] University education is reserved for the elite. Here the Church operates about one-third of all universities and faculties and produces 42% of the college graduates. The conclusions are obvious: the Church predominantly focuses on the middle classes.

In the 1930s, the Church–society relationship reverted to a comprehensive framework. The basic values, symbols and perhaps even beliefs had been derived from a Catholic mold even after 1891, but the political elite had not allowed their manifestation in structures and charters. Now, however, the state openly encouraged the integration of Church and state. The government promoted the symbols through the large number of Catholic holidays; religious celebrations in all sectors of the bureaucracy including the blessing of new buildings; the pointed reference to Catholic beliefs in discussing policies; the allocation of state money for Church projects; and, of course, the use of state structures for Church influence. The relationship between Church and state at the national and regional level was at the least one of cooperation.

At the local level, the Church remained integrated with families and local power groups. As a religion, Catholicism was simply a part of local culture, taking much from this culture and giving it some orientation.[33] As an institution, in the person of the priest, the Church was a part of local power groups and as such did not have to create its own organizations, as it relied on the structure of other social orders. However, implicit in this integration is a situation in which the Church was largely controlled by these orders. A sociologist who studied a particular Church system in the Northeast observed:

As an integral part of the patrimonial – paternalist domination system and, naturally, as instuments for its preservation, the clergy played a role subordinate to the economic and political control of the ruling 'colonels'. Despite their religious function and high status, the priests could not oppose patrimonial domination. Their roles were correlated to the structure of domination and adjusted to its asymmetry.[34]

The instruments or mechanisms for exercising and generating influence became broader and more diffuse after 1930. Organizational development continued with increased ecclesiastical divisions, parishes, priests and religious orders. The mechanisms continued to include administration of the sacraments, schools, pious groups and associations. But with the advent of the Estado Nôvo and government finances, the mechanisms broadened and embraced

---

[32] CERIS data gives 2,074 out of 7,254; most other sources give higher figures.
[33] For a discussion of this integration see Alceu Ferrari, *Igreja e Desenvolvimento* (Natal, R.N.: Fundação José Augusto, 1968), p. 29.
[34] Procópio Camargo, *O Movimento de Natal* (Brussels: Centre de Documentation sur L'Action des Eglises dans le Monde, 1966), p. 214.

numerous state structures as well. The Church, in its 'rightful position' in state and society, relied on extensive mechanisms for influence.

As an illustration, a brief discussion of charity and health will suggest the breadth of the Church influence mechanisms. A research project showed that of the total population of Salvador, Bahia, in 1966 some 40% were receiving charity from Church organizations. This figure is high compared with most of Brazil, but the fact that the Church distributes state and international charity is taken for granted. In fact, of the twenty-seven schools of social welfare in Brazil, twenty-two or 81% are operated by the Church.[35] In health, some 54% of all the nursing schools function under Church auspices. In 1963, the government at all levels operated 416 hospitals directly. Of the 2,854 private hospitals in 1968, 800 were run by the Church and another 300 were Santa Casas, which are affiliated with the Church through *irmandades*.[36] Of the 285,000 hospital beds in Brazil, some 150,000 were attended by members of the religious orders. That is, from the 1930s on, sectors of the Church were once again allowed to enter into all levels of society (the orders could not have managed hospitals before 1934) and were given state resources to do so. The Church thus had multiple structures at all levels to work through, and in fact the whole framework of institutions became to some extent instruments of influence.

It is clear that the change in the autonomy relationship after 1930 caused a return to an influence model similar to that of the Christendom form. This model was distinguished by its comprehensive nature, its links with all levels of society and its reliance not only upon the government but also upon local groups. In terms of the Church's perception of influence, the institution had prevailed: the Constitution was declared in the name of God, religion was taught in public schools, government funds were used for Church structures and the symbols were used by the political elite. However, this model, like the original one, does not require mobilization, autonomous generation of resources or any real life in the institution. It is defined through structures which may or may not have content. Indeed, by achieving reintegration some processes of innovation, which promised to give content to the structures, were impeded. The Church leaders may have considered the institution influential after 1930, but sociologists or anthropologists would have come to conclusions similar to Thales de Azevedo:

It is well accepted, even among ourselves, that in general terms,' our Catholicism is a Catholicism of pretty words and exterior acts' that 'does not live in the conscience' of the people but is transmitted from generation to generation, continually losing its influence.

He went on to cite examples of low influence which were extremely similar to

---

[35] Pe. Domingos Armando Donida, unpublished research report on Salvador prepared for Ação Misereor, Rio de Janeiro: CERIS, 1967. CERIS 1962 on schools.
[36] Interview with the head of the medical sector at Conferência dos Religiosos do Brazil (CRB) 20 February 1968. It is important to point out that the Santa Casas not only provide medical care but in many cases have educational institutes and some form of charity dispensaries connected with them.

those in Leme's 1916 pastoral, i.e., a population (including the elites) generally ignorant of the religion, a lack of vocations, a weak Catholic press and a mixed and confused religion. And he concluded from a study based on many research projects, '…the Church is no longer the organ of social control which it was in other periods of Brazilian history'.[37]

[37] Thales de Azevedo, pp. 26 and 58.

Section II: The Church faces the modern world, 1950–64

3. Socio-political threats of the modern world

Brazilian economic, social and political institutions were vastly different by mid-century from what they had been a mere decade or two before. In the abstract, this statement is not particularly remarkable, but the evidence on specific instances is rather surprising; its impact on Church influence is quite dramatic. After World War II, the country experienced a tremendous spurt of change, following decades of relative stability or even stagnation. I characterized the Old Republic (1891–1930) in terms of compromises, balances and lack of mobilization. Politics was based on extremely decentralized political and economic groups, which did not encourage broader participation by the people, and the political system at the national level was a balance between the three most powerful states. As João Camillo de Oliveira Tôrres points out 'One of the most impressive conclusions that one reaches in analyzing Brazilian society during the period known as the First Republic or "Old Republic" as it is called, is that of social stability.'[1] He continues by characterizing society in the following manner: a feudal structure in the rural areas (69% of the population as late as 1940) with the patriarchal clan in control, the family as the economic and political unit and the workers in a state of actual serfdom; a meagre middle class and domestic industry which was rural in character.[2]

The long era of Getúlio Vargas (1930–45) was a time of stability, while the world outside was being torn apart by mass mobilization, the conflict of ideologies and ultimately war. Vargas was a benevolent dictator in the tradition of authoritarian regimes, who did not have to rely on ideologies, a mass party, or much of a secret police to stay in power, because he was not seriously opposed by any important group in society. Initially he eliminated the potential threat of the Communists, then used the Fascists as a justification for his Estado Nôvo and proceeded to rule easily for the next eight years. During his time in office Vargas weakened the rural power centers, directed more control to the national level, encouraged a nascent industrialization process and organized the urban proletariat. All of these measures, however, contributed more towards maintaining stability than anything else. Given the initially low level of political and social mobilization, Vargas was able to buy off all relevant groups and then play them off against each other to preserve his own position. The Vargas regime came to an end in 1945 by means of a straightforward and bloodless military coup and not because of a mass-based movement of national revulsion.

Following the end of the war and the ousting of Vargas, all sectors of Brazilian society began to change and by the late 1950s the term 'The Brazilian Revolution' was current. These changes have been catalogued and analyzed so many times by Brazilians and foreigners that I will not cover the same ground again,

---

[1] João Camillo de Oliveira Tôrres, *Estratificação Social no Brasil* (São Paulo: Difusão Européia do Livro, 1965), p. 151.
[2] *Ibid.*, p. 178.

let alone seek to explain causation of change in one order *vis-à-vis* another.[3] It is necessary only to give a brief outline of the process of change in order to indicate the implications of this process for the Church.

What stands out most vividly in a review of post-World War II Brazilian society is the mixed and even paradoxical nature of change. On the one hand there is a dramatic leap forward in most sectors, but on the other a crisis is confronted and a regression occurs.

After 1950, Brazil experienced tremendous economic growth. Few other Latin American countries could have made the following claim: 'In short, the degree of industrial development achieved by Brazil makes it possible for the country's demand for consumer goods to be met almost entirely by domestically produced goods, and allows investment based chiefly on the internal supply of capital goods...the country's level of domestic activity is no longer chiefly dependent on the quantity and prices of the products exported.'[4] For the decade of the 1950s, Brazil's real *per capita* growth was about three times that of the rest of Latin America. The basis for this growth was an extraordinary increase in industrial output, as can be seen in the indices shown in Table 1.

TABLE 1   *Real growth indices of agriculture and industry*

	1947	1951	1956	1960	1961
Agriculture	100	114	142	172	187
Industry	100	146	213	327	362

Source: Werner Baer, *Industrialization and Economic Development in Brazil* (Homewood, Ill.: Richard D. Irwin, Inc., 1965), p. 71.

Between 1947 and 1961, the average annual rate of economic growth was 5.8%, which amounted to about 3% per capita. Between 1957 and 1961, the rate increased to some 7% or 3.9% per capita. Again, this growth was based on the industrial sector, and primarily on the more 'modern' divisions at that. Thus between 1955 and 1961, while overall industrial production grew by a relatively impressive 80%, output in the steel industry increased by 100%, in the mechanical industries by 125%, in the electrical and communications industries by 380% and in the transportation equipment sector by 600%.[5] In short, during this decade Brazil's economy developed very rapidly and mainly on the basis of industrialization.

[3] See Werner Baer, *Industrialization and Economic Development in Brazil* (Homewood, Ill.: Richard D. Irwin, Inc., 1965); Juarez Rubens Brandão Lopes, *Crise do Brasil Arcaico*; John W. Dulles, *Unrest in Brazil: Political-Military Crises, 1955–1964* (Austin: University of Texas Press, 1967); Celso Furtado, *Diagnosis of the Brazilian Crisis*, trans. Suzette Macedo (Berkeley: University of California Press, 1965); Thomas Skidmore, *Politics in Brazil, 1930–1964*; and Emilio Willems, *Followers of the New Faith* (Nashville, Tenn.: Vanderbilt University Press, 1967).

[4] Furtado, p. 80.

[5] *Ibid.*, pp. 88–9.

In 1962, however, the rate of growth declined and continued to drop through 1963. Due to the nature of the industrialization process itself, the policies of President Juscelino Kubitschek up to 1960 and the response of President João Goulart to the decrease in growth, inflation increased tremendously. During the 1950s the cost of living increase in Rio de Janeiro was roughly 20% per year. In 1959 it soared to over 50%, decreased the following year and then took off into the stratosphere with an 80% increase in 1963; in 1964 prices increased 25% during the first three months alone.[6] By early 1964, the economy had stagnated; inflation averaged at least 8% per month; foreign reserves were depleted; investment dropped; and in general the economy was in a shambles. In addition, sound analyses suggested that the economic problems were structural in nature and that only deep-seated social and political change could enable Brazil to recover economically.[7]

By 1960 Brazil had changed from being a predominantly rural society to being almost urban (see Table 2).

TABLE 2   *Urban population in Brazil* ('000)

	Population	Urban	Per cent urban
1940	41,089	12,868	31
1950	51,576	18,721	36
1960	70,976	32,471	46

Source: Derived from IBGE statistics.

Unlike many Latin American countries, this urbanization was not confined solely to one or two cities, but was spread among at least half a dozen.[8] It was a positive factor that the urban population was distributed over most of the littoral but it did not lessen the demands on the government both for new services and for increased political attention. If the aggregate data for Brazil in this period are consulted, it is evident that some significant demographic and social changes were taking place and at a very rapid pace. According to the census data, a great many more people were literate in 1960 than in 1950 (60.6% versus 48.4%); more had moved out of agriculture and into trades and services; they were using more than double the amount of electricity, etc. In 1960, a respected

[6] For one of many good discussions of growth and inflation, see First National City Bank, 'Brazil: Special Economic Study', (New York: The Foreign Information Service of City Bank, April 1971), pp. 12–16.
[7] See the excellent article on import substitution, the dual economy and political obligations, Maria Conceição Tavares *et al.*, 'The Growth and Decline of Import Substitution in Brazil', *Economic Bulletin for Latin America*, 9 (March 1964), pp. 1–59.
[8] For example, the 1960 populations of the most important cities were as follows: São Paulo – 3,825,000; Rio de Janeiro – 3,307,000; Recife – 797,000; Belo Horizonte – 693,000; Pôrto Alegre – 641,000; and Salvador – 655,000. To these could be added various other state capitals which were slightly smaller. See *Anuário Estatístico do Brasil* and other Instituto Brasileiro de Estatística (IBGE) publications.

and cautious observer of Brazil wrote: 'At present, Brazil is in a frenzy of continuous crisis as the traditional gives way to a new type of society.'[9]

The most widely accepted characterization of the process I want to depict is that of social mobilization. 'Social mobilization can be defined, therefore, as the process in which major clusters of old social, economic and psychological commitments are eroded or broken and people become available for new patterns of socialization and behavior.'[10] Once social mobilization has begun political institutions and practices are forced to change, as indeed they did in Brazil at this time. Even in the traditionally secure and passive rural areas, peasant leagues were appearing and demanding long overdue reforms. The suffrage expanded rapidly in the period and the number and variety of political parties grew even faster.[11] This was the first time that Brazil had experienced an open democratic system and the results, given the process and time, were radicalization of the parties, mobilization of the masses and a general questioning of the established structures. Some of the action was channeled through parties and other institutions but much of it was not. In the cities, and even at a national level, a populistic form of politics was followed, which did not give rise to the institutionalization of groups or structures. The legacy of Vargas had been a system of informal compromises and balances and his successors did not develop new means of channeling political action in a more effective manner. With the great economic and social changes after the war, this system could not cope and finally fell apart.

A simple chronology of political events for the period 1945 to 1964 would indicate the paradoxical and crisis-prone system of Brazilian politics. Vargas was deposed by a coup in 1945 and was followed by President Eurico Gaspar Dutra, whose five-year term saw little action and even less innovation. Vargas was elected in 1950 and initiated some changes in society, but he committed suicide in the face of scandal and a threatened coup. Juscelino Kubitschek could not take office in 1955 until a preventive coup was staged to counter another coup, but once in office he did largely fulfill his promise of fifty years' development in five. Kubitschek was succeeded by the enigmatic Jânio Quadros, who came into office to make politics moral and the bureaucracy functional. After seven months of no progress, he quit office and left the country. Not only did his unexplained departure demoralize and disillusion a great many Brazilians, but, even more seriously, it led to an immediate crisis as his vice-president, João

---

[9] Charles Wagley, 'The Brazilian Revolution: Social Changes since 1930', in Richard Adams ed., *Social Change in Latin America Today* (New York: Random House, 1960), p. 188.

[10] Karl Deutsch, 'Social Mobilization and Political Development', *American Political Science Review* 55 (September 1961), p. 494.

[11] In the elections for the 1934 assembly 2,659,171 people voted; in 1945 7,459,849 were registered, in 1954 11,455,149 and in 1960 15,543,332; Wagley, in Richard Adams ed., *Social Change in Latin America Today*, p. 207, and IBGE, p. 765. There were usually twelve or fourteen parties, the three main ones being the União Democrática Nacional (UDN), the Partido Social Democrático (PSD) and Partido Trabalhista Brasileiro (PTB), but there were also Christian Democrats, Socialists, illegal Communists, etc. For an excellent insider's interpretation of the economic, political and social components of the crisis see Furtado's *Diagnosis of the Brazilian Crisis*.

Goulart, was currently visiting the People's Republic of China and was completely unacceptable to the military.[12] A coup was frustrated; the governmental system was changed; Goulart sabotaged its operations and in January of 1963 received full powers, but he accomplished in effect little more than radicalization of all political groups.

Since this scenario did little to inspire confidence in the political system or its leaders in Brazil, several statesmen suggested that the system could not cope with the needs of the economy and society in this period, but the proposals they submitted varied so tremendously that there was no chance of compromise. The Cuban system was considered a particularly attractive alternative and was looked to by many political groups and student movements. However, the military found this alternative only slightly less desirable than Goulart's government and, for the first time in this century, assumed power on their own rather than returning it to civilians. With 1964, the legacy of Vargas was finally interred and the military since that time have been formulating their own system, according to their ideology of national security. They have, in effect, revolutionized politics in eliminating all vestiges of the Vargas system. The past two decades in Brazil have certainly been filled with action, drama and confusion. The reaction of the Church to the processes and events before the coup of 1964 must be analyzed.[13]

As noted above, social mobilization foreshadows a change for established political institutions and practices. The same could be said of religious institutions and practices. The Brazilian Church after World War II had to confront the twentieth century with an influence model which was at least a hundred years out of date. Obviously, all churches have had to cope with the changes associated with the process of social mobilization, modernization, or whatever one wishes to call the transformation of western civilization since the Reformation and Renaissance. However, due to particular historic circumstances, the Brazilian Church's process of response and innovation was cut short with its entry into the public realm in the 1930s. Leme's success in the 1930s merely served to aggravate the problem of change once the 'Brazilian Revolution' took hold twenty years later.

Central to the neo-Christendom model are its comprehensive aspirations, monopolistic tendencies and reliance upon structures. Further, there is the need for state power to both promote and support it. The crucial elements of personal commitment, autonomous resources and an effective independent institution are

---

[12] João Goulart was Vargas' Minister of Labor from 1953 on. As head of the labor system, he had the means for mass mobilization at his disposal. He rapidly became the *bête noire* of the middle classes, including the military, and was branded as a opportunistic demagogue. As Minister, he legally increased wages by 100% in 1954 and on the same day Vargas was forced to dismiss him. Elected vice-president in both 1955 and 1960, he never enjoyed the confidence of the military and was hated by many sections of the middle class. See Skidmore, pp. 113–15, 123–31.

[13] For a very thorough analysis of the background to military intervention and the crumbling of the old regime, see Alfred Stepan, *Patterns of Civil-Military Relations: The Brazilian Political System* (Princeton, N.J.: Princeton University Press, 1971).

lacking. These missing elements are not so important as long as the Catholic culture can buoy up the religion and state resources can support the institution. This was no longer possible, however, with the aforementioned changes which took place after the war.

At the end of the last chapter, I quoted a few sentences from Thales de Azevedo, in which he expressed doubt about the influence of the Church. Since Azevedo wrote those lines twenty years ago, a great deal of sociological research has been carried out which confirms his perception. The important point here is not how the Church institution defines influence, or whether Churchmen perceive influence, but what kind of base this influence has in Brazil. We must consider this base in order to be able to determine how changes in society affect it and why Churchmen must rely on political strategies to define it.

At the broadest level, the base of religion in Brazil is in the culture itself; this is confirmed by the vast majority of anthropologists who point to the essentially sacral nature of culture. After all, the society was founded in part by the Church; the Catholic religion gave early content to it; and through some four centuries of evolution Catholic symbols, beliefs, and formulas have remained dominant. The sacral nature of the culture has diminished somewhat in urban society today, but it is still very strong in the rural areas.[14] However, once the homogeneity of the Catholic culture is probed, it becomes evident that its content is extremely heterogeneous. Among sociologists of religion now working in Brazil, this heterogeneity is taken as a basis on which to develop classifications and indices of different types of Catholicism and Catholics. The only question among sociologists is on particular forms of classification.[15]

The sociological research on religious adherence in Brazil is almost unanimous in showing that the religion most closely associated with the Church as institution – with the sacraments, the cult, doctrine, theology, Church as intermediary with God – is extremely limited and weak. This finding in itself is extremely important, but it becomes, if anything, more significant when one recalls that in the Catholic religion, quite possibly more than in any other major faith, the structure is emphasized to the detriment of the individual or the group. It is the structure that links man with God and without this link man cannot be saved.[16] Yet research shows that only a small minority are linked to God through the Church as intervening structure. In a research project carried out by CERIS in 1968 in Rio de Janeiro, it was found that although 181 groups of mothers and children declared themselves Catholics, only 8.8 % of the mothers and 6 % of the

[14] As Emilio Willems notes for a rural village, 'It would be difficult to identify one sphere of life that was not impregnated with a faith in the supernatural, in which they did not employ means to assure the aid of supernatural powers.' Emilio Willems, *Uma Vila Brasileira*, p. 134. For further substantiation of the point regarding the Catholic basis of the culture, see Charles Wagley, *Introduction to Brazil* (New York: Columbia University Press, 1963), p. 232.

[15] See the excellent review article and conceptual statement on Catholicism and Catholics in which the most important authors are discussed and evaluated, Francisco Rolim, 'Catolicismo no Brasil', *Limiar* 26 (April 1970), pp. 93–153.

[16] Rather than entering into the history and the theology of the question, simply see the excellent discussion on the Church in McKenzie: especially p. 22.

children would be defined as Catholics in the eyes of the Church.[17] In a more comprehensive comparative study in two towns, the results were similar. After defining three different syndromes of religious behavior, the researchers interviewed large numbers of Catholics and found their practices extremely heterogeneous. One of the alternatives was religious practice through the religious institution, that is, by means of the seven sacraments which form the core of the Church's activities. However, the findings showed this to be the weakest of the three, mentioned in only 14.5 % of the interviews, and always linked to another syndrome which was not mediated through the structure. The alternatives which were the strongest were those which could be termed 'popular religion', and included such things as special relationships with the saints and a whole series of promises and obeisances. In sum, what this excellent and comprehensive research project demonstrates is that the Church as institution has very little direct influence on the religious behavior of individuals and what passes for the Catholic religion is a mixture of heterogeneous beliefs and syncretic elements.[18]

The research cited has been carried out in the past few years, but there is no reason to believe that its conclusions would be any different for the period now under discussion (up to 1964). What is particularly serious about this low base of influence, and of the influence model through which it is defined, is the fact that it tends to diminish with the changes described earlier in this chapter. So from a low base of real influence there is a decrease, and in many cases it is quite dramatic.

At the most general level, the sacral culture of Brazil has been becoming more secular. With the expansion of education, the improved means of transportation and the mass media, closer connections with other countries, secularization has increased greatly in Brazil.[19] In the neo-Christendom form of influence, total territorial coverage is expected. The Church could deceive itself as long as Brazilian culture was essentially Catholic, but increasing secularization made it difficult to believe that the culture was in fact Catholic. By the early 1960s it became impossible to continue to believe what had always been believed, in the intense ideological debate which centered on nationalism or other secular beliefs such as Communism.

At local levels, the Church has traditionally been fused with groups such as rural clans and the family. Following World War II, a combination of industrialization, political centralization, droughts in the Northeast and overall inflation caused a general migration to the urban areas. As the Church has always been allied with local groups, when people moved from these groups they also left

---

[17] The research project was not overly rigorous in defining who was and was not Catholic and there is no reason to believe that the results would be any different in other big cities. For the definitions and the research, see C. A. de Medina and Alice Rangel, 'A Transmissão de Valôres Religiosos Entre Duas Gerações', unpublished research report for CERIS, Rio de Janeiro, 1969.

[18] For a very perceptive analysis of religion in Brazil see Pedro de Assis Ribeiro de Oliveira, 'Catolicismo Popular no Brasil', unpublished research report for CERIS, Rio de Janeiro, 1970.

[19] Juarez Rubens Brandão Lopes gives special attention to this process of secularization in his book, *Desenvolvimento e Mudança Social*, pp. 112–18.

their religion, at least insofar as mass attendance indicated religious adherence. 'And it did this because the Church for the practicant was nothing more or less than a local institution, intimately united to the society which served her for support.'[20] Even if the individual remains in the same location while the society around him changes, mass attendance again decreases. Rolim's study of the Diocese of Ribeirão Prêto showed that in the traditional areas of low urbanization and archaic farming methods, the mass attendance was about 50%. In the sections of the diocese with urbanization and advanced agricultural technology, mass attendance varied between 18% and 24%. As he noted, 'These facts reveal to us that the cities where little change has occurred conserve high indices of Sunday mass attendance, whereas in the others, where there are obvious signs of transformation, these indices are low.'[21] Equally significantly, in the face of social changes the activities (such as sacraments) connected with the Church as institution decreased, whereas they did not decrease in the popular religions, or those religious activities associated with Catholicism but beyond the control of the Church.[22]

In this neo-Christendom form, the Church defines all strata of the population as being within its sphere of influence. With 'popular' Catholicism, it might be possible to preserve the illusion that all groups were included; however, on account of the growth of other religions, the monopoly of groups and strata in society is patently false. Even today, the census shows that approximately 94% of all Brazilians declare themselves Catholics. However, the number of Protestants has increased rapidly in the 1950s and the increase is particularly obvious among the Pentecostals. The data on religious affiliation are notoriously bad in Brazil but the figures shown in Table 3 are indicative and are not contradicted

TABLE 3   *Growth of Protestantism in Brazil*

Year	Members	Percentage of total population
1925	101,454	–
1938	241,128	0.58
1949	1,657,524	3.26
1957	1,755,929	2.86
1961	4,071,643	6.06

Source: Godofredo J. Deelen, *Sociologia a Serviço da Pastoral* (Petrópolis, R. J.: Editôra Vozes, 1966), p. 62.

[20] Francisco Rolim, 'Diocese de Santos: Levantamento Socio-Religioso', unpublished research report for Sociedade de Pesquisas e Estudos Sócio-Eclesiais (SPESE), Rio de Janeiro, 1966.
[21] Francisco Rolim, 'Em tôrno da Religiosidade no Brasil', *Revista Eclesiástica Brasileira* 25 (March 1965), p. 13. Obviously mass attendance is not the greatest indicator of Church influence, but it is easily obtained and easily compared. Further, attendance in the Catholic Church is obligatory and thus gives some indication of influence.
[22] Rolim, 'Catolicismo no Brasil', p. 101.

anywhere by any other data. The Pentecostals represented 9.5% of all Protestants in 1930; in 1958, they had increased to 55%; and by 1964 they were 73.6%.[23] The growth of the Pentecostals is important in this context, because their main attraction is in those areas where levels of industrialization and urbanization are highest. This form of religion, it is argued, fulfills a gap created by the lack of primary group ties in the cities. That is, as people break away from local groups in the rural areas and leave even a token Catholic Church attendance behind, they become available for resocialization by the Pentecostals. The implication is obvious: with more urbanization and industrialization, there will be more members for the Pentecostals.[24]

What applies to the Pentecostals also holds true for the Spiritists, although many priests undoubtedly believe that these people are basically Catholics. Brazil is today considered to be the world center of Spiritism. The two main Spiritist groups in Brazil are the Kardecist and the Umbandas, but all have a certain affinity with syncretic Catholic-African religions. The data on Spiritism are, if anything, worse than those on the Pentecostals. Again, however, all agree that they have increased rapidly in recent years.[25] The data on the city of Salvador are indicative and are probably even surpassed by the situation in Recife. In 1950 there were 6,831 admitted members of Spiritist groups; in 1960 this had increased to 15,330; and is estimated for 1965 to be 19,580.[26] The average increase over a decade for the state of Bahia was computed at 187.3%, but in the cities and episcopal sees it was 224%. From these differences it has been concluded that a social rupture, a migration or other change increases the adherence.[27] In conclusion, by 1960 it would be difficult to say that the Catholic Church held a monopoly of religious commitments. Even then the Protestants and Spiritists could claim more than 7% of the total population, their members were more active and committed and it could be anticipated that with further social change the number of adherents would continue to increase.

The last category of a model of influence deals with mechanisms and organizational development. A central consideration at this point concerns the number of clergy administering the sacraments to the faithful. A religion which emphasizes the priesthood to such a high degree must be concerned with the low number of vocations, and vocations to the clergy in Brazil have never kept up with Church requirements. The present ratio of one priest to 7,272 Catholics is very low

[23] Beatriz Muniz de Souza, 'Aspectos do Protestantismo Pentecostal em São Paulo', in Waldo A. Cesar et al., Protestantismo e Imperialismo na América Latina (Petrópolis, R.J.: Editôra Vozes, 1968), p. 105.

[24] Willems observes, 'The assumption that the diffusion of Protestantism has been roughly parallel to the processes of industrialization and urbanization, and that the largest concentrations of proselytically minded Protestants are found in areas where these processes have been most intensive, is supported by figures concerning the growth of the industrial labor force and its distribution within Brazil.' Followers of the New Faith, p. 71.

[25] Frei Boaventura Kloppenburg says that 30% of all Brazilians are in some way affiliated. 'Spiritism in Latin America: A Growing Threat', paper given to Catholic Inter-American Cooperation Program (CICOP) Chicago, 19–21 January 1966.

[26] CERIS, Boletim Informativo, 2:3 (July–September 1966), p. 79.

[27] Ibid., p. 83.

indeed, even without considering the enormous problems of distance and poor communications. Moreover, approximately 40% of the clergy in Brazil have come from abroad. Vocations have decreased absolutely and relatively since the late 1950s (Table 4).

TABLE 4   *Decrease in priestly vocations*

Year	Secular	Regular	Total	Percentage of vocations per 100,000 of population
1958	205	190	395	0.60
1959	164	198	362	0.53
1960	152	172	324	0.45
1961	111	186	297	0.40

Source: Gustavo Pérez *et al.*, *O Problema Sacerdotal no Brasil* (Rio de Janeiro: CERIS, 1965), p. 23.

If one examines the sources of vocations in Brazil, they are largely from rural areas (57% in 1960), from large families (48% from families of seven children or more), and from the lower strata of society.[28] It is also clear that as society changes, these sources will be seriously affected. The groups which represent what Brazil is becoming (urban, smaller families and middle class) do not provide their proportional share of vocations. Traditionally, a vocation was also a means of social mobility. Today with the differentiation of society and more channels of mobility, the priestly vocation is apparently less attractive. Even if rural vocations increased, which is most unlikely, there would be a question of quality; as society becomes more urban and industrial and also more complex, can rural vocations cope with the demands?

A traditional mechanism of influence for the Church in Brazil was education above the elementary level. With the social changes taking place after World War II, the middle classes expanded and the government committed more resources to public secondary schools; this was an unusual response, because the Church had traditionally borne the brunt of secondary education, but in this instance it was unable to continue doing so. As Church schools were private and charged tuition fees and many middle-class families were faced with a serious rate of inflation which increased near the end of the 1950s, they found themselves increasingly less able to afford parochial education and opted for the

[28] Gustavo Pérez *et al.*, pp. 147–60, on all these issues. Interestingly enough, research undertaken in the middle 1950s found that the priesthood was the third highest ranked profession, after doctors and lawyers and ahead of 27 other occupations. If this were so at that time, the researcher should have looked into the explanation for the low number of priests amid an abundance of lawyers and doctors in the urban areas. On the basis of superficial observations in the late 1960s, I would be willing to argue that the priest is no longer third. See Bertram Hutchinson, 'The Social Grading of Occupations in Brazil', *The British Journal of Sociology* 7 (June 1957), pp. 176–89.

free public schools.[29] One source indicates that whereas in 1950 78% of all secondary school students were in private schools (the vast majority of these were operated by the Church), by 1959 this number had dropped to 66%.[30] Consequently, given a continuance of the same social and economic patterns, the Church could be forced out of secondary education within a few decades.

There is an abundance of data pointing in the same direction. Most simply, the base of Church influence in a strictly sacramental or cult sense is very weak in Brazil. More importantly, this weak base grew weaker with the types of changes taking place in the 'Brazilian Revolution'. The awareness of this fact, depending upon how it is perceived, could lead to different strategies to gain and develop influence. In the face of threats, the Church again relied on political strategies to gain and exercise power, rather than turning to evangelization to increase its influence. There are several reasons why this was the case. In the first place, the process of evangelization or deepening the faith would be slow and almost impossible given the lack of priests. It would take decades to purify the faith through catechism, courses and personal contacts and at this time, before the Second Vatican Council (1962–5), the instruments for such a task were not particularly flexible or quickly effective. Further, the secondary organizational principle was the use of political strategies to guarantee influence. This was the legacy of the Christendom Church, which had worked in the 1930s, and by now was part of the institution's self-image. In time of need, the Church's immediate reaction was to use political strategies to fight divorce laws, guarantee morality, discourage the Protestants and ensure finances for Church projects. Finally, the most obvious threat to the Church at this time was in the political realm, and the perception of its importance was merely increased by the secondary organizational principle.

The political confusion of the pre-1964 period has already been described. It is an understatement to call the period turbulent and the Church was inexorably involved. For example, as the Church relied upon state structures and resources for its definition of influence, it was unable to stay on the sidelines while President Kubitschek pushed the country along, while Quadros equivocated and finally left, and while Goulart let Brazil drift towards increasing radicalization. The Church necessarily had to be involved in the process of obtaining more power. Even at the local level things were changing, as the old power groups in the rural areas were becoming increasingly caught up in national networks and thus relied less on the Church for legitimacy. In the cities and at the national level, the more common pattern of politics was becoming populism, i.e. a system in which a demagogic figure forms a direct relationship with the masses and trades off bread and butter issues in return for votes without the intermediary

[29] For a good discussion on education, the middle class and inflation, see Charles Wagley, 'The Brazilian Revolution: Social Changes Since 1930', pp. 177–231. On inflation and its effect on the middle classes and the Church schools see: G. Beaulieu, P.-E. Charbonneau and L. Arrobas Martins, *Educação Brasileira e Colégios de Padres* (São Paulo: Editôra Herder, 1966), p. 87 and J. Roberto Moreira, 'Sociologia Política de Lei de Diretrizes e Bases da Educação Nacional', *Revista Brasileira de Estudos Políticos* 9 (July 1960), p. 207.
[30] Cited in Beaulieu *et al.*, p. 87.

of a party or ideology. Again, there is no particular place for the Church in such a system and it is worth mentioning that the greatest populist of them all, Adhemar de Barros, was elected Governor of São Paulo in 1947 with Communist support and against the adamant opposition of the Church.

The Communists were an additional threat in the realm of politics. The Party was founded in 1921, the same year as the Centro Dom Vital, and was illegal from 1935 until 1945. In the 1945 elections it won some 9 % of the vote and made a decent showing in municipal elections. The Party was again declared illegal in 1947 but continued to operate actively through other parties. In addition to the Party there were the emerging elites of this period, which the Church viewed with equal distrust. For example, Francisco Julião was a Socialist, but he posed a threat as great as a Communist, and by the time of Goulart's presidency his number was legion. In fact, Goulart's brother-in-law, Lionel Brizola, was a Leftist demagogue who opposed the Church in Rio Grande do Sul and became a potential national liability. The danger from the Left became even more immediate after the successful Cuban Revolution in 1959 and the lesson for the rural areas of Brazil was obvious. In short, the period under discussion was a difficult one for the Church.

There is no doubt that the threats were perceived and that those which were most readily discerned were political. Indeed, the first commentary by a bishop on the need for rural reforms was made in terms of threats, when in 1950 the Bishop of Campanha, Minas Gerais, Dom Inocêncio Engelke, made a public statement entitled: 'With us, without us, or against us will be made the rural reform.' In the statement, he noted the great changes then taking place in the rural areas of Brazil due to the expansion of the mass media. With exposure to new ideas, the rural people would be available for revolutionary thought. And he argued, 'We have already lost the workers of the cities. We cannot commit the stupidity of also losing the workers in the fields.' Statements of this sort were made repeatedly, with particular emphasis on agitators in the rural areas (the 1952 statement of Vale do São Francisco), international Communism (Amazônia in 1957), indigenous Communists in the rural areas (Central Commission of Conferência Nacional dos Bispos do Brasil [CNBB] in 1961), and irresponsible political leaders (Central Commission of 1963).[31]

In conclusion, the Church entered the post-war era with a weak base of influence and an archaic influence model. There were tremendous changes taking place and it was a period of political crisis. With increased social change, the Church's base of influence diminished even further and the political instability of the period threatened its reliance on power for the exercise of influence. There were perceptions of the gravity of the situation and some very important responses, but as far as I can ascertain, only at the political level. What is most interesting, and most important for post-1964 developments, is the fact that the responses were different and in some respects contradictory. On the one hand,

[31] I have copies of these statements but to the best of my knowledge they are not easily available anywhere. Some excerpts, however, may be found in Márcio Moreira Alves, *O Cristo do Povo* (Rio de Janeiro: Editôra Sabiá, 1968).

sectors of the Church followed a political pressure group strategy to guarantee influence through education and in effect attempted to secure the *status quo*. On the other hand, sectors of the Church acted at a more basic level and worked politically to bring about structural changes in society through a new set of doctrines and mechanisms. A fascinating element of these divergent responses is that it was precisely the same institution going in two different directions. In 1958 the Brazilian hierarchy met in Goiânia and issued a statement to the nation. The statement noted the confusion and crises, the evil qualities of demagogic politicians, the problem of totalitarianism and the weakness of the political system. Then it went on to support with equal fervor two contradictory strategies.[32]

---

[32] My thesis included a chapter on the Church's political pressure group activity concerning a 1961 education law. The study showed that even at that period the Church still operated with a Leme-like strategy and attempted to preserve the status quo in education. I have excluded that chapter from this book because of length considerations and because it simply shows that there was continuity in political activity, which latter point is easily grasped.

4. In search of a new approach to influence: promotion of social change[1]

Before discussing the Church's involvement in programs and strategies of social change, a few words are required on the traditional role of the Church in maintaining or destroying the *status quo*. In the first instance, it should be remembered that most religious practices and beliefs are out of the institution's control. The common forms of religious practice are termed 'cultural Catholicism', 'primitive Catholicism', 'syncretic Catholicism' and so forth. Virtually all students of these forms of religion have noted their narcotic or pacifying characteristics, pointing out that they direct the adherent's attention to other-worldly or external sources of control. The individual cannot affect his own destiny; it is beyond his competence – it will happen 'se Deus quiser' (if God wishes). Further, this form of religion directly supports the patron–dependent relationship, whereby a few are entitled to rule and the many to follow. What is practiced in the civil and political field is directly legitimized in the religious.[2] Next, the Church in education had never sought change and had in fact merely supported the established elites and their social system. Further, it is obvious that the Church legitimized the government during the Vargas regime; this, of course, was the basis of the trade-off between Leme and Vargas. This role continued after 1945, and, if anything, became more clearly defined as the fear of Communism increased during the Cold War. As the Church opposed Communism it increasingly favored the *status quo*. In its arrangements with the state and other political elites, the Church also allowed itself to be used for almost any purpose; it has been part of the folklore of politics to utilize the symbols and messages of the Catholic religion in justifying dubious political actions. The Church in Brazil, as throughout the world, formally adopted the ideas of justice, a fair wage and other social equities of a capitalist society, at least from the time of Pope Leo XIII and his 'Rerum Novarum' and the 'Quadragessimo Anno' of Pius XI. However, as already noted, many of the ideas emanating from Rome were not particularly relevant to Brazil at this time: in this case, for example, the urban proletariat was

---

[1] The topics treated in this chapter have given rise to a fairly extensive literature in English and Portuguese. However, this literature is fairly specific in range, in that most researchers have dealt with the same subjects. While a decent amount of material exists on Catholic Action and Ação Popular (Sanders and de Kadt), rural unionization (de Kadt, Ferrari, Hewitt), MEB (de Kadt) and regional programs (Ferrari and Camargo), there is very little on the CNBB, the Christian Democrats and intellectual supports. The authors have not explained to my satisfaction the bases of the new social change programs or how it was possible to make them national. By missing the broader level of explanation, some authors have been misled as to the real sources of the new approach to influence.

[2] There is extensive material on the above points. See for example: Juarez Rubens Brandão Lopes, *Desenvolvimento e Mudança Social*, p. 115; Emanuel de Kadt, 'Religion, the Church, and Social Change in Brazil', in Claudio Veliz, ed., *The Politics of Conformity in Latin America* (London: Oxford University Press, 1967), pp. 194–7; and Leers *passim*.

neither large nor relatively exploited. The irrelevance of the papal social encyclicals to Brazil led to an interesting reversal, in that several high churchmen justified their support for the Estado Nôvo by a belief that Vargas was implementing this exact social doctrine.[3] Therefore, because of the distance between fact and theory in the Universal Church's social doctrine, due to lack of control over much of religious behavior and through express intent, the Brazilian Church, in this century at least, has always supported the *status quo*. One might cite the cases of Pes. Cicero and Ibiapina, and a few other isolated instances of individual clergymen who promoted change in their respective areas, but the overall impact of the Church has unquestionably been a conservative one.

However, this is not to argue that the Church was unaware of poverty and did nothing to ameliorate the plight of those who suffered. The Church received state resources to act in the social field and one important part of this field was charity. The Church assisted the poor in the best traditions of Christian charity, and many orders of nuns existed in Brazil for no other reason than to comfort the suffering. However, charity is one thing; social change another. This chapter analyzes how the Church came to replace charity with attempts to achieve social justice. That there is a great difference between charity and social justice is indicated in the following statement by Dom Helder Câmara.

Through our own experience, we know that the treatment received by those who work in a social field varies completely according to whether they limit themselves to simple charity or whether they feel the need to go beyond this to fight for the development of people who now vegetate in a sub-human situation. . . They will be suspect, and will be accused of being extremists and 'fellow-travellers' the moment that they realize charity is not enough, and that one must struggle in order that one's brethren, now debased by poverty, may achieve a measure of humanity.[4]

While all the threats to Church influence outlined in Chapter 3 are relevant to the social change strategy of influence, it is clearly the political threats posed by the Communists, demagogues and assorted rural agitators which really induced it. At a later stage, the clergy would be able to claim what the pastor of a small Northeastern village said in explaining the new approach.

It is not the fear of Communism, nor the desire to preserve traditional positions or to guard the faithful, that force our bishops to this new undertaking. On the contrary, it is the concrete, modern-day expression of true charity: the development of the human person, created in God's image. This development is achieved by eliminating obstacles

[3] See for example Dom João Becker, p. 30 and Pe. Leopoldo Brentano, SJ., *A 'Rerum Novarum' e seu Quinquagésimo Aniversário* (Rio de Janeiro: Gráfica Olímpico, 1941), in which it is argued that the labor union system was precisely what Pope Leo XIII had in mind in his encyclical.
[4] Dom Helder Câmara, *Revolução Dentro da Paz* (Rio de Janeiro: Editôra Sabiá, 1968), p. 180. Even while adopting a new response to misery and poverty, Dom Helder and those around him in the new approach to influence did not give up charity as a temporary help. In fact he and Dom Távora were instrumental in founding Caritas Brasileira in 1956 and incorporating it into the Bishops' Conference. It distributed in Brazil the resources of the Catholic Relief Services of the U.S. bishops.

which impede a deeper evangelic experience in an unjust social order contrary to God's design and – what is more appalling – in a land that is part of Christendom.[5]

But to reach a stage where Catholicism could legitimate the idea of social and political change required a catalyst which was political. In present day Brazil, it is clear to most clergy and laity that there is nothing in the religion which necessarily forces it to support the *status quo*. However, it is not the doctrine as such but rather the way it is interpreted in a social context which lends it a conservative or progressive orientation. For the religion to move from the middle of the road, so to speak, required some form of threat and the most serious form of threat to the Church was a political one.

Some elements in the Church would later argue that they became involved in social change programs simply because of the demands of the Gospel in a social situation they knew to be unjust. However, this argument does not explain why they suddenly took the Gospel to heart at this time or why the whole national Church also followed. My argument is more coherent and powerful for I can show evidence on the role of threats in documents of the time, in sectors of involvement, in regions of the country and in the causes of the later demise of this approach. If the above-noted elements were correct, the question would have to be put: Why was the Gospel considered in a social context before 1964 but not after?[6] The most succinct statement on threats leading to awareness is that made by the priest who was the main organizer of the Church's rural unions in Pernambuco. In the face of the awakening of the masses, with the rapid expansion of the *ligas camponesas* (peasant leagues), '...we opened our eyes, as members of the Church and as priests. We saw that the people in the rural areas were completely abandoned and easily stirred by political slogans that offered no hope of resolving the problem'.[7]

The topic of rural unionization has been well researched and it was not difficult to locate documents regarding the Church's position *vis-à-vis* rural workers and its perception of the potential loss of influence. The other programs are not so well documented and, moreover, much of the Church's response grew out of a generalized feeling of threats. However, the response on social change

[5] Msgr. Expedito de Sobral Medeiros of S.P. de Potengui, quoted in Procópio Camargo, *O Movimento de Natal* (Brussels: Centre de Documentation sur L'Action des Eglises dans le Monde, 1966), p. 125.

[6] For a justification of social action by the Church according to a 'reading of the Gospel' see Ferrari, *Igreja e Desenvolvimento*. It is worth noting, however, that on page 106, n. 24, there is some suggestion that the Church acted in part because of leftist threats. For another analysis of the same movement which gives emphasis to the threats see Camargo, *O Movimento de Natal*.

[7] Pe. Crespo of SORPE, 'Pequeno Resumo do Movimento Sindical Rural em Pernambuco', unpublished mimeographed bulletin. (31 May 1966), p. 1. Camargo states, '...the competitive example of the *ligas camponesas* was certainly important in the determination of the moment in which the rural unions were created and in the positions they came to assume.' p. 141. Precisely the same point is made by another priest in Pernambuco, who was also involved in rural unionization. See Father Antonio Melo, *The Coming Revolution in Brazil*, trans. and intro. Robert Menzel (Jericho, N.Y.: The Exposition Press, 1970), p. 32.

can be roughly correlated with those areas of the country where the threats were greatest.

The poorest area of Brazil is the Northeast. It is also the area of the most traditional agriculture and power relations and has the greatest social problems. It was in the Northeast where the *ligas camponesas* under Francisco Julião began, where a very progressive governor was elected (Miguel Arraes) and where the Communists became most active in organizing. In short, there were more threats of a political nature to the Church in the Northeast than anywhere else in Brazil.

It was also in the Northeast that the Church responded first and most positively to the threats. The bishops' manifestoes of the period are illustrative. The most progressive originated from the Northeast – those of Natal (Rio Grande do Norte) in 1951, Campina Grande (Paraíba) in 1956 and Natal again in 1959. In the rest of Brazil a few similar manifestoes were issued much later. (Minas Gerais in 1961 had one progressive manifesto and one conservative; São Paulo in 1960 produced one progressive statement in favor of the goverment's agrarian bill.) A contrast might be useful here. In the 1956 Campina Grande or the 1959 Natal manifestoes, the bishops of the Northeast observed that man was body and soul together; that the structures of society were unjust; that the Church must participate in changing the structures; and they mentioned several courses of action to remedy the various situations. In 1959, the bishops of Rio Grande do Sul met and issued a statement on social problems:

Unemployment causes hunger and despair in many homes. It is not within our scope to improve this situation. We are completely incapable of affecting the economic policy of the government, the outrageous expenditures at the federal level, the lack of incentives in agriculture, and other causes of the severe crisis.[8]

Thus while the bishops in the Northeast had been threatened by all sorts of enemies, had become aware of social problems and had committed themselves to act, the bishops in the relatively peaceful South noted that some problems existed but interpreted the Church's role in exclusively religious terms: their influence did not extend to the social. It is interesting to note, however, that when a counterpart of the *ligas camponesas* was formed in Rio Grande do Sul, the bishops then decided that social influence did fall within their domain and founded opposition rural unions, the Frente Agrária Gaúcha (FAG). This happened in most of Brazil: as the threats of *ligas componesas* or agitators increased, the Church became active in opposition movements or organizations which also sought to promote social change.

The Church became most active in those sectors of society where the threats were greatest. The social change response was found mainly in the fields of rural unionization, basic education, the university and secondary schools and the left wing of party politics. That is, the Church responded most actively either where it perceived that it had influence to lose (rural areas and education)

---

[8]   Made in Uruguaina (R.S.) November 1959, quoted in *Revista Eclesiástica Brasileira* 19 (December 1959) p. 992.

or where there might be possibilities of obtaining influence (left wing politics). There was little response where there did not seem to be a credible threat to past influence (e.g. urban labor). In short, there is an overall correlation between the Church's reaction in a social change direction and the threats of a political nature to the generation and exercise of influence. The function of the threats was to awaken sectons of the Church to a responsibility concerning social change. The awakening and resultant responsibility are vividly documented by the following statement of Dom Helder Câmara, leader of the group most concerned with social change.

Ever since the 'day of the discovery', Latin American society has grown and developed under the influence of the Church. Its social, economic, political and cultural structures were cast within the mold of Iberian Christendom. The struggles for independence did not cause any structural changes. Now for the first time, we are living in an era of substantial changes. The Church is inseparably bound to the entire history in its values, its true achievements and its moments of glory, but also in its failures, its false values and its contradictions.

This places on the Church an inescapable responsibility in the face of new challenges, and presents demands that cannot be ignored. The Church cannot allow the true value of our civilization, which she helped create, to be destroyed by structural changes rapidly coming into effect. The Church should denounce our collective sin – the unjust and stagnant structures – not as someone who judges from the outside, but as someone who accepts a share of the guilt. She must be bold enough to identify with the past, and thus to feel herself more responsible for the present and the future.[9]

The Church intentionally attempted to shift the nature of its power from maintaining the *status quo* to supporting social change *in order to continue to exercise religious influence*. The Church developed a strategy of pre-influence so that religious influence could then have meaning. This was no simple shift and it led to grave political problems for the institution, which became more serious after 1964.

Ideology formulation at the hierarchy level

The active promotion of social change by the Church was preceded by th formulation by a group of bishops of an ideology designed both to justify and to necessitate such action. The formulation of this ideology was a conscious policy of Dom Helder Câmara, the moving force behind the progressive sector of the Church. He was aware that any institution, including the Church, must have leaders who will draw guidelines and set goals.[10] He was such a leader, surrounded by a group of about ten other bishops, two or three score of priests and about the same number of young and active laymen. This ideology did not develop in the abstract but rather in a direct and dynamic relationship with the environment: with the Universal Church, particularly as evidenced in the

---

[9] Dom Helder Câmara, *Revolução Dentro da Paz*, pp. 31–2. From Mar del Plata speech of CELAM, but said many times before.
[10] Interview with Dom Helder Câmara in Recife, 25 October 1967.

relevant papal encyclicals 'Mater et Magistra' of 1961 and 'Pacem in Terris' of 1963, with the Brazilian government during its period of development and radicalization (1955–64), and in contact with the confusion and effervescence throughout Brazilian society in this period.

I use the term 'ideology' advisedly, in order to suggest more than the term 'theology' connotes. 'Theology' indicates a rather general, abstract, otherworldly set of principles which endures forever in only the broadest applications. 'Ideology', on the other hand, implies rationality of intent, an organized, or particular application and with definite action imperatives. It can be said that the neo-Christendom model included an ideology, but what I am emphasizing here is the intentional, deliberate orientation towards action in the post-1950 Church. It was a particular formulation of selected elements of a larger Catholic theology in relation to, or with particular relevance for, Brazil at a special historical point. The ideology was formulated in a process of questioning: questioning of the past role of the Church, the nature of change in Brazilian society and the proper role of the Church. Out of this questioning arose the basic justification of a new influence model, one which was radically different from the past in its action imperatives.

Chart I indicates the formulation of a new Church ideology after about 1950. To break down the components of ideology, I use the definition of Mary Matossian, which views an ideology as a pattern of ideas providing for the adherent a description of the surrounding environment, a self-definition within it and action imperatives deduced from the foregoing.[11] My sources for this ideology are largely national and regional statements of the hierarchy. However, these statements are only indicative of similar statements being made and implemented at all levels of the Church. The bishops are usually the most conservative element in the Church, so that when they make statements it can be supposed that other levels have already reached the point and passed beyond it. I use these statements because they were published in the press during the period, because they were made publicly and intentionally to legitimate change, and because they were recognized at the time as justification for change in the Church's role in society.[12]

The pre-1950 ideology follows directly from the neo-Christendom influence model. It comes through clearly in the statements and literature of the Church during this time. The statements were made in response to the threats presented

---

[11] Mary Matossian, 'Ideologies of Delayed Industrialization: Some Tensions and Ambiguities', *Economic Development and Cultural Change* 6:3 (April 1958), pp. 217–28.

[12] See de Kadt's brief comments on some of these documents. He takes a less serious view of their overall orientation than I do and in part this is caused by his main focus on the Catholic youth movements. In comparison with the evolution of the youth, the bishops were very slow indeed. However, I must diverge from de Kadt where he argues that the pronouncements remained 'circumscribed by the traditional doctrine of the church'. I have shown that Universal Church doctrine was not always either the doctrine of the Brazilian Church or in fact implemented. In contrast with past positions and statements in the Brazilian context, many of the statements were radical. Emanuel de Kadt, *Catholic Radicals in Brazil* (London: Oxford University Press, 1970), pp. 72–7.

CHART 1 *Formulation of a new Church ideology by the Brazilian hierarchy*

	Pre-1950	1950–61	1961–3	1963–4
Environment	A Catholic country (94%). Friendly government which cooperates in return for support. Stable or calm environment, but a few threats by politicians (e.g. divorce) and Protestants. Communists considered a menace.	Communists and rural agitators a real threat as the rural areas are socially and economically deprived and backward. Feudal structures exist; agrarian reform essential. Workers in all areas need assistance. Politics often demagogic and/or dishonest.	Possible guerrilla warfare in rural areas as structures so unjust. No credit, high prices, backward industry, etc. Basic reforms necessary. Minimal popular participation in politics; most people in power ignore the problems or profiteer.	Brazil is underdeveloped country thus has great problems by definition. Social order is terrible. Marxists want to replace it, but their solution is no better. Reforms vital on voting, taxes, business, administration and education.
Self definition	Monopoly in orienting norms and values for all. Defender of the faith in Brazil. An integral aspect of society at all levels, thus entitled to receive public support to carry out public services.	Religion obliged to associate body (social) with soul (doctrine), thus must see norms and values in terms of justice. The Church able to lead in social change; independent of government and siding with needy and oppressed.	Emphasize vital and legitimate role in social field. Must appeal for a just social order in a positive way. Can stimulate basic education, establish guidelines for change, and create a general mystique for change especially in rural areas.	Church is autonomous from government and political parties. In a social sense, everything concerns the Church and must be done by the laity. Must stimulate the necessary reforms.
Action Imperatives	Work publicly to ensure public support and act against Communists. Denounce Protestants, administer the sacraments, advise pious groups and avoid social concerns. Educate the middle classes. Distribute charity.	Legitimate values of justice, thus speaking out for change and supporting other groups as well. Demand reforms. Cooperate with government in change oriented programs. Help create rural union, co-ops, colonies, health projects, etc.	Generalize regional programs for change to a national level and unify the whole Church behind them. Specifically, promote MEB, *ligas*, JAC, etc.	Church should act through laity, thus they must be stimulated and educated. Until laymen ready the Church must act directly and as an institution. Continue to support rural unions, Catholic Action, etc.

Note on Sources: The pre-1950 formulation is put together from general sources, a series by *Vozes* on bishops, and a 1945 statement by the bishops led by Dom Jaime Câmara, 'Pastoral on Social and Political Situation in Brazil.' The 1950–61 stage is from the Natal statement of 1951, declarations of the bishops of Amazônia and Vale do São Francisco in 1952, the first and second statements of the bishops of the Northeast (Campina Grande in 1956 and Natal, 1959), the statement of CNBB in Goiânia in 1958, and the São Paulo bishops' declaration on agrarian reform in 1960. The 1961–3 stage is taken from the declaration of the Central Commission of the CNBB on the rural situation in 1961, the bishops' statement in Goiânia in 1962, and the declaration of the Central Commission of the CNBB in June, 1962. The fourth stage, 1963–4, is drawn from the May 1963 statement of the Central Commission, the declaration of the bishops in Recife in 1964 and the São Paulo episcopate declaration in May 1964.

by social and political change. It was a reaction along traditional lines, and the Church continued to maintain this ideology as power was sought in order to promote influence.

The 1950–61 period is the most important in the formulation of a social change ideology. Due largely to the threats of agitators in the rural areas and demagogues in the towns, the Church became aware of the backwardness of many societal structures and injustice in general. For example, in the earliest statement (that of Dom Inocêncio Engelke in 1950), the rural workers were referred to as 'infra-human...Do the shacks in which they live merit the name homes? Is the food they eat really nourishment? Can the rags they wear be called clothing? Can their unhealthy vegetative existence, without expectations, vision and ideas, be called living?'[13] Along with the awareness of injustice came the realization that man is composed of body and soul, and the Church must thereby be concerned with the temporal order. By confronting the unpleasant reality in which millions of humans existed with some elements of Catholic social doctrine, an awareness arose that the Church had something to say about society and its transformation. 'Nobody should be surprised to see us involved with problems concerning the temporal order. For man, as a union of body and soul, the relationship between material and spiritual questions is constant.'[14] The Church thus has a role as a leader in legitimating or advocating programs of social change. First, however, it must dissociate itself from the injustices of the past.

There are tremendous injustices inherent in structures of our political organization and our economic system. The Church is forced to dissociate itself from, and refuse any responsibility for, these injustices. Moreover – by virtue of her own evangelic mission – the Church...places itself on the side of the downtrodden, to co-operate with them in the task of rehabilitation and redemption.[15]

After declaring its independence, the Church further defined its line and expressed a desire to cooperate with the government in change-oriented projects; that is, cooperation was recommended but on an intentional and rational basis for particular goals and particular programs. The desire for specific cooperation was recognized by the then President of Brazil, Kubitschek, when he attended the 1956 meeting: 'It did not occur to any one, least of all to me, that the Catholic Church was moving out of its proper area. On the contrary I perceived from the beginning, that with these events [the cooperation for development programs a new relationship was developing between the Church and state in Brazil'.[16] Even by 1961 the Church formulated an ideology of 'pre-influence': there was no point in acting solely to evangelize or influence man until he had the conditions in which he could be a man. That is, when so many people exist in sub-human conditions, the first task is to change the structures so that conditions can be improved.

In the next period, the descriptions of environment, self-definitions, and

[13] Quoted in Moreira Alves, *O Cristo do Povo*, p. 48.
[14] Statement of Campina Grande, 1956.
[15] *Ibid.*
[16] Quoted in Camargo, p. 132.

imperatives become more concrete and a good deal more emphatic. The Central Commission began one of their messages: 'No one can ignore the outcry of the masses who, martyrized by the spectre of starvation, are reaching the point of despair in some places.' While the Communists are exploiting the situation, 'There was never in this country a greater or more criminal domination by the economic powers.' In this situation, the Church can 'cry out for a social order based on the principles of revealed truth and the norms of justice and equity.'[17] The Church can create a mystique to counter that of the Communists. 'To establish Rural Catholic Action is to guarantee to the rural area a sufficiently strong mystique to counterbalance and supersede the Communist mystique.'[18] In the present context in Brazil, the Church must act in a unified manner to assist attempts and programs to improve the situation of the lower classes. At this time such efforts were mainly through Church organizations such as the Movimento de Educação de Base (MEB), Juventude Agrária Católica (JAC), and efforts at rural unionization.

In the last period (1963–4) the ideology of social change became more emphatic, sophisticated and self-aware. For the first time Brazil was characterized as an underdeveloped country, 'in which the masses do not participate, where misery and premature mortality are common and where rural and urban realities generate extremely serious depersonalization'.[19] The social order might be stable, but it was immoral. The Marxist solutions were no better than what already existed. Yet something had to be done to change this social system. 'No one is entitled to presume that such an order of things can be a Christian order. To achieve a Christian order, deep and sweeping changes are needed and can no longer be postponed; otherwise we must be prepared for days of catastrophe.'

In the 1963 statement, the bishops examined and criticized six different sectors of society and indicated that serious change was needed. They found it necessary in all the documents of this period to emphasize that the Church was independent of both government and political parties, although willing to cooperate for the common good. The Church must continue to promote reform. For the Church, all aspects of life are important. However, it has to make its influence on social matters felt through the laity. 'The presence of the Church in the transformation of the temporal takes place through free and responsible laymen who, with all men of good will, show "the spirit of comprehension, unselfishness and disposition to cooperate loyally in pursuit of objectives which are inherently good, or at least lead towards the good".' The Church needs to educate and stimulate the laymen, and until the latter are ready the Church as institution must act. 'Because of certain urgent demands in a social situation which is infrahuman, the Church, as an institution, is obligated to intervene directly in support of certain temporal activities.'[20] And, all the while, the Church will continue to support the efforts of MEB, rural unionization and Catholic Action.

[17] Central Commission statement of July 1962.
[18] Central Commission statement of October 1961.
[19] Central Commission statement of 1963.
[20] *Ibid.*

The threats by the Communists and others, principally in the rural areas, but also by unscrupulous politicians throughout the country, led to an awareness in some parts of the Church that all was not well in Brazil. While it was true that the Communists were attempting to exploit this situation, the capitalists and politicians were doing little to improve the overall predicament. The country was in serious need of basic reforms. For the bishops, an underdeveloped country by definition could not offer the conditions under which man could be fully human. The Church was now interested in the human aspect, for it somewhat belatedly admitted that man is both body and soul and not just the latter. Consequently, the Church had to take an interest in the temporal welfare of its people and speak out for the necessary reforms. While compromising connections with the government and local power groups were criticized, the Church made clear its willingness to cooperate selectively with the government on development projects. The necessity of operating in the social field made the Church realize that the laity had to be mobilized to help. The help was concentrated mainly in efforts in the rural areas through programs of basic education, unionization and cooperatives. As an institution, the Church cooperated with the government in its program of development and made continual legitimation statements on the necessity and propriety of change. As noted earlier, this ideology in formulation established the basis for a model of 'pre-influence': the Church had to help in effecting structural change so that influence in the more limited religious sense could be meaningful. The Church was still seeking power in that the solutions suggested worked on the basis of structures, instead of individual conversion, and most of them concerned either utilization of state resources or the mobilization of individuals in opposition to other political groups. However, the focus was now in a progressive direction – for change – and the ideology seems to have served at least three functions along these lines.

The Church in Brazil in recent times had intentionally or otherwise favored the maintenance of the *status quo*. Charity was pleasant but it did not alter an unjust society. In this perspective, when the new ideology of social change was formulated and broadcast at the top level of the Church, it meant that one of the most conservative institutions in Brazil opted for change.[21] The Church came out publicly and vigorously to denounce injustices in society, to demand basic reforms and to offer help in implementing the necessary programs. Clearly, then, the Church gave support to other elements in society which were attempting to promote structural transformations, rather than denouncing them as Communists or agitators, as had been done previously and as was happening in other countries at this time. The Church served as a legitimating ally of progressive forces and opposed those who would deny the necessity of various types of change. A good example of the intentional legitimation function was the statement of the hierarchy in São Paulo in December 1960, explicitly favoring the agrarian reform project then being discussed in the State Legislature,

---

[21] The national statements, especially those of the Central Commission, were signed by the Cardinals of Rio, Bahia and São Paulo and the important Archbishop of Pôrto Alegre; that is, the top level concurred.

which was strongly opposed by conservatives. 'Providence is allowing us, by an evolutionary process, what other countries obtained only through bloody revolutions. The project is, with regard to São Paulo, a reply to the anxiety of the Holy Church for a reform of the agrarian structure with a just measure of safeguarding the right of property in its individual and social functions.'[22] In short, this new ideology legitimated change in its general aspects as well as in specific programs. It was formulated partly with this function in mind.

The next function was intentionally to stimulate the formation of change-directed programs. Internally, this resulted in several significant programs. For the society and government in general, the ideology recommended proposals ranging from the formation of labor organizations to all-inclusive programs of regional development. Superintendência do Desenvolvimento do Nordeste (SUDENE), the regional development program for the Northeast, is an example of the latter. SUDENE grew out of Operação Nordeste (OPENO), which was initiated when the Northeastern bishops suggested to the government of Juscelino Kubitscheck that the various ineffective programs in the region be coordinated. It was the bishops, and not the technicians, who first proposed an overall plan for the area and made specific recommendations as to its features and general character.[23] In 1956, Kubitschek met with the bishops at Campina Grande and began to coordinate government and Church personnel and plans in order to create a coherent developmental plan: SUDENE evolved from this meeting. Kubitschek also attended the 1959 bishops' meeting in Natal and stated:

It must be acknowledged that this initiative of the Federal Government (OPENO) is due to the inspiration of the Church and the energetic dedication of the Northeastern Bishops, ever since the first meeting at Campina Grande, to save our courageous fellow countrymen from destitution and misery.[24]

The President also made the larger legitimating function of the ideology clear in the same speech:

How could the regional planning of Operation Northeast be executed if the moral force of the Church did not assist the government to stimulate and engage public and private groups; although in the same region, they did not help or complement each other, but rather worked with a great waste of funds and personnel?[25]

Other examples of this stimulating function are the programs for assistance to migrants, slum clearance and other regional plans.

The third and final function of the new ideology was to prepare a legitimating framework or system for a new model of Church influence. As will become clear later in this chapter, the Church did not ignore its goal of embracing the

---

[22] São Paulo statement, December 1960.
[23] Compare Albert O. Hirschman, *Journeys Toward Progress* (Garden City, N.Y.: Doubleday and Co., 1965), where the role of the Church is played down, with Aníbal Teixeira de Souza, *Os Bispos do Nordeste e As Migrações Internas* (Rio de Janeiro: Instituto Nacional de Imigração e Colonização, 1961), p. 34, which supports my position.
[24] Speech of 24 May 1959, as quoted in *II Encontro dos Bispos do Nordeste* (Rio de Janeiro: Presidência da República, 1959), p. 12.
[25] *Ibid.*, p. 14.

whole of society, but there were rather serious modifications in the nature of this coverage. The new focal strata were the poor, especially the rural poor. Independence from national and local groups was declared, but cooperation of certain sorts was encouraged. The instruments of influence changed, or at least expanded, so that unions, basic education and other such programs which encouraged change were important mechanisms of influence. In conclusion, as a result of this new ideology of 'pre-influence', the overall influence model of the Church began to change. The ideology both stimulated the change and determined its nature. Through it the Church dealt actively with threats posed by society to the traditional model by in fact superseding this model.

Social change projects promoted by the hierarchy

The Movimento de Educação de Base (MEB) was the largest program in Brazil dealing with basic education.[26] Basic education is concerned not only with literacy training but more importantly with social mobilization or politicization through the concept of *conscientização*. *Conscientização* is basically an awakening of consciousness. The masses in Brazil lack an awareness of their intrinsic value as humans, of their ability to learn and grow and of their capabilities in bringing about changes in their situations and those of others. Basic education seeks to create an awareness so that people can begin to control their own destinies. The method involves the use of symbols and phrases, whereby an individual becomes aware or 'conscious' as he becomes literate. If the nature of the patrimonial-paternalistic society in Brazil is recalled, one can begin to appreciate the implications of a program such as MEB. The society is elitist; the masses do not participate; and reforms are not enacted. Illiterates, comprising the majority of the population, cannot even vote. Basic education, which gives literacy and awareness, would undoubtedly threaten the socio-political structures of Brazil and especially those in the rural areas.[27] MEB was located in the most underdeveloped areas of the country: North, Northeast, Centerwest and northern Minas Gerais, precisely those areas where the traditional patrimonial-paternalistic system was still intact. Clearly, a basic education program such as MEB was designed to bring about changes in society. 'MEB was not born to be another tradition loaded movement, to sustain what exists, at any price. It stands for the necessary changes. It stands for the full participation of the

---

[26] Others were Serviço de Extensão Cultural (SEC) of the University of Recife in Pernambuco directed by Paulo Freire, and several smaller 'popular culture' groups. See Carlos Estevam, 'A Questão da Cultura Popular', *Revista Tempo Brasileiro*, 1963; Paulo Freire, *Educação Como Prática da Liberdade* (Rio de Janeiro: Paz e Terra, 1967); Thomas G. Sanders, 'The Paulo Freire Method: Literacy Training and Conscientizacion', Field Letter (TGS-12) to Richard H. Nolte, Institute of Current World Affairs, New York, 6 June 1968; and Paulo Freire, 'Cultural Action for Freedom', *Harvard Educational Review*, Monograph Series, No. 1 (1970).

[27] In 1950 illiteracy in some Northeast states was very high: Alagoas – 76%, Piauí – 74%, Ceará – 60%, and Pernambuco – 68%. The rural areas alone are far higher.

peasant and urban worker in all the matters that concern them.'[28] But once fully understood, it posed a threat to the *status quo* and to those who profited from the archaic structures.

MEB was a national program which grew out of the experience of the radio schools pioneered by Dom Eugênio Sales in Natal, beginning in 1958. Dom Eugênio had visited Dom Salcedo in Sutatenza, Colombia, and on returning to Rio Grande do Norte established radio schools similar to those of Sutatenza. He went beyond the Colombian experience, however, in encouraging participation, whereas Radio Sutatenza was strong in literacy and catechism, but weak on the political side.[29] The radio schools in Natal were reasonably successful and the Bishops' Conference (CNBB), through their section on social action, decided to generalize the venture. By 1960, the CNBB was coordinating a system of radio schools in some five dioceses (Natal, Aracaju, Crato in Ceará, Bragança in Pará and Penedo in Alagoas). In that year, a presidential candidate, Jânio Quadros, visited Aracaju and was quite impressed with the radio schools operating there. The Bishop of Aracaju, Dom Távora, told him that the CNBB could expand the system but lacked resources. When Quadros was elected he signed a decree (No. 50,370 in 1961), whereby the government would finance radio schools under the direction of the CNBB for five years. After this date, MEB expanded rapidly. By 1963 it was operating 59 systems, using 25 radio transmitters and reaching some 7,353 schools in 57 dioceses in 15 states. Approximately 180,000 people attended the schools. By 1966, 400,000 students had completed one or more courses and 13,771 leaders had graduated.[30] MEB was then a going concern with substantial finances, dedicated organizers and a rather sophisticated and evolving technique.

At the local level, MEB functioned on the basis of a radio-school system (a group of schools receiving the broadcast from one transmitter), and the fundamental elements included a daily program designed for the particular region, local monitors at each school who organized and supervised their community and a room somewhere with a receiver which could be called the school. The system was quite simple, but because the local natural leaders were recruited as monitors and the students were stimulated toward awareness, the implications were a good deal more complex.

At the national level, the movement was overseen by the Conselho Diretor Nacional (CDN), composed of nine bishops. Yet from the national to the decentralized local level, the movement was entirely organized and administered by laymen. This fact suggests that it is necessary to mobilize the laity when the

---

[28] Marina Bandeira, 'MEB – "Movimento de Educação de Base",' paper given at CICOP, Chicago (23 January 1964).

[29] 'In Natal, however, the program differed from the Colombian model, by adopting the orientation of basic education, that is, integral education of the rural populations, seeking more than mere alphabetization, politicizing the consciousness of the rural man, giving him notions of his rights and how to achieve them, introducing notions of hygiene and health, more rational agricultural techniques, etc.' Camargo, p. 98.

[30] See 'MEB Em Cinco Anos: 1961–1966', a report in two volumes (Mimeographed), published by MEB, Rio de Janeiro, 1966, for all data.

Church wants to change its influence in relation to a temporal situation. This pattern began to result in new roles and structures for the Church which made for internal differentiation. Most of the laymen who worked with MEB came from the Catholic Action sectors.[31] This was important, for it not only meant that MEB would be carried along by the infusion of a young and dynamic personnel, but that these people would have a meaningful outlet in the Church, into which they could channel their time and energies. If they could continue with a Church-related program, their skills and energy would not then be lost to the Church.

Given the neo-Christendom model of influence and the past political activities of the Church, MEB was something unique indeed. Despite the bishops' statements in favor of structural change, their actions as individuals often belied their progressive stances. MEB was a very ambitious program, extremely serious and sophisticated, and was strictly aimed at bringing about structural change in society through the medium of individual actions. Most observers of MEB in this period agree that it did attain some acceptable degree of success, despite the fact that it was cut short in 1964, only three years after its founding.[32] Because it was such a change for the Church to be engaged in activities that might be considered radical (and in fact were), problems arose for the institution as well as for the movement itself. Initially these were of an internal nature, as tensions surfaced between the cadre of MEB, some of the clergy and many of the bishops in whose dioceses the schools were located. Originally the pastors had selected the monitors for the local schools, but it soon became clear that the priests usually selected more traditional types whom they could control, rather than the actual leaders. MEB thus devised a different method of selecting the monitors and many pastors became discontented and considered the movement a threat to their authority.[33] MEB was established in 57 dioceses, but it is impossible to know how many of the bishops fully appreciated the revolutionary potential in the process of *conscientização*. Some of them wanted the movement for prestige, others for catechism, some liked its health and agriculture aspect and some were apparently in favor of its revolutionary function. Because the movement meant different things to different elements in the Church, it was bound to cause problems and misunderstandings, as indeed it did.[34]

The tensions within the Church over the meaning of MEB were minor in comparison with the problems which arose in the society and politics generally. Change in the Church cannot remain an internal matter, simply because the Church is linked in a most complex manner with all sorts of other structures and

---

[31] Marina Bandeira, CICOP paper, p. 6.
[32] See de Kadt's *Catholic Radicals* for a very complete and critical analysis of the strengths and weaknesses of MEB. Even though de Kadt is not exactly caught up in the mystique of the movement, he does admit at times that it achieved worthwhile results.
[33] Interview with an important official in MEB on 13 November 1967 in Rio de Janeiro.
[34] On bishops' views, I interviewed Dom José Távora, President of the movement on 23 October 1967 in Aracaju. He told me that at least ten bishops, mainly those around Dom Helder and himself, were aware of the larger aspects. De Kadt's book covers the tensions in detail.

groups. To illustrate what happens when change occurs, the incident involving Carlos Lacerda in Rio de Janeiro during February 1964 is worth reviewing.

Carlos Lacerda, who had been a newspaper publisher and deputy, later became Governor of Guanabara, the state in which Rio de Janeiro is located. On information that Communist textbooks were being printed for imminent distribution, Lacerda authorized the confiscation of three thousand copies of MEB's new primer, 'Viver e Lutar' (To Live is to Fight). While some sections in the primer might have inspired class warfare, it generally described in a more or less objective way the unfortunate social situation in Brazil. In addition, this primer was but one of four texts which were to be used only in preparing the radio programs and were not for general distribution. Lacerda's use of the police, without warning the MEB through other Church sectors, suggests that he intended to demoralize the movement. A number of MEB's officials were forced to make statements to the police as though they were common criminals. These included Dom Távora, President of the movement, Msgr. Hilário Pandolfo, Vice-President, and Marina Bandeira, Secretary. The debate in the news media is indicative of what many thought of MEB and the social change strategy of the Church that it represented. The important conservative Rio daily, O Globo, of 28 February is typical. Under the heading, 'The Psychological Booby-Trap' they note:

The primer confiscated by the Rio police in a printing shop in Lapa is further proof of the intentions and plans of the Communists and their accomplices with regard to the Communization of Brazil. [If the Church was involved]...it would not be the first case nor unfortunately the last, in which some priest, or even some bishop, through ingeniousness or through a poorly understood social zeal or any other motive, becomes an involuntary accomplice of the Communists and an instrument of their subversive plans.[35]

That conservatives would oppose change-oriented programs such as MEB was understandable, for they were also against the government of President Goulart. MEB was not, however, a Goulart program and was far more responsible than he was in seeking change. What caused real difficulties for the movement was the equivocation and lack of support within the Church itself.

On the night of the raid, Lacerda tried to contact the Cardinal of Rio, Dom Jaime Câmara, probably with the intention of clearing his action with his longtime friend. The Cardinal was ill but replied through his secretary that the Governor should follow the law. Lacerda interpreted this as a sign of approval and went ahead as planned. On the 25 February Lacerda declared: 'Dom Jaime Câmara approved the action of the police,'[36] whereupon the Cardinal responded that he 'did not have anything to do with the primer ordered by MEB and that he was not responsible for everything that was done of the first floor of the Palácio São Joaquim.'[37] Dom Jaime had been President of the CNBB and,

[35] O Globo (Rio de Janeiro), 28 February 1964. For documentation on the issue, see MEB's 'O Conjunto Didático "Viver é Lutar" ' a mimeographed report, Rio de Janeiro, July 1964.
[36] Correio da Manhã (Rio de Janeiro), 25 February 1964.
[37] Where he was based and MEB had its offices. Diário de Notícias (Rio de Janeiro), 27 February 1964.

since MEB was part of the Conference, he could have been expected to know about it. Dom Távora came to Rio and spoke with the Cardinal, but Dom Jaime nevertheless came out against the movement in a radio broadcast. With the incident, a split became clear within both society and the Church regarding social change. Despite the fact that the Cardinal of Rio had signed the progressive documents, he was not willing to support MEB at a critical time. Opponents to the social change orientation could thus begin isolating the particular group behind it. Typical is a statement by the Secretary of Security of Guanabara, Colonel Gustavo Borges,' "To Live is To Fight" was prepared in the cellars of the Palácio São Joaquim by the radical bishops who hang around Dom Helder and without the slightest knowledge of the Cardinal.'[38] The primer was withdrawn from circulation, and MEB along with the CNBB was demoralized.

Later in the year, and after the coup, MEB cadres confronted far more serious problems; many were arrested and their teaching materials confiscated. While the bishops most closely associated with MEB at the national level defended it against charges of Communism and although the CNBB officially declared the movement safe, some local bishops allowed the military to harass and persecute the MEB militants.[39] The Church, through MEB, did become actively involved in promoting social change.

Rural unionization was the next important program of the hierarchy to promote social change. Whereas the Church became very active and important in the formation of rural unions, the experience in the urban unions was slight.[40] The difference in involvement is due to the overall nature of urban unionization as well as the initial Church experience in this field. Urban unions were 'captured' in a governmental system and consequently offered fewer opportunities to agitators who might make them threats to the Church. Further, the Church entered in this field early and became committed to a particular strategy. There was, consequently, little need to respond in this area and commitments had already been made in a particular form.

The system of urban unionization was designed and dictated by Getúlio Vargas during the Estado Nôvo period and was codified in the labor laws of 1943 (No. 2,162). This system brought labor under the government's control through the Ministry of Labor and has continued until the present time. The system is one of 'bureaucratic unionism', in which the government dominates the movement and in which a special type of *pelego* makes his career through the unions, into the labor party (Partido Trabalhista Brasileiro, PTB), and finally into the Ministry of Labor.[41] Because of the governmental controls, which are

---

[38] *A Notícia* (Rio de Janeiro), 21 February 1964.
[39] Interviews with Dom Távora and important official in MEB; Moreira Alves, pp. 163–210 deals with MEB and its problems.
[40] 'The work of Christians in urban unionization although much older was less profound and infinitely less effective than in the rural areas.' Moreira Alves, p. 132.
[41] Leôncio Rodrigues, *Conflito Industrial e Sindicalismo no Brasil* (São Paulo: Difusão Européia do Livro, 1966); *Sociologie du Travail*, December 1961, has a series of articles on Brazilian labor by Fernando Henrique Cardoso, Azis Simão, Alain Touraine and Juarez Rubens Brandão Lopes; see also Juarez Rubens Brandão Lopes, *Crise do Brasil Arcaico*.

reinforced by a lack of professionalization among the workers with the influx of rural migrants, the unionized workers cannot be called a class: they are instead a *masse de manoeuvre*. An important instrument in keeping them in this position are the relative advantages the unionized workers have over the non-unionized and especially the rural workers. With such provisions as minimum wages, social security, retirement benefits, medical benefits and so forth, the unionized worker is indeed a privileged individual. In this context, the Church did not feel compelled to enter and combat the subversives as had been the case in much of Europe. The movement in Brazil was very largely safe; Getúlio Vargas created it with precisely that intent.[42]

The Church entered the urban movement early and located itself comfortably within the Vargas system. The Círculos Operários were founded in 1932 by Pe. Leopoldo Brentano, SJ, and are still today the largest single Church group in the urban movement, with some 400 chapters and a claimed membership of a half million. Pe. Brentano, as the Church in general, was extremely satisfied with the Vargas system of labor relations and social order and oriented the Círculos to accept it fully. The movement became attached to the Vargas type of system and adapted poorly after his demise. The Círculos continued to be concerned with questions of catechism, moralism, the encroachments of secularism and the distribution of charity. After 1960 there were a few innovations regarding programs of leadership training, but these did not amount to much. The Círculos remained linked to their special past and were largely ignored by the more dynamic elements within the Church.[43]

After 1960, Catholic Action became involved in urban labor. Ação Católica Operária and Juventude Operária Católica (ACO and JOC) began in this period under the hierarchy to evangelize the worker milieu. Both movements remained limited in size, generally lacked resources, but did at times enter into alliances with Communists to pressure for some structural changes.[44] Neither were very important before 1964, but became larger and more active later, although they are now being eliminated by the government.

One final Church labor organization must be mentioned. The Frente Nacional do Trabalho (FNT) was founded in 1960 after a very long and difficult strike against the Perus Cement Company in São Paulo. Founded by a disciple of Pe. Lebret, Mario Carvalho de Jesus, the Frente waged a number of long-lasting strikes, most of which were successful. The movement spread to other areas, mainly around São Paulo, and a total membership of 10,000 was claimed. It was para-Church and para-union, attempting to change the union system while

---

[42] Urban unions in Brazil are not unique in Latin America in their privileged positions and subsequent reliable support for the government. See the general article on urban labor in Latin America: Henry Landsberger, 'The Labor Elite: Is it Revolutionary?' in Seymour Martin Lipset and Aldo Solari, eds., *Elites in Latin America* (New York: Oxford University Press, 1967), pp. 256–300.

[43] The most complete discussion of the Círculos is Howard J. Wiarda's, 'The Brazilian Catholic Labor Movement', University of Massachusetts, Labor Relations and Research Center, 1969.

[44] Moreira Alves, p. 133.

in the process evangelizing the milieu. On a limited basis the FNT succeeded, but due to lack of funds did not expand.[45]

In conclusion, the Church involvement in urban labor was neither particularly active nor important. The labor system was controlled by the government in such a way as to preclude serious threats to the Church's perception of its influence. In this context, the Círculos Operários were enough to ensure continued Church influence. When after 1960 even the urban labor field became rather turbulent, the responses were limited. While the hierarchy aided Catholic Action (ACO and JOC) and to a lesser degree the FNT, it did not do so in a strategic or significant manner.

In contrast, the Church became the largest and most important agent in the field of rural unionization. Critical in this involvement was the complete absence of any organization prior to around 1957 and the subsequent rapid growth of the *ligas camponesas*. The Church had always considered the rural areas secure. The rural people were out of touch with national society, illiterate and firmly attached to forms of 'cultural Catholicism'. When Francisco Julião began in the late 1950s to organize and mobilize the rural workers, the Church perceived that this secure area of latent or passive influence might simply disappear or, worse yet, be mobilized in direct opposition to the Church. Once the Church was aware of the threats posed by the *ligas*, it responded and found that a traditional form of influence (in this case, the maintenance of 'cultural Catholicism') could be converted into other forms, but that, as in the case of MEB, some support with the traditional political groups would have to be surrendered.

The formation of rural unions had been possible in Brazil since 1903 (Decree Law No. 979, expanded by Decree Law No. 637 of 1907). Like so many formal provisions, however, this one did not reflect the reality of the situation in the rural areas and by 1960 only six rural *sindicatos* (unions) had been formed. As Márcio Moreira Alves put it, the law did not go beyond the walls of the Legislative Assembly nor beyond the frontiers of the asphalt highway.[46] To appreciate the importance of the lack of rural unions in a predominantly rural country (64% of the population was rural in 1950, 54% a decade later) where the majority of the population is involved in agriculture (57.8% in agriculture, livestock and forestry in 1950, but producing only 27% of net domestic product in 1960), the pattern of land ownership and the structures of rural power must be understood.

The system of land-holding in Brazil is similar to that in other countries of Latin America, except that the distribution is more extreme. Table 19 in the Appendix clearly indicates that many people own very little land while a few own a great deal. In the Northeast in 1960, *minifúndios* comprised 55% of the total holdings but included only 2% of the land, whereas the *latifúndios* made up

---

[45] Interview with President of FNT, on 11 December 1967 in São Paulo. *Jornal do Brasil* (Rio) 11 June 1967, has an article on FNT. See also *O São Paulo*, 16 May 1970 for a report.

[46] Moreira Alves, p. 69. See also Clodomir Moraes, 'Peasant Leagues in Brazil', in Rodolfo Stavenhagen, ed., *Agrarian Problems and Peasant Movements in Latin America* (Garden City, N.Y.: Doubleday and Co., 1970), p. 456.

2% of the holdings with 47% of the land. The percentages of 1950 and 1960 show a change in the size of holdings and distribution of the land. However, these changes are not as significant as might appear at first glance. As the study by Comitê Interamericano de Desenvolvimento Agrícola (CIDA) stated in 1966, 'The trends concerning the large *fazendas*, as revealed in the preliminary data of the Census, indicate that the structure of agriculture changed little during the last decade and continues to be characterized by the predominance of a small number of large *fazendas* over the resources of the land.'[47] Intricately related to the system of land-holding is the structure of power within it.

The system historically established and maintained in the rural areas was along the lines of a patrimonial-paternalistic society, with a patron–dependent relationship between master and worker. By and large, this system remained intact in the rural areas through the decade of the 1950s. It is characterized by complete and diffuse authority on the part of the master and a lack of any self-determination on the part of the worker. In describing the relationship of owner to worker in *fazendas*, the CIDA study observes:

What distinguishes this power is its almost absolute and vast character. The decisions of the owner of the *latifúndio* are orders. The *latifúndio* is perhaps similar to rigid organizations in which the higher level holds the exclusive privilege of making decisions on all questions concerning the activities of the subordinates and in which the delegation of powers occurs only within certain limitations – limited always by the right of intervention.[48]

In short, the power of the owner over the workers is autocratic, complete and pertaining to all activities, whether directly related to work or not.[49] In this

---

[47] Pan American Union, *Posse e Uso da Terra e Desenvolvimento Sócio-Econômico do Setor Agrícola: Brasil* (Washington, D.C.: CIDA, 1966), p. 105. This study, conducted by Brazilian sociologists and agrarian specialists in conjunction with Americans, is a wealth of information on all aspects of rural society. The contributors are highly respected internationally and are not known for their radical views. I will use this study extensively.

[48] CIDA, pp. 147–8. The literature on the patron-dependent relationship, traditional politics, obstacles to mass mobilization, non-ideological nature of movements and the problems of change in the rural areas of Brazil is now very extensive. The latest summary and discussion is de Kadt's *Catholic Radicals in Brazil.* See pp. 10–24 for not only a synthesis but references to other sources.

[49] The following statement by a landowner in Sapé, Paraíba, gives a feeling for the nature of the relationship between owner and worker: 'The obligation of my tenants is to work for me three days a week without pay. In the time of cane cutting, six months in Summer, they must work up to six days, but then they have already taken in their own crop. The thirteen tenants can plant at least fifteen blocks, but there are some who are not interested in planting. They stop after a quarter of a block and then drink...They make flour out of manioc in my mill and give me one litre out of every ten. I usually work with only my tenants. In the time of cane-cutting...I use two or three from outside. They are tenants of neighboring landowners who finish their cane-cutting before I do. I pay 20 cruzeiros for each load cut. There are some who cut 25 loads a day. They earn 500 cruzeiros and on the following day do not appear. As they are not my tenants, I cannot force them...After the cane-cutting begins, I give a party for them and customarily give a piece of clothing to each. At the end of the cutting, I kill a goat and give another party. When the mill works out the accounts for me, I give them the greatest thanks, 500 cruzeiros for one, 1,000 for another.

system of land-holding and power relationships, the individual rural worker has absolutely no rights beyond those defined for him by his master – the landowner. There still exist in Brazil a number of institutions which disappeared in Europe with the great revolutions. One of these is the *cambão*, which is similar to the French *corvée* and means the unpaid labor of the worker for his master; another is the *meia*, which is the giving of half the crop to the landowner for the use of a piece of his property. Antônio Callado expresses very well the overall nature of power relationships in the Northeast: 'If a responsible agency would solicit the United Nations to do an investigation concerning working conditions in the Northeast of Brazil we would be greatly shamed. The United Nations would include us among the zones of the world where slave labor still remains in force.'[50] A general conclusion regarding the rural worker and his predicament must be similar to the following: 'Although some enterprises allow the workers to enjoy some liberty and security and a slightly higher standard of living, the entire country considers a natural phenomenon to be the existence of cheap labor, which is submissive, "secure", illiterate, and lacking any initiative.'[51]

The problem of land-holding and power relationships is clearly political. Those who have owned the land are also those who make and enforce the laws, control the Church and orient social values. If rural reform laws were occasionally passed, the rural owners were able to impede their enforcement. The rural system changed hardly at all before about 1960. Despite national political changes, depressions, booms, urbanization, industrialization and so forth, the traditional rural system remained amazingly static. After 1960 or so, SUDENE began to initiate some modifications in various aspects of this system, and the same configuration of national political forces that led to SUDENE also allowed room for the formation of rural unions. In the traditional rural system there was no room whatsoever for the formation of unions: this was anathema to the owners and they simply would not tolerate such threats to their authority.[52] What was important in the initial formation of rural organizations was the breaking-up of traditional society within the context of overall social change in

---

If they get sick I give them medicine, if they die I take care of the burial. When I do not buy their cotton, I send it to be sold at the neighboring *fazenda* where they make the payment. . . The tenants obey me. I make all the decisions. They cannot make improvements on the property. The only indemnity that I could pay would be in the case of a tenant who leaves without gathering his crops. In that case, I pay for his work.' CIDA, pp. 154–5 from a study done by Mário Afonso Carneiro in Sapé.

[50] Antônio Callado, *Os Industriais da Sêca e Os 'Galileus' de Pernambuco* (Rio de Janeiro: Editôra Civilização Brasileira, 1960), p. 33.

[51] CIDA, p. 326.

[52] 'The rural workers are too intimidated and poor to affiliate themselves with the unions for their individual and collective rights because they fear the loss of their job or even their life. Furthermore, without adequate resources it is difficult to maintain a union of workers in conditions of effectiveness. Also in the economic, social and political conditions of Brazil, it has been difficult to find union leaders who are dedicated and competent.' CIDA, p. 335.

Brazil and the instability in national politics, which created room for various innovations as different groups and leaders searched for power bases.[53] Once rural groups were formed, the Church became aware, responded and created a large network of rural unions with which to promote social change.

The *ligas camponesas* sprang up near Recife in Pernambuco when a group of tenant farmers decided to cooperate.[54] The *engenho* (sugar mill) Galiléia had been closed down since before 1940 because of low sugar prices and the owners, the Beltrão family, had moved to the city. The land was put into tenancy but in the late 1950s the cost to the tenants increased rapidly, with the result that many had fallen behind in their payments. It occurred to one *Zezé* (Zezé da Galiléia, José Francisco de Souza), who had been exposed to the outside world, that they should form a society and create a fund to keep up the payments. From this initial idea, they founded a society with the impressive title of, 'The Agriculture and Livestock Society of the Planters of Pernambuco', and the owner was very pleased since it appeared that his rents would be more secure. His son, however, who was more removed from the traditional authority relationship, recognized a threat in the organization and called in the police to remove them, although the most recent arrival had been there for some fifteen years. The tenants thought they had some protection in the law and went to Recife to find a lawyer who would defend them. In Recife, they came upon Francisco Julião, who was a Socialist (Partido Social Progressista, PSP) member of the state legislature. 'It was the encounter of the spark with the dry twig, with an ambitious deputy, a man then of less than 40 years of age (now 43) [1960] but suffering from that chronic illness of Brazilian socialism: lack of a cause.'[55] Julião realized the possibilities of organizing in the rural areas, defended the Society successfully and from then on organized similar groups throughout the Northeast.

Julião was able to get himself elected to the federal assembly and the *ligas camponesas* spread beyond Pernambuco. (The *ligas* are civil entities, or societies, with certain jurisdiction regarding wages, negotiations and not much more.) By 1960, the *ligas* were established in 26 municipalities in Pernambuco and in the states of Paraíba, Piauí, Ceará and Alagoas. Once begun, the idea of rural organization caught on and threatened to mobilize the peasants all over Brazil. Given the tremendous backlog of potential grievances, the barest suggestion of rural organization offered the spectre of revolution to the established classes.

Church involvement in rural unionization began in 1959 when Maria Julieta Calazans, who had been concerned with changing the regressive and unjust rural structures for a decade, spoke to Dom Eugênio Sales in Natal on the need for such a movement. Dom Eugênio gave his full support to unionization through

[53] For various interpretations of the causes of rural organizations and their formation, see for example: de Kadt, pp. 24–30; Moraes, especially p. 472; and Cynthia N. Hewitt, 'Brazil: The Peasant Movement of Pernambuco, 1961–1964', in Henry Landsberger, ed., *Latin American Peasant Movements* (Ithaca, N.Y.: Cornell University Press, 1969), pp. 374–98.

[54] See Callado, *Os Industriais da Sêca e Os 'Galileus' de Pernambuco*, pp. 33–7; and Manoel Correia de Andrade, *A Terra e o Homem no Nordeste* (São Paulo: Editôra Brasiliense, 1963). For what seems to be a unique view, see Moraes, pp. 462–5.

[55] Callado, p. 36.

his movement the Serviço de Assistência Rural (SAR), an organization which had been active since 1949 in working to promote social change at the local level in Rio Grande do Norte. Beginning in Natal, the movement caught on and by 1961 had also become established in Pernambuco. In July of that year, Dom Eugênio Sales and a few bishops from Pernambuco (including Dom Carlos Coelho and Dom Manuel Pereira) promoted a meeting of some 26 rural pastors and founded Serviço de Orientação Rural de Pernambuco (SORPE). From these two states, the movement of Church unions spread very rapidly to other dioceses and other states, as the whole institution seemed to develop a unity and momentum behind the program. Nationally, the CNBB published statements of justification for the movement as well as providing legal information on its organization and recognition; the MEB established a special sector on unionization and directed the local schools to prepare the students for it; regionally, bishops made supportive statements and asked their priests to assist in the formation and growth of unions, and at the parish level priests encouraged their parishioners to found unions and at times did so themselves. By 1964 there were Church rural union movements in about half the states, including all those of the Northeast.[56]

All observers of the rural unionization taking place in Brazil during this period agree that the Church was an important agent in the movement. The potential importance of the unionization movement was greater than that of any other Church program and it led to severe conflicts with local power elements, to which the parish priests had always been closely linked. The bishops' statements, albeit progressive, were in fact still words; and MEB, at least initially, was undoubtedly perceived by most of the bishops as an innocuous radio school program to teach catechism and some ideas on hygiene. However, the unionization program left no room for doubt that the Church was making a distinct break with the past in the rural areas. Instead of helping the local *patrão* control his peasants, the Church now militated actively to organize the workers to demand a better situation. The more radical departure from past social functions (latent although they may have been) required serious reasons indeed.[57]

Historically, the Church had taken its influence over the rural masses for granted, although the institution rarely exercised it and largely accepted the

[56] These included SAR in R.N., SORPE in Pernambuco, FAG in R.S., FAP in São Paulo, FAG in Goiás, MEB in Maranhão, many in Minas Gerais and variations of MEB and Ação Popular in several other states. Data are unreliable. However, Hewitt notes that in late 1963 there were 280,000 members of peasant associations in Pernambuco and the Church claimed 200,000 of these. Hewitt, p. 374. The Church unions were dominant in Rio Grande do Norte as well. The organizations increased rapidly after January 1963; there were not always as many members as the various unions claimed, and organizations' representatives might not accurately reflect the size of the membership. For a very realistic and perceptive study of unionization from the perspective of SAR, which was the beginning, see Ferrari, *passim* but especially pp. 90–6.

[57] See Ferrari for a discussion of these conflicts with local elements and the realization that there was in fact a break with the past. For an account of what it meant personally for a priest to make the break, see the semi-fictitious account by Estanislau Fragoso Batista, *A Revolução de um Padre* (Salvador, Bahia: Editôra Mensageiro da Fé, 1966).

'primitive' or 'cultural Catholicism' as valid. With the formation of the *ligas* in these rural areas and their subsequent rapid spread, the Church's influence was no longer so secure. Many in the hierarchy were doubly aware of the gravity of their predicament, for they had studied in Rome during the pontificate of Pius XI, who had often pointed to the great tragedy of the Church's loss of the urban workers in Europe. These bishops did not want to see a similar tragedy occur in their country and were ready to upset the *status quo* if necessary.[58] In fact, the initial bishop's pastoral of 1950 raised this point even before the *ligas* had been formed and when the rural areas were only beginning to awaken. It took on increased urgency with the *ligas*, and particularly with the success of the revolutionary movement in Cuba in early 1959. To add insult to injury, many in the Church were incensed by Julião's usurpation of religious symbolism in his mobilization of the *ligas*. He compared himself to St Francis and on one occasion stated, 'Pope John XXIII was the first pope of peasant origin. The Encyclical that he just issued ['Mater et Magistra'] is proof that the Pope approves of the *ligas camponesas* and the "using in our preaching the words of the Bible. Yes, because the Bible is a revolutionary book",[59] Julião and others of his ilk threatened not only to diminish the influence of the Church, but in fact to replace the institution completely in the rural areas, and, if the precedent of Cuba followed, quite possibly to eliminate it from the whole country. With threats of this magnitude, the Church had to respond.

I do not want to suggest that the Church's response to the *ligas* was simply reactive. It is a fact that the SAR in Rio Grande do Norte was involved in rural programs for a decade before 1959. The *ligas* served as the spark to make the clergy realize that the gospel could be interpreted differently than had been the case in the past; they 'opened the eyes of the Church', as Pe. Melo, one of the leaders of the movement, has stated.[60] Once the eyes were opened, so to speak, the movement assumed a momentum of its own, which was supported by Pope John's encyclical of 1961 as well as by the statements emanating from the national and regional bishops' conferences. The Church was not reacting in a purely negative or defensive fashion when it became involved in the unionization program. The *ligas* had recognition only in the Civil Code and were not officially labor organizations under the extremely complex Labor Code. They had, in the words of one informant, 'the same jurisdiction as a football team'. It was felt by people in the Church, and subsequent students have supported this, that the *ligas* were at best limited to making the peasants aware and at worst mere tools for the middle-class agitators that organized them. Later analysis has shown that Julião and others lacked a consistent ideological basis and really did not have

---

[58] Interview with one of the key bishops in the unionization movement in Fortaleza on 10 January 1968. This view is also supported by the lay head of the national movement. Interview in Rio de Janeiro on 9 February 1968.
[59] Cited in Correia de Andrade, pp. 245–6. See also Gondim da Fonseca, *Assim Falou Julião* (São Paulo: n.p., 1962).
[60] Father Antonio Melo, p. 32.

defined goals. They could mobilize the peasants, maybe win a few issues, but could not go much further.[61] The Church opted for the union form over the *liga*; with jurisdiction and organizational stature, they could accomplish far more for the peasants. The Church too demonstrated a tendency towards middle-class leadership, but there was an awareness of the problems involved in becoming a 'new *patrão*' and serious efforts were made to turn control over to the workers themselves. Various groups and individuals became active with the Church's programs for different reasons. In the Northeast the largest element was apparently genuinely concerned with matters of social justice and structural change. In some areas the priests formed organizations to defeat the Communists, and lay militants were attempting to 'make the revolution' in the rural areas, realizing that the urban area was too tightly controlled by the government. In Rio Grande do Sul the hierarchy formed FAG to oppose the rural organizations of Brizola, the brother-in-law of Goulart.[62] While there were mixed reasons, some more noble than others, it is a fact that large sectors of the institution did become extremely active in and committed to the formation of rural unions.

The Church had a number of resources which could be used to promote this new mechanism of influence. The basic religiosity of the peasants was important in bringing them into the Church unions. Priests retained prestige with the people, which was useful in motivating them to join a Church union. And while it did not take long to alienate the land-owners, the Church as institution could stand up to them as a nascent group of peasants could never hope to do. Further, in some cases the Church unions were more acceptable to the owners than the *ligas* of Julião. And, of course, the Church was already an established institution with personnel, centers, lines of communication and some elements of central coordination (in the CNBB). All of these factors could be brought to bear on the unionization of the peasants.[63] In a sense the Church, at least in the first stages of social change, has important traditional resources which can be redirected for new and radically different goals.

The Church unions for the most part were not the 'revolutionary' ones. By this I do not mean that their goals were any less radical, for in the context of the backward rural areas with their ignorant and exploited peasantry almost anything was radical. And further, although it is difficult to break down and compare the goals of all the *ligas* and all the Church unions, there were many obvious similarities.[64] But by 'not revolutionary', I mean that the techniques or strategies were less violent, less polarized, less dialectical than those of the *ligas*.

[61] Interviews with lay head of unions in R.N. in Rio de Janeiro on 22 November 1967; and with priest head of SORPE in Jaboatão, Pernambuco on 20 January 1968. See also Hewitt, pp. 389 and 393 and de Kadt, pp. 30–1.

[62] Interview with bishop who had been head of FAG in Pôrto Alegre on 28 November 1967.

[63] As Camargo puts it: 'The transfer of the Church's prestige and sacredness as the expressed objectives of the action program of the Movement, was one of the principal aspects of the adopted strategy. Essentially, the prestige and sacredness of the clergy were transferred from their traditional functions of supporting the "status quo" to activities more in line with the concrete Christian values and the strategic intention of the Movement.' p. 154.

[64] See Hewitt, pp. 385–6 for a list of 15 goals common to Church and Communist unions.

The Church unions attempted most often to enforce the existing laws, for if these could be implemented most of the serious problems of the peasantry could be resolved. To enforce the laws, the unions had to unite the peasants. This was probably the main function of the Church involvement in unionization: educating, mobilizing and organizing a completely disorganized mass of downtrodden people. To accomplish this end courses were given, meetings promoted, legal papers arranged and so forth; anything to stimulate unification. Once begun the unions operated at a number of levels: they pressured the government and landowners for compliance with existing laws, lobbied for new and improved laws and educated the peasants in working for an improved situation at all levels. The overall goal was of course a change of structures, but from the bottom up rather than focusing upon revolutionary action at the top while neglecting the bases. In the Brazilian situation, everything is executed (or not executed) through detailed and elaborate legal procedures, which need not be observed by those with money and power, but must be closely followed by those with neither. Thus an important issue in rural unionization was that of the laws.[65] The *ligas* had minimal jurisdiction, so the union form was adopted. However, a union had to be recognized by the government to be legal, and if the government did not favor a particular organization legality could be most difficult to achieve.

By 1962 the Church had organized about 50 unions, but none had been recognized by the government. In May of that year, these unions promoted a meeting in Itabuna, Bahia, entitled the 'First Congress of Agricultural Tillers and Workers of the North and Northeast' and invited the Minister of Labor, Franco Montoro, a Catholic and important figure in the Partido Democrata Cristão (PDC). After a certain amount of pressure and bargaining, the Minister agreed to recognize some 22 Church unions. After the initial recognition, formation of new unions increased rapidly. The *ligas* still continued, but the real action and competition was at the union level. By 1963, the Church was competing in the founding of unions with several others, including President Goulart, Governor Miguel Arraes of Pernambuco, various Communist affiliates and a few independent agitators or individuals seeking power bases. The rural area became a veritable field of battle for groups attempting either to bring on the revolution or to establish their own positions in the government. And in all instances, the legality of the situation prevailed; it was necessary to be recognized and this recognition ensured privileges concerning dues and ultimately questions of control of larger organizations. Unions begat federations, which in turn gave rise to the creation of a confederation; this was the grand prize.[66]

[65] 'Simply applying the existing laws would completely modify the situation of misery in the rural zone.' Serviço de Orientação Rural de Pernambuco (SORPE), 'Pequeno Resumo do Movimento Sindical Rural em Pernambuco', p. 11. Camargo points out the importance of this on pp. 180–1; see also Brandão Lopes in *A Crise do Brasil Arcaico, passim.*

[66] The number of laws passed dealing with rural unionization is indicative of the increased interest in the area. These included: Portaria 209 A of 25.6.1962, Portaria 355 A of 20.11. 1962, SUPRA decree 1879 of 13.12.1962, Statute of the Rural Worker of 2.3.1963, Portaria 346 of 17.6.1963. See Antônio Callado, *Tempo de Arraes: Padres e Comunistas na Revolução Sem Violência* (Rio de Janeiro: José Alvaro, 1965), for description of union formation.

In August 1963, the Church unions held an election for the control of the recently formed Confederação Nacional dos Trabalhadores na Agricultura (CONTAG). At this time there were five legal federations (state level organizations of the unions): those of the Church in Rio Grande do Norte, Pernambuco, and Sergipe; one of the Círculos Operários in São Paulo; and one run by the Communists in Parana. The Church won control of the Confederation, but the government of João Goulart refused to accept the results, declaring that Paraná had not been invited in time and that many federations were then in the process of being recognized by the Ministry of Labor and elections at that time were thus unrepresentative. Another election was scheduled for December 1963 and the formation of federations increased rapidly.[67]

By this time the unionization movement was largely neglecting the bases as it concentrated on the scramble for power at the national level. The goal was to form as many unions and federations as possible in order to gain control of CONTAG. By the time of the second election in December the Church was directly represented by six federations, indirectly (through MEB and Ação Popular or some combination) by another eight, and the Communists of various hues had ten. The Church representatives met before the elections with the MEB–AP group, but could not come to any agreement on a slate of candidates because of personal and ideological differences.[68] In the election itself, the Ação Popular (AP) and the Communists shared control of CONTAG. The Church groups, including SAR, SORPE, FAG, Círculos Operários and some of the MEB, achieved no control in the confederation. From then until the coup some three months later, the Church unions worked at the local levels while the Communists largely controlled the national organization. The gains in most respects were significant for the peasants but, because of the in-fighting and bureaucratic politics, they were not consolidated. With the coup all rural unionization came to a halt. Most of the unions were placed under intervention; their leaders were removed; strikes were prohibited and laws no longer implemented; conditions in general were no longer conducive to rural organization.[69]

Even before the coup, but most certainly after it, the experience of the Church in rural unionization was similar to that of MEB. The involvement indicates a change in the approach to influence, and while initially the Church could use traditional resources to move ahead rapidly in organizing, the long-run effect was to create animosity and tensions among the traditional supporters of the institution. The Church's involvement in the rural areas came to be seen in the same light as that of the Communist agitators, who sought to bring about a

---

[67] Ferrari notes that by 31 December 1963 the Ministry of Labor had recognized 256 unions and 10 federations; at the same time there were another 557 unions and 33 federations awaiting recognition, p. 93. Before the early 1960s there were only 6 rural unions in all Brazil.

[68] Interview with lay head of Church's national program in Rio de Janeiro on 9 February 1968.

[69] See Hewitt, p. 398 for a brief discussion of post-coup situations; see Wiarda, p. 19 which shows how the Círculos benefited from the coup.

violent revolution.[70] The militants, even in the clergy, suffered persecution to a greater degree than did the Communists. In the first place most of them were sincere and naive and, secondly, they were regarded by the military and the owners as heretics who used the traditional name and appeal of the Church to attempt things fitting an antichrist.

As with MEB, the period of action in this new line of influence was too short to be amenable to evaluation with any degree of certitude. Camargo, in his study on Natal, seems to think that the rural unionization had several important effects in promoting social change. Ferrari also carried out a sociological study and comes to similar conclusions. The land owners and the military apparently considered unionization effective or they would not have acted so quickly and harshly to stop it. My interviews, in various parts of the Northeast, indicated a general feeling that something important was being accomplished in educating and mobilizing the masses. At the very minimum, in adopting this new form of influence the Church differentiated itself from the status quo – from the patrimonial-paternalistic system of domination – and encouraged people to break out as well. One would imagine that the Church involvement in organizations, legal matters and other secular activities tended to decrease the sacred element of the religion and introduce some secular aspects. In theory, at least, with increased secularization the 'cultural Catholicism' of the masses will break down and they will be less passive.

It is clear that Church involvement in rural unionization was still highly structured. Other experiences in social change, such as the Natal Movement, various experiences in colonization, or the São Sebastião Crusade of slum clearance in Rio, also display a tendency toward bureaucratization.[71] Essentially, the Church was opting for a different role in society but following traditional methods. A religious basis was not being created for change, but instead individuals were encouraged to participate in new groups and movements, whereby the Church could continue to exert influence; the element of power played no small part in this transformation. Power was still necessary to exert influence, but now this influence carried an intentional progressive orientation rather than an intentional or neglected regressive tendency. A dominant force in helping the Church to shift its orientation and in crystalizing the conflicts and tensions inherent in this change was Ação Católica Brasileira (ACB).

Brazilian Catholic Action as the vanguard of ideology and action

Catholic Action was reorganized in 1950 on a basis different from the format adopted under Cardinal Leme. The new structure was based on the French or Belgian (as opposed to the Italian) model, which promoted the sectoral penetration of the movement into various milieu. Thus, instead of the fourfold division

---

[70] See Camargo, p. 143.
[71] See Camargo; and Mauro Roberto da Costa Souza, 'Igreja e Desenvolvimento', unpublished research report No. 1.18 of PPC of CNBB, Rio de Janeiro, CERIS, 1968.

into adult/youth and male/female, there was established the format of adult/ youth and secondary schools-Juventude Estudantil Católica (JEC), universities- Juventude Universitária Católica (JUC), rural areas-Juventude Agrária Católica (JAC), working class-Juventude Operária Católica (JOC), and other-Juventude Independente Católica (JIC).[72] During the period under consideration (1950–64) JUC and JEC, the youth in universities and secondary schools, were by far the most important. Despite the modification in format, the movement was still an integral part of the institutional Church, being mandated by the hierarchy.[73] Catholic Action was allowed a great deal of autonomy during the decade be- tween the mid-1950s and the early 1960s and became heavily involved in the milieu. This involvement on the part of JUC and JEC led to an awareness of various problems in society and a subsequent desire to change its structures radically. As I have argued, the bishops became aware because of various threats against Church influence, which brought them to perceive injustice, misery and so forth. Catholic Action enjoyed freedom from the Church because of these threats and the need for sectoral movements to counter them. The move- ments themselves developed a particularly acute awareness, because of their involvement and firsthand exposure to problems.[74] The movement was guided by a group of young and very progressive clergy, most of whom had been trained in Europe. This group included such figures as Pe. Henrique Vaz, Pe. Luís Sena, Pe. Emery Bezerra, Frei Carlos Josaphat, Frei Mateus Rocha and the French- man Frei Thomas Cardonnel; they were the most active and advanced priests in Brazil at this time. Through them the movement was introduced to the advanced lines of European, primarily French, theology associated with the names of Louis Joseph Lebret, Emmanuel Mounier, M. D. Clenu, Henri de Lubac, etc. Frei Thomas Cardonnel, for example, was a follower of Mounier and helped to introduce the concept of 'established disorder' in Brazil.

We can never insist enough on the need to denouce natural harmony, class collabora- tion. God is not so dishonest, so false as a certain kind of social peace, consisting in the acquiescence of all in an unnatural injustice. Violence is not only a fact of revolutions. It also characterizes the maintenance of a false order.[75]

The combination of direct involvement in the milieu, progressive priests as leaders and exposure to advanced European theology caused members of JUC

[72] The adult equivalents of JOC (ACO) and JIC (ACI) were founded later.
[73] A typical definition of the movement's position in the Church is the following: 'Above all it [JUC] is, in its operation as a movement, a cadre of militants and directors of Catholic Action mandated by their pastors [bishops] to participate in their apostolic and missionary action of evangelizing, of spreading the truth, giving testament to their sanctity, and keeping intact the treasure of the Faith.' 1961 statement of Comissão Episcopal da ACB e Apostolado dos Leigos.
[74] The development of awareness and meaning is suggested in this 1966 statement of justifica- tion. 'What JUC is today – and consequently the position it takes – did not arise as any *a priori* thing nor as the decision of a moment. It was constructed on the experience of mili- tants which was continually examined by the whole movement over several years.' XIV Conselho de JUC Antônio Carlos (M.G.) 'Anexo II Documento de JUC Dirigido aos Srs. Bispos Membros da Comissão Central da CNBB' 18–26 July 1966. Mimeo.
[75] Quoted in de Kadt, p. 65. See pp. 58–80 for his discussion of Catholic Action.

and JEC to question the society and their role as Christians within it.[76] The event which indicated this awareness was the tenth annual meeting of JUC in July 1960, and the basic document which it formulated and studied, 'Minimum Bases for the Historic Ideal of the Brazilian People', demonstrates that the movement had attained a high point of fulfillment or maturation. At this point, JUC and JEC came to the vanguard of the Catholic Church, in actively seeking the promotion of socio-political change. By 1962 a large number of the Catholic Action militants had founded Ação Popular, which by the time of the 1964 coup was the most revolutionary organization in Brazil.

The formulation of an ideology of social change for the bishops took place mainly between 1950 and 1961, with certain modifications and refinements after that period. In the case of JUC and JEC, the decade of the 1950s was one of involvement and adaptation of sociological and theological concepts to the Brazilian situation. 1960 saw a full ideological formulation which went far beyond anything the bishops had discussed. A recurring point in my material on the movement and in my interviews is the fact that the ideology grew with the involvement.[77] The militants needed an ideology to define the movement's goals, promote coherence and broadcast an image. Prior to 1960 it did not have one; rather, it was included within the hierarchy, as one part of the bishops' strategy of influence in the neo-Christendom model.

Originally, the environment for JUC and JEC was defined in purely spiritual terms of evangelization in the school milieu. The movement sought to counter secularization within that environment and protect members from the hazards of various non-Catholic appeals. Later the milieu was no longer only the schools but the whole society, and evangelization now meant change in the temporal and not just the spiritual sense. The following statement from a 1963 JUC bulletin suggests the environment and how it was regarded after 1960.

At the present time the student movement, and particularly its leadership, is becoming conscious of the fact that university reform is part of the [more general] Brazilian process, intrinsically articulated with the socio-economic and political structures. This being so we could not simply start with university reform and move on to achieve [changes in the wider society]; university reform has to become part of the Brazilian Revolution.[78]

The previous exclusively spiritual environment was now seen in concrete terms of structures which impeded evangelization; men could not be Christian unless they were wholly human. Therefore in the 'established disorder' structural

[76] Interview with leader of movement during this period in Rio de Janeiro on 22 November 1967; also supported by other interviews, by de Kadt and by Thomas G. Sanders, 'Catholicism and Development: The Catholic Left in Brazil', in Kalman H. Silvert, ed., *Churches and States: The Religious Institution and Modernization* (New York: AUFS, 1967), pp. 81–99.
[77] 'The involvement demands a definition. Demands certain objectives to attain. Demands, in sum, a vision of man and of the world, that through the requirements of a determined time and place carry on to an ideological option.' XIV Conselho de JUC Antônio Carlos (M.G.) 'Síntese da Experiência Atual da Ação Católica Especializada como Movimento de Leigos para a Evangelização no Brasil', July 1966, p. 4. Mimeo.
[78] Quoted in de Kadt, p. 69.

changes would have to be made, and the school milieu was only a part of the overall picture.

The movement's original self-definition was minimal, since it was a mandated extension of the hierarchy and consequently had the same goals and methods, being only more specialized in its milieu. After 1960, the movement totally redefined its identity in both structure and purpose. While not immediately breaking with the bishops, JUC and JEC calculated their relationship in terms of an autonomous organization. That is, they considered the movement theirs, but the relationship with the hierarchy was useful for support and legitimacy.[79] Structurally, therefore, the movement was considered a creation of the members; it was an autonomous organization. The movement's new purpose was to humanize before attempting to evangelize; to promote structural change so that evangelization would be possible and realistic. The new self-identity was inseparable from action and at times it invaded the temporal sphere of politics.

Whereas the previous action imperatives were largely of a spiritual or cate-chetical nature, such as retreats, processions, etc., which aimed at deepening the faith, after 1960 they became political. At the minimum, the imperatives were to convince and convert others to the necessity of serious structural change. Beyond that, they directed the student organizations so as to promote fairly radical political change and worked in Church movements for social change such as MEB and unions. In sum, the members operated in almost any way or in any organization to promote socio-political change in Brazil, justifying their action by the belief that evangelization would be possible only through such change.

The radically different JUC and JEC ideology was broadcast all over the country by a variety of means. Each year they held at least one national meeting and several regional ones; they issued statements and documents as part of the action imperative to promote awareness of the necessity for change; and each individual militant was to be a carrier of the reformulated message or truth.[80] Insofar as JUC and JEC were still connected to the Church (and in the eyes of the public they were), they put it in the forefront of the movement for social change in Brazil.

The movement was extremely active in pursuit of its goals. In 1961, a JUC militant was elected president of the União Nacional dos Estudantes (UNE) thus bringing to an end the long-term Communist domination of this important

---

[79] Interview with a JUC militant in Rio on 6 September 1967. De Kadt's observation is also interesting: 'Too bad that the hierarchy had originally given them a mandate; intolerable that the bishops now wanted to control them. JUC was their organization, they had shaped it into what it now was, they made use of its structures to think and act together. In short they were JUC.' *Ibid.*, p. 79.

[80] Typical is the title of the theme of the 1961 national meeting: 'The Gospel, Source of the Brazilian Revolution'; in the same year, JUC militants published a long statement at the Catholic University in Rio on revolutionary themes, which is found in Luís Alberto Gomes de Souza, ed., *Cristianismo Hoje* (Rio de Janeiro: Editôra Universitária, 1962). Statements can also be found in *Boletim da ACB*, *Brasil Urgente* (São Paulo) and *O Metropolitano*.

organization. The movement became the center of attempts to promote university reform, and it is interesting to note that the members actively opposed the Church-supported education law of 1961. The militants worked in MEB, rural unionization and various regional programs, not to mention non-Church and even anti-Church programs. In many cases the mere participation of these militants led to a subtle, or not so subtle, modification of programs. What might have been a formal and ineffective plan became with their energies and commitment something with content. This observation might be generalized to the Church itself. Through intention as well as occasion, the militants related to younger bishops, priests and laymen, and in a sense educated them in social awareness.[81] Contact of an educational sort was made in seminars, meetings, discussions, particular visits to seminaries, and through the conscious elaboration of an advanced theology of social involvement and an ideology of social change.

Being in the vanguard of the 'Brazilian Revolution' created several problems for Catholic Action and the Church. As the militants of Catholic Action very often staffed MEB and the other programs, the problems were often faced by the same personnel. However, ACB's importance lies in the fact that it showed the problems of change earlier. Whereas the other programs experienced difficulties from late 1963 or early 1964, ACB had internal and external problems at least a year earlier.

In the face of external criticism of the advanced positions of JUC and JEC, some in the hierarchy became aware of the changes which had taken place in the movement and attempted to counter them and return it to the previous 'safe' orientation. The bishops should have known all along about the changes, but they were often hopelessly ignorant of the movements' real orientation. In 1961, the bishops in charge of ACB and the apostolate of the laity issued directives to clarify the position and goals of the movement vis-à-vis the hierarchy. They pointed out that Catholic Action was a mandated extension of the hierarchy and not an organization unto itself. Therefore the line or orientation which Catholic Action assumed had by definition to be identical to that of the bishops. 'Nobody, neither from within JUC nor from without, can present interpretations or establish a line of conduct which carries the JUC movement or one member of it to disregard the orientation which the Catholic hierarchy gives it.'[82] On the two critical features of the new self-definition – an autonomous organization interpreting its own mission – the bishops rejected out of hand what the movement had become. The bishops also rejected the action imperative which led JUC and JEC into political activities. For the hierarchy, ACB's evangelization was still largely spiritual, although militants could work in Church programs of social change. As members of Catholic Action they could not run for National Students Union positions nor participate in other movements of social change. Clearly, then, the movement and most of the hierarchy had gone their different

[81] Interview with leader of movement during this period in Rio de Janeiro on 22 November 1967 and with the hierarchical advisor of JUC and JEC between 1962 and 1964, in São Paulo on 18 December 1967.
[82] 1961 statement of Comissão Episcopal da ACB e Apostolado dos Leigos.

ways. However, the group in the CNBB around Dom Helder Câmara tried to assist the movement and served as a bridge between it and the majority of the hierarchy. In order to escape from the authority of the hierarchy over Catholic Action and to establish their own independent identity and goals, in 1962 many of the JUC militants founded the Ação Popular, or AP. AP was not founded as a political party, but as a movement with a vanguard composed of workers, peasants and students, who sought to prepare for the revolution through a process of overall mobilization.

> Popular Action thus opts basically for a policy of revolutionary preparation, consisting in a mobilization of the people, on the base of the development of their levels of consciousness and organization, securing this mobilization in a struggle against the double domination of capitalism (international and national) and feudalism.[83]

It was anticipated that violence would be necessary to bring about the structural change to which the movement was committed. AP was composed not only of ex-JUC members, but also included professional people and many non-Catholics. The movement apparently grew to between 300 and 500 members between June 1962 and April 1964, yet all observers note that it was influential beyond its numbers in movements for change such as MEB, Paulo Freire's group, Popular Culture circles, Goulart's programs and those of the reform governments of Pernambuco and Goiás.[84] AP was in existence only two years before the coup of April 1964, and it is therefore impossible to evaluate its impact on the 'Brazilian Revolution'. Most observers point out that its ideology was utopian for Brazil and the leaders probably lacked a deep appreciation of the society's resistances to structural change. But the fact that it could mobilize 300 to 500 members of the established classes to revolutionize society is in itself significant.

Despite efforts by AP, by the militants who remained in Catholic Action and by the CNBB bishops, JUC and AP were regarded as synonymous by the general public, by many of the bishops and certainly by the military. That is, the most revolutionary group in Brazil was confused with Catholic Action and many within the institution were implicated with revolutionary action. For this reason many Catholic Action militants suffered severe persecution after the 1964 coup.

The JUC and JEC experience had some positive effects on the Church's new role in social change. The militants helped to create an image of a Church interested in improving an unjust society, they educated bishops and others in social change orientations and they worked in the Church's programs of MEB, rural unions and so forth. However, the overall impact on the new influence approach was quite negative. As I indicated at the beginning of this chapter, the bishops formulated their ideology of social involvement over a period of more

---

[83] Sanders' unpublished translation of Ação Popular, *Documento de Base*, position paper for the organization, Goiânia: Centro de Cultura Popular, January 1963, p. 28.
[84] Sanders gives a high estimate of 3,000 in Silvert's *Churches and States*, p. 96. Interviews with knowledgeable opponents put the number at 200. A candid interview with organizer of AP put the number at a maximum of 500. MANAUS, 13 July 1970.

than a decade and were 'in tune' generally with events in society and in Rome. In historical perspective, the bishops' ideology was radical, but in comparison with others in the society it was moderate; it simply put the Church on the side of change, though not in the vanguard of violent revolution. With time, this ideology would probably have pervaded the whole of the hierarchy and consequently the whole of the Church. However, when Catholic Action 'came of age' in 1960 and jumped to the forefront of revolutionary statements and activity through AP, attention was focused on the progressive sector of the hierarchy and criticism followed. Dom Helder Câmara and his group in the CNBB were singled out and received special censure both from the news media and even within the hierarchy. The statements and actions of Catholic Action were traced back to the CNBB and the latter held responsible. Dom Helder was removed from his position as national assistant to Catholic Action and replaced by another bishop, who ultimately came to sympathize with the movement and thus was seen in a similar light. Before the progressive sector of the bishops had a chance to consolidate their position through the CNBB and make the pre-influence model of influence general for the whole Church, they were isolated and attacked, largely because of association with JUC and JEC. The new influence model became obviously that of a particular group against which opponents of social change in the society could direct their attacks. After the coup the military felt free to persecute the progressive elements, as there was no unity within the Church on their position. In spite of the divisions and animosities created within the Church over JUC and JEC, the new influence strategy of social involvement might have been a long-term success if there had been a buffer between the Church as institution and social change statements and programs. It is in this perspective that the Christian Democratic Party must be studied.

The Christian Democratic Party as an intermediary between power and influence

In Chile the Church had supported the Christian Democrats both directly and indirectly, promoting progressive goals of social change, yet not becoming directly involved in what could be termed radical politics. The Church thus encouraged the Party to act in a particular direction in the temporal sphere while the institution as such remained at a higher level of religious significance, aloof from political controversies.[85] In Brazil the Party never became an important buffer and the Church chose to act directly in the temporal sphere, thus suffering the erosion of tensions and a loss of prestige after 1964. It appears from a study of the Brazilian case that the Church might be well-advised to support social change by a two-stage model: first, to organize movements such as the Christian Democrats and Catholic Action, which can act in the temporal sphere

---

[85] See Ivan Vallier's discussion of the Party as 'buffer' between Church and politics, *Catholicism, Social Control, and Modernization in Latin America*, pp. 142–6.

while the Church itself makes supportive statements; and then, after change is accepted and the institution can develop new resource bases, to enter into programs, if necessary, to support change directly. In Brazil, these two stages were fused and led to involvement without any buffers.

Cardinal Leme's strategy of seeking power through the LEC, or the pressure group model, continued to be used in Brazil into the 1960s, although in 1958 the name had been changed to Electoral Alliance for the Family. This body was largely diocesan-based, run on *ad hoc* lines from election to election, was primarily concerned with issues such as divorce and Communist affiliation of the candidates and was effective only in the more traditional states of the South. The LEC did not lead to the formation of a Christian Democratic Party. The bishops who followed the LEC strategy relied upon it at election time and the rest of the year relied directly on candidates, the bureaucracy and other personal contacts for their political needs. These bishops were concerned with their authority and thus opposed a PDC form in the fear that it might in some way lessen it; the party might compromise their positions. Also, the Church was to 'keep out of politics' and supporting a PDC would amount to an overt denial of this detachment.[86] Furthermore, the PDC was vaguely associated with Maritain and in Brazil throughout the 1950s there was a battle between the semi-progressives (mostly within the Centro Dom Vital and for Maritain) and the reactionaries (who were against him). The bishops were usually conservatives and for all these reasons did not want to support a PDC.

A PDC was, however, founded in Brazil in 1948. During the first few years the presidency of the party was held by Msgr. Arruda Câmara in Recife, but by 1958 control had shifted to the South in São Paulo, where Franco Montoro and Antônio Queiroz Filho were the most important leaders.[87] The party had little direct stimulation from the Church and became a party much like all others in Brazil, even while formally adhering to Catholic social doctrine. The PDC varied in orientation from area to area; made alliances usually to the right; and grew so that by 1962, with 5.7% of the congressional vote, it was the fourth largest party in Brazil.[88]

Because the PDC was in no way unique, it did not appeal to the progressives who had become active in the Church by 1961. It was too much like all the parties, was too compromised and was not considered a base from which important changes could be promoted in society. The group around Dom Helder Câmara did not go out of their way to support the party and the activists of Catholic Action went into AP instead.[89] In sum, the party was backed neither by

---

[86] All the while, this neglects the compromises involved in dealing with candidates and the bureaucracy, which are traditional and thus apparently assumed.

[87] On the PDC, see Sanders in Silvert's *Churches and States*, and Moreira Alves, Chapter 11. Interview also with ex-leader of PDC, in Rio de Janeiro on 20 March 1968.

[88] After the PTB, PSD, and UDN. After 1962 it had 19 federal deputies, one senator, two governors, 120 state deputies and about 10% of the mayors.

[89] Sanders, in Silvert's *Churches and States*; interview with ex-leader. Wiarda notes that the same phenomenon occurred with the Circulos; the new progressive elements bypassed the old organizations as they thought these too compromised and not worth changing, p. 77.

the traditional Church nor by the newer sectors; it was so much in the middle that it appealed to neither group.

There were, however, two progressive Catholics in the PDC who published a very advanced social document, which could be interpreted as contradicting my argument. Paulo de Tarso and Plínio de Arruda Sampaio had been active in JUC but affiliated with the PDC. They were members of the party in order to run under a party banner and to attempt a change in its orientation. The high point of their involvement came in 1960 with the document of the party convention in Aguas de Prata. This was an extremely progressive statement on social change, but to have it approved they had to compromise on the election of traditional-conservatives for the important positions (Ney Braga as President and Marechal Juarez Távora as Secretary). The overall significance of these two individuals and their document was small. At the local level in the states of Guanabara, São Paulo, Minas Gerais and Paraná, some elements in the party promoted community organization and courses in leadership training. These were not part of the national program, however, and by and large the party was rather undistinguished.

In conclusion, the PDC did not serve as a buffer between the Church and programs of social involvement. Unlike in Chile, the militants of Catholic Action did not join the PDC. More often than not they joined AP, thus associating the movement with the revolutionary organization and the institutional Church with both. The new model of influence thus brought the Church face to face with direct action of a radical orientation in the temporal sphere, and it suffered by association with the revolutionary vanguard.

Conclusion

My discussion in this chapter is by no means a comprehensive historical treatise on Church involvement in the promotion of social change in the post-war era.[90] What has been covered is sufficient to indicate that the Church was engaged in rather different activities compared with its past history and traditional orientation. A new model or approach to influence was being formulated at this time, as will become clear using the four categories. The dominant ideology, as expressed in the bishops' statements and supported in action through MEB, regional development programs, rural unionization and so forth, was to provide

[90] I could have offered a content analysis of the new publications, or 'reformed' old ones, which sought to convince the reader of the need for change. See *A Ordem* of Natal, R.G. do Norte; *Síntese* of the Catholic University of Rio; *Brasil Urgente* of Frei Carlos Josaphat, which had articles by Dom Motta and Dom Helder Câmara; (see Manoel Cardoso, 'The Brazilian Church and the New Left', in *Journal of Inter American Studies* 7 (1964)), or books such as: Juracy Andrade, *A Igreja na Cidade* (Rio de Janeiro: Tempo Brasileiro, 1965); Pe. Aloísio Guerra, *A Igreja Está com o Povo?* (Rio de Janeiro: Editôra Civilização Brasileira, 1963); Michel Schooyans, *O Comunismo e o Futuro da Igreja no Brasil* (São Paulo: Editôra Herder, 1963); Frei Carlos Josaphat, *Evangelho e Revolução Social* (São Paulo: Livraria Duas Cidades, 1963); Luís Alberto Gomes de Souza, ed., *Cristianismo Hoje* (Rio de Janeiro: Editôra Universitária, 1962).

a legitimation for change based on religious principles. Quite possibly the motive of continued territorial coverage was lurking somewhere in the background, but it seems to have been largely overlooked while the Church became concerned with the general topic of change. The groups and strata focused upon were mainly the rural poor. Although to a much lesser degree there was some consideration of the urban areas, the statements, programs and movements all dealt with the underprivileged groups of society and sought ways to improve their situations. The Church–society relationship at the ideological level remained comprehensive, but now promoted rather than discouraged change, in that the bishops made statements as though they could orient the values of the whole of society. And the values they advocated were a radical departure from the Church's traditional orientations. At the local level, sectors of the Church were forced to define their independence from local power groups as they entered into conflict with them over opposing positions regarding the *status quo*. Priests and lay militants, and finally some members of the hierarchy, were forced out of traditional resource bases and obliged to search for new ones. At the national level there was a growing awareness that the institution was compromised with the government and efforts were made to define its independence. The mechanisms for exercising influence de-emphasized the cult, ritual devotions, sacraments and other traditional forms. Those most relied upon were new and included regional development programs, radio schools, rural unions and even lay organizations.

This new influence model never had time to become fully defined. Most of the important statements, programs and movements were formulated only after 1960 and were severely discouraged after the coup in 1964. A question might be raised as to how effective any of these new elements of the approach to influence were; only generalizations can be made in reply. The studies carried out on particular movements, such as the one in Rio Grande do Norte, MEB and rural unionization, suggest that they were effective. The bishops were important in the creation of SUDENE. More could be said, but I would still conclude that the programs accomplished much, in spite of a large number of problems and lack of time to fulfill their most basic goals. What is most important is the fact that the Chuch acted in a novel and progressive manner, rather than reacting blindly and condemning all change as dangerous and Communistic. The Church in fact opted for change in a most active manner and became an integral part of the nascent 'Brazilian Revolution'.

It should be obvious that the social change response was still on the basis of power and politics and not religious influence. The strictly religious element was, if anything, down-graded, because MEB was basically uninterested in catechism; the unions were political organizations seeking legal gains; ACB left its spiritual element behind with the metamorphosis in 1960; and the bishops talked mainly about structures rather than personal religious beliefs. Influence was redefined as pre-influence, in which the Church had to work simultaneously on changing structures so that man could be more amenable to spiritual concerns, and on religious influence. Given the pressure of events and the nature of threats, the religious element was neglected while the political was concentrated upon. This was probably inevitable. Had the new approach continued for a few more years quite possibly the religious element would have been emphasized, but at this time it was largely overlooked.[91]

[91] The distinction which I want to underline between power and strictly religious influence can be illustrated by reference to the Pentecostals. In Brazil some 70% of the Protestants are included within the general title of Pentecostals, but even so the Protestants compose only 5% of the population. For practical reasons of small size, lack of historical prestige, few political connections and a popular suspicion of their goals, as well as theological reasons, the Pentecostals do not seek power. They do, however, seek (and achieve to a remarkable degree) religious influence through evangelization. This influence may well be more powerful than that of the Catholic Church, and the Church/sect dichotomy is partly responsible, but the Pentecostals are not concerned with changing social structures nearly so much as changing the 'inner man'.

Section III: The Church after 1964

5. Institutionalization of strategies for social change: the CNBB

This chapter analyzes the conditions under which the strategy of pre-influence became possible. The crucial difference between Brazil and most other Latin American countries in this period was that in the majority of countries one or two bishops and several priests might have been involved in social change programs, whereas in Brazil these programs became national. The bishops' statements were both regional and national; MEB became national in 1961, as did rural unionization by 1962; and Catholic Action was also national. In short, the institutional Church in Brazil was apparently promoting a new role which supported elements of modernization in the society at large. However, the disputes over MEB, rural unionization and Catholic Action indicate that there was something less than unanimity on the Church's mission to promote social change. Yet the national Church appeared to agree upon the approach to pre-influence and it behaved accordingly. The Brazilian Church was socially more advanced than any other Latin American Church (except perhaps that of Chile).

A closer examination of the bases for the new approach to influence, as described in the last chapter, will show that the CNBB was behind it, either directly or indirectly through the person of a member of its core group. The CNBB was the body which promoted regional and national assemblies (six national general assemblies prior to 1964 and eight regional assemblies and several meetings of its elite Central Commission); it backed and organized MEB; rural unionization was sponsored through its auspices nationally; and the ACB was mandated to the hierarchy through the CNBB. Therefore it was not 'the Church' which created and supported the pre-influence strategy, but rather one body within it and a small one at that.[1]

The CNBB was founded in October 1952 by Msgr. Helder Câmara and approved by Msgr. Giovanni Montini, of the Vatican's Secretariat of State. The idea and plans for the organization grew out of discussions between the two in the early 1950s and it is safe to say that the CNBB was well within the structure and priorities of Rome.[2] Shortly thereafter, Helder Câmara was nominated Auxiliary

---

[1] My analysis resolves a latent contradiction between Ferrari's research and my own. He indicates that the Natal Movement was largely indigenous and a response to local conditions based on a new reading of the Gospel; I have taken a different tack. Whereas his research is accurate for the particular situation in Rio Grande do Norte, it is not applicable to the whole of Brazil. My inquiry shares Landsberger's concern about how a small group of progressives can influence the whole hierarchy. In this sense, my analysis could have policy implications for those countries where the Church has not yet adopted a progressive position. See Henry A. Landsberger, 'Time, Persons, Doctrine: The Modernization of the Church in Chile', in Landsberger ed., *The Church and Social Change in Latin America* (Notre Dame, Indiana: University of Notre Dame Press, 1970), pp. 80–1.

[2] See the brief history in Pe. Raimundo Caramuru de Barros, *Brasil: Uma Igreja em Renovação* (Petrópolis, R. J.: Editôra Vozes, 1967). Dom Helder's friendship with Montini, later Pope Paul VI, dates from this period.

Bishop to Cardinal Dom Jaime Câmara (no relation) of Rio and elected General Secretary of the CNBB, a position he was to retain for more than a decade. Dom Helder's goals in founding the organization were twofold: there had never been any national coordination of the Church beyond what a strong figure such as Cardinal Leme could effect, and as the early 1950s saw a rapid expansion of dioceses, such coordination became imperative; and he felt a national organization, such as the CNBB, would encourage the whole institution to take an active interest in social change. By now Dom Helder's ideas on the Church, politics and social change should be clear. During the period before 1964, these ideas infused the CNBB and to some extent the whole Church.[3]

Dom Helder was the moving force behind the organization during the period under consideration, but he was not acting alone. Indeed the CNBB was presumably the conference of all the hierarchy but, as is the case with any group, a few individuals were more active and concerned than the rest. From interviews with bishops and priests, from books, a content analysis of the CNBB organ, *Comunicado Mensal*, and other sources, I have compiled a list of eight other bishops who were the initial 'CNBB group'.[4] These bishops were also the most socially concerned in the pre-1964 period, and thus there was a duplication of personnel, in that the organization brought together those bishops who were active in social change programs in their own dioceses and who through the CNBB made their interests those of the whole institution. Within the Church there is a stereotype concerning the social propensities of the bishop: those from the Northeast are the most socially concerned and those from the South the least concerned.[5] This stereotype, like most, seems to be at least partly correct and the following list shows that the majority of CNBB bishops were from the Northeast.

1. Dom Helder Câmara	Ceará
2. Dom Carlos Carmelo Motta	Minas Gerais
3. Dom Carlos Coelho	Paraíba (deceased)
4. Dom Luís Mousinho	Pernambuco (deceased)
5. Dom José Delgado	Paraíba
6. Dom José Távora	Pernambuco (deceased)
7. Dom Eugênio Sales	Rio Grande do Norte
8. Dom Fernando Gomes	Paraíba
9. Dom Manuel Pereira	Pernambuco

[3]   Interview with Dom Helder on the reasons behind the CNBB in Recite on 25 October 1967. See his *Revolução Dentro da Paz* and also José de Broucker, *Dom Helder Câmara: The Violence of a Peacemaker*, trans. Herma Briffault (Maryknoll, N.Y.: Orbis Books, 1970).
[4]   For this sort of material on bishops also see *Visão*, 24 March 1967 and 16 August 1968; for data concerning origins and other variables see Godofredo Deelen, 'O Episcopado Brasileiro', *Revista Eclesiástica Brasileira* 27 (June 1967), pp. 310–32.
    To determine why the Northeastern bishops are more socially aware is beyond the scope of this book. The usual observation by the individuals concerned is that conditions of life are so bad in the area that they feel intensely the need to improve the situation. In other words, poverty and misery lead to awareness. See for example Dom Antônio de Almeida Lustosa, *Terra Martirizada* (Rio de Janeiro: Imprensa Nacional, 1958). The observation holds if we see the obverse, i.e., life is best in the South and thus those bishops do not feel any need for

Eight out of the nine are from states in the Northeast; one is from the center (Minas Gerais); and none come from the South. The predominance of the Northeastern bishops becomes more impressive if their ratio is compared to the total hierarchy. The data for 1966 (the most accurate, which are also correct for the previous period, because trends in diocese founding have been basically identical throughout Brazil) show a total of 178 native-born prelates. There are an additional 65 foreign-born, but they are relatively unimportant in terms of participation, ecclesiastical politics and other relevant concerns of this book. In the eight states of the Northeast (this excludes Bahia, which functions differently for historical reasons) there are a total of 35 bishops, or about 19 % of the native-born hierarchy. Minas Gerais, with 43 bishops, comprises 24 % of the total. The South, with Rio Grande do Sul, Santa Catarina and Paraná, has 36 bishops, about 20 % of the total.[6] It is evident that the vast majority of the CNBB and socially concerned bishops came from the Northeast and in substantially higher proportions than would be predicted. Further, it appears as though the organization gave national prominence to members of the hierarchy who traditionally were somewhat marginal. In this century the important Church 'statesmen' – Dom Arcoverde, Dom Leme and then Dom Jaime – as Cardinals of Rio, as well as other strategic members of the hierarchy, were all from the South or Center. Through the CNBB, Northeastern bishops became the most strategic and prominent in Rio as well as nationally, by means of its statements, programs and movements.

It is appropriate at this point to relate ACB to the CNBB, although there is a formal and real distinction made between lay organizations and an episcopacy. During this period, however, the two organizations were structurally and ideologically very similar. The CNBB, like the Natal Movement, grew out of Catholic Action as Msgr. Helder Câmara was national assistant of ACB from 1947 and used this organization to call the first two meetings of the hierarchy. Many in the CNBB group had been involved with ACB as assistants and remained in contact with the movement in key positions. The contact between the Catholic Action militants and the CNBB bishops was reciprocal: they aided each other in the formulation of a new influence model. The CNBB financed ACB and, as I noted previously, it was largely the members of the latter organization who worked in the Church's projects. What was critical for ACB was the fact that the CNBB existed. Previously Catholic Action had been on the highly centralized Italian pattern, under the direct jurisdiction of the local bishops. Now, Catholic Action was national, being directly affiliated (or mandated) to the new and national Bishops' Conference. Thus the lay organization was not constrained by the priorities and regulations of each local bishop. The leaders

---

change. There are, however, other factors, such as the ethnic origins of the bishops, formative role of a particular seminary and the influence of particular bishops over the younger ones. For example, Dom Mousinho had a role in influencing two later progressives, Dom Picão and Dom Miele.

[6] For the full description of data see Deelen, *Revista Eclesiástica Brasileira* 27.

could function at the national level and be concerned with the problems of general interest. It was at the national level that meetings were held, guidelines set and resources distributed. The national level was progressive, as it was part of the progressive CNBB. In short, Catholic Action had more autonomy than ever before and could respond to its involvement in the milieu and develop its own orientation and priorities. Later, with the problems of ACB and the bishops, many in the hierarchy realized the importance of the national element in ACB. They praised the local members of the organization (often largely because they did not know what they were doing), but denounced the national leaders for giving a 'false line' to evangelization and the mandate relationship. Despite official approval (or disapproval) of the new Catholic Action goals and behavior, all agree that the national scope under the CNBB was strategic in allowing – and encouraging – the evolution of ACB into a lively, *avant-garde* organization.[7]

It is necessary to study the legal stature of the CNBB within the institutional Church to understand how it could play a central role. The CNBB was founded in 1952 and recognized by the Holy See to 'A. study problems of interest to the Church, particularly in Brazil; and B. present norms, approve and coordinate measures, which facilitate and promote the unity of orientation and the convenient actualization of the pastoral.'[8] Dom Helder had precise aims in founding the organization, but its legal stature was slight. Legally, the CNBB had but the barest recognition in this period, which is commonly (but incorrectly) termed its 'pre-history', before the Second Vatican Council expanded the jurisdiction of national episcopal conferences. If Canon Law is consulted the limited stature of a national conference becomes apparent: at the basis of the hierarchy are the bishops;[9] at the top is the Pope and the secretariats of the Holy See; in between these levels there is little. Provision is made for Provincial Councils every twenty years, but they are of limited jurisdiction and not relevant for continual operations. The papal nuncio is the Pope's religious and civil representative in a country. He communicates between the bishops and Rome, makes recommendations for nominations and transfers, makes suggestions, relates to the government, but is in no sense a national representative of the hierarchy. Strictly speaking, there is no such thing as a national Church. There are the bishops, who rule a territory called a diocese and are endowed with wide powers in virtue of their office and not by delegation. At the same time, the Pope has ultimate authority, so that every member of the faithful is under a double jurisdiction. While there are entities

---

[7]   All informants in both the ACB and the hierarchy agreed that 'going national' was critical for evolution. Interviews with several ex-assistants noted that the diocesan bishops did not know what ACB was doing. CERIS research supports the observation that ACB was removed from direct contact with the local bishops. They note that often the movements lacked assistants and were not well linked in communications with the bishops. See Carlos Alberto de Medina and Dimas Furtado, 'Participação e Igreja; estudos dos movimentos e associações de leigos', unpublished research report for CERIS, 1969, pp. 6–10.

[8]   Article I of CNBB statutes, in CNBB, *Plano de Pastoral de Conjunto 1966–1970* (Rio de Janeiro: Livraria Dom Bosco Editôra, 1966).

[9]   'They have the right and duty to govern the diocese both in temporal and spiritual matters, with legislative, judicial, and coercive power, to be exercised according to law.' Canon 335.

called nations or countries and the Holy See receives ambassadors and sends out legates, there simply is no explicit provision made for national Church organizations.

In the Second Vatican Council the minimal jurisdiction of national conferences was expanded slightly. One finds in 'Cristus Dominus', No. 37:

This most sacred Synod considers it supremely opportune everywhere that bishops belonging to the same nation or region form an association and meet together at fixed times. Thus, when the insights of prudence and experience have been shared and views exchanged, there will emerge a holy union of energies in the service of the common good of the churches.[10]

The Council referred ambiguously to national conferences in 'Cristus Dominus' No. 36–8; Pope Paul VI emphasized their value in his motu-proprio 'Ecclesias Sanctae' No. 41, and did so at least once again in his speech of 24 November 1965 to a meeting of the Latin American bishops (CELAM). And today theologians are able to state that the formation of national conferences is a logical outcome of the modern world.[11] In Canon Law national conferences barely exist and, after the Council, they are slightly recognized and most certainly have no claim to the authority of the bishops. Even so, they enjoy more legality today than they did when Dom Helder founded the CNBB in 1952 and used it to redirect the whole institution.

Despite its slight legal stature, the CNBB possessed an elan, a spirit, a value unto itself. The organization lacked finances, had no proper headquarters and was really centered on one individual, Dom Helder, but for those associated with it it had meaning and they were willing to give their time and energy.[12] Essentially, the CNBB was able to supersede its limited jurisdiction and give a new orientation to the whole Church because it became an institution.

Referring to the CNBB as an institution conveys a particular impression of value or meaning, of dynamic instead of limited structural arrangement for a particular goal. The organization became, in the words of Selznick, laden with value, at least for those who worked with it, if not for the whole Church. It became more than a utilitarian instrument (or organization); it was a living entity centered on the charismatic figure of Dom Helder and other active, involved bishops.

The study of institutions and institutionalization is an historic concern of sociology and organization theory. Despite the long and illustrious tradition of study associated with it, the concept seems to mean something different to each author and there is usually a tremendous degree of confusion regarding both the

[10] Walter M. Abbot, S. J. and Msgr. Joseph Gallagher, eds., *The Documents of Vatican II* (New York: Guild Press, 1966), p. 425.
[11] J. Hamer, 'Conferências Episcopais', in Dom Helder Câmara et al., *Novas Estruturas na Igreja* (Lisbon: Livraria Morais Editôra, 1966).
[12] Interviews with Miss Nair Cruz, pre-1964 CNBB staff member, in Rio on 14 November 1967; Marina Bandeira in Rio on 13 November 1967; Otto Engel, pre-1964 CNBB staff member, in Rio on 8 August 1967; Dom Timóteo Amoroso Anastácio in Salvador on 18 October 1967; and Miss Cecília Monteiro, former personal secretary to Dom Helder, in Rio on 29 February 1968.

terminology and suggested indices of measurement. For our purposes the best interpretation of institutionalization is one which reflects the linking of personal and motivational elements to a structural entity for the achievement of a goal which has significance for the members of that entity. That is, an institution is more than an impersonal organization in which the members make calculations on their contributions *vis-à-vis* their benefits. In an institution the members neglect the calculation, because they have linked their personal goals with those of the entity and thus the institution has personal meaning for them. The importance of the value and commitment dimension lies in the fact that because of it an institution can do more than it might have been intended to, is dynamic, is innovative and is alive.[13]

In order for institutionalization, or institution-building, to occur at least four conditions are required: autonomy, leadership, ideology and coherence. These categories are not original to this work, but are recognized by specialists as common necessities.

Autonomy looms large in discussions of institution-building. It indicates a relationship involving structures and goals which can be seen in levels of independence of one entity from others. Presumably if an entity has its own structures and can generate its own resources, it can also define its own goals. Conversely, when it relies upon another's structures or resources its goals will be determined in conjunction with the other. Autonomy is most important in a new movement (group, organization, entity, or other type of social formation) for it is necessary in order to define a distinctive identity.[14] Autonomy can refer either to the entity as a whole or to its elites; here I will deal with both.

Ideology is necessary if a distinctive identity is to be defined. Ideology not only 'explains' the organization's environment, self-definition and action imperatives, but also creates the 'myth' which integrates its various elements and makes it a single whole. Ideology is thus important in creating a unified understanding of the enterprise and in facilitating communications. Without an ideology there can be no institution. An ideology also relates an institution to others, defining them and their relationships.

Leadership is central to all discussions of organizations and groups. Statesmanship (versus the politics of compromise or bargaining) is the institutional equivalent of leadership (versus the role of bureaucrat). In a highly structured organization like the Church, leadership means the creation or change of structures, by which the leader embodies the ideology in the organization. Leadership in normal Church structures is most difficult, because of the precise

---

[13] See the various works of Durkheim, Tonnies and Weber. See also Philip Selznick, *Leadership in Administration*; David Moberg, *The Church as a Social Institution* (Englewood Cliff, N.J.: Prentice Hall, 1962); Max Weber, *On Charisma and Institution Building*, ed. and intro. by S.N. Eisenstadt (Chicago: University of Chicago Press, 1968); Samuel Huntington, 'Political Development and Political Decay', *World Politics* 17 (April 1965), pp. 286–430; Ivan Vallier, 'Church "Development" in Latin America: A Five-Country Comparison', *Journal of Developing Areas* 1 (July 1967), pp. 461–76.

[14] Selznick, *Leadership in Administration*, p. 121.

regulations concerning all aspects of action and the need to control charisma. Leadership involves some element of charisma and this is one thing the Church seeks to monopolize completely. Only through the creation or change of structures, which require autonomy, is leadership possible. On the other hand, only through leadership can the other conditions of autonomy, ideology and coherence he brought together in order to make an institution. Leadership stresses the rational element in institution-building.

Coherence means integration, unity, consensus on goals and means. Coherence necessitates the other elements: autonomy indicates that other, alien sectors have not penetrated the institution; ideology provides the basis for coherence; and leadership is the art of forging unity and consensus. Coherence does not imply the absence of internal conflicts, but rather circumscribes them, so that unity is not threatened. With coherence an institution can confront other institutions without fear of disintegration or decay. Essentially, three of these conditions prevailed because the fourth applied only internally; internal coherence was present in the CNBB but lacking in the larger Church.

Autonomy. Despite its minimal legal jurisdiction, the CNBB was able to function and develop because it was separate from the traditional Church structures of diocese, curia, parish and others. It had no precise position in the hierarchy and could seek its own level of significance. The significance reached a high level because in the face of threats, mainly perceived at the political level, the bishops allowed the CNBB to respond for them to demagogic politicians, leftist organizers, the incompetence of President Goulart and the like. That is, the CNBB did not fit neatly into the traditional system, but its inroads into the bishops' authority were tolerated by the bishops because they felt a response was necessary in order to assert a 'Church position' on social and political affairs. In its supra-Church position, the CNBB could manipulate the former's resources, such as personnel, contacts, communications and prestige, for its new and different goals. Also in the line of resources, well-prepared and dynamic people who generally had little to do with the Church were willing to donate their time and talents to the institution simply because it was dynamic and doing worthwhile things. As it was independent of the larger institution, the CNBB also escaped the traditional relationship with the state. It negotiated a new relationship with the state, which brought in resources without the historic compromises.

Leadership. All observers of Dom Helder have noted his charismatic capacity to stimulate, innovate and inspire.[15] He could exercise these gifts to the full in Rio, for he was auxiliary bishop and thus without the fixed pastoral duties of an ordinary (or bishop who has specific jurisdiction). After founding the CNBB in 1952, he was able to devote much of his time to its growth and development, for essentially the same reason that it had autonomy; the Church was confronted by threats of various kinds and the Cardinal and other bishops allowed Dom Helder considerable leeway in forming a response. He directed this response through the CNBB, thereby institutionalizing what could have remained a very personal

---

[15] See for instance Richard Shaull's foreword to de Broucker, pp. vii–xii.

program or movement.[16] The other members of the CNBB group were generally younger and certainly more active than most of the hierarchy. These groups complemented Dom Helder's charismatic leadership with a further impetus in the same general direction.

Ideology. In the last chapter I described the CNBB ideology as formulated after 1950; this ideology distinguished the CNBB from the larger Church body. If any aspect of the CNBB could be termed unique, it was its ideology of social change, which justified a crucial role for the Church in helping to form a new Brazil. Through it other groups, such as ACB, the state and political parties, could be related to in ways different from the past, and because of it new elements in society were induced to participate in novel Church programs. This ideology was possible, though very radical compared to the past, because again it was the Church's response to the threats of the times.

Coherence. This obtained within the CNBB because of its autonomy, ideology and active leadership. The body was not large; it was new and not yet compromised; and it attracted people with essentially the same ideas and goals. Coherence was to be expected and it did indeed exist. However, within the larger Church coherence was absent *vis-à-vis* the CNBB. The new body was legally and structurally an anomaly and reactions to it could not therefore be fitted into standard patterns. Moreover, the CNBB and its ideologies were diametrically opposed to the Church's traditional views on social change. Tension arose within the hierarchy not only over the ACB (mainly JUC), but over MEB as well, and also involved some conservative lower clergy and laymen. Many of the bishops did not know what the CNBB represented; those who did thought it necessary given the demands of the times; and in comparison with other groups it did not seem radical. However, it is important to realize that there was no conscious consensus or agreement on its goals and certainly not on its means. In fact in 1961 a group of bishops and conservative laymen attacked a CNBB policy on agrarian reform and from about this time Dom Helder's relations with some members of the hierarchy (including the Cardinal of Rio) began to deteriorate.[17]

The CNBB became an institution despite its minimal legal stature, because of a perception of threats by some of the hierarchy and the ignorance of the rest. They allowed the charismatic Dom Helder Câmara to exercise his leadership freely in creating and building an autonomous body and infusing it with an ideology of social change. The conditions for institutionalization thus existed for the same reasons that the Church was stimulated to respond in general: the Church was threatened by all types of social and political processes which diminished its influence, and many sectors perceived at least the political aspects

---

[16] His successor, Dom José Gonçalves da Costa, made a point of the 'living' character of the pre-1964 CNBB in an interview in Rio on 17 November 1967, and Dom Helder himself spoke of his 'mission' in the interview of 25 October 1967.

[17] He became the focus for attack after a well-publicized appearance on U.S. television, in which he expressed doubt that the holders of power in Latin America would willingly make changes as stipulated in the Alliance for Progress. An interview with Dom Helder which appeared in *Última Hora* of Rio on 8 August 1967 made the estrangement between Helder and Dom Jaime clear.

and allowed a response. Given these conditions the CNBB institutionalized, allowed the ACB to evolve and become very *avant-garde* and generally gave a new orientation to the whole Church. Instead of remaining a small group of like-thinking and progressive bishops, the CNBB imposed its goals on the legally non-existent national Church.

The reorientation of the whole Church by the CNBB, however, required more than the institutionalization of Dom Helder's group. In fact, institutionalization itself necessitated support from beyond the national Church and it was forth-coming from both the state and the Holy See. While the timing is difficult to establish, it seems best to argue that the processes of change in the Church happened simultaneously. That is, from the early 1950s both the state and the Holy See encouraged institutionalization, the social change influence model and its generalization throughout the larger institution. Or, translating into the terms of the introduction: Church influence was transformed because of general environmental changes (decreasing influence which, when perceived, created conditions for institutionalization) in interaction with both the state and the Holy See, but made possible in the first instance by the new entity. The new institution was able to take advantage of new and different facets of both the state and the Holy See, which the larger Brazilian Church could not.

The relationship between the state and the Church (particularly the CNBB) was probably the more important and events after 1964 support this contention. Initially, it is worth reiterating that the changing political conditions after the War stimulated a perception of the loss of influence and allowed the CNBB to develop. The political system was 'opening up', new political elites were forming and there was much consideration given to structural change, agrarian reform, development and other dramatic programs and processes. Through statements as well as programs the government in Brazil, at least during the period 1955–64, showed its concern with change and reform. In some instances the statements seemed serious (particularly those of Kubitschek) and in others they were merely political tactics aimed at securing a power base (Goulart's presidency seems to me best understood in this way). Regardless of sincerity, the whole political atmosphere was pervaded by talk of structural change; the Church added one more voice of consent and was in no way out of line with other elements in society. As Moreira Alves notes, 'Excepting the case of the MEB, what we see is that the pronouncements of the Catholic hierarchy on social problems are concomitant with or after the projects and pronouncements of the govern-ment.'[18]

The CNBB cooperated with the government on programs for change. For example, the hierarchy of São Paulo intentionally provided legitimacy for the state's agrarian reform bill in 1960 and the bishops of the Northeast, under CNBB auspices, stimulated the formation and development of SUDENE and continued to work with it at the local level. Instead of pretending that the Church was still 'above politics' and representing 'all that was best in Brazilian tradition',

[18] Moreira Alves, p. 47.

the CNBB group realized that they were cooperating with the state. By understanding the relationship they could presumably control it.[19] The neo-Christendom Church was not aware of the political link and was therefore dominated by
it. The CNBB group were closely allied with important political leaders of this
period; leaders who were progressive and presumably promoting change.
Cardinal Carlos Carmelo Motta of São Paulo and Dom Helder Câmara were
very friendly with President Kubitschek and had close contacts with President
Goulart.

However, the relationship of cooperation with new elements was not the sum
total of Church–state contacts in this period. The CNBB was in competition
both with the more radical goals and programs of Goulart and with traditional
power bases that had always been aligned with the Church. Regarding the
former, it can be recalled that rural unionization began in competition with the
ligas of Julião and remained active in the field against the unions of Goulart and
the Communists. As to the latter, the CNBB in its programs supported change in
opposition to the political elements that had always relied upon the priest for
support in the *status quo*. In short, what was most critical for the Church was the
institutionalization of the CNBB, which allowed for a variety of autonomy
relationships. Instead of relying upon the traditional links with the state and
local power elements, the CNBB could choose and thereby promote its own
orientation as well as that of like-thinking elements in the state.

Our discussion on the relationship between the CNBB and the Holy See
indicates several points concerning the Universal Church and its bonds with the
local and national Churches: change did not begin with the Council; papal
statements can have an impact; and internal Church compliance is a very tricky
matter. The relationship will be discussed along two main lines: the part played
by the papal nuncio and the encyclicals and letters of Pope John XXIII. Papal
nuncios in Latin America have been very important in giving particular orientations or colorations to the national Churches. In the first place, national Churches
do not theoretically exist whereas local Churches do, and the nuncio as the
only fully national figure can communicate with the Vatican as though he represented the bishops of a particular country. The nuncio, of course, is the Pope's
representative and cannot interfere with local Church affairs without a mandate,
but in fact he often does assume a national religious role. Secondly, the Latin
American bishops are all too frequently poorly educated, usually isolated in their
rural dioceses and concerned exclusively with local rather than national Church
affairs. In this context, the nuncio with his national position, international links
and 'Roman diplomatic skills' can run the national Church. The nuncio assists
in the nomination of new bishops, arranges for transfers, provides the communications link for most issues between a diocese and Rome and is involved
in policies at all levels. Further, with his civil as well as spiritual status he possesses an added element of persuasion over individual bishops. In sum, a nuncio

[19] For example, the 1956 Campina Grande statement notes, 'Nor should it seem peculiar to
see us apparently linked to the organs of public powers. At the opportune time the absolute
independence of the spiritual power from the temporal power will be quite clear.'

with his central position can easily dominate an amorphous Church and give it a coloration which local conditions might not seem to warrant.[20]

The papal nuncio in Brazil from September 1954 until his death in May 1964 (almost the entire period under consideration) was Dom Armando Lombardi. Dom Armando was involved in the almost total renewal of the hierarchy during this decade. He helped create 48 new bishoprics, 11 archbishoprics and 16 *prelazias*. These figures become quite significant when compared to the previous ten years, during which only 8 bishoprics, 3 *prelazias* and 1 *abbe nullius* were created. He handled the nominations of 109 bishops and 24 archbishops and these, in comparison with the total number of dioceses (116) and archdioceses (31) of the period, indicate that he was intricately involved in nominating a vast majority of members of the hierarchy.

While most of my informants on the relationships between Rome and the Brazilian Church were critical of the Roman Curia, the Secretariat of State and the 'Roman way' of the Universal Church, they were all very much impressed by Dom Armando. They noted that he was intelligent, active, aware of the problems and responsibilities of a Church in a developing country such as Brazil, and saw as his role the renovation of the Brazilian Church. His channel of renovation was the CNBB. The nuncio met weekly with Dom Helder and worked out strategies for change; he attended the majority of CNBB meetings at which advanced social statements were formulated (for example, Campina Grande in 1956, Natal in 1959 and São Paulo in 1960) and publicly supported this orientation; Dom Armando was involved in the nomination as bishops of a large number of obviously progressive young men who have since become the leaders of the post-1964 active sector. The nuncio also defended the 'excesses' of the ACB to critical bishops, and in several meetings made clear his support for the organization. In general, he supported the CNBB as an institution as well as the individuals who constituted the group, attended its meetings and made use of its organ, the *Comunicado Mensal*, for his communiques. It is impossible to determine whether in this support of the CNBB and its orientation Dom Armando was simply representing the three popes (Pius XII, John XXIII and Paul VI), or if he acted with some degree of independence. It was probably more the former than the latter, given the time involved and the fact that there were no serious reversals during the period. Certainly Popes John and Paul favored Dom Helder and the activities of the CNBB; this is particularly clear with regard to the encyclicals and letters of Pope John. The same could be said later for Pope Paul and his message, but this comes under a different period.[21]

[20] Interview with Msgr. Mario Tagliaferri, secretary of the papal nuncio, in Rio on 25 March 1968, concerning formal powers of nuncio. McKenzie notes, 'It is a known fact that a papal representative may have as much influence as he chooses to wield. He is in a position both to promise and to threaten'. p. 51.

[21] On support of the popes, see David E. Mutchler, 'Roman Catholicism in Brazil', *Studies in Comparative International Development* (St Louis, Mo.: Washington University, 1965) 1:8, 103–17. On the nuncio see Sanders in Silvert, *Churches and States*, p. 87. Interviews with the Provincial of a religious order, a Catholic journalist who knows about the international level and the former head of the Brazilian Religious Conference (CRB).

Papal encyclicals are not specific directives to the Church on particular matters, but messages to the world on the Popes' views. Their status regarding compliance is rather ambiguous, but they undoubtedly indicate a preference and can help in creating an atmosphere in favor of general policies. The support given to the CNBB and its influence model is clear in the case of Pope John's 'Mater et Magistra' of 1961 and 'Pacem in Terris' of 1963.

'Mater et Magistra' was the first papal encyclical that dealt specifically with the necessity of reform in rural areas and many attribute its emphasis to the rural background of the Pope.[22] Until 'Mater et Magistra', all the progressive CNBB statements were made on a regional basis and without precise organization backing. After the encyclical, and because of it, the Central Commission of the CNBB met in an extraordinary session in October, issued a very advanced document dealing with the necessary changes in rural society and political structures and committed MEB, ACB and rural unionization to assist these changes. Not only were the various regional programs encouraged to spread to other parts of the country, but important members of the hierarchy beyond the CNBB group signed the document. It was recognized by all involved that the encyclical gave impetus and support to the still incipient national influence model.[23]

If anything, the next encyclical was more important in supporting social involvement. Pope John's 'Pacem in Terris', issued at Easter 1963, was the occasion for another Central Commission meeting. In it they prepared the most advanced and critical social statement ever issued by the Church in Brazil; important again was the fact that it was signed by the two cardinals as well as the influential archbishop of Pôrto Alegre, Dom Vicente Scherer. With this statement the Church (and presumably the whole Church, since the most important prelates signed it) was placed clearly on the side of serious socio-political change. It is doubtful whether the more conservative prelates would have agreed to such a progressive and forward statement had Pope John not issued his advanced encyclical.[24]

In addition to the encyclicals which Pope John issued to the whole world, there were at least two letters to the bishops of Latin America which emphasized the same social concern and desire for the Church to act positively to bring about change. In November of 1958 Pope John directed a letter to the Latin American bishops in which 'he made an appeal for an awakening to the grave situation of this continent, and of the challenges and demands to be confronted

---

[22] E.E.Y. Hales, *Pope John and His Revolution* (Garden City, N.Y.: Image Books, 1966), p. 67.
[23] Cardinals Dom Jaime of Rio and Dom Augusto of Bahia also signed the document. Interviews with Marina Bandeira on 5 March 1968 and José Kosinski Cavalcanti, a journalist concerned with Church affairs and active in some spheres of Church involvement, in Rio on 4 August 1967 indicated the importance of this encyclical.
[24] On the role of the encyclical on the 1963 Central Commission document, Alceu Amoroso Lima notes, 'When and how is it that our Episcopacy would write such a thing if it were not for our John XXIII. What a force the Pope has!' *João XXIII* (Rio de Janeiro: Livraria José Olympio Editôra, 1966), p. 114.

by the Church'.[25] In November 1961, with the example of Cuba very much in mind, the Pope made a dramatic appeal:

That the bishops should demonstrate to the governments and all those responsible the urgency of structural reforms and improvement for the underdeveloped masses; that the hierarchy and the Church, in a subsidiary function, should cooperate in this improvement and participate actively in it.[26]

The Holy See, then, both directly and indirectly supported the CNBB and its approach to influence. The general relationship of the Holy See to the whole Brazilian Church was one of coalition: they had identical goals and structures. However, there was the possibility for a completely new series of relationships, because the Universal Church was then experiencing a process of change which would become manifest in the Council (1962–5) and the CNBB was an institution somewhat apart from the traditional Brazilian Church. The most advanced lines of the Universal Church, then, were able to relate to this new institution, and in many respects the Council and even 'Populorum Progressio' of 1967 were manifest in Brazil before their time. Therefore a pardoxical situation occurred, in which two coalition relationships existed but with different, and in some respects contradictory, goals. This was possible, again, because the Universal Church was in a process of transformation and thus amenable to contradictions. Essentially the same situation held true for the Brazilian state: the relationships were not so close as they were with the Holy See, but they were at least cooperative and the CNBB aligned itself with the most progressive elements, while most of the Church remained linked with the more traditional and conservative sectors. The lesson of the CNBB shows that Church change is possible even while the larger institution remains traditional, if some sort of platform exists by which national and international progressive elements can promote their goals. The continuation of the new strategy of influence, however, depended on the continuation of the CNBB and this became impossible after the coup of 1964.

The literature on the military coup of 1 April 1964 is extensive.[27] The combination of President Goulart's political incompetence and the various attempts at structural change was enough to cause the military's intervention. The political role of the Church in the coup was limited. The social change activities described in the last chapter promoted political mobilization and the response to it was a military dictatorship. Again, as noted before, there was something less than complete unanimity within the Church on the social change role and this led to crises which became serious after the coup. A rather dramatic piece of evidence on the lack of unity was the series of 'Rosary Marches' that were held in late 1963 and early 1964. The largest of these marches took place in São Paulo on 19 March 1964 and brought more than half a million people out onto

[25] Quoted in Caramuru de Barros, *Brasil: Uma Igreja em Renovação*, p. 24.
[26] *Ibid.*, p. 25.
[27] For general political information regarding the coup, see Skidmore, *Politics in Brazil, 1930–1964*. See also Amaury de Souza, 'Março ou Abril? Uma Bibliógrafia Commentada Sôbre O Movimento Político de 1964 no Brasil', *Dados* 1 (1966), pp. 160–76, for an extensive bibliography on the coup.

the streets for the feast of St Joseph, patron of the family. These marches in São Paulo, Rio, Belo Horizonte, etc. were organized by upper middle-class Catholic women belonging to the Democratic Women's Campaign, São Paulo Civic Feminine Union and similar groups. They were often encouraged from the pulpit and Cardinal Dom Jaime was known to favor them as well. However, the nuncio opposed them, officially the Church dissociated itself with the marches, many of the clergy spoke out against them and in fact Cardinal Dom Motta specifically discouraged them in São Paulo – all to no avail.[28] There is some evidence that the rosary marches were an important stimulus for military intervention, as they showed that the good Catholic ladies of Brazil had had enough of the government of João Goulart.[29]

Even while the ladies were marching two members of the CNBB group apparently gave support to Goulart. Dom Helder Câmara and Dom Carlos Carmelo Motta were photographed together with the President at a friendly luncheon just about a week before the coup; the picture and story circulated everywhere in Brazil. This was an attempt by Goulart to use the legitimacy of these bishops for his support. In fact, Helder and Motta had gone to see Goulart to warn him of the inevitable outcome of his irresponsible policies; while they were there he invited them to lunch. In the middle of it, they were photographed and assured that their picture was only for 'the family album'. The bishops were taken completely by surprise when the picture came out in the papers, and the conclusion that most people drew was that Dom Helder and Dom Carlos still supported Goulart, despite his radicalization.[30] Thus not only had MEB been demoralized by the Lacerda attack, rural unions sabotaged by the Communists at the top and the owners at the local level, Catholic Action vilified for its radicalization, the leaders of the CNBB photographed with Goulart, but the Catholic women were marching against them all.

The first public statement by the hierarchy on the political change of April was a joint declaration in May, which was signed by 26 of the most important bishops (including cardinals and archbishops) from all parts of Brazil. At this time, the CNBB group was still dominant at the national level, but the necessity of conciliating other sectors of the hierarchy led to the publication of a vacillating, not to say paradoxical, statement. Very simply, after the coup the conditions which had favored institutionalization disappeared and, as unity or coherence was established throughout the Church, the CNBB's continued survival became extremely problematic. The statement in May was an attempt to demonstrate that unity existed within the Church, despite the fact that previous crises had revealed its absence. Thus, on the one hand, the bishops welcomed the military intervention in no uncertain terms:

In response to the widespread and anxious expectations of the Brazilian people, which saw the quickening pace of communism's rise to power, the armed forces came to the

[28] Interview with Amoroso Lima on 7 July 1967, regarding the nuncio and Dom Jaime.
[29] Clarence W. Hall, 'The Country That Saved Itself', *Reader's Digest* (November 1964), pp 135–48.
[30] De Broucker's reporting of the episode is accurate enough. pp. 48–9.

rescue in time to avoid the implantation of a bolshevik regime in our country... In offering our thanks to God, who heeded the prayers of millions of Brazilians and delivered us from the communist peril, we thank [also] the military that, with grave risk to their lives, rose up in the name of the supreme interests of the nation, and grateful are we to them for cooperating to liberate the nation from the imminent abyss.

Then they went on to defend the militants of the Church for their 'misplaced idealism' and specifically stated that MEB and ACB were not communistic. Bearing in mind that there were at least 300 lay and clergy activists in jail at the time, the bishops spoke out for decency and justice in their treatment. And so the statement continued: on the one hand welcoming the coup, and on the other attempting to defend the militants who had suffered because of their involvement in Church projects.[31]

The statement indicated the prevailing climate and generalized orientation of society and of the majority of the hierarchy. Quite simply, with the coup the political threats of a leftist and a demagogic nature were eliminated; the military talked of reforms, but only in terms of their paternalistic and watchful direction and statements of social change became dangerous. On the one hand, therefore, there was no longer a need to respond and, on the other hand, the types of responses that the Church had made (MEB, rural unionization, ACB, etc.) were illegal. The future of the CNBB and the approach to influence were obvious, as a brief review of the changes in the conditions for institutionalization will indicate.

Within the CNBB *coherence* was eliminated, as elements from the larger Church interfered to bring it under control. Externally, it was re-established, as the CNBB was quickly reintegrated into the institution.

Even before the coup, Dom Helder's *leadership* had been attacked. He was accused of 'doing the work of the Communists' and his relations with many in the hierarchy were tense. After it, Dom Helder and his group (including Dom Eugênio Sales of Natal) were attacked in the press and identified with the government of the deposed President Goulart. In April one of the group died (Dom Carlos Coelho) and Dom Helder was nominated to replace him as the Archbishop of Olinda/Recife. By the end of April he had left Rio for good and was established in the Northeast. The President of the CNBB at this time was Cardinal Carlos Carmelo Motta of São Paulo, an early member of the group. Fifteen days after the coup the Cardinal was transferred from São Paulo to the relatively unimportant pilgrimage town of Aparecida. Most reliable sources indicate that the Cardinal had wanted to move for some time on account of age and ill health, but the transfer at this crucial time was construed as a move by Rome to hurt the CNBB and its orientation.[32] Within a month, therefore, the

---

[31] For the statement see the newspapers of 30 or 31 May. A good analysis of the statement, entitled 'Unity of the Church', can be found in the *Correio da Manhã* of 4 June 1964 by Hermano Alves. On persecutions see Moreira Alves, *passim*.

[32] *Comunicado Mensal* No. 141 of June, 1964, states that he had been requesting his transfer for some time. Interviews in Rio with informed insiders support this, although there is no complete agreement.

leadership of the CNBB was moved from central, strategic positions and was isolated. Then, too, because of attacks, the CNBB group was demoralized and its strategy became impossible.

The CNBB *ideology* was one of social involvement for structural changes. After the coup, this ideology became not only precarious but illegal.[33] Several of the movements which were logical action imperatives of the ideology were suppressed (MEB, rural unions, student organizations) and it was simply no longer possible to talk about basic changes and the need for radical reforms. When others in the society ceased being concerned with change, the great majority of the bishops felt no need to have the Church so involved.

The *autonomy* of the leadership disappeared with the coup. Dom Helder left Rio and became involved in the affairs of his archdiocese; the bishops became aware of what the CNBB had been involved in under their auspices and withdrew the authority which the institution had gradually usurped. Further, without continued threats they felt there was no longer a need for such an entity and as a consequence forgot about national responses and focused exclusively on local affairs once again. Therefore the autonomy the CNBB had enjoyed because of threats and the benign neglect of the hierarchy simply disappeared.

The conditions which allowed institution-building in the CNBB disappeared with the political change of April and it became a mere organization. The distinction here is described by Selznick in terms of self-maintenance, which 'refers to the preservation of central values and purposes as well as to the bare continuity of organizational existence'.[34] The CNBB as an organization did in fact grow; it obtained more finances, established a proper center and began to publish more documents on various topics, so that, if anything, it appeared more important than before. Several members of the hierarchy seemed honestly to believe that there was no difference between the pre- and post-1964 CNBB. However, it can simply be noted that no more national statements on social change emerged from the body, it no longer promoted rural unionization and the mood of those involved changed. I interviewed most of the activists (both clergy and lay) in the pre- and post-1964 organization and there was a general consensus that the CNBB was not what it used to be. Even a content analysis of the *Comunicado Mensal* before and after shows a very definite change; a change of focus from larger social concerns to those of a purely organizational character.[35] If any doubt could exist regarding the difference between the pre- and post-coup CNBB, a discussion of decisions made during the Second Vatican Council in Rome should dispel this.

---

[33] On precarious values in an institutional context see Selznick, *Leadership in Administration*, pp. 119–33.

[34] Philip Selznick,' Institutional Vulnerability in Mass Society', *American Journal of Sociology* 56 (January 1951), pp. 320–31.

[35] Best seen in November/December 1964 versus March/April 1965. An interesting comparison might be made here between the pre-1934 *A Ordem* of the Centro Dom Vital and the issues after political success. Those before in both cases were active, relevant and specific, whereas those after were very inward looking, alienated and superfluous.

In retrospect the 'Church of Vatican Two' is very similar to the Church of the CNBB. The Brazilian Church during this period, with its emphasis on the Church in the world, discovery of neglected strata of the population, participation of the laity and other such renewal topics, bears a strong resemblance to the model which emerged from the Council. I noted before that the minimal legal jurisdiction of national conferences was expanded somewhat by the Council. Further, if there is an archetype of the 'bishop of Vatican II', it would be Dom Helder and others of the group. With all these points of identification, the Council should have given considerable support to the CNBB and its model of influence. After all, the model was legitimized by the two papal encyclicals and Dom Helder was on close terms with both Popes.

However, precisely in the middle of the Council the coup occurred and the conditions for institutionalization disappeared. A discussion of the Brazilian bishops' actions in Rome with regard to the CNBB and ACB suggests to me that in the short-run at least national political conditions and a concern with power are more important than links with the Universal Church (in this case seen in the decisions of the Council, which of course had to be recognized and legitimized first by the Pope). Thus to return to a point I noted at the beginning of the discussion on the Holy See and the CNBB: internal Church compliance is a very tricky matter. What the bishops did was simply to certify a lack of conditions for institutionalization by changing the CNBB into a simple organization which could serve no significant purpose in the larger institution. They did this despite what was taking place in Rome and in opposition to its so-often-hailed spirit of renewal and reform. At best, the results were unanticipated consequences of immediate concerns and fears in the Church resulting from the coup. At worst, they were based on personal concerns with power and a feeling of rancor against Dom Helder.[36]

The great majority of the two-hundred-odd Brazilian bishops attended the Council and during its second session they held the VIth and VIIth meetings of the CNBB General Assembly. If the decisions made on leadership, structure and programs are examined one can see how the CNBB and ACB were totally altered.[37]

Leadership is critical in any institution, but especially in new ones. I have stressed the importance of Dom Helder in the role of Secretary General of the CNBB, from 1952 when he founded it, and the fact that it brought together the more progressive hierarchy, mainly from the Northeast. Elections were held in

---

[36] Merton has given four limitations on the correct anticipations of consequences of action. The CNBB case seems to fit two of the limitations very closely. Number 3 is 'the imperious immediacy of interest', which refers to those instances where the actor's paramount concern with the foreseen immediate consequences excludes the consideration of further or other consequences of the same act. And Number 4 is similar: where there is no consideration of further consequences because of the felt necessity of certain action enjoined by certain fundamental values. Robert Merton, 'The Unanticipated Consequences of Purposive Social Action', *American Sociological Review* 1 (December 1936), pp. 901–903.

[37] September/October 1964 and September 1965. See *Comunicado Mensal* from Nos. 142 to 157 for the topics discussed.

Rome in late 1964 for all the CNBB positions. The CNBB group expected that Dom Helder would be elected once again. However, the opposition to Dom Helder and his line was organized by the arch-conservative bishop of Pouso Alegre, M.G., Dom José D'Angelo Neto, who brought together the prelates from the outlying areas (that is, bishops from *prelazias*, who are usually foreigners), the conservatives, the moderates who were worried about radicalism and those who could not attend because of ill health. Not only was Dom Helder defeated, but so were two other members of the CNBB group, Dom Fernando Gomes and Dom Eugênio Sales, who attempted to save the election. The bishop elected to be Secretary General, Dom José Gonçalves, was from Minas Gerais and had three main virtues: he was auxiliary to and intimate with Cardinal Dom Jaime, as it were, 'his man'; he was a bureaucratic type in Church affairs; and he knew German, which was important because the German bishops through Adveniat and Misereor were to finance the CNBB for the next five years. For President of the CNBB the group ran Dom Fernando Gomes, but he was defeated by Dom Agnelo Rossi of São Paulo, who was known to have no particular line of his own. Dom Fernando Gomes was again defeated for the positions of First and Second Vice-President, these positions being won by Dom Avelar Brandão and Dom Penedo. Thus the previous CNBB group was displaced from all the top positions; their places were taken by individuals who had no previous experience in the institution and no particular interest in the social involvement form of influence. This election represented a complete change in leadership, not just in individuals but in the character and type of leaders. Now a bureaucratic type headed the organization and none of his Vice-Presidents and advisors had any commitment to what the CNBB had previously represented. This was, of course, intentional and in terms of personnel alone the changes were great enough to transform completely the institution. In the less important positions of national secretariats, the CNBB group was able to maintain some continuity. Dom Helder was narrowly elected to be head of Social Action; Dom Fernando Gomes became head of Special Pastoral, Dom Padim of Education and Dom Eugênio Sales of Public Opinion.[38] But even with these personnel concessions, the CNBB was radically changed by the elections.

The structure of the pre-1964 CNBB was that of a small group of progressives with substantial independence from the larger Church body. It was a small elite leading and educating the rest, and as such could sponsor programs and represent the whole Church in social matters. At the VIth Assembly, however, the structure was radically changed and the name of Dom José D'Angelo Neto came up again. It is true that the CNBB began to decentralize gradually after 1962 and that there was a desire on the part of Dom Helder and his group to diversify and expand beyond the Northeast, but in Rome the institutional core in the Central Commission was expanded from 7 to 37, which meant that it could scarcely

---

[38] On results, see *Comunicado Mensal* Nos. 146–7 of November/December 1964. Dom Padim became part of the CNBB group by mid-1963.

function any longer. Instead of representing a progressive minority, it now included all the hierarchy.[39] The Central Commission was not intended to speak independently of the hierarchy, but only with their total agreement and, as the Secretary General told me, 'I am too official to take stands'.[40] Later the regions of the CNBB (its 13 territorial divisions formed after 1964) were emphasized to the detriment of the central organization and the whole operation was decentralized on the basis of these regions and the dioceses themselves. Structurally, therefore, the CNBB became precisely the sum of its parts: it was no longer 'supra-diocese' or 'supra-bishop' but an amalgam of these parts. As such, the CNBB could not be autonomous, progressive or lead an independent existence.

The most important CNBB program had been in its lay sector, the ACB. The ACB developed and became significant because of its national character and the autonomy granted it by the hierarchy through the CNBB. When conditions for institution-building in the CNBB disappeared, it followed that the ACB would also suffer. The first important decision made in Rome on the ACB was the election of Dom Vicente Scherer as national secretary of lay affairs. Dom Vicente was the most important Archbishop (today Cardinal) in the South, remained very concerned with Church authority and was not known to be especially interested in the laity or in Catholic Action. This election meant that a very influential member of the hierarchy who was not particularly concerned with the lay movement was now in charge of it. The next important decisions on ACB were made at the viith Assembly in late 1965, at a meeting called specifically to deal with the problem of the movement. At this meeting there were two distinct groups: the CNBB circle, including Dom Helder, Dom Padim, Dom Távora and Dom José Delgado, and the anti-group, including Dom José D'Angelo Neto, Dom Scherer, Dom Brandão and Dom Edmundo Kunz, who was one of Dom Vicente Scherer's auxiliary bishops in Pôrto Alegre. The former group attempted to relate ACB to recent decisions in the Council on the laity and the right of lay militants, as individuals, to take positions on temporal matters. The other group was disturbed by past problems, radicalism and compromises of the ACB and wanted the movement either controlled more closely by the hierarchy or done away with entirely.[41] The anti-group won; ACB was defined in a special way so that it was linked very tightly to the hierarchy and the militants consequently could not take positions on temporal concerns. Further, the movement was decentralized to the diocesan level and the national assistants removed. ACB

[39] As the change was explained in official statements: 'In October of 1964, the CNBB was restructured, with the intention of giving it a more collegial functioning, capable of responding to the new demands, new threats to the pastoral action, in this historical situation in which the country is found.' *Nacionais Informam*, 15 June 1967. Certainly it became more collegial in form but for this very reason could no longer respond. One of the CNBB bishops in June 1970 emphasized that the CNBB group had wanted to decentralize in order to broaden the base of the institution. However, he did admit that the opponents of the CNBB wanted to expand its central body in order to have it better 'represent' all the hierarchy. In São Paulo on 16 June 1970.

[40] Interview with Dom José Gonçalves in Rio on 17 November 1967.

[41] See *Comunicado Mensal* of October/December 1965, and June/July 1966.

was, therefore, right back to where it had been before 1950 and consequently was again destined to atrophy.

The ACB militants recognized the full significance of the decisions and at the XIVth meeting of JUC in Antônio Carlos, M.G. on 18–26 July, 1966, they declared their independence from the hierarchy and their commitment to an involvement in the milieu as individuals.[42] That is, they wanted nothing further to do with the hierarchy as an officially mandated organization. Dom Vicente Scherer responded to the JUC statement and made it very clear that ACB (specifically JUC and JEC) had been eliminated. In sum, with deinstitutionalization in the CNBB the conditions for a viable ACB disappeared.

The conclusion is clear that, with the removal of the conditions for institutionalization, the CNBB had to become simply one more organization in the Church. The decisions made by the Brazilian hierarchy in Rome regarding leadership, structure and ACB completely verified this conclusion. As might be expected, with the reintegration of the CNBB into the larger Church, both the state and the Holy See ceased cooperating with it. The pattern *vis-à-vis* the state fell into the traditional mold of bishops and clergy contacting their political intermediaries for particular benefits. And in regard to the Holy See, despite the increased legal jurisdiction of episcopal conferences, the CNBB decreased in jurisdiction, and the nuncio as well as the Roman Congregations bypassed it and dealt directly with the bishops once again.[43] In both respects, of course, the situation was different: the state was no longer the same and the nuncio had died.

There was much positive in the CNBB experience. It showed that at least a sector of the Church could adapt to a changing environment, respond to political threats and innovate. Regardless of the initial stimulus to response, I find enough to support a contention that the Church was assisting the marginal sectors of society. It is true, however, that the response was still on the basis of power and structures and no individual religious conversion, but given the definition of pre-influence the structural change would have had to occur either before or during the conversion process. There simply was not time for the strategy to reach the conversion stage for a judgment as to whether or not it ever would. The CNBB was the precursor of the Vatican II Church in Brazil but it was isolated, dismantled and its members scattered throughout the country. There was, therefore, no ready base for implementing the post-Vatican II Church in Brazil and at the same time a memory lived on of the positive things that the Church had done even before the Council. Arising out of the experience of the CNBB was the spark whereby the whole Church–state system would change and with it the definition of influence by means of power.

[42] See documents of XIV Conselho de JUC Antônio Carlos, M.G. 18–26 July 1966; 'Resolução', 'Síntese', 'Anexos I, II', Mimeo.
[43] Interview with religious sociologist working with CERIS in Rio on 30 June 1967.

6. Demands of the times and responses in the hierarchy

The CNBB was an anomaly in the larger Church because it was able to form new autonomy relationships with the Holy See and the Brazilian State. With its elimination the Church reverted to the concerns proper for the neo-Christendom body. The nature of these concerns becomes clear from the VIIIth General Assembly of the CNBB, which was held in Aparecida, São Paulo, in May 1967. The VIIIth meeting was the first since the Council; it came shortly after the very progressive encyclical 'Populorum Progressio', and was held at a time when widespread unemployment and misery suggested to some observers that social problems still existed despite the military coup. The meeting convened more than 200 bishops for a few days; it was by and large concerned with matters of internal Church administration and doctrine. They discussed 'The Year of the Faith', minor seminaries, presbyterial councils and the university pastoral. Dom Helder did present a statement on 'Populorum Progressio and Brazil', but there was little discussion and no public statement. Many observers realized that the Church, judging by this meeting, had retreated not only from social concerns but from all innovative activity. One journalist correctly noted that the meeting was an attempt to maintain coherence at the price of action. And another, who had been involved in the CNBB, analyzed the problem perceptively when he noted that the CNBB had once been a head without a body, but was now a body without a head.[1] This meeting, three years after the coup, merely verified what most observers already realized: there was no specific institutional means whereby the Church could relate to changes in the environment and in its absence the body would flounder.

There is no reason whatsoever to assume that the social processes which caused Church influence to deteriorate diminished after 1964. Further, whereas in the past the institution may have lacked religious influence, it was at least a viable organization and could mount political offences. After 1964, however, the combination of the Council, which created an awareness of problems and the need for 'renovation', and the coup, which forced a regression in the Brazilian Church, amounted to an institutional crisis to which the body was unable to respond.

The Second Vatican Council stimulated questioning of the very nature of the Church. This is not to say that the Council went beyond the advanced theologians of an earlier generation, such as Congar and Rahner, but in accepting their questions and studying their answers a great deal was in fact thrown up for debate. In Brazil, the Council was followed avidly, numerous books and articles being published on its every aspect and the implications for Brazil.[2] The Council

---

[1] Otto Engel in *Jornal do Brasil*, 4 May 1967. Other articles on the same topic by Engel and Frei Marcelino in *Jornal do Brasil* 18 May 1967.

[2] For example, see Frei Boaventura Kloppenburg and Frei Guilherme Baraúna, *As Grandes Tensões na Igreja Pós-Conciliar* (Petrópolis, R.J.: Editôra Vozes, 1969); Kloppenburg's orientation of *REB* on precisely the questioning line and his two volumes on the Council.

has not found an organizational basis in the Brazilian Church, but it certainly has stimulated a sense of uneasiness. In general terms of structures, for example, there is a questioning of the relevance of past forms. A meeting of regional secretaries of the CNBB noted in 1967, 'Society is changing each day more quickly and the ecclesiastical structures don't always accompany this change. The parish and the diocesan structures require, in a general sense, profound modifications.'[3] Many have concluded that the parish form in Brazil is not the most appropriate means whereby the link between the faithful and the institution can be made. So far, however, alternatives have been minor and still operate as pilot projects.[4]

The same sense of drift can be observed in the Church and education. The declaration on Christian education, 'Gravissimum Educationis', is but one of the Council's results related to the Church in education. The Council and subsequent meetings at all levels have gone against the orientation of traditional Church education in Brazil and thus against what for all intents and purposes is still being promoted. The resulting tension has led to a considerable amount of confusion regarding what should be done and what can be done, given the present compromises with the state in education.[5]

Brazil has always lacked vocations but today matters are even worse. What is important here is not the decree on the ministry and life of priests, 'Presbyterorum Ordinis', but simply the open-endedness of the Council itself. The traditional factors making for the small number of vocations have been joined and superseded by factors arising from questions of relevance and meaning. The Pro Mundi Vita study observes that the Church in Brazil 'is witnessing, powerless, a drastic drop in priestly vocations, perhaps because she has lost hope of finding a solution or because she is convinced of the uselessness of her work under present conditions'.[6] There seems to be unanimity that the problem with vocations is due to questions of relevance, meaning, goals and of faith itself. The problem of vocations is extremely serious in Brazil; more so than in Europe or other Latin American countries. In 1964, there were a total of 4,604 parishes for about 80 million Catholics.[7] Even this low number of parishes could not be fully staffed with priests. Five hundred and twenty-four had no priests at all and 860 lacked pastors.[8] There are about 12,500 priests in Brazil and while the population

---

[3] 'Regionals em Foco' in *Nacionais Informam* (CNBB publication) 10 March 1967.
[4] 'Both the Catholic Church as well as the classic Protestant Churches are incapable of penetrating and organizing the pastoral within the framework of their present institutions in the suburban regions and the industrial complexes where modern Brazil is being forged.' *Pro Mundi Vita*, 'Brazil: The Church in Process of Renewal', Bulletin No. 24, Brussels 1968, p. 59. See also CERIS series No. 6 on Parish and No. 7 on large cities and Pe. Raimundo Caramuru de Barros, *Comunidade Eclesial de Base: Uma Opção Pastoral Decisiva* (Petrópolis, R.J.: Editôra Vozes, 1967).
[5] Interview with head of education section of CRB in September 1967; interview with ex-head of Secondary Education in Rio on 6 March 1968.
[6] *PMV*, 'Brazil: The Church in Process of Renewal', p. 59.
[7] Compared to Portugal with 4,142 for 8 million; Spain with 19,562 for 30 million; France with 38,312 for 30 million; the U.S. with 18,000 for 40 million. *Ibid.*, p. 35.
[8] CERIS *Boletim* January 1967. See Michel Schooyans, *O Desafio da Secularização* (São Paulo: Editôra Herder, 1968), Chapter 6 on the 'recruitment crisis'.

increases some 3.1 % per year, the vocations are roughly 3 % per year. Interviews in various parts of Brazil suggest that vocations are considerably less than this, but even given the above figure the ratio of priest to parishioners grows worse. Suggestive is the case of São Paulo: with 6 million people and one priest per 4,589, in order to maintain this ratio during the next ten years there is a need for an additional 857 priests. However, in the 1957–66 period only 34 diocesan priests were ordained. Even if the numbers of new religious clergy were doubled or tripled, which is unlikely, the problem would be almost as serious. Foreign priests (43 % of the overall total) have been imported to help the Brazilian Church. However, for various reasons, including the same questioning after the Council, importations are decreasing and will continue to do so in the future. Priests are also leaving the ministry as never before. A conservative estimate is that between 1960 and 1967 120 priests left the active ministry; one would imagine that this number would increase in the future. With an already poor ratio of priest to parishioners, the Brazilian Church is entering an ever-deepening crisis of personnel.

Intricately related to the confusion generated by the Council are the results arising from the Church's reaction to the coup of 1964. Only by stretching the term beyond meaning could it be claimed that a laity exists in Brazil, when the term laity means a body of Christians connected to the institution by more than the sacraments and the cult. The vast majority of the faithful can be called 'massified', which denotes their ritualistic link to the Church. There are, of course, still traditional pious groups, but they have little meaning in the Church or in society. After the CNBB and ACB were virtually done away with there was no means whereby the layman could relate to the Church in any significant sense. Thus people who were mobilized before 1964 and who wanted to take the Council and its 'People of God' talk seriously simply had no place to go. The current mode is to form small groups of laymen, often with the support of an understanding priest, and to make 'little churches'. These laymen are estranged from the larger Church, become more and more distant, and the institution loses talents which were valuable before 1964 and could be so today. Whereas in most countries after the Council the role of the layman tended to increase, in Brazil it decreased, thereby forcing the layman out.[9]

Before 1967 the public campaign to demoralize the Church was directed mainly at Dom Jorge Marcos, Bishop of the proletarian city of Santo André outside São Paulo. In the press, in other media and by individual statements, a great deal of abuse was heaped upon the bishop without the other bishops realizing that the whole Church was suffering in the process and coming to his aid. In fact, a couple of the more important archbishops even joined in the

[9] See Thomas C. Bruneau, 'How to Demoralize the Laity', *America*, 22 June 1968; interviews with Pe. Angelo Pino, with lay section of CNBB, on 18 July 1967; a Msgr. in Recife who headed the local lay sector on 26 October 1968; a Bishop, activist in the hierarchy on 15 December 1967.

attack and thus became unwitting allies of enemies of the Church.[10] In early 1968 the campaign against progressive bishops spread to the Northeast, with the case of the misused German aid money. Many bishops in the area had received funds from Germany through Misereor and Adveniat to promote various types of projects. Some of these bishops wanted to increase the amounts and invested the funds in a semi-shady deal which turned out to be an outright swindle. They lost the money and enemies of the progressive elements made use of the issue to attack Dom Helder and others of his group, although they had not been involved at all. Given the facts of the case, and noting that Dom Helder had advised the bishops against playing with the funds, one can only agree with Dom Helder's public statement: 'It is nothing but a game to alienate the people from their pastors just at the time when the prelates come to demand basic reforms and to protest against those who think they are above the law.'[11] In sum, past social involvement and present statements by a few progressives have encouraged strategies on the part of conservative sectors which seek to tarnish the prestige of some elements in the Church, but in fact hurt the whole institution. Before the social involvement decade of Dom Helder and his group such attacks were unheard of, but today they are very common.

The combination of the effects of the Council and of the coup suggest that there are some serious problems facing the Brazilian Church. However, the two series do not combine by addition, but by multiplication, because of the contradiction in the results of the Council at precisely the same time that the coup made its effects on the Church obvious. While the Universal Church went ahead in statements and doctrine, the Brazilian Church retreated; while the layman was promoted in Rome, he was suppressed in Brazil; while bishops' conferences were given jurisdiction in Rome, in Brazil one was put down; while the progressives in most countries were encouraged by the Council, in Brazil they were isolated and attacked. While the Universal Church attempted to update its influence through the Council, in Brazil the critical mechanism for updating influence was eliminated. The contradiction and the many problems which have resulted from it, as well as the two events, add up to a real crisis in the institution.[12] This crisis occurs while the same social threats to Church influence remain. Thus when the Church needs most to respond to the changing environment, there are definite institutional impediments in doing so.

[10] See Dom Jorge's letter to Castelo Branco in May 1965; he was criticized in the press now and again by Cardinal Dom Rossi and Cardinal Dom Vicente Scherer for his positions.

[11] *Jornal do Brasil*, 18 January 1968. See also the article on this topic in *Visão*, 12 April 1968.

[12] See Michel Schooyans, *O Desafio da Secularização* (São Paulo: Editôra Herder, 1963), passim. The January 1970 number of *Limiar*, No. 25 is entitled 'Crisis in the Church?' and gives a useful discussion of different facets of this crisis. However, this discussion suffers from the same narrow focus and resulting optimism as does the otherwise excellent book of Thomas F. O'Dea, *The Catholic Crisis* (Boston: Beacon Press, 1968). O'Dea neglects the political dimension of impediments to change in the Church, as he focuses mainly on the Universal Church with particular reference to Europe and the United States. The 'crisis' that O'Dea analyzes is serious enough without the political dimension and given the optimism of the Council, but with politics added and a certain pessimism arising from the Brazilian Church's reaction at the time of the Council, it becomes much more serious.

One of the most serious results of the contradiction of Council theory and post-coup practice is the erosion of episcopal authority. Despite all the support for social involvement and the statements in Brazil by some bishops, there is really minimal action in pursuance of social change on the part of the whole Church. When younger clergy demand that the Church should play a more active role, they come up against their bishops and are rebuffed. As this happens the priests question authority, which is very clearly diminished because the bishops are caught in the contradiction between their theoretical guidelines and what they actually allow. The deterioration of authority has become manifest in the past few years with the publication of several letters from the clergy to their bishops. The most important of these letters was signed by 300 priests and published in the secular press on 24 October 1967. It protested against the social, religious and pastoral situation in Brazil and pointed precisely to the contradiction: 'the discrepancy between the doctrine of the Church and real action which doesn't correspond to this doctrine: the continuation of traditional action is a counter-testament'. The fact that the letter was published outright and not previously negotiated with the bishops indicates in itself a certain problem of authority.

Moreover, there have been at least two well-publicized cases in which the clergy were not willing to accept the nomination of a bishop with whom they did not see eye to eye. These instances, which took place in Botucatu, S.P., and Amargosa, Bahia, show that the episcopal jurisdiction over the clergy is weak, and the results of the cases suggest that it is definitely on the wane.[13] If the Church cannot rely on authority to keep the institution together, one wonders what there is to maintain coherence. To the outside observer the crisis is obvious and to many within the Church who are studying it or attempting to change it the crisis is also evident.

As noted previously, the basis of the Church is the diocese and the bishop 'is master in his diocese, under the authority of the Pope, and has legislative, judicial, and coercive power within the limits laid down by the law'.[14] With the elimination of the CNBB complete and total formal authority returned to the bishops, who, having rashly relinquished it earlier, resolved to be more cautious in the future. The authority was also increased, if only in tone, by the decisions of the Second Vatican Council which directed the hierarchy to stimulate renewal in their dioceses. Of the 2,217 discourses made during the Council, no less than 311 (14%) were on the nature and functions of the bishops.[15] In addition to the emphasis in the Universal Church on the role of the bishops, it is worth remembering that Brazil is a very elitist society. The point is important because unlike democratic societies, where the layman has broad opportunities for participation in civil society which may be reflected in spiritual society, in Brazil participation is very limited and there is little or no demonstration effect

[13] For documentation, see *Serviço de Documentação* (*SEDOC*) (Petrópolis, R.J.) May 1970.
[14] Metz, p. 106.
[15] Frei Boaventura Kloppenburg, 'A Perigosa Arte de Ser Bispo Hoje', in *REB* 27 (June 1967), p. 257.

between society and Church. In other words, the decision as to whether the Church will change rests almost entirely on the bishops. They themselves realize this fact, as they stated in a document on Church renovation: 'It is up to the hierarchy to begin it, to promote it, and to determine its character.'[16] Since the bishops are so critical in the Church and change, what can be expected from them? The bishops are central to any institutional study of the Church.[17]

To describe the hierarchy as a whole and to do this systematically, categories are useful. Administration involves relating the internal dynamics of an organization to a changing environment. As the elite of the Church, it is up to the bishops to direct this relationship. What primarily concerns me in Thompson's discussion of administration[18] are the limitations. The limitations are particularly useful because they include not only individual facets but also the systems or situations within which individuals operate. Critics of the bishops frequently fail to relate them to their environment and blame their shortcomings on purely personal features. Bishops are clearly not free agents; they operate within a context, are constrained by it, and while they have some room for innovation, it is extremely circumscribed.[19] The four limitations on administration are: when the organizational elite is sheltered and/or captive; the absence of an inner circle; a bias toward certainty; and a lack of knowledge or know-how. As all the data tend in the same direction there should be no difficulty in describing the limitations, categories or no.

The Brazilian episcopacy in 1966 consisted of 243 prelates in the following categories: 4 cardinal-archbishops, 32 archbishops, 122 residential or titular bishops, 37 auxiliary bishops, 41 prelates for the mission territories, 5 apostolic administrators, 1 abbot nullius and 1 bishop of the Ukrainian rite.[20] The total of 243 included some 65 (26.7%) who were born in 13 foreign countries; all

---

[16] Central Commission of 8–10 November 1966.

[17] I had fourteen long interviews with bishops in the initial field period and another five during my return visit in 1970. In addition I assembled all the available CERIS research on the bishops, did a content analysis from data in the *Anuário Católico*, *REB* and the special Vozes series on bishops, and verified my conclusions through interviews with members of the clergy and laity. Unfortunately nobody in Brazil has done anything as comprehensive as Sanders' study on the Chilean Episcopate. See Thomas G. Sanders, 'The Chilean Episcopate', a newsletter to Mr Richard H. Nolte of the Institute for Current World Affairs New York, 6 July 1968. Sanders interviewed 23 of the 29 Chilean bishops and obtained very significant results. The Brazilian hierarchy is ten times larger, more difficult to reach, and this investment of time and energy might not be necessary anyway.

[18] Thompson's discussion of 'administration' (Chapter 2) fits my data precisely. See James Thompson, *Organizations in Action* (New York: McGraw-Hill, 1967).

[19] A similar point concerning constraints on bishops' actions is made by John J. Kennedy in his study of Argentina. He notes that one bishop could oppose the government because he did not have a diocesan responsibility in Argentina. 'Had Andrea been governing a diocese, his attitude would probably have been the same, but his freedom of action as an individual might have been much less. The diocesan bishops were in a quite different position.' *Catholicism, Nationalism and Democracy in Argentina* (Notre Dame, Ind.: University of Notre Dame Press, 1958), p. 205.

[20] Deelen, 'O Episcopado Brasileiro', p. 310 supplemented from more recent CERIS data. See also *Realidade* (January 1970) for a series on the cardinals which is popularized but useful for an insight into their personalities.

41 of the prelates for the mission territories are foreign-born. Generally these 65 are not distinguished by any particular characteristics, at least not in episcopal politics, and here they are included as a neutral body within the general discussion.

The bishops tend to be sheltered from competition and from contact with the 'real world'. In taking seriously the figure of 94% of the population with a Catholic religious affiliation, the bishops seem to think they have a virtual monopoly on things religious. In this misleading sense, the bishops simply do not perceive competition. The pre-1964 political threats are gone and today co-operation with the Protestants is officially encouraged, so they are less frequently considered as competition. Apart from the institutional aspect of low competition, however, the isolation of the bishops from real life must also be discussed.

The bishops are quite isolated in their dioceses and have very little contact beyond their strictly circumscribed worlds. An article in the bishops' journal (*REB*) suggests the same thing: 'It isn't just a few Brazilian dioceses whose bishops still embody the figure of members of the nobility – untouchable, divorced from the people to whom they only incline their heads.'[21] Or, as a work on bishops and priests noted in an interview with a professor in a major seminary: 'The bishops are alienated from the Brazilian reality.'[22] There is a good deal of agreement on the observation that bishops are sheltered to a considerable degree from the outside world.

The majority of the present bishops were trained in seminaries, which patterned their programs and education according to the Modernism scare of the early part of this century. By design, therefore, they were removed from the world and taught that it was to be approached only with extreme caution. The education they received in these seminaries was based on a formalistic classical orientation which gave a set interpretation to all reality, without the necessity of experiencing this reality through direct contact.[23] Once graduated and ordained, most of those who would later become bishops were involved in the Church bureaucracy (curia, seminary work, etc.) rather than direct pastoral duties in the parishes. The most common channel of recruitment to the hierarchy was through managerial positions in the seminaries, since these were important for the bishop and he would thus put the priests 'of confidence'. Deelen's data on the bishops support the existence of a lack of contact in the pastoral. In analyzing positions held immediately before becoming bishop, Deelen found that of the 243 only 73 had been in direct pastoral roles and of these 63 were either pastors or vicars of cathedrals; again, a position which involves little but administration.[24] An interesting light can be brought to bear on the CNBB group when it is noted that a good many of them had been involved in the Catholic Action movement before becoming bishops. At least two of them

---

[21] Kloppenburg, 'A Perigosa Arte de Ser Bispo Hoje', in *REB* 27 (June 1967), p. 278, quoting from *Visão*, 28 April 1967.
[22] Deelen, unpublished manuscript.
[23] Interview with a bishop in Fortaleza on 12 January 1968; he had done a study of the classical routines in seminaries.
[24] Deelen, 'O Episcopado Brasileiro', p. 319.

attributed their 'more enlightened perspectives' to their experience in a direct pastoral relationship with students and workers.[25]

On becoming bishops the vast majority move into a settled role in a generally static rural diocese. Usually the bishop comes from the same area, and when he takes over his position he automatically becomes a notable in the area, does not face an active clergy or laity and relates to the other power elements in the region as one of them: police, civil and religious. In short, the long path of isolation from seminary to diocese is maintained with few deviations along the way. The bishops are, in Merton's terms, locals and not cosmopolitans, and information on transfers bears out this appellation. Of the 243, at least 152 have never been transferred, and of the 91 who have the move is usually within the same regional area.[26]

The bishops tend to be captive in their local situations and systems of control. Just as the Church in the neo-Christendom model lacks independence from the government, the same applies to the bishop in his diocese. This means that the bishop not only fits into a role in local society, but is in fact strictly constrained by it, largely because of his own background. There is enough sociological material to support the contention that those who achieve considerable social mobility tend to be satisfied with the *status quo*. In some Latin American countries it is assumed that the hierarchy is drawn from the upper middle class. In Brazil the bishops come from predominantly lower middle-class families. Further, they are predominantly from the rural area. Deelen in his analysis found that of the 178 native bishops only 36 were from the capitals of states. The rural orientation of the bishops is in fact far greater than this and they are usually from regions far removed from active society. And, depending upon the area, many of them are from first or second generation immigrant families.[27] This combination of factors means that achieving the position of bishop, even in a nondescript diocese, is a considerable gain in prestige and social status. In short, having moved so far up the hierarchy, they are much less likely to question the circumstances within which they and the institutional Church operate. Interestingly enough, one informant, a bishop's aide, suggested that this particular bishop's higher class origin made it far easier for him to bring about changes in his diocese. She contrasted him to other bishops of lower class background, who would have had great difficulty in doing the same thing.[28]

The relatively satisfied bishops inhabit a structure which has traditional commitments to the local power structure. The diocese, like the parish, is largely integrated with the society around it, supports this society and receives

[25] Interviews with Dom José Delgado on 10 January 1968, and Dom David Picão on 15 December 1967. Dom Helder had been a priest of this kind as were Dom Távora, Dom Padim, Dom Fernando Gomes and Dom Maria Pires.
[26] Deelen, 'O Episcopado Brasileiro', p. 321 for figures; Robert K. Merton, *Social Theory and Social Structure* (New York: The Free Press, 1957), pp. 393–403.
[27] See *Realidade* for descriptions of the immigrant background of Cardinals Rossi and Scherer.
[28] Interview with Maria de Lourdes Santos, secretary to Dom Eugênio Sales, in Salvador on 21 October 1967.

resources from it. The bishop has his clearly defined role in the local situation, which he is unlikely to question or confront. A crisis occurs when a bishop, for one reason or another, attempts to assert his independence. A good study of this would be the case of Dom Picão (a second generation CNBB group type). This bishop attempted to assert his independence from the landed elements in the diocese in order to bring about the formation of unions. In doing so he encountered direct opposition from the local power structure, which he resisted. The question is not why he resisted, but rather whether the same reaction on the part of local elements would follow in every case where the bishop tried to assert his independence. The reaction would indeed follow and in this case the bishop was later transferred, although there are contradictory views on the reasons for the move.[29] In later chapters the lack of autonomy of bishops and dioceses will be further illustrated, but here I can conclude by stating that the bishops do indeed tend to be captive: their roles in local communities are well-defined before arrival; the expectations are clear; and given their backgrounds the bishops are not prone to question their captivity, because it is a pleasant one.

The bishops are definitely biased towards certainty. The hierarchy is very largely composed of individuals who might be called 'organization men', in that they fully accept the norms and values of the institution and consequently are certain in their adherence. McKenzie notes that the Church generally elevates to the bishopric those priests who have been considered 'safe'. If anything, this characteristic is heightened in Brazil because of the monopoly position of the religion and the recognition of the bishops' high social position. If there is any sociological truth in the research project which showed that priests have the third highest occupational prestige in Brazil, then bishops must surely be placed higher than the scale could measure.[30] One informant noted that the bishops do not tolerate ambiguity or innovation: 'The bishops want everything from Rome, already worked out, without confusion, and anyone who attempts to innovate is not to be trusted.' The data suggest some reasons why the bishops may be so certain. It can be assumed that older people, and particularly those who have been within an institution for a considerable period, are more likely to be sure or certain. Some 72.4% of the bishops are over 50 years of age and 32.5% are over 60.[31] To the factor of age must be added some information on those individuals who are nominated for the position of bishop in the first place.

Several interviews with bishops and important members of the clergy indicate that those who are nominated are known for staunch defense of the faith, clear records, lack of notoriety and balance. In other words, those who become bishops are the most certain in the institution; true organization men who do not

[29] Interview on 20 June 1967 with religious sociologist who studied the diocese. He said that the transfer was due to the reaction. Dom Picão said otherwise, that he was in fact promoted; interview on 15 December 1967.
[30] McKenzie, p. 73; Bertram Hutchison, 'The Social Grading of Occupations in Brazil', pp. 176–89.
[31] More specifically, those aged 60 and over constitute 32.5%; those between 50 and 59 39.9%; 40–49 23.8%; and 30–39 1.6%. Deelen, 'O Episcopado Brasileiro', p. 316.

question.[32] No one doubts the faith and dedication of the hierarchy, but there is some question whether this suffices in a changing society.

The bishops lack knowledge or know-how in areas which might assist change or, for that matter, which might corrode their certainty. As one bishop voluntarily pointed out: 'The Brazilian hierarchy, like the society itself, is underdeveloped.'[33] It must be pointed out that their educational background is rather limited. Of the 243 only two have bachelor of arts degrees, in science and letters. There are no degrees at all in such fields as social science, history and so forth – not to mention technology or science. In philosophy there are one *licenciado* (between a B.A. and an M.A.) and six doctorates; in theology, there are five *licenciado* and ten doctorates. In analyzing this data Deelen concludes that 'While we don't have an episcopacy composed of bishops specialized in other areas, beyond philosophy and theology, pastoral changes are more difficult. Apparently, because of the method, there is a great difficulty for the theologican to penetrate sociological and psychological motives in pastoral reflection.'[34] Clearly some of the bishops who are younger and who have been involved in particular programs have developed their ability in many fields. Most of these, however, are in the CNBB group or are among those who follow the same lines. For the most part, the clergy and laity in positions of advisors to the hierarchy noted that the bishops were simply ignorant of much which would facilitate an understanding of change and direction. In sum, the bishops are clearly lacking in the sort of knowledge which is necessary for administration.

The episcopacy lacks a single inner core or inner circle because it was eliminated in 1964. Thompson states that, 'The organization with dispersed bases of power is immobilized unless there exists an effective inner circle.'[35] The Church does indeed have a dispersed basis of power. There is what might be termed 'an inner circle' in the Northeast among probably twenty bishops who are centred around Dom Helder. Another such circle exists in the South around Dom Vincente Scherer. Beyond these two, and including the national level, there is no inner circle and precious little coordination.[36]

The conclusion which can be drawn from this discussion of the bishops as a group is obvious. Because of background, formation, the nature of the institution and the sociological position of the Church in society, the bishops individually are not well-suited to innovate and respond. As a result of their close ties with their local situations and because it lacks an inner core, the hierarchy is not capable of acting in new, and potentially disruptive, ways.

At this point, it is useful to offer a case study to illustrate how the hierarchy does in fact act and the implications of this action for Church influence. The

---

[32] Interviews with Dom Tiago Cloin on 20 October 1967; Dom Valfredo Teppe on 19 October 1967; and Msgr. José Maria Tapajós on 2 August 1967.
[33] Interview with Dom Tiago Cloin on 20 October 1967.
[34] Deelen, 'O Episcopado Brasileiro', p. 323.
[35] Thompson, p. 141.
[36] This assertion is supported by Frei Francisco Rolim's, 'Estrutura da Igreja', unpublished research report for CERIS, 1968, pp. 187–96.

following description of some events and issues in São Paulo should demonstrate that the Church is in a dynamic situation which poses threats to influence, that bishops respond poorly in not exercising leadership and that a reliance on traditional responses is bound to fail. São Paulo was selected for several reasons: the city is not only the largest in Latin America, but is also the biggest diocese in the world; the social processes of industrialization, urbanization and communications which take place there now represent what will be happening elsewhere in Brazil in the future; from 1964 until his appointment to the Sacred Congregation for the Evangelization of the Peoples in Rome in late 1970 the Cardinal-Archbishop was President of the CNBB, which nominally represents the third largest hierarchy in the world; what was happening to the Church between 1967 and 1970 was obvious and widespread among observers. The problems of 'administration' or leadership are similar throughout the Brazilian Church; what makes them outstanding in São Paulo is the fact that the city is so big, busy and complex in all respects and everything is exaggerated and laid bare.[37] One informant touched upon this point in an arresting way by contrasting the very successful tenure of the Cardinal-Archbishop while he was bishop in Volta Redonda with his period in São Paulo and noted that he was a bishop suited for a small town.

Shortly after the coup the Cardinal-Archbishop of São Paulo (Dom Carlos Carmelo Motta) was transferred to the nearby town of Aparecida and was replaced by Dom Agnelo Rossi. Dom Rossi was elected President of the CNBB in October 1964, both because he was Archbishop of São Paulo and because he was known to have no particular orientation: he was neither progressive nor reactionary and had never been in the CNBB group. In early 1965 Dom Rossi was made Cardinal; thus within a year he had become the most important member of the hierarchy, as he was Cardinal-Archbishop of the largest city and head of the CNBB.

Dom Rossi, in not adhering to any particular set of orientations, kept well within the traditional lines. He sought to maintain a 'balance' and was therefore non-innovative, non-controversial and malleable. For example, the Cardinal met on frequent public occasions with military and civilian government leaders, as was Church custom. At one point a group of businessmen were promoting a venture to make the shrine of the national patron in Aparecida (where Cardinal Carlos Carmelo Motta is located) into a paying affair. The gist of the proposal was to exploit popular religious sentiment for financial gain and neither the Cardinal in Aparecida nor the order entrusted with the shrine were in favor of the plan. Despite these obstacles, Dom Rossi visited the headquarters of the business group on 6 January 1968 and gave his public and official blessing to the plan. Literally scores of other illustrations could be offered to show how the Cardinal

---

[37] The population estimate for 1970 is 6,600,000. In 1967 São Paulo had 253 parishes, 1,625 priests and 2,300 female religious. For data on São Paulo and other Latin American cities see Segundo Galilea *et al.*, *Pastoral de Grandes Cidades* (Petrópolis, R.J.: Editôra Vozes, 1967). My interviews in São Paulo were extensive. Those interviewed included three bishops, about a dozen priests, several nuns and a score of lay people involved at all levels of the Church.

fitted into the strictly traditional mold of the Brazilian Church: he had no particular orientation and was thus available for friendly contacts with business and government without much apparent concern for the subsequent abuse of Church prestige. Balance here implied an absence of controversy within the old expectations of society and the Church.

Behavior of this type might have been sensible before the 1950s, but after the Council and a decade of CNBB type of activities it was positively detrimental to influence. One case arises from the imprisonment in 1967 of students who attended a meeting of the illegal União Nacional dos Estudantes. The seminarians in the order seminary Instituto de Filosofia e Teologia (IFT) protested against the behavior of the military police by picketing the police headquarters. The Cardinal would not allow the seminarians in the secular seminary to participate, but several did nonetheless. This demonstrated for those involved that the Cardinal was more concerned with the appearance of order and good relations with the police than with a fairly obvious case of injustice; many seminarians questioned his authority.[38]

Another long series of cases can be illustrated from the relationship of Dom Rossi with the outspoken bishop of the nearby town of Santo André, Dom Jorge Marcos. At one point Dom Jorge was asked by the managers of an automobile plant in his diocese to celebrate mass in the factory. The bishop refused to do so until the poor working conditions were improved. The managers then contacted Dom Rossi who said mass there without any questions asked.[39] Again, this instance reinforced many observers' view that the Cardinal was more concerned with order and the traditional links with the society than with his own brothers in the hierarchy or questions of social justice. It is evident that the Cardinal, in attempting to follow the traditional role of a bishop in a complex and dynamic situation, is bound to create more problems than he solves.

Even on less controversial and purely internal matters, the Cardinal's strategy of doing little and doing it traditionally could not succeed in securing Church influence. To respond to the problems of size and complexity, the Cardinal divided his archdiocese into six episcopal regions and created 50 new parishes. That is, he offered a simple bureaucratic solution to the problems of bringing influence to bear, even when almost everyone in the Brazilian Church had concluded that the parish structure was outdated and ineffective. Although President of the CNBB for six years, the Cardinal did not support the body or its planning program in his archdiocese.[40] In 1965 a plan was prepared by several priests to organize and adapt the Church in the archdiocese. The Cardinal, however, refused to approve it because it involved a clear commitment to Church change, which he was unwilling to accept. By 1970 the regional CNBB had effectively disintegrated. The Cardinal had put a bishop in charge of the body who was very conservative in all respects and not at all involved. Further, the

[38] Interview with teacher in the IFT in Rio on 5 March 1968; interestingly enough on my return in June 1970, the Cardinal had closed down IFT.
[39] Interview with activist in the clergy in São Paulo on 15 February 1968.
[40] Interview with coordinator of planning of CNBB on 25 August 1967.

Cardinal, in not supporting the body, simply starved it financially and in personnel. Those still in the CNBB in São Paulo were convinced that the CNBB had died because of the Cardinal's lack of support and even active opposition at times. What becomes very clear in São Paulo is that the traditional episcopal approach to administration or leadership is not functioning. Even one of the auxiliary bishops, not a radical one at that, stated that the Church is falling behind in its attempts to keep up with change in the city.[41] São Paulo is an exaggerated example of the Church in a changing society faced with a serious institutional crisis. Cardinal Dom Rossi is no worse than many bishops and probably more conscientious than most. He has even been forward and outspoken at times, but then seems constrained because of his past and that of the institution. Given the social and political changes, the Council and coup, the institutional crisis and weak religious influence, the traditional pastoral line simply cannot succeed, but it is difficult to see how any individual bishop can supersede it without external support from some other institution. Cardinal Dom Rossi did not supersede it, for he was 'kicked upstairs' and out of harm's way in October 1970.[42]

When the Brazilian bishops were assembled in Rome for the second session of the Council (1965), they not only voted to dismember the CNBB but paradoxically approved a five-year plan which had as its goal: 'To create means and conditions so that the Church in Brazil can adjust, as rapidly and as fully as possible, to the image of the Church of Vatican II.'[43] That is, they simultaneously eliminated the institution which most closely represented the Church of Vatican II and adopted a plan which sought to implement this form through 'the organic and global renovation of the Church'. Between 1966 and 1971 this plan was to be the predominant focus or coordinating center for the whole Church in Brazil. A review of the plan's origins in the pre-1964 CNBB and the role of the Holy See explains this paradox.

In the two letters from Pope John XXIII to the hierarchies of Latin America in which he stressed the role of the Church in social concerns, the Pope also suggested that the bishops should formulate plans to respond to the demands of the times. The CNBB of Dom Helder responded to the appeal and at the vth General Assembly of April 1962 adopted a rough draft of a project which was entitled the 'Emergency Plan'. This plan was to be of limited duration; it dealt only with selected areas of Church renewals and its implementation was entrusted specifically to the CNBB.[44]

The Emergency Plan lapsed in 1964 and was replaced by the Plano de Pastoral de Conjunto (PCC), as a logical continuation which showed both elaborations

---

[41] Interview with Dom José Lafayette in São Paulo on 15 December 1967.

[42] Most people in Brazil seemed to think that the Pope was giving support to the more progressive elements by this move. See even the *New York Times*, 21 October 1970. His replacement was his best auxiliary, Dom Paulo Evaristo Arns, who so far seems very astute.

[43] CNBB, *Plano de Pastoral de Conjunto 1966–1970* (Rio de Janeiro: Livraria Dom Bosco Editôra, 1966), p. 25.

[44] 'It is a plan centralized around the CNBB.' 'Plano de Emergência,' *Cadernos da CNBB* No. 1, 1962, p. 11.

and improvements. It was a five-year plan, provided for the division of the country into 13 regions, stipulated an extensive research program through CERIS for a discovery of social and religious problems, and through six main lines of activity aimed at the total renewal of the Brazilian Church 'in the image of Vatican II'. A review of the PPC documents and extensive interviews indicated that the PPC was a plan but did not involve planning. 'Planning' means a process whereby a rational system of choices is related to several alternatives, and planning cannot be separated from implementation. The PPC was an alien venture, without any real body to implement it and with goals so amorphous that there was no possible way to enact them, even if the whole Church agreed. There was no selectivity in aspirations, no specific provision for support and most of the hierarchy remained uncommitted. Basically the PPC is a response to the plea of Pope John XXIII, a logical continuation of the Emergency Plan and a statement of optimistic intent; it was most certainly not planning.[45]

Despite the deficiencies of the PPC, many priests had great expectations of its potential effects. Those responsible for the PPC at the national and regional levels believed that the processes of the PPC would generate commitments in the hierarchy. The PPC was formally the main focus of the Church for five years (1966–71), involved all levels of the body and drew on the thought and action of a great many good people at the national and regional levels.[46]

Originally the PPC was a continuation of a pre-1964 CNBB plan encouraged by the Pope, but most of the bishops had little interest in it and no commitment to its vague and ambiguous goals. In order to analyze the possibilities for the PPC to generate commitments to its goals and to expand its institutional basis, it is useful to organize the data according to a set of categories: initial character and expansion of the central organization; importance of the tasks assigned to the organization; and degree of expansion of these tasks. On the basis of these categories a rapid evaluation can be made of the PPC's potential in assisting the hierarchy to overcome its many constraints.[47]

The central organization entrusted with implementing the PPC was the CNBB. In the last chapter I showed how the bishops withdrew their authority, so that its functions became strictly limited. Functions within the CNBB regarding the PPC have been divided in such a way that the organization could not develop so as

---

[45] See the critique of the PPC as planning in *PMV*, 'Brazil: The Church in Process of Renewal', pp. 57–8.

[46] My research on the PPC *vis-à-vis* the CNBB was extensive. I interviewed and reinterviewed all those involved at the national levels and interviewed at least once, sometimes two or three times, those involved in 8 of the 13 regions. These interviews concerned people at all levels of the institution, from archbishops downwards. Then too I reviewed all the publications of the PPC–CNBB and any secondary literature that was available.

[47] These categories are informed by the concepts and conclusions of the literature on political integration. A comparison between dioceses and nation states is not as far-fetched as it might seem at first and at the minimum the categories are applicable. For an introduction to this literature see Leon Lindberg, *The Political Dynamics of European Economic Integration* (Stanford: Stanford University Press, 1963), and Ernst B. Haas, 'International Integration: The European and the Universal Process', *International Organization* 15 (Summer 1961), pp. 366–93.

to increase the commitments of bishops. From 1964 until 1968 the Secretary-General, Dom José Gonçalves, maintained a strict bureaucratic and legalistic interpretation of the organization and its roles. A priest, Pe. Raimundo Caramuru de Barros, was in charge of implementing the PPC and had little support or cooperation from the larger organization. Had the CNBB been serious about the PPC they would have put a bishop in charge and given him some authority; this was not the case and the link between plan and organization was very tenuous. Indicative of the CNBB's neglect of the plan is the viiith Assembly in Aparecida in May 1967. This was the first meeting of the Assembly since the PPC was adopted, yet in the reports of the meeting there was no mention of the plan, which was supposed to provide the main focus and orientation of the CNBB during the 1966–71 period.[48] If the connection between the CNBB, the bishops and the PPC has been so weak then why do the bishops support the plan? In fact, they do not. The German bishops have been financing the PPC through Adveniat; the Brazilian bishops contribute but a small share of the expenses.[49]

There were changes, however, between 1968 and June 1970. During these two years a new Secretary-General, Dom Aloísio Lorscheider, who had begun as a fairly uncommitted bishop, promoted the development of the CNBB. Through his efforts, the CNBB became more dynamic and assumed a larger role than it had during the previous four years. In addition, he linked the promotion of the PPC more closely with the organization itself and at the national level at least there was some growth in functions. Further, in the 1969 and 1970 General Assemblies of the CNBB the plan was studied and approved for further elaboration, and the CNBB was restructured. Now instead of the structural estrangement between the plan and the organization there is a central body of nine bishops, of which three handle administration and six the pastoral plan. In short, immediately after the PPC was adopted, there was no growth in the central organization and the plan was not linked to what remained. However, from 1968 on there has been some development of an organization and it seems that with the recent restructuring there will be more of the same.[50]

In theory the PPC encompasses all tasks related to renovating the Brazilian Church in the image of Vatican ii. In the plan itself, the implementation of these tasks is formally divided into six main lines of pastoral action, which are further formally subdivided into approximately 30 smaller assignments.[51] In fact, however, the tasks that the PPC has been working on are of a most limited and insignificant nature. The priest in charge of the plan up until 1968 told me in 1970, after his departure from Brazil and the priesthood, 'The plan couldn't deal

---

[48] See *Telepax*, No. 98 of 12 May 1967 and No. 99 of 31 May 1967 on the meeting.

[49] Interview with Dom José Gonçalves on 17 November 1967. The Germans gave $1,045,154 for five years of the plan; *PMV* 'Brazil: The Church in Process of Renewal', p. 55 notes that it is largely foreign financed.

[50] Interviews with three bishops, two priests and one layman involved in the plan in 1970 suggest that the organization has a dynamic quality which is likely to increase.

[51] CNBB, *Plano de Pastoral de Conjunto 1966–1970*, pp. 51–89 or *PMV*, 'Brazil: The Church in Process of Renewal', pp. 55–7.

with social issues because of previous controversies and thus it focused exclusively on internal matters.'[52]

Without exception, the sectors implemented were catechism and liturgy. Those ignored were the laity and social action. Catechism is not very significant in the overall process of renewal in the Church. Certainly it is good to update methods of training and dissemination of information, but in the various regions most bishops emphasize the catechism part of the PPC simply because it requires minimal commitments; it was the least controversial section of the plan. The same attitudes apply to the plan and liturgy; most of the regions adopted the sections on liturgy and even sent their personnel to liturgy courses sponsored by Instituto Superior para Pastoral de Liturgia (ISPAL). The priest in charge of the ISPAL stated that what the bishops meant by liturgy was simply the traditional doctrine with the same emphasis on rote learning. The bishops were willing to adopt the plan's section on liturgy as long as it fitted traditional patterns; when it diverged into something new or important, it ran into direct opposition.[53] In short, liturgy is acceptable as long as it does not become an important task.

Mobilization of the laity is clearly a vital task in the Brazilian Church. Today the Movimento Familiar Cristão (MFC) is really the only group which is actively encouraged, mainly because it is composed of well-established couples and is thus 'safe'. The archbishop who was in charge of the section of the PPC dealing with the subject, Dom Vicente Scherer, is not known for his interest in the laity, and his secretary in the CNBB informed me that 'there is no plan for the layman'.[54] This priest left his position with the PPC after more than a year of frustration. Very few of the 13 regions have anyone in charge of the section on the laity, and when they do it is usually someone organizing the traditional pious groups. This section on the laity has been so neglected that even official CNBB documents, which are usually euphoric about everything, point out the bishops' neglect. 'We can say that the promotion of the layman will require new approaches for its implementation. What has been done – even the new perspectives – appear timid in the face of the demands of the moment and of the options to be taken.'[55]

Since the CNBB was put down in 1964 mainly because of its role in social action, this is another facet which was previously important but is negligible today. In the 1965 elections in Rome Dom Helder Câmara was made head of the social action sector of the PPC, but because of conditions in the hierarchy and in the politics of the country he could not fill a national role. Instead he worked locally within his archdiocese of Olinda-Recife and internationally to promote the role of the Church in social change. His secretary in the CNBB could not find enough support from the Brazilian bishops and left in late 1967.[56] He was replaced by another priest, who has many commitments locally and on a

[52] Interview with Raimundo Caramuru de Barros in Montreal, Canada, on 7 November 1970.
[53] Interview with Pe. Domingos Sanchis on 26 March 1968.
[54] Interview with Pe. Pino on 18 July 1967.
[55] 'Regionais em Foco', of Nacionais Informam of 15 March 1968, p. 16.
[56] Interview with Pe. Gonzaga Melo on 22 July 1967.

continental basis in CELAM. Nationally no PPC program exists dealing with social action and most regions have done nothing at all in this area. (Bahia and Recife are exceptions.) The trend today is for individual bishops to promote social action programs in their dioceses, which means that the CNBB group do and all the rest do not.

Between 1968 and 1970 there was some change in personnel in the various national secretariats, but programs for the laity and social action were still neglected. Although not directly linked to the plan as such, these topics of laity and social action are now discussed in the national and regional meetings, so that a strong possibility exists that they will be introduced into the plans. Even now, however, the tasks are not significant; this is deliberate policy on the part of the bishops, because they do not wish to give up any authority or become involved in controversial programs.

In the case of the PPC expansiveness would mean that in attempting to reach a goal of low commitment, such as liturgy reform, the bishops would be forced to rethink and then change other sectors, such as the seminaries; to do this they would have to restructure the local curias and so forth. Any plan, including the PPC, can be formally adopted but implemented in such a manner as merely to reinforce the traditional pattern. A very good example of reinforcement exists in the CNBB division in the state of Paraná. Here they adopted the PPC in its formal aspects, but not in spirit. Thus the sections dealing with social action meant just the traditional charities and orphanages, the laity sector was translated into pious associations, public opinion meant the diocesan papers, and so forth.[57]

A very thorough and impressive study has been carried out by a sociologist priest, Frei Francisco Rolim, O.P., of the effects of PPC programs on local structures. Since the Church in Brazil is really just the sum of all the local and regional units, what applies at this level adds up to the national level. Rolim studied 38 parishes in 5 dioceses and looked at PPC programs such as parish councils, administrative councils, presbyterial councils and pastoral councils, as well as social works, religious associations and interdiocesan relations.[58]

He studied the way in which the new structural aspects of the PPC programs had transformed the traditional structures and relationships. His conclusion, after analyzing a good deal of data, is that they have not transformed these traditional elements, but have been incorporated within them. In guarded terms (since the document is destined for the bishops), he observes:

These new things, like the parish pastoral council, diocesan pastoral council or even the so-called basic communities, might well involve a strategy of simple imitation, or the addition of the new to the old, and do not imply any transformation of structure at all.

[57] Interview with pastoral coordinator in November 1967 and also a review of the sections' documents.
[58] Frei Francisco Rolim, O.P., 'Estrutura da Igreja no Brasil', unpublished research report No. 1.2 of PPC of CNBB. (Rio de Janeiro: CERIS, 1968). For summaries of the same material see 'Igreja em Dimensão Estrutural', *Convergência* 1:7 (August/September 1968), pp. 14–18; and 'Estrutura da Igreja no Brasil', *Paz e Terra* 2:6 (April 1968), pp. 35–49.

Only to the point that they can originate new relations can they create conditions for structural transformations.[59]

The local versions of the PPC are not expansive because they are mere imitations of a national plan, which is not really implemented.

They try to follow the general lines of a plan or a model which has not come from the local reality. They transfer, in this way, a great part of the responsibility for what is done. The imitative process, because it is not creative, ends up reduced to the traditional line. And what is put forward as renovated ends up non-renovated.[60]

The tasks of the PPC are not expansive and they may be detrimental to any innovation. That is, many elements in the Church seem to adopt the plan and then presume that they have made the 'renovated Church', the 'Church of Vatican II'. They are not encouraged to innovate on their own and in fact are positively discouraged, due to the misconception that there is nothing left to be done. In a sense Frei Rolim makes the same observation when he notes that in one of the five dioceses some of the goals of the PPC are being attained but the plan itself is not being followed. What was important here was not the plan but a willingness on the part of the bishop to bring about change in his local Church.[61] In sum, the manner of implementation does not encourage the expansion of tasks associated with the PPC; perhaps they could be expansive, but it most certainly does not follow automatically. In 1970 there was more discussion about the plan, its structures, the need for renovation and so forth, but it did not seem to be expanding in actual implementation. Seemingly, the initial commitments were so low that expansion was not possible, let alone necessary.

The overall conclusion from this review of the PPC in terms of commitments and expansion is mixed. Initially, at least until 1968, there was no increasing commitment and no growth of a central institution. However, with the changes in leadership, and because of strategies of persuasion which will be discussed later on, the central organization has taken on new life and the plan is apparently being seriously considered. However, up to now the plan has not really caught on; the commitments are still largely formalistic or only being discussed; and its components do not seem to involve much institutional growth aside from the present personalities of the leadership. Even with more activity at the central level, it does not seem likely that the bishops will allow their authority to be absorbed into the national organization. The main impediments to commitment and institutional development seem to lie in the memory of past compromises and the ensuing problems, a premature focus on exclusively internal and bureaucratic matters and a minimal initial commitment to the goals of the organization. Therefore, while the CNBB and PPC will probably continue, they still will not come to represent that institutional core or platform whereby the Church can be lifted from its present predicament and propelled to change in order to increase its influence.

[59] Rolim, 'Estrutura da Igreja', p. 214.
[60] *Ibid.*, p. 205.
[61] *Ibid.*, pp. 164–9.

7. Strategies for the promotion of change in the church

In the pre-1964 period there were few explicit strategies for promoting change in the Church. The innovators already had an institutional basis in the CNBB and ACB and related organizations, so that the question did not concern change *per se*, but rather its specific direction. With the coup, regression in the institutional Church and the lack of a central core to promote reforms and change, the innovators came to realize that it was up to them to transform the Church. The bishops and the institution in general first had to be convinced of the need for change before anything significant could be expected. Two main strategies of change emerged.

The groups described in this chapter do not feel that the Brazilian Church has been completely unresponsive to internal and external demands for change. Indeed mass is now said in the vernacular; there is a great deal of talk of renewal and renovation; the hierarchy is committed (formally at least) to renewal through the PPC; some seminaries are modifying their programs; there is debate over a different Church role in education; and so forth. These innovators feel that the Church has an important role to play in Brazil but profound and rapid change is necessary before it will be able to act. They total no more than 500 at all levels of the Church; this estimate excludes those who have left the Church, either out of apathy or to fight 'the system' with more flexibility. It also excludes those who are still satisfied with the Church and its role in society, as well as those who were satisfied but are now mobilized in order to fight against change and the change agents. A comprehensive study of the current actions in the Church's pursuit of change suggests that categories – arbitrary though they may seem to the individuals included – are sufficient to describe the most essential ingredients.[1]

Although trying to achieve similar goals, the innovators follow different strategies according to their perception of the nature of the Church and its involvement in society and politics. The goals are alike because most of the personnel come from similar backgrounds in youth movements, social action programs and groups in the hierarchy. Also, the goals and their attainment are at a very rudimentary level, as there has not been sufficient stimulus to further differentiate them. Those following the 'people' strategy believe that the institution can change when its personnel become convinced and tend to neglect the external commitments of the Church and its traditional role in society. Those working on the 'structural' strategy are pessimistic both about the chances of convincing the personnel and about modifying the institution and its role, because of the past commitments and roles.

---

[1] Most of my 200-odd interviews tried to probe the informant's ideas and strategies of change. I did a content analysis of almost all the literature currently emanating from Church sources and studied various groups and organizations which seemed to have explicit strategies. This discussion is selective in that I have included only about half of the strategies and elements I could have surveyed.

All the innovators want a more influential Church, in the sense that they feel the institution should have a greater impact on society. As a prerequisite, there need to be modifications in various sectors of the body. The influence includes a strong social change element, but in most cases the formulation of this element is vague, simply because there is little chance now to implement it. Aside from the consensus about more influence – necessitating change – and a progressive social role, there is both ambiguity and disagreement. The ambiguity exists because in the present institutional crisis and political predicament people often seek change for the sake of change, i.e., anything is better than the present situation. Disagreement comes about as a result of the perception of obstacles and the location of the innovator in the institution.

The PPC, in its original formulation in the Emergency Plan, spoke specifically of changing the Church in order to increase its influence.[2] The PPC itself emphasizes change in order to transform the Brazilian Church into an approximation of the image of Vatican II. While aspiring to total transformation, it is likely that the PPC as a plan will not achieve very much. However, a strategy revolves around the PPC as a process and the groups who promote it do have particular goals. They seem primarily concerned with pastoral reform; in other words, encouraging the bishops to begin modifying some structures and processes in order to 'open up' the institution to new forces from within. They stress particular structures which must be modified, including those which relate to the layman, to the clergy and to the orders-all relationships within the institution. For the most part they neglect external variables and the past role of the Church in society and politics. To summarize, their goals include a renewal and reformation of the Church through efforts to gradually weaken and transform the traditional structures.

The *Conferência dos Religiosos do Brasil*, or CRB, is the conference of major superiors. Its primary constituency is the body of 60,000 religious of more than 500 orders located in Brazil. Through their publications (mainly *Convergência*), courses and assemblies, however, they reach beyond the members of religious orders. Even so, the goals of the innovators in the CRB are predominantly formulated in terms of the impediments to change found in the orders. The emphasis is thus upon a weakening of structures through a change in mentality. As an article by the editor of the journal noted: 'The whole problem [of change] is a question of mentality. The goals are not the same as the ones they traditionally had.'[3] The idea is to encourage all members of the orders to update their functions and structures. As with the PPC, the main stress is upon internal variables, though external factors are not completely neglected. However, the innovators in the CRB are primarily concerned with openness, questioning, and change in mentality as leading to a change of structures both within the orders and within the Church in general.

The letter signed by 300 priests and sent to their bishops while being published simultaneously in the popular press is the last example of the goals

[2] *Cadernos da CNBB*, 'Plano da Emergência', 1962, p. 9.
[3] *Convergência*, 10 November 1967, p. 5.

being sought by innovators. This letter is one of many during the last few years and represents a different form of strategy from that of the PPC and CRB.[4] In it the priests stress the necessity for Church change because the environment is no longer the same.[5] The priests who wrote this letter embrace the goals of the PPC and CRB but go beyond them. They want change, through a change in mentality and a weakening of traditional structures, but they emphasize external over internal obstacles. Essentially the letter is a protest against the current social, political and religious situation in Brazil. And the social mission of the Church is clearly the crux of the argument for change. To improve life for the people the Church must change its form of influence, must adopt a 'prophetic mission', and to do these things the whole institution needs change.

In sum, I find similar aspects in the various goals expressed by the innovators. However, there are variations in emphasis and stress. The PPC and CRB are internal strategies; indeed, those who promote them are well within the institution. The letter of the 300 is external and the priests who signed it are for the most part rather outside the center of the institution.

The 'people' strategy of Church change

Strategy suggests a plan, a program, or a sequence whereby particular goals are to be implemented. For present purposes, all the strategies can be broken down into two main categories: the 'people' strategy and the structural. Within both categories there are various tactics or different series of emphases. Those who subscribe to the people strategy focus mainly on the bishops and their inability to perform a leadership function. The innovators following this strategy work principally on the hierarchy but do not completely exclude other levels of the Church in their attempt to reach the bishops. They believe that if the elite can be changed, then the whole institution will be also; if only the elite can be persuaded, then change in the institution will follow *ipso facto*.[6]

The innovators who follow the structural strategy are not optimistic about change in the present institution. Rather, they believe that the impediments are so integral to the whole history and structure of the Church that it will first have

---

[4] Other letters are: April 1967, signed by 30 priests in Rio de Janeiro; July 1968, signed by about 350 from Rio, São Paulo, and Paraná; and another signed by 110 in Rio at about this same time. I have seen no other letters since late 1968 and presume that this is attributable to the strict government censorship.

[5] 'We feel that the life of Faith, lived and transmitted in the past within a social context of a colonial society, is gradually disappearing with change, and is too weak to create new attitudes of Faith in the face of new realities in Brazil today.' Quoted in *Última Hora* of 24 October 1967.

[6] 'The people approaches try to change organizations by first changing the behavior of the organization's members. By changing human behavior, it is argued, one can cause the creative invention of new tools, or one can cause modifications in structure (especially people structure).' Harold S. Leavitt, 'Applied Organizational Change in Industry: Structural, Technological and Humanistic Approaches', in James G. March, ed., *Handbook of Organizations* (Chicago: Rand McNally, 1965), Chapter 27, p. 1,151.

to be broken down before change – in the form of another group or institution – can be possible. That is, they focus on the whole model of influence and institution and do not bother with any particular group or sector. In a sense, this strategy is the simpler of the two, for its adherents do not have to be clever. They can attempt various tactics of disruption and need not be as sensitive to nuances and rules of the game. However, these innovators are not irresponsible; they are seriously concerned with change and believe that it can be realized only in this manner.

It is impossible to be consistently specific on the groups, because what is treated analytically here is really quite complex in action. In some cases, there is an individual or group working mainly with the people strategy, but at the same time tending toward the structural. Or sometimes a bishop deals with the people but will support a priest who inclines toward the structural approach. Because of the complex relationships of the groups and individuals involved, the focus of analysis will be first on the strategies and then on those behind them.

The people strategy is most significant and difficult at the level of the bishops. There are two main groups of innovators working at this level: the CNBB group of bishops (with additions since 1964, now totalling around 25) and the PPC coordinators and assistants. There is considerable communication and cooperation between these two groups. The bishops carry out this strategy in personal contact with other bishops at various meetings, but primarily at the CNBB meetings at the regional and national levels.[7] Depending on which commission the bishop belongs to, he will encounter other bishops at these meetings up to ten or fifteen times a year. The tactics used vary from general discussions with other bishops, course-type seminars, the presentation of formal statements for progressive programs, etc. Their tactics are basically personal persuasion, combined with providing ideological orientation and 'hints' to the other bishops. In scope, if not in tactics, their strategy is essentially the same as the PPC coordinators whom they support.

The last chapter concluded that not much could be expected from the PPC, either as planning or as a process which might lead to commitments and institutionalization. There is, however, another way of interpreting the PPC and thus the optimistic propaganda which emanates from it and CNBB. Nationally, and in about a half of the 13 regions, innovators work with the PPC in order to persuade the bishops and others of the need for change. Instead of a set plan or a process involving commitments, the PPC is used as a medium of communication to convince the bishops of what they had already agreed to in accepting the plan. The PPC and documents relating to it do not represent a description of present reality but a means of propaganda whereby the bishops can be influenced. Some elements of this strategy can be seen in the initial documents on planning in the Church. For example, one of the formulators of the plan suggested that the importance of the PPC was in its questioning, as this might lead to the desired

---

[7] For a list of these meetings, see *Nacionais Informam* 47/48, January 1968 and for 1969 No. 75 and for 1970 No. 93.

renovation or change.[8] Planning, in this case through the PPC for the coordinators and assistants, is basically a process of persuasion; the terms used are 'education', 'questioning', 'stimulation', but what it all boils down to is clearly persuasion.

The 'people' strategy of the PPC begins with the innovators convincing the bishops of the necessity of planning. Although the bishops agreed to the national plan (the PPC), this did not necessarily bring about the formulation of regional or diocesan plans. In some areas the innovators had to 'sell' the idea of a plan as a service to the bishops, for they often still associated the CNBB with radicalism from the time of Dom Helder.[9] Once a plan was 'sold', they could follow through in educating the bishop. The innovators who use the PPC are, by the way, both clergy and laity in the confidence of the bishops and quite closely associated with the Church. They tend to be young and usually have been involved in some lay movement.

The PPC is used as a 'vehicle of change', in the words of one of the innovators. Through meetings at all levels in the Church, teams which visit the dioceses for discussions, sessions on specific parts of the plans and assessment services rendered to the regions and the dioceses, they work to persuade the bishops that the change proposed by the PPC is both right and necessary. When it is recognized that the strategy is persuasion through education and personal contact, the fetish for meetings and numbers of plans becomes clear. 'And it is in the meeting that the Pastoral Plan develops, for the meeting is vital for the PPC: its programs ...blossom forth in its shadow...the meeting, in itself, is always valuable.'[10]

Essentially the people strategy at this level consists of communication and education and is intended to expand the leadership capabilities of the hierarchy. The sheltered nature of the Church leaders is attacked through written and oral communications, by meetings with other bishops and by contact with the PPC group at frequent intervals. Certainty is directly attacked by education. The bishops are introduced (or reintroduced) to the reformulated goals of the Church after the Council; goals which can only be achieved through change.

8 'To submit our actions to a system of planning corresponds to submitting them to an attitude fundamentally of questioning. By questioning, and questioning always severely and humbly our actions and thus creating an atmosphere of profound revision, we will be preparing ourselves to fulfill the hopes of renovation in line with the Second Vatican Council.' Francisco Whitaker Ferreira in 'Planejamento Diocesano São Paulo', (São Paulo: n.p., 1966), Mimeo, pp. 6–7.

9 In Minas Gerais this was clearly the case. Interview with pastoral coordinator of CNBB in Minas Gerais, in Belo Horizonte on 14 March 1968.

10 *Telepax* 93/94 (14 April 1967). Further, to emphasize this obsession with meetings: 'On only the *regional* level (not counting the national, diocesan, etc.) of *the CNBB sectors* (and only these without including the Episcopal Commissions, annexed organisms, etc.) there are on the average more than 100 meetings annually! By averaging conservatively the participation of 20 persons per meeting, we will have two thousand "thinking heads", during a minimum of three days engaged in discussions about pastoral problems. The national and diocesan levels will perhaps triple this "intellectual statistic"; and the cost of all these meetings comes to be around two million cruzeiros [$700,000].' *Ibid.* (their emphasis). The PMV monograph notes on the PPC: 'In our opinion, it exercises its most important influence in a series of national and regional meetings and congresses which have contributed to an awareness and an anxious search for solutions to the problems of the Church in Brazil.' p. 55.

They are also shown that even the traditional goals are not being achieved by the Church. This is accomplished by educating them in religious sociology, or at least by presenting its findings to them. What the innovators try to do is to make the bishops appreciate the negative stimuli for change. For example, by the use of information on the low level of vocations and low mass attendance, they persuade the bishops that solutions must be sought. Through communications the formation of core groups becomes possible. When the bishops are isolated in their rural dioceses there is no possibility, given the sociological bases of the institution, for the formation of core groups. But once they are brought together at regular intervals there is at least the possibility. The 'lack of knowledge' characteristic is obviously a focus of the education process. In the meetings and through the various publications (*Nacionais Informam, Telepax* [until 1969], *REB*) data are presented on the society, the Church and various international topics, which should give the bishops information needed to make better decisions. This information is all oriented toward change so that the general concept should come through even if the particular pieces of data do not. In sum, through education and communication the innovators attempt to persuade the bishops to change, by focusing on their limitations in the leadership or administrative process.

Evaluating the success of the persuasion strategy at the elite level is no simple matter. While the PPC has run its five-year course, the results will take considerably longer to become fully manifest. In 1970 some regions were more active and some less than in 1968. However, it did seem as though the bishops in general were at least mouthing the formulae with more conviction. Then, too, as indicated in the 1970 General Assembly, they wanted the PPC to continue and seemed to respond favorably to questions such as 'crisis in the Church', the role of the layman and the problem of vocations.[11] Even so, the informants interviewed in 1970 were no more convinced than they had been in 1968 as to the direction of this strategy. The optimists thought it worked; the pessimists did not.

Communication and education are relied on for persuasion. Thus the potential for change is only as strong as education and communication can make it. What these innovators demand is that the bishops change radically in perspectives, perception and then action. There is real doubt that men of this age and training can be so easily altered; it is simply too late for most of them to be persuaded that they should become different people. Possibly if they could take a year or two off from their dioceses and be encouraged to take special courses in leadership, religious sociology, etc. they might be convinced to change their ways and attitudes. So far this has not been done and the meetings, visits, correspondence and so forth only temporarily change their approach – but for how long and with how much conviction?

Even if the bishops took the year or two off, although they would probably talk more progressively in meetings they would still act in much the same way

[11] For results of Assembly see *SEDOC* 26 (July 1970), pp. 77–96.

once they were back in their dioceses. We must recall that the bishops have to be seen in the context of their dioceses and other Church structures, within which they were educated and continue to function. Even if persuaded, they would not be free agents, for they fit within a historical Church model and historical structures. Rolim has studied several instances where the bishops were persuaded to create new organizations or structures in their dioceses; in the majority of cases these organizations came to be absorbed by traditional structures or were simply ignored.[12] The persuasion strategy at the elite level is in itself insufficient to bring about actions aimed at changes which the innovators desire. Communication and education probably are not enough, and when considered in the context of dioceses they are clearly inadequate.

Several groups of innovators attempt to persuade the clergy (as well as the male and female members of the religious orders) on at least four main principles. The first and most obvious is the fact that even a 'persuaded' bishop must rely upon his clergy to implement changes. Several of the younger bishops have brought up this important point. They personally may desire to transform the local Church, but if the clergy and religious in their dioceses are unwilling then it is very difficult to make headway.[13] Of course a bishop does have authority over his priests, but if he must exercise it to implement change then this belies the very goals he seeks. In addition, forcing change programs on an unwilling clergy might well cause a reaction and lead to further delays in implementing programs and policies. Therefore a certain level of agreement on change must exist before a bishop and his clergy can implement new goals.

A second reason why the innovators focus on the clergy is in order to stimulate and support possible changes at the hierarchy level. In other words, to complement the tactics they pursue for the hierarchy, they create a larger body around and under the bishop. In the case where a bishop is already inclined to be persuaded, the constituency of the clergy can be useful in encouraging him further. Where the bishop is relatively unreceptive, the clergy can possibly introduce him to the spirit of change. Perhaps they will be unsuccessful in convincing him, but if there are gaps in his control or areas where his administration is incomplete then the clergy can act in a new manner.[14] There are, however, certain definite limits on this tactic of the progressive constituency. Studies carried out on the role of constituencies in a democracy show that a representative largely selects his image of the constituency and permits communications accordingly. The Church does not claim to be democratic and one wonders how effective pressures from below can be in influencing a bishop. By and large the bishop has certain confidants among the clergy, and he confers with them rather than consulting all members. Then, too, innovators are likely to be most suspect and thus the last members of the clergy to have the ear of the bishop. Rolim's

[12] Frei Francisco Rolim, 'Estrutura da Igreja no Brasil', unpublished research report No. 1.2 of PPC of CNBB. (Rio de Janeiro: CERIS, 1968), pp. 186–7.
[13] Interviews with Dom Fragoso, Bishop of Cratéus, in Fortaleza on 10 January 1968; Dom David Picão, Bishop of Santos, in São Paulo on 15 December 1967.
[14] This tactic was suggested to me in an interview with Jair Martins, a sociologist, in Rio on 20 June 1967, and by 1970 seemed to have become very common.

research is relevant to this point, since he studied the occasions on which the bishops met with the priests in five dioceses. He found that in 73.7% of the cases the contacts were for exclusively religious or administrative purposes. In only 7.9% of cases did the contacts involve pastoral affairs; it would be in these instances only that a constituency pressure would be relevant. He concluded from this study, 'The individual contacts with the bishop did not significantly weaken the net of bureaucratic and juridic relations which are maintained through the diocesan curia.'[15] This tactic seems to be very limited in actually persuading the bishops, but it may be effective in bringing about a different form of behavior without the participation of the bishop. In many instances where a bishop known to be conservative or apathetic took a stand at variance with his past actions, it was because the clergy simply overwhelmed him by their arguments and strategies.

A third reason for dealing with the clergy is the fact that sooner or later some of them will become bishops and the problems will be solved. This makes some sense, but will certainly take time. However, the success of this tactic depends on who is nominating the bishops. If the nuncio is concerned with stability in the Church and if conservative bishops are involved in the process (as they are now), then the changed clergy will be passed over in nominations. Also, persuaded clergy upon being made bishops will still have to confront the structures and routines of the local churches. They may or may not be able to overcome the pressures of the environment, depending upon their personalities and the nature of their clergy.

A rather broad last reason for acting in this direction is that if the clergy are persuaded then they will influence new clergy, who will in turn influence others until all the Church is changed. This argument crops up from time to time, but seems to neglect considerations of strategy and timing. I question the validity of this reasoning, which assumes that all the clergy can be changed, by asking why so few are presently in this 'fortunate' state. This reason seems to neglect the problems really facing the Church.

The four reasons certainly differ in significance. The most important are the second and third, which focus on the clergy as an intermediate step to the bishops, because of the power of the elite over the institution. If change is to come about in this generation, it will have to be with the encouragement, or at least tacit support, of the bishops.

The PPC attempts to persuade the clergy through a series of meetings, institutes and courses. One begins to appreciate how it functions by noting the following excerpts from one of Pe. Marins' books.

In only four days we went over 16 council documents: 4 constitutions, 9 decrees, 3 declarations. There was discussion on the basis of pastoral materials concerning theology, scripture, and ethics. Everything was related to the six lines of the Joint Pastoral Plan [PPC] of the Brazilian Bishops (CNBB). The groups presented good reports and then the final plenary [session] took over. It was worth all the effort.

[15] Rolim, 'Estrutura da Igreja no Brasil', pp. 176–7.

The dominant activities were meetings, reunions, training, and actualization courses. The regions sent a great deal of material to the dioceses – bulletins, mimeos, books, etc. The coordinators visited almost all the ecclesiastical divisions of their territory and in this way opened new paths and suggested unanticipated cooperation.[16]

Aside from the frenetic activities of meetings and reunions, the PPC sponsors institutes for further training of the clergy. The best known of these are Instituto Superior para Pastoral de Liturgia ISPAL (for liturgy) and Instituto Superior para Pastoral de Catequese ISPAC (for catechism). At the national level the former had given courses to some 255 priests by 1966 and the latter to 353 by 1967.[17] The limitations of age noted in the case of the bishops would be less relevant here since the clergy are a good deal younger and thus somewhat more likely to learn and be persuaded; Table 5, giving the breakdown by ages, appears below. Here again, however, it must be pointed out that after the meetings and

TABLE 5   *Clergy and bishops by age*

Age	Clergy	Bishops
Over 60	14.0	32.5
50–59	18.0	39.9
40–49	27.1	23.8
30–39	32.2	1.6
Under 30	8.8	0.0

Source: Pe. Godofredo Deelen, 'O Episcopado Brasileiro', *Revista Eclesiástica Brasileira* 27 (June 1967), p. 316.

courses the priest returns to the same parish, curia and bishop. Whether the force of persuasion is sufficient to overcome past behavior and training is questionable. Rolim's data are again relevant. In the PPC, an example of change in the parishes is the adoption of a pastoral plan and pastoral council. However, in the 27 parishes which had one or both, only 6 (22.2%) of the priests had taken the specialized courses. On the other hand, 16 (59.3%) had not taken the courses. Apparently the courses had nothing to do with the adoption of change-oriented parochial bodies. However, age was an important factor in the adoption of the bodies.[18]

When the CRB was founded in 1954, its original functions were, in effect, to assist the orders and congregations in extricating their government grants (*verbas*) from the various ministries and to purchase goods wholesale which were sold to the members at discount. Since there are some 60,000 members of orders, congregations and institutes in Brazil, both these functions (from which a

[16] Pe. José Marins, *Presbítero Hoje* (São Paulo: Editôra 'Ave Maria', 1966), pp. 22–3, 65–6.
[17] *Nacionais Informam* 41/43 (October 1968), p. 62.
[18] Rolim, 'Estrutura da Igreja no Brasil', pp. 37–8.

percentage was retained) tended to make the CRB a very extensive and profitable enterprise. The Conference is well-organized, effectively administered, and has branched out from Rio to 21 regional centers. Like the CNBB, it has no real jurisdiction over the orders affiliated with it, but because it is useful and effective as a service most of them adhere to it.[19]

Following several years of preparations, an innovating group took over direction of the CRB in the 1965 elections and further consolidated their position in the 1969 elections. Since then they have maintained the profit-making activities, but have added another dimension which seeks to persuade the Church, and especially those in the religious orders, to change. An inherent limitation of the CRB is that only some 36 of the 500 religious superiors are to be found in Brazil. Further, the religious are largely at the disposition of the local bishop and to a large extent dependent upon his orientation or priorities. The case here is that of a 'people approach'. The CRB seeks to persuade the religious through a broad range of activities. Each year there are several national and regional week-long meetings, in which the various levels of superiors are 'educated'. At all levels, the CRB promotes courses independently as well as in combination with the PPC. The organization is divided into sectors; each produces material and statements for the use and persuasion of members of the orders.

The tactics of persuasion through education and communication followed by the CRB have basically the same limitations as those of the PPC. However, the financial independence and high-level organization and coordination of the CRB, in combination with the high quality and drive of its elite, suggest that it may be more successful. The fact that an obvious innovator group is directing the organization is indicative of the ability of these people. In this position they have considerable resources at their disposal for promoting their tactics.[20] The religious are usually more independent than the seculars, they are better educated, more secure financially, more cosmopolitan and in general provide better material for persuasion. The people strategy for the religious will be quite successful at least in the long run, i.e. over a decade or more. By this time the older and more conservative superiors will have been replaced by those who are now most influenced by the persuasion strategy.

The two approaches so far discussed are forms of education 'after the fact'. They are intended to persuade or convince existing clergy and religious that change is necessary. A logical concurrent tactic is to educate the priests and

---

[19] I conducted a long series of interviews on the CRB, including interviews with Irmão Cristóvão on 3 January 1968, Pe. Angelo on 8 September 1967, Pe. Filipelli on 18 May 1967, and Pe. Zolim on 18 June 1970. All of these were at the national level and another dozen interviews were at regional levels.

[20] It is necessary to note that after four years of rather peaceful and covert persuasion the CRB was publicly attacked in 1969. A group of religious who were not in agreement with the leadership's orientation wrote a long document, sent it to the Sacred Congregation on Religious in Rome and also had it published. The criticism followed a pattern common in Brazil, in that in combined elements in its attack on: doctrinal error, lack of discipline, weak morals and social subversion. The CRB was able to defend itself nationally and internationally with apparently no serious effects from the episode. Interview at CRB on 18 June 1970. For the documentation see *SEDOC* 2:11 (May 1970), pp. 1385–418.

religious in this orientation while they are still in the seminaries and convents instead of waiting until they emerge. There are serious drawbacks, however, in the type and quality of seminary education.[21] The innovators who pursue this tactic argue that while it may not have been imperative to worry about the training of clergy in the past, because the ministry was simple, today it is vital to improve training because the environment is changing and the demands are greater.[22] They point to the Council's statement on clergy formation, 'Optatum Totius', compare the society of today with that of the past and argue that a rather different type of priest is now necessary if the Church is to respond effectively to change.

In Brazil the clergy is trained in archdiocesan and regional major and minor seminaries throughout the country.[23] During the past few years there have been various crises in education and vocations so that several seminaries have closed.[24] Innovating groups have taken over the training of clergy in at least two places and considerably modified its format and content. The Regional Seminary of the Northeast in Recife is under the direction of the Northeast bishops, headed by Dom Helder. The Institute of Theology and Philosophy in Belo Horizonte is largely under the direction of CRB affiliated groups. In these two examples of changed formation, the idea is to give the seminarians the best possible basis in 'renewed' theology and philosophy (often taught by foreign priests from France, Holland and Belgium) and to introduce them to the world by making them live outside the seminary, or take jobs, or both.

The tactic used in relation to the other seminaries is the same as in the cases of the PPC and CRB: that is, to convince the bishops and religious superiors in charge of the seminaries that the institutions and routines should be modified

---

[21] See Gustavo Pérez et al., pp. 155–60, and Marins Presbítero Hoje. A recent research project on the clergy supports this view. 'We discovered that in the opinion of the priests interviewed, the quality of the priests is a more serious problem than that of their numerical weakness in Brazil...we discovered that the priests do not feel sufficiently prepared for the exercise of their ministry. In general, they attribute this deficiency to the seminaries in which they studied.' Pedro de Assis Ribeiro de Oliveira, 'Pesquisa Sobre O Clero – Sumário,' unpublished research report for CERIS in 1968, from a survey of 203 priests in 7 dioceses. See also the research report in REB 29 (March 1969), pp. 121–38.

[22] For example, 'In the Christendom regime it was relatively easy for the priest to fulfill his mission. The social structures supported his position and reinforced the faith of the Christians. Generally, it was enough to be a good follower of canon norms and executor of liturgical rubrics. The bishop demanded correctness in these matters. The diocesan curia... would consider him a good functionary in the dioceses insofar as he would fulfill the norms.' Msgr. Marcelo Pinto Cavalheira, 'O Tipo do Padre Que A Igreja Espera Apos O Concílio Vaticano II', unpublished report Serviço de Apostilas No. 5 (Recife: CNBB, Northeast II, 1967), p. 7.

[23] In 1968, there were 13 secular and 43 religious major seminaries. From statement of Secretário Nacional dos Seminários, CNBB.

[24] Fortaleza and Mariana closed because of internal crises. Interview with Pe. Carlos Alberto, head of CNBB secretariat of seminaries, in Rio on 21 March 1968. Belem, João Pessoa, and Maceió have closed because of a fall in the number of vocations. See Thomas G. Sanders, 'The Regional Seminary of the Northeast', Field Letter (TGS-3) to Richard H. Nolte, Institute of Current World Affairs, 5 August 1967.

according to Council documents and the needs of Brazil. This tactic is again implemented through meetings, courses and a great deal of published material.[25] Its chances of succeeding are about the same as for the persuasion of the bishops in general. However, one point must be noted which somewhat improves the potential for success: the 'crisis in vocations' and the attrition rate of seminarians are powerful negative stimuli in persuading the bishops that something needs to be done. On this point the innovators argue that a better program in the seminaries would most likely encourage more prospective priests to remain until ordination, and that priests trained in the new system would be more valuable than those trained in the old. That is, quantity would probably increase and quality certainly would.[26]

Other tactics associated with this people strategy at the clergy level could be mentioned. What can be expected from these tactics in persuading the clergy, and then the bishops, that change is necessary? It seems that a combination rather than any one tactic induces a significant movement which will assume a greater magnitude and depth with time. This movement consists not only of its particular elements, but, perhaps more important, is accompanied by an ideology or mystique of change which will surely generate new tactics. An increasing number of priests and religious people are talking about change and after a while it may come to mean something. There are, however, certain problems involved in the strategy at this level. If the clergy and religious become highly change-oriented, and if the bishops are convinced more slowly, as is to be expected given their age and position in the Church and society, there may well be a sharp increase in tensions and crises so that this strategy will not be effective vis-à-vis the elite. In effect between 1968 and 1970 there was a sharp increase in these tensions and in the 'crisis of the institution'. An increasing number of priests began to ignore the bishops, to criticize them and to do all they could to bypass the hierarchy by doing what *they* felt to be right and necessary. If, on the other

---

[25] See 'Comunicado' of the Secretariado Nacional dos Seminários of CNBB which lists meetings and materials. *Igreja*: *Vocação* of CNBB–CRB also supports persuasion of future clergy.

[26] Interviews with Pe. Carlos Alberto on 21 March 1968, and Pe. Olinto Pegoraro from São Paulo IFT on 5 March 1968. One must remember that $40\%^+$ of the clergy, secular and religious, are foreign-born. Thus the type of training these 'imports' receive either in their own countries or upon arrival in Brazil is important. Traditionally, the largest groups are the Italians (1,173 of 3,894 foreign-born), the Dutch (902), and the Germans (856), *Pro Mundi Vita*, 'Brazil: The Church in Process of Renewal', Brussels, Bulletin No. 24 (1968), p. 37. It is difficult to generalize on the kind of training these priests receive for they come from 13 countries, are young and old, secular and religious. What might be considered is the training given before, or just after, their arrival in Brazil. Many of the Northern Europeans receive training in Louvain for their future ministry in Brazil. The Spanish, Portuguese and Italians do not apparently receive special preparation. The CNBB–CRB created Serviço de Colaboração Apostólica Internacional (SCAI) as an organization to coordinate the introduction of new personnel in Brazil. This organization deals mainly with locating the individuals and not with their initial preparation. Ivan Illich founded Centro de Formação Intercultural (CENFI) outside Rio for preparation, but SCAI is not supporting CENFI, because many bishops would rather have their new recruits a bit more malleable than the education at CENFI leaves them. From interviews with Maria de Lourdes at CENFI on 22 February 1968. See Illich's article in *America* in January 1967.

hand, the bishops and clergy are persuaded but the laity is excluded then there will be a 'changed' but even more clerical Church.[27]

The existence and efficacy of a strategy at the laity level are minimal; rather, the innovators are attempting to persuade the bishops and clergy that there should be a laity. It is, therefore, a strategy once removed. There is little chance that a lay movement will be created without a serious and intensive program on the part of the Church. The fact that such a laity never existed, except for the anomaly of Catholic Action before 1964, is suggestive.

It seems doubtful that the Church will of its own accord allow, let alone stimulate, lay participation. The tradition of the clerical Church which does not include the layman is still very much present. Then, too, the Church has never really relied upon the laity for resources; it is no secret that the parishioners give little support to their Church. There is the continued expectation that the institution will receive resources from the government, from abroad and from a few wealthy members. This applies to vocations as well as finances, but it apparently has not occurred to the bishops that a new contact with the laity might generate indigenous resources for both. Probably most important is the hierarchy's fear that if it stimulates a relevant and active laity it will 'go political' as Catholic Action did before 1964. The fear seems to be well founded. In this predicament, all statements about lay stimulation notwithstanding, there is little likelihood that it will be formed.

When new structures are formed which are intended to allow lay participation, they ultimately operate in the traditional manner of a clerical Church. Where aware and mobilized laymen from the pre-1964 period exist and demand a role in their Church, they are either isolated or ignored.[28] The Church is, then, clearly facing a dilemma. To modify its stand regarding the layman, change is first necessary. Substantial numbers of laymen are needed to pressure the Church through tactics which affect the resource base. However, such a group does not exist, nor could it threaten the resource base if in fact it came into being. The groups dealing with the people strategy for the laity are minimal.

Several priests in different regions attempt to work with the laymen and are searching for useful methods and approaches. Focusing on the hierarchy and the clergy, there is mainly the group around the PPC. In some regions, they try to bring laymen of 'proven confidence' together with the bishops for meetings and reunions in order to show that the species is not dangerous and to give these

---

[27] Already some researchers are aware of this problem, as are some of the more sophisticated laymen I interviewed; few priests seem to think about it. See Rolim's 'Estrutura da Igreja no Brasil', p. 194. The project on the clergy notes that while many priests are unhappy with the way authority is exercised by the bishops, they are unwilling to include the laity in the democracy they demand from the bishops. 'However, this 'democratic' appeal [participation with the bishops] pertains only to the level of the clergy; only a minority wants the laymen to participate more actively in the decisions of the Church. The priests in general think that the absence of laymen in Brazil is a serious matter, but want to maintain an attitude of tutelage over them, that is, their action must always be guided by the priests who makes the decisions.' de Oliveria, 'Pesquisa Sobre O Clero', p. 4.

[28] See Rolim, 'Estrutura da Igreja no Brasil', p. 42 for a case study of the activities of Catholic Action individuals in parishes.

laymen the chance to convince the bishops themselves. At the CNBB General Assembly in 1970, there were laymen present who were allowed to speak to the group. A further element of hope is the fact that the bishops discussed several propositions concerning the laity and more or less came out in favor of more work with and support for them.[29] At the local level several of the isolated lay groups attempted to work with priests in order to develop larger roles for themselves. By 1970 some of these groups had disintegrated (Valhinos in São Paulo for example), but new ones had formed which were also searching for some institutional support. With very few exceptions, this is the extent of the strategy regarding the layman. It is still at an incipient stage and history, tradition and political considerations all hinder its development. Some people believe in a limited strategy (a low profile strategy) regarding the layman. They argue that it is most effective first to persuade the bishops and the clergy, while largely ignoring the layman, and then the layman will be included naturally in due course.[30] Whether the clergy and the bishops will be persuaded is, of course, one initial consideration. Then, if they are, but without the layman as a participant, the sophisticated clericalism will be extremely difficult to break down. And if the layman could be included now, there would be greater chances of success in persuading the other two levels; the laity might serve as a form of constituency and thus buttress other innovators.

Theoretically the Church maintains contact with society through the laity.[31] If such a laity does not exist then it is probable that change at other levels of the Church will not be the most appropriate, given the transformations in the larger society. Several priests and bishops have been aware of the problem. They have felt that even with ecclesiastical change the Church might well remain alienated from the dynamic sectors of society. In short, without direct contact with the environment through an effective laity the changing Church may be changing in the wrong ways.

Assuming that the Church changes in a progressive direction requiring social involvement, the priests will then be heavily involved in programs which should be administered by the laity. There is a tremendous shortage of priests in Brazil; everyone agrees about this, but they usually fail to appreciate the fact that the priest wastes a great deal of his time in non-pastoral tasks. The priests almost completely monopolize the administrative and bureaucratic duties of the parish. Rolim's findings are typical, that of the social work (charities, groups, etc.) in the parishes, some 80% was directed by the priests.[32] And it should be mentioned again that a problem in the pre-1964 social involvement was that the Church

[29] For the propositions and voting see *SEDOC* 26 (July 1970), pp. 89–91.

[30] Interviews with two bishops in São Paulo and several CNBB insiders.

[31] Conservative bishops used this argument to justify the Church's non-involvement in society, but they failed to mention that they were doing nothing to encourage the layman.

[32] Thirty-five of the parishes had such social work. In 19 (54.3%) the pastor ran the activities; in 9 (25.7%) associations ran them; in 6 (17.1%) religious did; and in 1 (2.9%) a pastoral council did it. Since the pastor also directs the associations, this means that a total of 80% were directed by the priest alone. *Ibid.*, p. 57. And this direction is very close; the priests do not delegate authority well.

was directly, and not very often through the layman (except in the case of MEB), involved in programs which became controversial. Therefore, if the Church intends to play an active role in social involvement (which is anticipated in the changed Church) but fails to form and mobilize a laity, not only will the priest and the institution spend far too much time in this role but the Church will be directly compromised in activity which is of necessity political. The result will be a limitation on the institution's ability to operate as well as a position of decreasing moral legitimacy, caused by direct involvement in programs which will be attacked, which may fail and which may have little directly to do with the Church's mission. If the Church intends to play any role in social involvement, a lay movement simply must be formed.[33]

In conclusion, while the people strategy offers some possibility of change at the clergy level and considerably less at the hierarchy level, there is almost no chance of change at the all-important lay level. On the one hand, the innovators do not generally favor a formed and mobilized laity at this time; on the other, the mobilized laity of the past have almost no role in the present Church. Many of these people, partly because of their enforced isolation, want nothing to do with the Church. Others still have hopes but think that only the structural strategy is valid.

The structural strategy of Church change

The analysis formulated by those who support the structural strategy is much more incisive than that behind the people approach. Rather than regarding the institution in isolation and believing that persuasion can lead to changed structures and roles, they look at the situation in an historical perspective and realize that the Church is not now and never has been a free agent. The institution has been linked historically in multiple and complex ways with political and social systems of the country, and they hold that it cannot possibly be changed without support from these other sectors. Today, after the coup, these spheres are strictly and staunchly in favor of the *status quo*, so that Church change is not just a simple matter of convincing a few bishops and priests that it is desirable. Then, too, they correctly note that the Church has always been compromised, so that if a social change role is adopted it must criticize past and present society, of which the Church forms an integral part. Maybe some of the hierarchy have the courage to criticize their past roles and actions, but most do not.[34] As a result of this analysis of the obstacles to change, most of the

[33] This is a point that Vallier continually makes in his work. If the Church gets involved as an institution in controversial programs, it either re-enters or stays within the political realm and short-circuits its possible autonomy. Then too the Church may well be most important in legitimating change at a more secure position of 'ethico-cultural leadership'. See Vallier, *Catholicism, Social Control, and Modernization in Latin America*: especially Chapters 3 and 7 for excellent discussions of this crucial point.

[34] For an excellent analysis of this dual criticism and its implications for Church and social change see Pe. Henrique Vaz, 'Igreja-Reflexo versus Igreja-Fonte', *Cadernos Brasileiros* 46 (March 1968), pp. 17–24. A shortened but similar article is available in English by the same author, 'The Church and Conscientização', *America*, 27 April 1968. As noted early in Chapter 4, Dom Helder has made such a criticism of the Church's historical role.

innovators feel that the institution must first be more or less destroyed in order to make room for the reconstruction of the Church in a form more faithful to its mission as they understand it. In their view the people strategy is at best a misallocation of time and at worst counterproductive, because it will ultimately serve to reinforce the traditional Church model.[35] Suggestive of their critique of the people strategy and indicative of their own views are extracts from a letter signed by 350 priests of Guanabara, Estado do Rio, São Paulo and Paraná in July 1968 and published in the secular press.

Many people in the Church (laymen, priests and bishops) try to sew patches of a new mentality on the old wineskins that are leaking from all sides. Is it sufficient to place principles of Vatican II in tired structures? Be it in the pastoral or in the liturgy; be it in official organs (CNBB, CRB, CELAM) or in the seminaries? [the clear response is no and thus persuasion is insufficient]. Nobody thinks that it is enough to write reform on paper. Reform will come through the deterioration (painful for many) of the old forms and through the genesis of a new Church, appropriate for this [time in] history... Many no longer think that it is possible to improve the present structure of the Church. Its structures were never questioned deeply. Do they serve the Gospel or impede its announcement? Our dioceses, parishes, convents, schools, superior institutions, what do they signify today for an underdeveloped country?[36]

In short, those who follow the structural strategy feel a need to destroy the old institution, which is interwoven with the whole of society, and begin anew with a different form of Church which presumably would be extremely flexible.

It is more difficult to pinpoint the groups and individuals engaged in this strategy than those using the other strategy. This should be obvious: whereas the latter may operate in a semi-covert fashion, they are still 'legal' and can function within the structures for their ultimate transformation. The structural strategy is 'illegal' and thus not recognized by the Church as valid; its supporters attempt to work through clandestine tactics, although at times public statements are made in pursuance of a particular part of this strategy. There seem to be no bishops who adhere to this strategy. Some may agree with its analysis and even its goals, but their positions of authority give them other forms of leverage to promote change; then, too, they are most involved with the institution and least likely to wish its demise. There are quite a few laymen formerly associated with Catholic Action who attempt to follow one tactic of this strategy, but because the layman is outside the institution his influence is limited. The overwhelming majority of those following the structural strategy are young priests, mainly in the orders, but some foreign-trained secular priests are also included. These priests are most often in their thirties or early forties, were probably affiliated

---

[35] This latter view is suggested in a review of two of Pe. Caramuru's books on Church change; Caramuru is an originator of the people strategy. 'However, the problem, ignored in both books, bothers all of us: that of questioning the structure itself [and] its validity in a society undergoing rapid change. Will a renovation that comes from the supporters of the institution be sufficient, or will it have to come from the outside, from dissident groups similar to what happened in the sixteenth century with the advent of Protestantism?' *Paz e Terra* 7 (1968), pp. 322–3.

[36] Reprinted in *Correio da Manhã* of 16 July 1968.

with Catholic Action (as members or assistants), have an education beyond the seminary – and very often abroad – and have most likely had problems of one sort or another with the bishops.[37] It is difficult to gauge their numbers, but in São Paulo there are at least 30, in Belo Horizonte some 20, 30 in Rio, around 20 in Recife and so forth. The letters which promote this strategy nationally are usually signed by 200 or 300, which indicates that the group of priests pursuing it amounts to around 2% to 4% of the clergy. They are, however, usually more active, more committed to particular goals for the Church, and as they are better educated they are in crucial positions in seminaries and universities, and in general can exercise their strategy fairly effectively, at least in convincing those around them of the validity of the approach. They have communications throughout the country but no coordinated plan or program for the implementation of their strategy.

The most popular tactic of the structural strategy is the selective abandonment of the institution or some parts of it. This desertion is not necessarily due to frustration or apathy, but is rational and intentional. The following quotation illustrates the type of calculation involved in this tactic: 'Realizing that the structure of the Church is an insurmountable obstacle to this evangelical mission (the original and pure mission of the Church), many priests and Catholic laymen are asking themselves if they should stay within it to promote its subversion . . . or, if they should abandon it, to create the model of the Church of the future.'[38] Those who follow this tactic deny resources of time and energy to the institution, while attempting to create parallel structures which will gradually replace the Church as it falls to pieces. Thus laymen who no longer work with any Church program still meet with others in small groups with a priest. They attempt to convince others to follow their example in order to present the institution with desertions *en masse*. Priests will leave their administrative, and even at times religious, roles in the institution (such as in the CNBB or in parishes or in parochial schools) and create new centers where they can meet with other priests and laymen. Other priests will opt out of the structure but will continue as priests and teachers, worker priests etc. There are a great many variations to this tactic, but the general idea is to deny resources to the institution – thus bringing about its demise – while at the same time creating something else to replace it.

This tactic is very easy for the layman; indeed, laymen are almost compelled to accept it if they want to follow what they consider to be their function as the

---

[37] Primarily because of their training abroad and resulting proficiency in other languages, but also because of further education itself and their affinities with similar elements in other countries, these priests tend to get more attention in foreign journals, books and other publications than they do in Brazil itself. Because of this, foreigners often think that the Brazilian Church is far more *avant-garde* than it really is. For a good selection of the more advanced statements and beliefs emanating from all the Latin Churches, see the *LADOC* series of the Latin American Bureau–USCC, Washington, D.C. See particularly the publications from the Latin American Bureau on CICOP (Catholic Inter-american Cooperation Program) meetings. The book based on the 1971 meetings is *Conscientization for Liberation* edited by Louis M. Colonnese (Washington, D.C.: Division for Latin America – USCC, 1971.)

[38] José Kosinski Cavalcanti, *Visão*, 12 April 1968.

People of God. It is rather more difficult, however, for the clergy. The order priests can use the approach without too much trouble (provided their superiors are willing), for the local bishops are then relatively powerless to force them into diocesan or parish structures. Given the lack of clergy, they also have a certain bargaining power to exert. For the secular priests, it is almost impossible: the courage, independence and security required for this strategy are found in only a few. This tactic is possible for the secular priests mainly in the more open and progressive dioceses; just those dioceses where the innovating bishops are attempting to accomplish something. It is important in giving the mobilized laymen and a few priests oases in the midst of frustration. Rather than opting out completely they have parallel structures to cling to and work from. However as a tactic for breaking up the Church it is not very satisfactory. The resource base of the Church does not rely heavily on the laity nor, for that matter, on progressive priests. The resource base in the government, in priests who originate abroad, and in a few rich people will not be seriously affected by this tactic. In a sense the innovators overvalue their worth to the Church in thinking that their withdrawal will threaten the institution.

Further, the parallel structures which are created are extremely weak. Without some form of institutional support (through progressive bishops, religious orders, etc.), they tend to experience mitosis, or an endless division into smaller and smaller groups, ultimately losing all contact with the Church in an institutional sense. The elements which make up the parallel structures are fully absorbed into secular society and their resources are lost not only to the institution but also to the impetus for change. In short, this tactic does not seem to offer great possibilities for destroying the institution. For a time it gives solace to disenchanted elements, but it does not offer enough contact to maintain any identification with the Church.[39]

While the first tactic attempts to rupture the institution by denying it resources and creating parallel structures, the next two focus directly on particular sectors of the Church and seek to break it by direct confrontation and disruption. The first of these might be termed 'the guerrilla variation' and has as its end the generalization of crises throughout the institution. But they are very subtle and covert, and probably effective only in the long term. This tactic creates less direct confrontation than the next and is more delicate in its disruption. A definition of this tactic is found in an article by Richard Shaull which has been widely circulated in Brazil.

Sudden pressures applied effectively in the right place and at the proper time can produce a surprisingly broad and profound impact; in this way, small changes can set in motion the forces that will produce greater changes in the future. In this situation, the

---

[39] My interviews which pinpoint this tactic were extensive, as these are the people one tends to gravitate towards when looking for 'new things in the Church'. At least 30 of my informants were working with this approach. On my return in 1970, I found that my criticisms of this tactic were accurate; there was a general decay of the parallel groups as they moved further and further away from the institution. As they peeled off, however, there were new groups, but I anticipate the same effect with them.

revolutionary strategy consists of developing the bases in which a decrepit system initiates greater changes insofar as they [the changes] become urgent or necessary and [the system] would be constantly bombarded by strong pressures, achieving small changes in different points.[40]

In the concrete situation of Brazil, an example of this tactic is the formulation of a compact ideology of development from Church material such as 'Mater et Magistra', 'Pacem in Terris', 'Populorum Progressio', and then inviting comparisons between this legitimate ideology and the statements, actions and orientations of certain bishops.[41] The comparison does not require much elaboration as the contradictions between theory and action, and even words, are glaringly obvious. In the Brazilian Church, with its rapid about-face in 1964 on both social and institutional matters but with its commitment to the previous CNBB ideology and the Council doctrines, this guerrilla tactic offers broad possibilities for aggravating the institutional crisis. However, it requires a highly sophisticated promoter if it is to be effective. Only a few individuals follow this tactic, and they are all in critical positions in institutes and seminaries. For the most part they promote it while preparing trained cadres who will also presumably follow the same tactic in the future. One of these priests suggested that it would be for the next generation to bring about the demise of the institution; the task for his generation is the preparation and training of the next.[42] This tactic can work in the Brazilian context, but it most certainly will take time and by then maybe the other strategy will have caught on and thus this tactic will not be necessary.

The second tactic of confrontation and disruption might be called the 'tension-inducing approach'. But individuals using this variation do not so much create tensions in ideology and action as exploit already existing stresses in the institution and its relationship to society. Internally they attempt to disrupt the institution by neglecting lines of authority, ignoring functions and roles of priests and bishops, side-stepping official programs and creating their own, defying official directives, and by other flagrant manifestations of a desire to accelerate the institutional crisis. At times they confront the Church directly with threats and demands, at other times they operate in the margins between structures and formal roles. If assigned as instructor in a conservative seminary, such an individual will teach the course as he wishes despite the opposition of the rector. If this sort of act is too flagrant, however, problems are aggravated and

---

[40] He is here speaking of the political process, but the tactic has been adapted to the Church as well. From 'Desafio Revolucionário à Igreja e à Sociedade', speech given to World Conference of Church and Society in Geneva, July 1966. Translated and published in CEI August 1967.

[41] For an introduction to this approach see Hugo Assman, 'Tarefas e Limitações de uma Teologia do Desenvolvimento', *Revista de Vozes* 62 (January 1968), pp. 13–22.

[42] Interview in Pôrto Alegre on 25 November 1967. The informant has since left the country and the priesthood. In general what has happened to the IFT in São Paulo, where this informant taught for a while, is typical of the problems such priests encounter. They attempt to work more or less within the institution, and covertly, to cause general disruptions, but are usually found out and in some way censured. Since they are on the fringes anyway they move further out and simply leave the institution.

the institution reacts.[43] The main difference between this tactic and the guerrilla approach is that the latter is more subtle, sophisticated and long-range. The tension-inducing tactic is blunt, obvious and designed to directly confront the institution. It is not just simple insubordination, although most critics see it as such, but a rationally designed plan to exploit tensions. The letters of priests to their bishops published in the secular press are examples of this tactic. What is most obvious about this tactic, but which is present in the other two variants of the structural strategy as well, is the realization that the institution cannot be separated from its environment. The recognition of a need for autonomy is an integral part in their evaluation of the necessity to break the institution. In 1968 a letter signed by 350 priests queried: 'Can the Church (institution) evangelize without first making a testament of justice? And does this testament in favor of justice require the "non-compromise" with the dominating and exploiting class?'

This tactic is the most drastic and outspoken. It would seem that with more support from within the clergy and given improper reactions from the bishops and state, they could indeed be effective in breaking the institution. However, this cure would appear to be a case of too much too soon. By rupturing the institution they will end up with nothing: no institutional basis for social involvement, no prestige, no religious authority and no further opportunities for other tactics. This tactic is most of all political and most of all external. By entering 'into politics', the priests become viewed increasingly as politicians rather than members of the clergy. They mark all the clergy with a political hue. Therefore one must question whether this tactic would be a success even if on its own terms it was successful. If these priests destroy the prestige and authority of the Church and thus most of its potential influence, what is the value of being associated with the institution at all? Why not ignore the institution and just form guerrilla bands which would leave the Church and proselytize for rapid socio-political change? In other words, while their tactic is probably effective in achieving its goals, they will obviate the long-range goals they have of using the Church to change society.

In conclusion, there are at least two main categories of strategies which seek to bring about change in the Church. There are others that could be included, and some that might fit partly within both but those discussed are dominant and the most representative at the present time. The people strategy is very uneven but probably could be effective in the long run, at least in convincing people. But it is partial in its neglect of the layman and thus tends toward self-defeat. These strategists want to change people but are naive if they believe that

---

[43] A good case of this occurred in Botucatu in São Paulo, where 23 of the 32 priests in the diocese refused to accept the nominated bishop because he had regressive views on most matters. After several months of battles back and forth, and the intervention of the nuncio and the civil authorities, the regressive bishop stayed and the priests went. See *Jornal do Brasil*, 26 July 1968; *Telepax* 143 (1968), pp. 4–5; *SEDOC* 2:2, p. 149. While documentation is now hard to come by, this type of crisis seems to have become much more common. See *SEDOC* 2:11 (May 1970) for documentation of a similar case in Bahia, pp. 1422–5. My informants in 1970 cited many such instances which have not been publicized by the news media.

as a corollary the structures of dioceses, curias, etc. will simply give in and become instantly renewed. This is not to mention the socio-political context, which for the structural strategist is really the most important obstacle. The tactics associated with this strategy seek to break the institution and its links with other orders in order to free it for change. There is some promise in the guerrilla tactic but progress between 1968 and 1970 appeared to be slight; there is no hope at all in the desertion tactic, and probably too much success in the tension-inducing tactic, which I hold to be very negative.

8. The 'experiences' of four dioceses: obstacles to change

This short chapter studies the attempted implementation of 'changed Churches' in four dioceses. The dioceses are Cratéus in Ceará, Itabira in Minas Gerais, Olinda-Recife in Pernambuco and Salvador in Bahia. These four were selected primarily because the bishops who have headed them are already convinced of the necessity for change, and in fact, try to promote its acceptance among other members of the hierarchy. These bishops have been suggested as models for emulation by those promoting the 'people' strategy of church change.

Dom Helder Câmara is Archbishop of Olinda-Recife, founded the CNBB, assisted in the founding of CELAM, is the most well-known progressive in the Brazilian Church and seems to be the spark behind most innovations nationally if not on a continent-wide basis.[1] The Cardinal-Archbishop of Salvador until April 1971, Dom Eugênio Sales, founded the Natal Movement, was crucial in the early days of MEB and rural unionization, provided stimulus for the early PPC, has sponsored leadership and unionization programs, is a member of various international and continental commissions for social development and was described by Pope Paul VI, we are told, as 'a true bishop of the Second Vatican Council'.[2] The Bishop of Cratéus is Dom Antônio Batista Fragoso; he came from a very large and poor family, spent 13 years in various Church labor organizations, was active in the rural reform programs as auxiliary bishop to Dom José Delgado in São Luís do Maranhão, is extremely politically aware and today seems to be vying with Dom Helder as the Brazilian bishop most famous (or infamous) abroad.[3] The Bishop of Itabira, until he resigned his see in 1971, was Dom Marcos Antônio Noronha, known as the most progressive in Minas Gerais. He is highly respected throughout Brazil for his institutional innovations at the diocesan level and generally progressive attitudes toward social matters.[4] These four are frequently referred to when the 'new Church' in Brazil is discussed.[5]

[1] The bibliography on Dom Helder is now extensive: de Broucker *Dom Helder Câmara*, gives a good idea of his thinking; this book is a sympathetic account by a foreigner, as is Frances M. Foland, 'Northeast Brazil: The Archbishop of Recife and Olinda', Field Letter (FMF-8) to Richard H. Nolte, Institute of Current World Affairs, New York, 4 October 1967; see also the article by Joe Page in the *New York Times Magazine* of 23 May 1971 for a reasonable evaluation of his work.

[2] *Realidade*, January 1970, p. 137. For further information on Dom Eugênio, a man who acts more than he writes, see Ferrari particularly pp. 57–8 and 233–4.

[3] On his orientation, see the coverage in *Fatos e Fotos*, January 1967; statements of his in *National Catholic Reporter* for 8 January 1969; an article of his for *Razón y Fe*, Madrid, May 1970, which is presented in *LADOC* 1:37 (October 1970); and several of his sermons, statements and explanations, all in mimeograph. See Dom Fragoso's *Evangile et révolution sociale*, trans, from the Portuguese (Paris: Editions du Cerf, 1969).

[4] Interviews with journalists in Rio and with informants in Belo Horizonte on the Bishop's position and actions. On his views see the coverage in *Convergência*, May 1968; he has published a book, *A Igreja que Nasce Hoje* (Petrópolis, R.J.: Editôra Vozes, 1970), which is a compilation of short articles and essays of reflection and is indicative of his line.

[5] I have had interviews with Dom Helder, Dom Fragoso and Dom Marcos Noronha; for Dom Eugênio I have relied on interviews with most of his close advisors as well as outside

In 1968 the process of renewal-or-change was more successful in Cratéus and Itabira than in Salvador and Recife. This observation still holds but events in both the former have forced a reconsideration of the level of success. There was a feeling in 1968 that Cratéus and Itabira had taken off into a process of sustained change, while any such process was extremely dubious in the other two. There were plans and programs at the diocesan and parish level, meetings of the clergy and laity, involvements of all sorts, and it appeared as though a momentum had been achieved. However, in late 1971 Dom Marcos Noronha resigned his see and he now works as a common priest; the reasons given are that he could not achieve enough cooperation with his clergy and suffered too much opposition from the local power elements. Dom Fragoso is still in his diocese, but during the past two years has become the focal point of attack by conservative elements in society and the army. He has been attacked repeatedly; foreign clergy who have worked with him have been forced out of the country; his priests are imprisoned; and by all manner of actions he is being impeded in his work. Cratéus and Itabira are indeed ahead of the other two, but the process of polarization has come to these rural dioceses and also impedes their progress.[6]

If this evaluation of the four dioceses is accurate, then how can the differences in levels of attainment be explained? If anything, Dom Helder and Dom Eugênio should be more experienced in promoting change activities, and they are more able to mobilize national and international resources for their purposes. The problems that Dom Eugênio and Dom Helder face are of a different magnitude both in quantitative and qualitative terms, although recent events show that they apply with almost as much force for the bishops of the other two dioceses. These problems are discussed in three general categories: the structural internal obstacles to change; the overall complexities of the regions in which the dioceses are located and integrated; and, because of the complexities, the political impediments to change. With regard to the last category Dom Helder and Dom Eugênio disagree, the latter still adhering to a power definition of influence, despite his otherwise progressive stance.

Itabira and Cratéus are new dioceses and in both the bishops are the first to be appointed. (The former was created in 1965 and the latter in 1964.) Thus these

---

critics, and on an interview that Thomas G. Sanders conducted with him in June 1970. I have visited Salvador and Recife several times, but am relying on other's research and observation for Itabira and Cratéus. To undertake the analysis of the four, I have collected everything available on the bishops and the dioceses in question, have conducted at least 20 interviews and have extensive documentation on all. For the best popular account of three of the four, excluding Dom Eugênio, see the interesting report by Henri Fesquet in *Le Monde*, 30 September 1970; what is significant is his choice of Dons Helder, Fragoso and Noronha for particular attention.

[6] Rolim's study covered Recife and Cratéus. Of the latter he noted, 'We would venture to say that in this renovation there are, undoubtedly, new relationships established. In this renovation, the human element is crucial – the bishop, some young priests and laymen favour a joint pastoral program involving reflection and action.' 'Estrutura da Igreja no Brasil', unpublished research report No. 1.2 of PPC of CNBB (Rio de Janeiro: CERIS, 1968), p. 148.

men did not have to confront many of the bureaucratic elements of the established Church when they took over. There was no bishop's palace, no creaky and compromised curia and none of the interwoven relationships which go to make up the structure of a local society in which the Church is an agent on a par with the civil and military authorities. The diocese of Cratéus in 1965 had only 12 secular priests in 11 parishes and 15 nuns in 2 schools. Fesquet states that in 1970 there were the same 12 priests, but 20 monks; he makes no mention of the nuns.[7] There are four lay groups surviving from the past and the description of the diocese in the *Anuário Católico* for 1965 takes up two pages. Itabira is somewhat larger and occupies four pages in the *Anuário*. It has 40 parishes, 52 priests and 12 religious. There are 12 schools, hospitals, orphanages and other such institutions; there are six lay groups.[8] Both bishops told me of their difficulties in bringing the clergy round to a new way of thinking, in getting rid of old institutions and groups and emphasized the general problems of internal Church change, but these problems are minor in comparison with what they would face internally in other dioceses.[9]

While Recife and Salvador do not approach the extensive and complex confusion that characterizes the archdiocese of São Paulo, they are still of another category from Cratéus and Itabira. It cannot be accidental that both Dom Helder and Dom Eugênio made symbolic gestures of leaving the old structure behind and adopting new ones; Dom Helder moved out of the archbishop's palace to a small house and Dom Eugênio had the old structure renovated while he also lived simply. In both cases, a great deal of publicity was given to these minor events, which represented poverty and a break with the triumphant past of the institution. Symbolic gestures are called for when organizational complexities alone do not allow anything more.

Recife was founded as a diocese in 1676 and Dom Helder is the 31st prelate (it became an archbishopric in 1900). Salvador was the first diocese in Brazil, having been founded in 1551, and Dom Eugênio was the 32nd prelate; the see has carried the cardinal's hat since 1953. Recife has 70 parishes, 107 secular priests, 14 male religious orders, 32 female orders, 64 lay groups (including *irmandades*), Church schools, hospitals, diocesan newspapers, radio stations, three movie houses, a university and six faculties. Salvador has 79 parishes, 75 secular priests, 20 male religious orders, 24 female orders, 17 lay groups (not counting *irmandades*), Church schools, hospitals, several newspapers, two radio stations, 11 movie houses, one university and five faculties. Recife occupies 16 pages in the *Anuário* and Salvador 14. The important fact is not simply that Itabira and Cratéus occupy six pages in the *Anuário* and Recife and Salvador 30. It is not just a

---

[7] Data from *Anuário Católico do Brasil*, 3rd ed. (Rio de Janeiro: CERIS, 1965). Fesquet in *Le Monde*.

[8] Material from *Anuário* and from interview with the Bishop. Fesquet states that there are fifty priests and monks, forty of whom are 'worker priests'.

[9] Interviews with Dom Fragoso on 10 January 1968 and with Dom Marcos Noronha on 1 July 1970. The personality factor is a problem in this analysis. The point to be made is the relative difficulty presented by the structural and political obstacles to change.

matter of the latter being 500 % more complex than the former; there are definite qualitative differences, which include old structures, complex because of various religious orders, groups, papers, schools, etc., and people in the Church have commitments to groups and structures which are not easily changed. In short, there are such organizational complexities in these old archdioceses that even highly dynamic and very committed archbishops find it difficult to make changes. There are several public instances in each case where tensions within the Church arose because the bishops were going too fast for some of the clergy; one can only guess about the number of such tensions that did not become public.

As noted above, the archdioceses have schools, radio stations, hospitals, movie houses, etc. – all features which represent the Church's traditionally broad-based approach to influence through a comprehensive and structural integration at all levels of society. Because of the age and size of these archdioceses, they have extensive relationships with other social orders and multiple levels of penetration into the societies. The newer dioceses have weaker structural links with the traditional influence approach, are not so restrained by the extensive institutes and groups, and in general are structurally integrated with less complex local societies. Not only are the dioceses much simpler than the archdioceses, but their local societies are very primitive in comparison. Cratéus and Itabira are not important cities like Salvador and Recife. Cratéus has a population of 250,000, is 80 % rural and has no industry. Itabira has 350,000, is both urban and rural and has considerable mining. Recife has a population of 1,600,000, is the most important port of the Northeast, the capital of the state and a focal point for all the region. Salvador is basically the same.[10] The point of the statistics is simple: most people until recently did not care what went on in Itabira and Cratéus, but they did care and know about what took place in Recife and Salvador. Because the Churches in the former two are structurally integrated with weaker societies in unimportant cities, the bishops have more flexibility in controlling their respective dioceses. There are obstacles to change nevertheless, but they do not compare with those found in the big cities.[11]

The Church has always been integrated into society, provided an essentially legitimating role for the political elites and is expected to maintain a certain

[10] To demonstrate the differences between the four, some facts from the *Enciclopédia dos Municípios Brasileiros* can be cited. The articles are not standardized, but some scattered facts are interesting. Recife is third largest city in terms of population in Brazil and Salvador is sixth. The other two are near the bottom. Cratéus is 80 % rural, exclusively agricultural; there are 4 doctors, 3 dentists and 3 pharmacists; and 2 banks have agencies. Itabira is 67 % rural (1950); only 7.3 % of the population is in industry; there are 7 doctors and 5 banks have agencies. Recife in 97 % urban, based mainly on manufacturing industry (metal, textiles and foods), there are 704 doctors, 248 dentists and 22 veterinarians; 7 banks have central offices and 23 have agencies. Salvador is 87 % urban, based on services (30 %) and industry; there are 986 doctors, 150 dentists; 32 banks have centers there and 17 have agencies. The first two have no newspapers; Recife has 7 dailies and Salvador has 4. Cratéus has an army railroad batallion; Recife is the headquarters for the 4th army.

[11] During my interview with Dom Marcos Noronha he discussed his problems, but noted that they were nothing in comparison with those of Dom Helder, for example. He specifically noted that there were no papers in Itabira and no army and thus his room for manoeuver was greater, although in retrospect not great enough.

image. A changed Church (and this must include a social change role after the decade of involvement, the papal encyclicals and formal commitments by the bishops) must of necessity have a different role vis-à-vis the status quo. This was vital to the strategies of change described in the last chapter and is just as essential to these bishops.[12] Many elements in society do not want the Church to change its role and assume a social change mission; these people were the ones who benefited from the military seizure of power in 1964, which has further buttressed the status quo during the past eight years. Thus when these committed bishops talk about change, it immediately assumes a political connotation, because it concerns such an integral institution in society and because the mere mention of topics such as unionization, political parties, etc. is very radical indeed. The Church, in attempting to redefine its role in society, mainly in order to reestablish influence, comes into contact with politics simply because the idea of religion today is no longer wholly divorced from the wordly reality in which men live. All the bishops face the same problem in a political sense when they attempt to change. However, the Churches in the dioceses are not so complex and important as in the archdioceses. Their political problems exist but they have not, until recently, been so grave as those of the archbishops.

Dom Helder's fame as a social progressive preceded him when he took over as archbishop of Olinda-Recife two weeks after the coup and this notoriety was immediately crystallized by two events: the document which he and 17 other bishops issued on 13 April, declaring their continued commitment to the CNBB ideology and programs of social involvement; and the fact that he gave asylum to the sister of Miguel Arraes, the imprisoned progressive governor of the state. Dom Helder has maintained his forthright position in favor of renovation within the Church, a social change role and a renegotiated position in the polity and society. Because of the latter two points he seems to have accomplished relatively little, as society's reactions seem almost to overwhelm his not inconsiderable energies and personal charisma. With regard to internal Church reform he seems relatively successful. He is forced to deal with an ossified bureaucracy, but appears to have mobilized it well enough, although it is clear that he gets along better with the younger and more progressive foreign priests than with most of the Brazilian clergy in the archdiocese. The PPC is being implemented in the area, there is a great deal of cooperation between Catholics and Protestants, and issues such as liturgy and seminary reform have progressed very well. However, in terms of social programs and overall dynamic the archdiocese is almost inert. Dom Helder attempts to cover the social field by promoting programs such as the Banco de Providência and Operação Esperança and deals with social reform in his weekly radio broadcasts, which relate the Gospel to the reality of the Northeast. Beyond that, except for a few small groups and minor programs, almost nothing

[12] If there is any doubt concerning their adherence to a social change role, see Revolução Dentro da Paz; Dom Eugênio's speech on 'Social Action of the Church' to the Escola Superior de Guerra, reprinted in SEDOC 2:1 (July 1969), pp. 61–75; Dom Fragoso's paper reprinted in LADOC; and Dom Marcos Noronha's frequent articles in Revista Vozes of Petrópolis.

substantiates the fact that this bishop has been known for some two decades as the most famous progressive in the Brazilian Church.[13]

Because he is known to be attempting to change the Church and extract it from its traditional role in society, Dom Helder is opposed on all sides by the strongest possible means and can barely survive.[14] As will become clear in the next chapter, the number of incidents which involve attacks on Dom Helder or his colleagues is almost limitless. The process began in 1966 and has grown to the point where his freedom of action is non-existent. When he has tried to mobilize groups of laymen the local authorities have made life difficult for them and they have ultimately given up. When he has tried to encourage novel experiments, such as priests living in the slums or working with the laboring class, they have been harassed and many actually expelled from the country. One of his chief religious aides, Msgr. Marcelo Cavalheira, a brilliant and responsible individual, was imprisoned for no apparent reason. Another aide, Pe. José Comblin, has been attacked over and over again in the papers and in early 1972 was not permitted to re-enter Brazil. Dom Helder's house has been machine-gunned four or five times; right-wing graffiti are written all over the outside walls; he often receives telephone threats to his life; and in May 1969 one of his closest associates, Pe. Antônio Henrique Pereira Neto, was brutally killed. The lesson of Pe. Henrique's death was lost on no one: it was a warning that Dom Helder must remain inactive and that nobody could work with him.[15] Today Dom Helder is not mentioned in the news media except in order to attack him. People living in foreign countries see far more of Dom Helder on television than do Brazilians.

The atmosphere in Recife is oppressive. Most of those around Dom Helder want to work to change the Church, but the difficulties are often insurmountable; also the bishop understandably finds it difficult to ask people to work with him as it could mean their assassination. The result is passivity and a 'waiting for better times'. In the meantime relatively little is going on in the archdiocese and one has the feeling that there will not be much improvement for a long while. All of this was brought about by Dom Helder's commitment to a social role and to a different position for the Church in society and politics.[16]

---

[13] My interviews in Recife in July 1970 left me with a very depressed and pessimistic view of possible progress. However, I have been informed that Operação Esperança has actually taken off as Dom Helder hoped it would and has mobilized the people themselves by its programs. Dom Helder's international and national roles will be touched upon in the next chapter.

[14] All of his documents make this point of extraction clear; the following statement by a foreign journalist captures the sense very nicely. 'The Archbishop is striving to shift the base of Catholicism's prestige from a static reliance on "The weight and tradition of the ecclesiastical institution" to a dynamic involvement in an ideology and cause attuned to the world's needs...And he would forfeit the advantages which derive from an alliance with the State in order to gain independence of action.' Foland, 'Northeast Brazil: The Archbishop of Recife and Olinda'.

[15] On the murder see documents in *SEDOC* 2:2 (August 1969), pp. 143–9, or any newspaper account.

[16] Page's article in the *New York Times* gives an accurate recent impression of the atmosphere of oppression and the impediments to Church change.

Whereas Dom Helder is vilified, shot at and slandered, Dom Eugênio was voted 'personality of the year' in 1967 by the Association of Political Writers of Bahia, meets with the President of the Republic for several hours at a stretch, became a Cardinal and is now Archbishop of Rio de Janeiro.[17] However, while Dom Helder seems barely to progress locally because of political threats and attacks, Dom Eugênio gets nowhere because he continues to play the political game. This is not to belittle Dom Eugênio and his accomplishments. He did, after all, create the Natal Movement, which formed the basis for many of the important reforms in the pre-1964 CNBB. However, at that time, the political climate was ripe for such innovations and a sociologist who studied the Movement noted that this atmosphere was an important factor in explaining its feasibility.[18] However, after the coup Dom Eugênio was denounced in the Rio Grande do Norte state legislature as a Communist and transferred to Salvador, where many referred to him as the 'socialist bishop'; he has since had the benefit of a learning experience based on the example of Dom Helder. The two archbishops are very close friends, say that they agree on goals, but work differently. They do indeed work differently and this distinction is worth discussing at some length.

Dom Eugênio is known by his critics as 'the youngest bishop of Christendom'. Obviously he is a prelate of a rather different kind from the model of the 1930s, or even from the majority of those currently holding office in Brazil, but his line is essentially the same on the all-important question of the position of the Church in society and politics. He clearly wants to direct the institution toward a larger social role, of a progressive as opposed to a revoluntionary kind, but he thinks he can do this *in cooperation with* the government and local elites. Dom Helder believes he cannot and the elites do not want much to do with him anyway. Dom Eugênio, however, points to the historical collaboration between Church and government and believes that the former has something to tell the latter, in the best Christendom tradition, about social change. According to Sanders, he thinks the Church can have a dialogue with the government and assist it in its role of improving society.[19]

Dom Eugênio has referred to himself on occasion as a '50/50 man', a phrase which refers both to religious and social concerns and to Church – state relations. In point of fact this relationship, in the present political context which reinforces the traditional relationships, comes to mean 80 % religious (as opposed to social) and 90 % state (as opposed to Church). He does not allow conflicts in his archdiocese and if they do occur he attempts to smother them. For example, the abbot of the Benedictine Monastery in Salvador has been involved in several conflicts

---

[17] See *Jornal do Brasil*, 23 January 1968 on his 'personality of the year' award; *Veja* of 27 May 1970 for his contacts with government; *Realidade* of January 1970 for his style and political operations. Sanders notes in personal communications that Dom Eugênio is undoubtedly the main episcopal contact with the government.

[18] Interview with a sociologist who has written on the Movement in São Paulo on 14 February 1968.

[19] See Dom Eugênio's paper for the Escola Superior de Guerra (the highest level military 'think tank'), which is moderate and fairly convincing. Both the audience and the paper itself are indicative of his approach. Reprinted in *SEDOC* 2:1 (July 1969), pp. 61–75.

with the local politicians and military. Dom Eugênio has in most instances attempted to smooth over the problems or convince the abbot to back down.[20] In 1966 he closed down the JUC, which still existed in the archdiocese, because of its political involvement. When a French priest got into political difficulties with the authorities in 1969, Dom Eugênio would not support him, but attempted to transfer him to a remote parish; the priest resisted and left the country. Dom Eugênio, in trying to cooperate with the government and local elites, will not allow problems to surface; if they do he seeks to suppress them or get the opponents to compromise, even if this means a concession against the presumed role of the Church. Because of his desire to cooperate and fear of problems, Dom Eugênio must direct everything himself rather than delegate authority (which seems to suit his personality fairly well) and cannot allow the setting up of controversial programs. Thus little or nothing has been done to mobilize the laity except for those in the highest social classes, and the social programs are such as can be supported by the government. This is not meant as a criticism; the leadership courses, programs for unionization and other such holdovers from the Natal Movement are useful but rather innocuous. Because he has kept all control in his own hands, Dom Eugênio has not allowed the PPC to become dynamic and the feeling of reform or renewal in the archdiocese, judging from extensive interviews over a three-year period, is minimal. For religious renewal, the big innovation in 1970 was the *Cursilhos de Cristandade*, which so far in Brazil focus only on the religious, deal exclusively with the upper classes and are alienating. Whereas Dom Helder has spoken out nationally and internationally on the necessity for social and political change and is attacked, Dom Eugênio offers courses for technicians, politicians, communications experts and the industrialists in order to convince them. In sum, Dom Eugênio's tactics are very different from Dom Helder's, because he cooperates with the local and national elites in order to convince them. In the process, however, it seems that his influence is eroded almost to zero, in that he accepts their system, within its limits, and becomes overly compromised. In his attempt to obtain status and influence for the Church by his high level political manoeuvers it seems that he is functioning normally for the neo-Christendom model: defining influence through the use of state power. He relies on the prestige of politicians for his programs, has plenty of government money for his projects, and when he became Cardinal the state government overdid itself in celebrations and publicity. In this way he gathers influence and the state maintains legitimacy, but it means that the Church remains as committed as ever to the status quo and internal innovations are squelched.[21]

In conclusion, then, the committed or innovative bishops meet varying degrees of success. Originally those in the rural areas seemed to make considerably more progress than those in the big cities, but the distinction seems less and less relevant. Because of the efforts of Dom Fragoso and Dom Marcos Noronha, they too have

---

[20] Interviews with the abbot, several priests and laymen in Salvador in 1967, 1968 and 1970.
[21] Interviews with priests in Salvador on 3 July 1970 on his becoming Cardinal; on accepting limits to his actions, interview with an important priest on 4 July and Sanders' communication with me.

had increasingly to confront the political impact of social opposition to Church change. Dom Marcos Noronha's solution was relatively clear, in that he simply resigned the see. Dom Fragoso is close to Dom Helder's approach in that he is trying to take it head on and, given his isolation and relatively minute area involved, seems to have had some success. Unless more and more bishops resign, however, the alternatives will be either to confront the opposition (assuming that the bishop desires change) or to follow Dom Eugênio's approach and compromise. In neither instance does the task of Church innovation appear so simple as in the people strategy; the structural model is more accurate. What is most interesting, however, is that, beyond the control of Dom Helder, Dom Eugênio and others, a process has been initiated which has conflict as its motor force and promises to sever the Church from established society.

Section IV: The Church and state in conflict

9. Origins and process of conflict

The decade of social involvement (up to 1964) showed that the Church could act to promote change. The participation in the 'Brazilian Revolution' distinguished the CNBB group and ACB from a long ecclesiastical tradition of splendid rhetoric and little action in the interests of the lower strata of society. In this case, action came to be defined as subversive, with the result that many priests and laymen were persecuted for their behavior. While the activists either went underground or dispersed after 1964, the government still remembered that Church militants meant what they said far more than did the traditional Churchmen, or even Communists for that matter.

The social involvement ideology formulated before 1964 was never repudiated by the Church. The vast majority of bishops simply ignored it; they could not regress as this would have resulted in a clear contradiction between Church orientation after the Council and Pope Paul's very advanced 'Populorum Progressio'. Within Brazil, progressives continued to promote the development of this ideology, although in a vacuum. The ideology remained, however, with support from Rome.

Some bishops, priests and laymen continued to act according to the ideology and in line with the pre-1964 programs. The large national programs disappeared (MEB might be construed as such, but after 1964 its orientation was less controversial), but a dozen or so individual bishops, including Dons Helder, Fragoso and Marcos Noronha, continued to do what they could despite government disapproval. Moreover there were individual priests working with student groups, organizing the workers milieu, attempting to promote local agrarian reforms and so forth. Laymen met in groups and made statements, talked about the relevance of 'Populorum Progressio' for Brazil, attempted to organize workers and undertook other similar social or political activities. There was no overall thrust or coordination to these activities, but the fact remains that they existed.

These observations on the post-1964 Church provide the foundation for understanding a process which could not take off without a favorable political climate. In a sense, this is a return to the discussion of the political situation after World War II, which provided the stimulus and the conditions whereby the Church could respond. Now, however, the situation is reversed, because the Church is providing the incentive and the government is reacting. Essential to an understanding of the conflict process is some appreciation of the Brazilian regime since 1964 and its increasingly hostile attitude towards the Church. The Church has been evolving in response to changes initiated by the regime, but the initial spark was caused by governmental reaction to previous Church change.

Numerous studies have been carried out on the coup of 1964 and the resulting military regime.[1] The military took power in 1964 because they thought the

---

[1] See for instance Alfred C. Stepan, *The Military in Politics: Changing Patterns in Brazil* (Princeton, N.J.: Princeton University Press, 1971); the very excellent analysis by Thomas

policies and personality of President João Goulart would destroy the country through inflation, corruption and incompetence, or because he appeared ready to hand the country over to the Communists. As the result of the decay of civil institutions and the formulation of an ideology which legitimized their rule, the military took over with the intention of remaining for some time, whereas in the past they had only played a 'moderating role'. Thus rather than attempt to legitimize themselves through elections or plebiscites, they relied on decree laws, or Institutional Acts, to justify their positions in civilian roles. While there have been high and low points during the past eight years, the general direction of the process of control is clear: the military has increasingly centralized political and economic power and has become more authoritarian and less open to external, or even internal, criticism. Under the Castelo Branco government (1964–7) it looked as though there might be an opening for political competition after some 'house cleaning' had been undertaken. During the Costa e Silva government (1967–9) the system did indeed open, partly because of Costa e Silva's vacillation, and chaos threatened, at least in the eyes of the hard liners among the military. In the face of increasing criticism, urban terrorism, protests and so forth, the right wingers reacted and the 'coup within the coup' came about on 13 December 1968, with the decree of the Institutional Act No. 5, which gave the executive power to close Congress and other legislative assemblies, remove citizens from office and political activities, eliminate the rights of habeus corpus and in effect subvert the 1967 Constitution, which itself had been dictated by the military.

Since that time the process of centralization and authoritarianism has continued.[2] Today in Brazil there is legal censorship of a very severe variety, the death penalty is applicable to crimes against national security, politicians as well as bureaucrats can be compulsorily retired without explanation and habeus corpus is non-existent. When President Costa e Silva became ill in August 1969, the military did not even bother to consult the people about the next president, but held an election within their own ranks and picked General Emílio Garrastazu Médici, who was a follower of the hard line and head of the Serviço Nacional de Informação (SNI – or military intelligence). This regime of illegality, or maybe super-legality, has given rise to a political situation in which the government can effectively do as it wishes and in which abuse and arbitrariness are rife.

The main reason for the military intervention in 1964, and probably the main motor force behind the increasing radicalization to the right, was the fear of subversion. Unfortunately, this type of concern can lead to paranoia and a vicious circle, creating groups of people who by definition are subversive and thus become such. Initially hundreds were persecuted, because the military feared the Communists had infiltrated all the urban unions, rural unions, political parties and the student movement. Then when these had been suppressed, the government came

---

G. Sanders, 'Institutionalizing Brazil's Conservative Revolution', AUFS Reports, 15:5 December 1970; and Ronald Schneider, The Political System of Brazil (New York: Columbia University Press, 1971).

[2] See Constituição da República Federativa do Brasil (São Paulo: Editôra Atlas, 1970).

to define almost any opposition as subversion and by the nature of their responses have closed all channels of participation and protest. Therefore individuals and groups which may not see eye to eye with the government on some matters have absolutely no platform for their criticism and seem to be driven either into apathy or armed rebellion. So goes the process of radicalization and polarization. Today in Brazil any criticism is taken as subversion, groups and organizations are disbanded and the people are continually intimidated.[3]

After the initial purges in 1964 there was little protest until about 1967. Since the 5th Institutional Act, however, protest, action and terrorism have been decreasing. The main instrument used by the regime in putting down dissent seems to be torture and its corollaries of intimidation and fear. There is a tremendous amount written about torture in Brazil and I do not want to discuss it, save in regard to the conflicts. The President does not perhaps condone torture, but in relying on the 5th Institutional Act, which he has the power to abrogate, he opens the way to arbitrariness, thereby presaging torture.[4]

The Brazilian military regime is not by any means a traditional conservative Latin American military government. Sanders refers to the system as a 'conservative revolution' and indicates several distinctive features.[5] The government is concerned with development and making Brazil 'a great country'; to accomplish this it has relied upon neocapitalism in a technocratic framework. Politics is not allowed because it only causes inefficiency and waste. The regime is closely aligned with the West (with Western and Christian Civilization) and very staunchly anti-Communist. Current today is an idea of security which focuses less on external than on internal threats and from this arises a mobilization to oppose guerrilla warfare. Although the regime is oriented toward the West, it is not subservient to the United States and is extremely nationalistic. Judging from the available national and international statistics, the government has been extremely effective in the economic sense, in that since 1969 the gross national product has increased 9% annually with even higher rates of growth for industry, and the annual rate of inflation has fallen to a tolerable 20%.[6] All studies have shown however, that this fantastic growth has not benefited the lower classes, and it is presumably because of this that it has been rapid. The lower classes have been forced to pay the costs of rapid growth and as there are no channels of protest, but only repression, they have no alternative.[7]

[3] Reference to the *New York Times, Le Monde, The New Republic*, etc. will illustrate these assertions.

[4] See the article by Ralph della Cava, 'Torture in Brazil', *Commonweal* 92 (24 April 1970), or any of the *LADOC*, Latin American Documentation (Washington, D.C.) series or even the *New York Times*.

[5] Sanders, 'Institutionalizing Brazil's Conservative Revolution'.

[6] *Ibid.*, p. 5. And *Brazil*, First National City Bank, April 1971.

[7] See City Bank, *Ibid.*, p. 15, which shows that real wages have dropped; Sanders in 'The Social Functions of Futebol', AUFS Fieldstaff Reports 14:2, July 1970, cites others' statistics, showing that the cost of living between 1966 and 1969 increased 117% and the minimum salary increased only 86%. Citing ECLA data, he indicates that Brazil has the most inequitable income distribution in Latin America. An excellent article by Zeno

The Brazilian regime is unusual in Latin America today. The elites since 1964 have put themselves squarely on the side of Western Christian Civilization and as Sanders notes, 'Brazil's conservative revolution exalts old-fashioned virtues'. Intricately linked with these virtues, and certainly with Western Civilization, is the Catholic Church. The presidents have affirmed their faith in Catholicism; Costa e Silva visited the Pope before taking office, his wife raised money to complete the Cathedral of Brasília, Médici is apparently a devout believer, as are those around him. The current President, like his two predecessors, has attempted at all times to demonstrate the agreement between the Church and state; this link has taken such diverse forms as masses on the day of the Revolution, the reception by Costa e Silva of the Pope's Rose of Gold in 1967, Médici's meeting with the Cardinals in Brasília and so on. Since 1964 the military leaders have looked to the Church for support in building a 'bigger and better' Brazil and in keeping down the Communists. As General Sizeno Sarmento, the Commander of the 1st Army, observed in a speech: 'The two basic supports of Western Civilization, the Church and the army.'[8]

There is no reason to doubt the Catholic beliefs of the present-day Brazilian elites. However, their Catholicism and their Church are not the ones that they put down in 1964, nor is it the Church of Vatican II or of 'Populorum Progressio'. It is true that the government outdid itself in welcoming the encyclical. Costa e Silva stated that the ruling doctrine of his government 'is the humanistic philosophy exalted by the last encyclical of Pope Paul VI'.[9] On the third anniversary of the coup the Minister of the Army, General Líra Tavares, stated, 'The predominant aspect of the meaning of the revolution . . . is contained in the higher and more expressive message of the encyclical "Populorum Progressio".'[10] The Chancellor, Magalhães Pinto, sent a message to the Pope congratulating him on the encyclical and stated that it represented the foreign policy of Brazil. But let anyone attempt to enact the teaching of this encyclical and then it becomes clear just how committed the government is to the 'humanistic philosophy' of the Pope. For example, in the case of one conflict, the military judged subversive a priest's statement in which he confessed that, 'he struggled for the non-violent transformation of our country by means of the revolution of the Gospel and he wanted our people to participate fully in the problems of our community'.[11]

Santiago, 'A Arrancada Econômica do Brasil: Custos Sociais e Instrumentalidades', *Dados* (1972), pp. 7–20 deals precisely with the economic miracle and who is really paying for it.

[8] *Notícias da Igreja Universal* (NIU), Numero Especial, 'A Hora da Opção', No. 68/72 (January and February 1969), p. 58. This publication has produced two special numbers on Church–state conflicts; the above and 'Uma Nova Questão Religiosa?' No. 46/47 (February 1968) as well as other relevant documents. Its material is taken from papers, interviews, etc., so it will not in all cases be possible to cite the initial sources. It ceased publication in 1969, but much of the coverage is to be found in Charles Antoine, *L'Eglise et le pouvoir au Brésil* (Paris: Desclée de Brouwer, 1971).

[9] *Jornal do Brasil*, 15 April 1967.

[10] *Ibid.*, 1 April 1967.

[11] *NIU* 68/72 (January and February 1969), p. 58.

The Church that the military elites have in mind is that traditional one which baptized them, educated them, married them, spoke for morality and against Communism, and in general supported the status quo. It is the Church of the 1964 Rosary Marches, of charity for the poor, and it is the one which 'finds strength in its traditionalism'.[12] However, this is not the Church that began to form in Brazil before 1964, nor is it the one promoted by the Council, nor the one that talks about violence in Pope Paul's encyclical. The position of the military on this false church, or even anti-Christ, is very bitter indeed. The commander in Belo Horizonte stated that the military was stunned by 'a spectacle . . . of some priests who defend the giving over of our country to one of the worst enemies of the Church'.[13] A syndrome emerges when the military confronts a slightly changed Church: Marxist principles have invaded the Church; a fifth column seeks shelter in the institution and acts as an anti-Christ; principles of morality and discipline have disappeared; and only a minority is at work in name of the whole Church. What becomes apparent is the bitterness and love–hate relationship on the part of the military. They did anticipate the Church's assistance in governing the country, but it seems that even this institution has been invaded by enemies and must be purged. On the one hand, they defend its importance and align themselves with its traditions; and on the other they attack it, imprison priests and persecute even bishops.[14]

It took two years for the first conflict to erupt. Immediately following the coup there were persecutions of clergy and laymen who had been involved in social change programs. After these elements were dealt with the government felt that it could rely on the Church. The change in the CNBB and elimination of ACB ensured that the platform of previous programs, which became illegal, was no longer viable. On the side of the Church there was an initial period of good faith, when even progressive elements were willing to see if this government was better than the fiasco before 1964. The bishops were content that a Communist revolution had been avoided and even those who opposed its manner of coming to power thought that the new government might enact some of the reforms which the previous government had promised. Of course most of the hierarchy welcomed a government that promoted order and stability. The state was certain of Church support in maintaining order once Dom Helder and his associates were isolated and the Church was willing to go along for the time being. However, with time it became clear that the government was doing nothing more than maintaining order by suppressing dissent, and was not carrying out those reforms which seemed necessary to maintain stability in the long run. After an initial period of waiting some sectors, mainly those related to the CNBB before 1964, felt it their duty to prod the government a little by criticism or by calling its attention to

---

[12] Quotation from the wife of the Governor of São Paulo, Sodre, in *Correio da Manhã*, 7 December 1967.
[13] *SEDOC* 1:9 (March 1969) p. 1,210.
[14] For an article that gives a good insight into how the military perceives the Church, see General Carlos Studart Filho, *Temas Sociais* (Fortaleza: Imprensa Universitária, 1969).

problems.[15] Once they began to speak out, even in a calm fashion, the military reacted very bitterly and the conflict was initiated.

Ten incidents before the 5th Institutional Act

A series of Church–state conflicts that occurred between July 1966 and early 1971 serve well to illustrate the changing relationship between the two institutions, as well as the various issues involved.[16] To maintain coherence some categories are followed: (1) the initiating factor(s) with attention to the particular party which brought on the conflict; (2) the manner, or tactics, whereby the conflict was enacted, which can range from talk to imprisonments, repression and torture, and include the levels of the institutions which become involved; (3) the manner by which the conflict was resolved, which varies from real resolution to a mere propaganda campaign to cover the issues; and (4) the immediate effects on the Church and state; that is, how the particular conflict immediately affected the relations between the two.

The first important conflict after 1964 took place in the Northeast and lasted from mid-July to the end of August 1966. It centered on the bishops of the CNBB region Northeast II (Rio Grande do Norte, Paraíba, Pernambuco and Alagoas) and especially on the personality of the Archbishop of Olinda-Recife, Dom Helder Câmara. To a large extent, therefore, this was an encounter involving the pre-1964 CNBB group. In March 1966, with lay and clergy participation, and with the blessings of their bishops, Ação Católica Operária (ACO) met in Recife for three days and studied the predicament of the worker in the Northeast. Their public statement at the end of the conference was critical.[17] Four months later,

---

[15] As Otto Engel said at the time of the first conflict in 1966: 'It has now become easier to analyse the silence of the bishops during the first two years of the revolution. It appears as though, without entering into the merit of the legitimacy of the revolution, the bishops, in an evident demonstration of good sense, gave their confidence to the new government. Brazil needs a strong government, capable of realizing social reforms as a preliminary condition to open the road for development. The bishops are not completely withdrawing their confidence, but simply insisting that what the Church wanted done was not done.' *Fôlha da Semana*, 18–24 August 1966.

[16] I have selected the most important and representative conflicts out of around one hundred. I have excluded five very important conflicts originating in Church support of university student movements, because, although they do not contradict anything stated here, they involve more explanation than necessary for my present purposes. For these five see *Notícias da Igreja Universal* 56/57 of July and 62 of October 1968; *Paz e Terra* 6, pp. 281–96. My sources on the conflicts include some interviews in 1967–8 and about forty interviews in June–July 1970, which sought specific information on conflicts and results; the *NIU* series; *Paz e Terra*; *SEDOC*; extensive documentation received from friends in Brazil; letters; and all the papers of this period.

[17] 'The encounter revealed that the working class in the Northeast is marked above all by a contempt for man. This contempt, of which the workers are victims, is manifested by persecutions of all types...There appears to be a plan to destroy people by eliminating their dignity and their rights...The working class in the Northeast is less a class and more a grouping of destroyed people.' *Paz e Terra* 2 cites most of the documents on this conflict; taken from pp. 242, 245. Statement made on 10 March 1966.

in July, Ação Católica Rural (ACR) and Juventude Agrária Católica (JAC) held a conference and issued a similar public statement on the situation in the region.[18] On 14 July, bishops of the Northeast region, with its center in Recife, met in an ordinary session and issued a moderate statement of support for the two Catholic Action groups. They offered their solidarity to the workers, especially those being exploited. They stated: 'If, through imperative of conscience, we condemn injustice, we do not want to increase the splits between men or between social groups: what we want is to unite more and more the People of God. However, the maternal concern of the Church has to be directed primarily to those who suffer.'[19] This statement was signed by the fifteen bishops attending the meeting.

General Gouveia do Amaral, the Commander of the 10th Military Region with its headquarters in Fortaleza, prohibited the publication and circulation of the bishops' statement. At about the same time the military distributed two clandestine notes to the clergy in the Northeast, violently attacking Dom Helder Câmara. Among other criticisms, the notes pointed out that Dom Helder was an agitator and took 'pleasure in appearing on television engaged in histrionic excesses and theatrical displays [and that] . . . the activities of Dom Helder particularly divided the Catholic flock, exacerbating the generation conflicts by throwing youth against their parents in arguments'.[20] Pointing to the signs of moral decay in society, the notes concluded that Dom Helder was behind it all, because of his demagogy and dangerous programs. The conflict was therefore initiated by the censorship and the notes; it was quite clear that elements in the military were attempting to isolate Dom Helder and others of the CNBB group from the larger institution. The conflict intensified soon after because of rumors that Dom Helder was to be removed as Archbishop of Recife.

The manner of enacting the conflict was exclusively by statements and testimonies in the regional and national news media, and this was front page material of national interest. The first conflict was important not only in showing the divisions and the forms of unity in the society and Church itself in relation to a social question, but also in establishing certain lines of argument which would appear again and again in later cases. Interestingly enough, after the military's action in initiating the conflict no more criticism was heard from them. This would not be the pattern in later cases.

On 21 August the well-known and elderly sociologist, Gilberto Freyre, published an article on the conflict. He argued that the Church had no right to criticize the government for failing to improve conditions in the Northeast, as the Church itself had done much to make the situation what it was. In fact, he speculated that

---

[18] 'The rural man gradually becoming aware of his dignity as a man and worker, finds himself a victim of a structure that reduces him to an infra-human.' *NIU* 46/47, p. 5. These movements in Catholic Action, ACO, ACR, and JAC had been innocuous and thus were not eliminated, as JUC and JEC had been. They had never been significant in size nor outspoken in criticism.

[19] 'Nova Questão Religiosa?' *Paz e Terra* 2, pp. 248–9.

[20] *Ibid.*, pp. 252–3.

the bishops' criticism was motivated by a guilt complex.[21] Of course, the Church's omissions in the past had been recognized by many of the bishops whom Freyre was criticizing, and Dom Helder himself justified the present need for social action partly in terms of responsibility for the past. Whereas the bishops understood past neglect as justification for present action, Freyre would not let them do penance for these sins. Specifically, he would not forgive Dom Helder either for his past as a fascist youth or for having changed into a progressive bishop. He compared Dom Helder with the Nazi Goebbels, in aspect, personality and technique. Noting that some people alluded to Dom Helder as a possible presidential candidate, Freyre observed that he would end up being the Brazilian Kerensky. In one article, then, Freyre attacked the Church for its past and for its present attempts to change, called Dom Helder a Fascist and then described him as a tool of the Communists. While Freyre was extremely outspoken, it was clear from others' statements that he voiced the opinions of a sizeable conservative section in Brazil. They simply could not believe that the Church would, in good faith, adopt a social role and if it did they wanted no part of this Church. In addition, many blamed Dom Helder personally for leading the Church astray.

The bishops of the Northeast were criticized from within the Church by Dom Castro Mayer of Campos, Rio de Janeiro, who is a member of the ultra-reactionary Tradição, Família, e Propriedade (TFP) group. He wrote a letter to the bishops criticizing the language of their document, which would surely have grave consequences 'for a country that desires to repel Communism in a decisive manner'.[22] He was disturbed because their statement did not show any appreciation of how the Communists might use it to promote class conflict. In short, Dom Castro Mayer was afraid that the Northeastern bishops were doing the work of the Communists: they were, in common words, *inocentes uteis* or useful innocents.

The very important conservative paper *Estado de São Paulo* used the letter of Dom Mayer in an editorial, in which it recognized in his words, 'that old Church, under whose protection our country lives and attempts to realize its destiny'. And the editorial was eager to interpret Church doctrine in stating that 'the intervention [of the bishops of the Northeast] is fundamentally in deviation from the spirit and significance of the words of Holy Father Paul VI'.[23] The *Estado de São Paulo* on this occasion and subsequently recognized the true Catholic Church in the traditional Church and took it upon itself to interpret the meaning and application of Church doctrine. The three points made by these conservative reactions to the conflict will recur repeatedly in later instances. They refuse to

---

[21] 'Perhaps it can be said that the manifesto of Your Excellencies is secretly animated by a guilt complex and that some of Your Excellencies attempt to transfer in block the pain of this terrible guilt, of your own venerable consciences, to the present Brazilian government.' *Paz e Terrra* 2, p. 267. As a young priest Helder Câmara was involved with the *Integralistas*. In order not to give this facet of his past more emphasis than it deserves, I will mainly refer the interested reader to others' discussion of it. Cf. José de Broucker, *Dom Helder Câmara* (MaryKnoll, N.Y.: Orbis Press, 1970), pp. 145–6; interview with *L'Express* in France of 15–21 July 1970, and reproduced in Portuguese in *SEDOC* 27 (August 1970), pp. 219–32.

[22] *NIU* 46/47, p. 9.

[23] Cited in *Ibid.*, 6 October 1966.

believe that the Church can change its traditional role as a supporter of the status quo; they claim that when it talks of justice and change, it is 'doing the work of the Communists'; finally all conservatives seem to regard themselves as experts on canon law and theology.

The statements in support of the Northeastern bishops far outnumber the negative ones. These statements are from fourteen bishops, three different clergy groups, two important lay spokesmen, two Protestant groups, members of the opposition party (MDB) and a petition signed by 20,000 laymen in one week. They have in common the following factors: solidarity with the Northeastern bishops and especially Dom Helder, support for their position on Church social involvement, a commitment to pursue the advanced social teachings of the Church, and criticism of the government for its role in this case and generally in society.

The statements indicate a realization that the military was attempting to isolate Dom Helder from the larger institution. The strategy was recognized by the Archbishop of Pôrto Alegre, Dom Vicente Scherer, who noted, 'An attempt was made to weaken the legitimate ecclesiastical authority in the eyes of the priests, something one would least expect from the military where order, discipline, and respect for hierarchy are inculcated and exalted almost like a religion.'[24]

Support for the social involvement of the Church came from all sorts of unexpected quarters. Dom Vicente Scherer stated that he would sign the bishops' document, for it was entirely compatible with Church doctrine.[25] He noted that he had signed the 1963 document of the Central Commission of the CNBB, which was far more wide-ranging and critical than the present one. It was pointed out by others that Church teachings on social matters had changed during the past few years, due to Pope John's encyclicals and the Second Vatican Council. In the concrete context this meant, as Alceu Amoroso Lima put it, 'The missionary Church, the Church present in the world, participating in the world to convert it, to reform it, to defend it against exploitation, misery and injustice.'[26]

The statements promised that despite opposition and even persecution the Church would carry out a mission in the social field. The clergy of Recife made this very clear in their statement and Dom Fragoso confirmed the point when he said, 'The Church of silence cannot exist in Brazil.'[27] In other words, despite opposition the Church would go forwards; as Dom Waldir argued in speaking for the bishops of Rio de Janeiro: 'A persecuted Church is better than a compromised Church.'[28] And in general, by demonstrating that social involvement was legitimate according to current theology, most of the statements showed that the Church would not stop talking and even acting accordingly. One interesting possible result of this action was suggested by Alceu Amoroso Lima, when he

[24] *Paz e Terra* 2, p. 264.
[25] 'Personally I would have no difficulty at all in signing the document which is entirely in conformity with the religious and social doctrine of the Church in all of its parts.' *Ibid.*, p. 264.
[26] *Ibid.*, p. 257.
[27] *Ibid.*, p. 251.
[28] *NIU* 46/47, p. 7.

compared the conflict with the Religious Question of 1874 and Dom Helder with Dom Vital, who was also Bishop of Recife. He raised the question whether this conflict signalled the end of one regime and the beginning of another.

The conflict was resolved through the initiative of the government and the cooperation of the Church. The day after the two clandestine notes were made public by the clergy President Castelo Branco flew to Recife and met with Dom Helder. Four days later it was announced that the Commander of the IVth Army would be transferred from Recife.[29] The new commander was General Souza Aguiar, who took a moderate stand on the prerogatives of the military in relation to the Church. He stated, 'I favor non-involvement in the areas which do not concern me . . . each one in his place and all working in the same direction toward the greatness of our nation, of the army, and of the country.' And upon taking command in Recife he elaborated by stating that it was legitimate for priests working 'in areas as complex as the Northeast to defend the rights of "creatures" oppressed through misery'.[30] Dom Helder met with the new commander personally and later visited his general staff as well. When the papal nuncio was questioned upon leaving a meeting with President Castelo Branco on 25 August he noted: 'There is no conflict between the government authorities and the Church. There have been some complications that we have attempted to eliminate.'[31] Finally, when the new president, Costa e Silva, met with the Pope at the Vatican in January 1967 (before taking office in March), he told him that the Church problems were of the past.

The immediate results of this first conflict were important, for they indicated where the Church and state stood in relationship to each other and established the lines which would be common in later encounters. The government had learned that Dom Helder and the Northeastern bishops could not be so easily isolated and attacked as they had previously seemed to think. When threatened, there was much more unity around the bishops than anyone had anticipated. This unity arose partly from a fear that the corporate entity of the Church would be destroyed, but at least it existed. And the justification for most of the defenses on the part of the Church was in terms of the social mission undertaken before 1964, legitimized by the Council and heavily documented by social encyclicals. The rapid response from the President, Castelo Branco, showed that the government was extremely anxious to moderate the conflict and to resolve the problems quickly and smoothly. The manner of this action suggests that the elite had the impression that the Church possessed something valuable for the regime.

After the resolution of this first conflict in late August, 1966, several problems, misunderstandings and tensions arose concerning the relationship of Church and state. There was nothing that could be termed a conflict until September 1967, and I think that the year of tranquility can be attributed to the initial

---

[29] He did not suffer in any way, however, as he was given a more important command at his next post in Rio and then became Commander of the IVth military region in Minas Gerais. Márcio Moreira Alves, *O Cristo do Povo* (Rio de Janeiro: Editôra Sabiá, 1968), p. 62.

[30] *NIU* 46/47, pp. 6–7.

[31] Moreira Alves, p. 62.

'honeymood period' of the Costa e Silva government. There was little criticism of him and his government until it became obvious that such criticism was necessary to point out problems and to stimulate action. Costa e Silva wanted to be a popular leader, whereas Castelo Branco apparently did not care, and his attempts to be well-liked led to equivocations and contradictions in policy. When it was clear that the government was neither effective nor reformist, people in the Church and outside became vocal in their criticism; this led to many conflict situations.[32]

The next encounter is minor in comparison with the first, for it remained largely regional, touched the national news media only briefly, did not involve individuals as well-known as Dom Helder or the President, and was settled in a week. It is important, however, to deal with this minor conflict so as to maintain continuity with the more important ones, and because they all contribute to the process.

On 6 September, 1967, the archdiocesan radio station in São Luís do Maranhão presented a program in its series 'Between Day and Night' in commemoration of Brazilian Independence Day of 7 September. The program raised the question, 'Is the independence we celebrate real? Is Brazil really independent? Or, on the contrary: is this independence we celebrate false?' After giving statistics and material for reflection, the conclusion was that Brazil was not independent. 'The truth, my friends, is very clear, but also very hard: Brazil continues to be exploited by other countries and by some Brazilians [that are] traitors and enemies of their nation . . . It is up to us [as] Brazilians . . . to make her independent. If we do not . . . then who will do it in our place?'[33] The regional subdelegate of the federal police in Maranhão did not appreciate this form of questioning, shut the radio down for eight days and demanded prior censorship of all the programs in the 'Between Day and Night' series. The police thus instigated discord in response to a provocative program on a Church station. The conflict developed through public statements from all sides. Dom Manoel Edmilson da Cruz, the auxiliary bishop, lodged a formal protest with the military, in which he defended freedom of speech. Dom João José Mota e Albuquerque, the archbishop, expanded this defense by supporting the right of the station to broadcast in accord with general freedom of speech. He stated that this freedom was fundamental to the progress of the country and noted that in this case, 'This Church announces the truth. The truth very often hurts.'[34] This line of defense was carried further in a letter from the archbishop of Fortaleza in Ceará, Dom José Delgado, in which he argued that the radio station was simply trying to help the country through constructive criticism and that silence would produce the opposite result. In this vein, he requested that the leaders of the country control those 'individuals dressed as soldiers who possess only the appearance of military men'.[35] He speculated whether this action of silencing the station was intended to mute one of the

---

[32] de Broucker also refers to this 'honeymoon period', suggesting that it was Dom Helder's opinion, p. 47. See Sanders' critical evaluation of the Costa e Silva regime, 'Institutionalizing Brazil's Conservative Revolution', p. 8.

[33] *Telepax* Documento No. 2, 27 November 1967.

[34] *Ibid.*, p. 3.

[35] *Ibid.*, p. 4.

last living forces in the country. All the statements in defense of the Church station argued for freedom of speech, especially if the speech was critical. Dom José Delgado turned the government's argument around, calling those who silenced a positive force the subversive elements. The conflict was reported in the national news media and briefly debated in the Congress.

The conflict was resolved with the termination of the orders for closure and censorship and the Church elements made nothing further of it. The result was to demonstrate that some sectors of the government were extremely touchy about criticism and likely to use authoritarian means to control it. It gave the Church an opportunity to refer to the Constitution in its defense of freedom of speech, and it successfully 'turned the tables' on the military to show that it was right. After all, the facts the program reported were accurate and when the military suppressed conclusions drawn from them their significance increased.

After the São Luís incident, there was a very minor conflict before the next important episode in November 1967. This conflict again involved Dom Helder with the government, and in particular with the Commander of the IVth Army, who had taken over the previous year in Recife. On 25 September 1967, Dom Helder was received in the state legislative assembly and given the honorary title of 'Citizen of Pernambuco' (he was originally from Ceará). In his acceptance speech he took the opportunity to make a few critical remarks. He compared the current period with that before the abolition of slavery in 1888. After describing the grave social problems in the state, placing particular emphasis on the land-owners' non-compliance with the agrarian reform laws, he stated: 'If tomorrow, Joaquim Nabuco [statesman and abolitionist] were to arrive in Recife and travel through, for example, our sugar cane zone, would he or would he not feel the need to reopen the abolitionist campaign?'[36] Inasmuch as the assembly was largely composed of landowners and industrialists, who were at least partly responsible for the sad state of affairs, the bishop's speech was not well received. Many of the deputies protested against it; the city council of Recife formulated a document in protest; and the Commander of the IVth Army, breaking protocol, left the assembly without greeting the bishop. Later, when this commander also received the title of 'Citizen of Pernambuco', he made a speech in which he stated, 'there is goodness in the masses and it is only when false preachers agitate that there is a possibility the masses will revolt'.[37] The reference to Dom Helder and his speech was not lost on the audience.

On the morning of 5 November 1967 the military (The First Battalion of Armoured Infantry) arrested four youths for distributing subversive pamphlets on the streets of Volta Redonda, an industrial city just outside Rio de Janeiro on

[36] *NIU* 46/47, p. 27. See also the insightful article on Recife and Dom Helder by Frances M. Foland, 'Brazil: Recife, False Gem of the Northeast' (FMF-9) to Richard H. Nolte, Institute of Current World Affairs, New York, 4 November 1967, which shows that his speech was very moderate, quite long and subdued in its criticisms.
[37] *Ibid.*, p. 28.

the road to São Paulo.[38] The four youths were using the automobile of the diocese of Volta Redonda and two of them lived in the bishop's residence. When the bishop, Dom Waldir Calheiros, heard about the arrests he tried to get information from the colonel in charge but received no satisfaction. On the 11th, fourteen armed soldiers invaded the bishop's residence in search of more subversive material. They found none and left without further arrests. The military would not discuss the matter with the press, and as there were several serious rumors circulating about the bishop's personal safety, Dom Waldir gave an interview on the matter to the *Jornal do Brasil*. At one point in the interview he stated, 'While Colonel Armênio [commander of the battalion] is preoccupied with discovering subversive people, I am concerned with . . .' And he then listed seven serious social problems in the region and concluded with an explanation for the childish subversive pamphlet. 'I am concerned with these and other problems, because it is better to combat the causes of dissatisfaction and revolt, poor counselors in the hour of despair, than to confront this or that person who no longer has patience . . . All these pastoral concerns . . . force me to see the causes of despair and subversion.'[39]

This edition of the *Jornal do Brasil* (14 November 1967) was quickly exhausted in Volta Redonda, either bought up or confiscated by the military. Dom Waldir then had his interview from the paper printed for distribution at the diocesan churches the following Sunday. However, three priests and five laymen were arrested while passing out copies of it. Clearly, then, this conflict was initiated and enacted with more serious means than those which had taken place in the Northeast. It began with the distribution of subversive literature and the response of the military in arresting the four, in invading the bishop's residence, and in arresting another eight for passing out a statement which had already been published in the national news media. Here, physical action in arrests and searches replaced words in the manner of enactment. The conflict lasted at least two months, was the most serious conflict since the Religious Question, and took place in an important part of the country between the two most important cities. It involved the national levels in both Church and state institutions and would have lasting effects.

The conflict sparked statements of support for Dom Waldir and his position from broader sectors than was imagined possible. This is due, it seems, not only to the previous momentum of the conflict process in the Northeast but to two other factors. First, as noted above, Volta Redonda is located between Rio and São Paulo and is similar to many other cities in the Central and Southern parts of Brazil; it is most definitely a quite different location from the Northeast,

---

[38] The pamphlet as reproduced in the press was possibly subversive, but given its infantile Marxist orientation should probably have been ignored. It is interesting that it was published in the national press, after the military arrested the four for doing just the same thing (i.e. publishing it) on a very limited scale. Some excepts are: 'In Brazil, 1,000 children die each day because of starvation. For each death that occurs as a result of starvation, misery, sickness and other consequences of U.S. exploitation, the American banks take the sum of CR$2,500,000...This government is a dictatorship at the service of AMERICAN IMPERIAL-ISM...IT IS NECESSARY TO FIGHT FOR LIBERTY.' *Jornal do Brasil*, 22 November 1967.

[39] Quoted in *Paz e Terra* 6, pp. 254–5.

which it does not outwardly resemble. And secondly, Dom Waldir did not belong to the pre-1964 CNBB group. He had been an auxiliary bishop in Rio de Janeiro before being moved to Volta Redonda and was never considered radical; he was known as a moderate pastoral type and one with whom the government should have had no cause to argue. The combination of these two factors not only increased the validity of the Church defense in the face of attack, but also made many in the Church wonder if indeed anyone was safe from such attacks. The statements of support show the new groups mobilized by this conflict and the increasingly lucid nature of their defense of unity and a social mission.

Most of the statements emphasized the fact that the Church had formally modified its goal of influence after the Council and 'Populorum Progressio'. The auxiliary bishop of Belo Horizonte explained that the series of conflicts was due to this altered approach on the part of the Church, which was not understood by the government:

Two important groups, in my view, cause crises: the military in their great fear of Communism and subversive movements and the conservative classes also fearful that the positions of the Church will take away their economic and financial privileges... We have different mentalities, a Church attempting to open itself to all the problems of man and the world, and the government often times tied to particular interests and caught by a situation that they themselves have created.[40]

In fact, many in the Church thought the conflict had healthy results in demonstrating that the Church was sensitive to the needs of the country and its people; in other words, that a new influence model was coming into being, which was more relevant than the traditional one.[41]

This conflict drew supportive statements on the social role of the Church from the conservative Cardinal of Rio, Dom Jaime de Barros Câmara, and the Cardinal of São Paulo, Dom Agnelo Rossi. Before this conflict both Cardinals had not been advocates of social involvement, but the incident involving Dom Waldir at least led to words of support from them. In his radio broadcast 'A Voz do Pastor', Dom Jaime stated that numerous papal documents show 'the most sincere interests of the Church for the happy solution of social problems; and therefore the priests that dedicate themselves to this difficult task do not deserve suspicion or recrimination'.[42] Dom Rossi wrote a long position paper, which was made public and in which he showed the historical contribution of the Church to the people of Brazil. He noted that the goal of the Church was to help individuals become 'complete men', for without such men the necessary social changes in the nation would not be possible.

[40] From interview with *Jornal do Brasil*, 16 December 1967. Or, as a member of the opposition party, MDB, said, 'The Church is opting for the future, while the military is caught in the past.' Osvaldo Lima Filho in *Jornal do Brasil*, 22 November 1967.
[41] The Bishop of Garanhuns noted, 'It [the conflict] will serve to highlight the social and religious functions of the Church in a country of Christian culture such as Brazil...The Church will not restrict itself to sacred functions, in that already involved in the world, it has to be sensitive to the necessities of the people of God.' *Estado de São Paulo* 15 December 1967.
[42] *Jornal do Brasil*, 16 December 1967.

The Church, therefore, is not content to transmit only a message. It wants its doctrine translated into practice and lived. [Consequently]...because we love Brazil and her people we have the right and the duty, as hierarchy, to bring our undeniable and urgent contribution in this grave hour of our nation, while the people still hope to obtain their social improvements through democratic means...the social transformations will come either with us or without us and therefore against us, Brazilians and Christians. [And, we must not blame those who are over-zealous in advocating the changes for]... inactivity is much more pernicious than the exaggerations of those who work with sincerity in the fields of social change.[43]

There are innumerable individual statements which reiterate the points about a social mission and opposition between Church and state, but rather than review them I want to turn to the very important statement of the Central Commission of the CNBB, because it represents important and moderate opinion among the Church elite in the post-1964 period. Until 1971 the Central Commission was made up of the most influential members of the hierarchy, including all four cardinals, and archbishops such as Dom Vicente Scherer, Dom João Resende and the apostolic administrator of Salvador, Dom Eugênio Sales. If an official statement of the whole institution existed regarding the conflict, it was certainly this one signed by 21 members of the hierarchy. The statement, entitled 'The Mission of the Catholic Hierarchy in Today's World', was issued in the middle of the Dom Waldir conflict and was the first Central Commission statement with a social content since the document of April, 1963. At this time and in this context, such a document indicated an important commitment by these members of the hierarchy and was well thought out and discussed before publication. The Central Commission was holding its semi-annual meeting in Rio from November 28 to 30 and on account of the gravity of the conflict invited Dom Waldir to attend and explain the situation in Volta Redonda. The document represents a watershed in the development of a self-definition for the hierarchy.[44]

In 'The Mission of the Catholic Hierarchy in Today's World', the Central Commission stated that the bishop must identify with his people, as he was committed to them in establishing the Kingdom of God. 'Not an abstract kingdom, but one which, in the words of Paul VI, the Church "must already establish in this world"'... The bishop cannot alienate himself from real problems that afflict his fellow men. The joys and agonies of men are our agonies and joys.' The functions of the bishop were threefold: to teach, to sanctify, and to govern. The commission repudiated the Marxist interpretation of religion as an opiate of the people, which offered a better life in the next world while condoning exploitation in this one. 'To affirm that the religious mission of the bishops cannot go beyond the limits of the so-called "spiritual life" is practically to accept the Marxist concept of religion. To proclaim the defense of "Christian civilization" and, at the same time, limit the teaching mission of the Church in defense of human values signifies the defense of masked paganism.' Also included within the teaching

---

[43] From 'The Church and State in Brazil', published in *Estado de São Paulo*, 15 December 1967.
[44] The document can be seen in *Paz e Terra* 6, pp. 260–6.

function was the prophetic announcement of the truth in concrete situations. The sanctifying function was set forth in terms that made it more than a mere social ritual: it must be dynamic to be true to its meaning. In his governing function the bishop must enjoy total liberty under the authority of the Pope. 'The bishop cannot accept beyond the legislation of the Church that others attempt to define and delimit his functions . . . Within their respective areas the Church and the state enjoy autonomy and independence, observing mutual respect.' In relation to the socio-economic problems of Brazil and with special regard to the poor, the commission asserted that they would educate and stimulate the people to bring about the necessary social transformations. This was not to be interpreted as subversion: indeed, the Comissão Central (CC) contended that groups which created confusion for their own political ends, as well as those which were served by unjust political and economic arrangements, were themselves subversive. 'We are conscious that broad sectors of our population look to the Church as one of their last hopes.' Unfortunately, the CC did not as an institution possess the resources to do much more than cooperate in programs of real human promotion. It criticized the government in this regard by noting that some Latin American countries put 25 % of their national budgets into education. In Brazil the proportion was about 9 %. Lastly, it expressed its solidarity with members of the Church who were attacked while carrying out their proper duties. 'We must express our solidarity to our brothers, bishops, priests, and laymen, when misunderstood and persecuted for their authentic apostolic action.' This document is indeed a signal statement for the Brazilian hierarchy. In it they commit themselves to an active social role in society, deny the abuse of religion as an opiate, defend the Church's autonomy and independence, show that they are aware of the problems in society and the suffering of the people, recognize their responsibility to do something and declare their solidarity with all those in the Church (and this now includes laymen) who are persecuted for their action in their religious duties.

A good take-off point for discussing criticisms of the Church in the conflict is a study of the Press' reception of the CC document. Most papers published the entire document, but the headlines are indeed revealing in their bias. The popular Rio paper *O Sol* headlined, 'Bishops: The Time is for Youth'. The conservative Rio daily *O Globo* titled it, 'Bishops Demand Respect for the Human Person and for the Public Authority'. And the moderate Rio daily *Jornal do Brasil* used the headline, 'Manifesto of Bishops Condemns Subversion'. The editorials are even more interesting in their interpretations. It can be assumed that people would not read the entire CC document, and if they did they would still be influenced in their interpretation by the papers' editorials. The editorials in *Jornal do Brasil* demonstrated that either the editor could not believe the Church would change its form of influence, or, if it did, the paper was against it. The most important editorial appeared in the issue of 2 December, 1967, and was entitled 'Balanced Word'. It noted that devious forces in society were at work to provoke conflicts between Church and state, in order to force an opposition between them. The editorial asserted that this in fact did not happen, but the truth is otherwise. There was a serious confrontation and the CC document was the result. The editorial went on to point out erroneously that the bishops had removed themselves from political matters 'which have nothing to do with the Kingdom of God'. Yet I noted above that the Kingdom of God in the CC document was broadly interpreted and began in the here and now. For the editorial, in its terms, this would be a fully political statement. The editorial then misconstrued a quotation from the CC document. In the original statement the bishops criticized those liberals and agnostics who so quickly come to the defense of a disembodied Christianity which had little resemblance to the Gospel. Here they were referring to politicians and writers who were basically irreligious but very willing to advise the Church on practically any issue of doctrine or morals. In the editorial, this quotation was transposed into an attack on the 'Catholic Left' who are really 'Communists in disguise'.[45] Another similar statement was misconstrued. The CC statement condemned two types of subversives: the usual kind and those who profit from unjust structures. In the editorial the second was omitted. Whereas the CC statement encouraged young people and stated that the Church desired more contact with them, the editorial observed that the Church would not seek to 'politicize' the youth. The contrast between the document itself and the editorial describing it is clear in the last paragraph. 'The pronouncement . . . is a document of great importance which comforts the Brazilian Catholic family, justly preoccupied with increasing infiltration and the discord of political-ideological dispute into the sacristies of our churches and the seclusion of our monasteries. This indicates that a new chapter of understanding and collaboration is opening now in the relations between the Church and government.' As should be clear by now, the editorial completely misconstrued the words and meaning of the CC statement.

The statements of those who opposed the Church made essentially the same points in this conflict as in the Northeastern episodes. They included the following arguments: the Church is a sacred and important institution and demands full respect when dealing with 'religious matters'; the involvement of the Church in social concerns is a form of Communism or subversion and must be punished accordingly; the Church is an integral part of the social system and cannot be allowed to oppose the regime. The following passages indicate these points and hopefully give a feeling for the spirit of the conflict. The editorial in the 23 November 1967 edition of *Jornal do Brasil* was entitled 'Red Vestments' and demanded: 'It is time to end once and for all this political-ideological action of some of our priests. The Church is worthy of all respect and her activities are sacred insofar as they are within the ministry of God. But when priests abandon the courtyards of their churches in order to enter the territory of the political revolutionary confusion, the cassock must no longer be a shield to protect them from the law.' And, if this political involvement continues they suggest, 'All will be simplified in a flamboyant red "regalia" more in accord with the convictions of some of our priests. All that remains is to substitute the cross with the hammer and sickle.' It is worth noting that the editorial referred to 'some of the priests' and not to the

---

[45] 'With reason the bishops were surprised at the transformation of self-declared agnostics into "defenders" of a Christianity bearing little resemblance to the Gospel.'

institution in general. The argument that a few subversives existed within a generally pure institution was used repeatedly. Earlier they were Northeastern bishops and clergy, but now they were spreading out nationally. And there was a plot behind the matter: 'Each day it becomes clearer that the intention of forces connected with the Communist movement in Brazil is to transform the Catholic Church into its instrument of action.'[46] Communist penetration would not be so serious, but the Church was perceived as a bulwark of the social system. An editorial in the *Estado de São Paulo* decried the penetration because of the supportive role 'of the Catholic Church in the defense of our threatened civilization.'[47]

The spokesman for the 'hard line' of the government in Congress, Clovis Stenzel (ARENA), stated: 'Certain priests – clearly a minority, but influential because of the publicity that is given them – want to persuade the faithful in Brazil to condemn the revolutionary government and subvert order.'[48] And he was ready to interpret the Church's function in society and judge the clergy: 'Misguided priests forget that it is not the mission of the Church to solve social problems. The priest cannot attempt to implant the Kingdom of God over the earth, for "His Kingdom is not of this world".'[49] Of course, only the previous week, the CC statement had pointed out that the Kingdom began in this world and thus the Church had to be concerned with social problems. The military concurred with the *Jornal do Brasil* and with their mouthpiece Stenzel, 'remaining irreducible in the belief that the Church must not move beyond the spiritual domain'.[50] The problem confronting the government was obvious. A situation existed in which more and more members of the Church had become concerned with social matters and spoken out. For the government this sort of concern was dangerous and the 'deviants' must in some way be discouraged. However, discretion was necessary for the Church was a desirable ally and could not be forced into active opposition. If the government had carefully read the CC document or Dom Waldir's statement at the meeting, they might have realized that opposition had already progressed quite far. Dom Waldir's statement is a classic and worth quoting:

Ever since the time of Pope Leo XIII, the Church has been preoccupied with the living conditions of its people. Today, she continues to be preoccupied with the people, but instead of supplying a few crumbs of bread, she attempts to teach how bread can be purchased with one's own effort; she does not only teach how to pray and meditate, but she attempts to create the conditions for prayer. A person with an empty stomach and unable to fight for his own rights cannot pray. The Church must defend them...we need deep reforms, we must renounce our complacency.[51]

A few days after the conflict became public, President Costa e Silva tried to resolve it behind the scenes, while repeatedly denying to the press that any

[46] *Jornal do Brasil* 28 November 1967.
[47] *Estado de São Paulo*, 13 December 1967.
[48] *Jornal do Brasil*, 6 December 1967. 'Revolutionary' in this context refers to those who came to power in the 1964 coup.
[49] *Ibid.*
[50] *Estado de São Paulo*, 13 December 1967.
[51] *Paz e Terra* 6, pp. 258–9.

discord existed. On November 27 he met with Dom Eugênio Sales, the unofficial spokesman in this case for the CNBB. On November 29 the President stated, 'There is no tension between the Church and the government. What exists are differences between some members of the clergy and some officers of the Armed Forces, but there are no differences between the two institutions.'[52] On 7 December the President appeared on television in honor of the 'National Day of the Family' and said: 'Brazilians can be sure that all the recent notices concerning frictions between the Church and the government are without basis. They are the result of interpretations by those interested in sowing discord or misunderstanding and lack of confidence in the spirit of what is most dear to the hearts of Brazilians. The government is composed of committed Catholic citizens who nourish only sentiments of sacred respect for the Church.'[53] On 11 December, the President met with Dom Waldir about the four youths who had been arrested and then somewhat forgotten in the excitement of the larger conflict. Problems in resolving the conflict were increased by a notice to the effect that elements in the military were attempting to have the papal nuncio replaced. These hardliners alleged that the nuncio supported the progressives in the hierarchy and clergy and was unwilling to transfer bothersome bishops. The notice was officially denied the next day, but the ensuing debate did little to help the government to play down the controversy.

The conflict, which was causing the President so many problems, should never have occurred in the first place. After the initial conflict in the Northeast in 1966, the Church and President Castelo Branco agreed to cooperate in resolving difficulties which could lead to persecution of the clergy. In this case, the military was either ignorant of the agreement or chose to disregard it.[54]

The conflict was finally resolved through efforts on the parts of the President, cooperation with the hierarchy, a decrease in attacks by the newspapers and politicians and a termination of military action. On 17 January 1968 (more than two months after the conflict was initiated) Dom Avelar Brandão met with Costa e Silva for a long discussion. The bishop gave the President six copies of 'Populorum Progressio' and requested that a government body be created to study the encyclical. With this the conflict *per se* was terminated, although the unfortunate four remained in jail. Dom Waldir still worked to have them released, and in late 1969 was indicted on charges of subversion on another issue to which I will return later in the chapter.

The results of this conflict were very important. They showed that it was not only the Northeastern Church or the pre-1964 CNBB group which had problems with the military. The CC document indicated how far the hierarchy had moved in defining a social mission and in declaring autonomy for the bishops. The conflict brought the Church to a new level of awareness and commitment in

---

[52] *NIU* 68/72, p. 7.
[53] *Jornal do Brasil*, 8 December 1967.
[54] Stepan makes a good point in showing that continuity was lacking between the Castelo Branco government and that of Costa e Silva, thus weakening one of the arguments made by the apologists for military rulers who praise the order and stability of such regimes.

Brazilian society. It also showed that the government was indecisive and lacked control over military elements. The President did not want problems with the Church, but apparently had little immediate power to restrain the colonel involved or to silence the hard line which wanted the papal nuncio removed. The conflict again reflected how far conservative or traditional elements would go in telling the Church where it did or did not belong in society. Despite editorials and statements to the contrary, the conflict indicated an increasing contradiction between the goals of the Church in regard to social questions and the perception of these goals by other elements in society. And, lastly, although this conflict was formally settled, in fact the issues of the four youths and the bishop himself were not resolved for more than three years.

Following the Dom Waldir episode instances of conflict increased in frequency, geographical distribution and intensity, as Brazil in 1968 teetered back and forth between increasing violence and recriminations from the right and left and as the government appeared immobilized. A discussion of two minor conflicts will serve to illustrate the new levels of definition and antagonism between the Church and elements in society and the government.

The bishops had long since lost their immunity from attacks in the press, and now members of the clergy lost immunity from arrest. Priests had been imprisoned at the time of the 1964 coup, but since then the government had been reluctant to arrest them. With deterioration in Church–state relations, however, hesitation disappeared and it was always for the same reason: social involvement defined as subversion. A minor conflict illustrates this point. For the first time since the coup, a workers' celebration was held in São Paulo on 1 May 1968. The thousands of workers who gathered for the celebration were not content with the official program, took control of the event and forced many political figures (including the governor) to flee. In the aftermath many were arrested, including two priests. In a subsequent statement on the arrests, members of the Catholic and Protestant clergy explained, 'Our position is at the side of the workers and the people in their just desire for liberty.'[55] It was, in fact, their position at the side of the people that led to their imprisonment. That is, as the members of the clergy moved away from traditional religious duties and into social action, they were prone to receive the treatment meted out to everyone else. It became a matter of either/or: either acting in traditional Church roles or operating subversively. There seemed to be no middle ground.

Because of the government's handling of conflicts, options became strictly limited for the Church. A minor conflict illustrates this point. On 3 May 1968, José Solero Filho, lawyer, father of ten children and national vice-president of the MFC, was arrested by the military police and kept in prison for four days. The MFC is anything but radical and José Solero Filho was considered by most people to be a politically conservative paragon of familial and professional integrity. While in prison he was visited by many friends, including Cardinal Dom Rossi. To the extent that there was a charge against him, it was that he had allowed a dangerous Communist agitator to remain in his house for an evening. The

[55] *NIU* 68/72, pp. 17–18.

conclusion to be drawn from this conflict is well stated by Dom Lucas Moreira Neves, auxiliary bishop of São Paulo and national assistant to the MFC. 'If the operations of national security result in the detention of men like José Solero Filho, I fear what may happen to this country. Who can be sure of not being held?'[56] The unexplained imprisonment of such an individual showed that the government was acting arbitrarily to say the least, and many came to the conclusion that one was prone to arrest if connected even indirectly with broad sectors of the Church. The Church no longer seemed to represent a secure refuge for people but rather a somewhat risky proposition. This incident forced people to become aware and to consider options.

The next conflict was more significant than the two just described. It demonstrates how touchy the military had become in the face of criticism from the Church and it further shows that criticism was being commonly accepted within the Church as a legitimate activity. On 8 May 1968, in São Luís do Maranhão, the Association of Ex-Combatants sponsored a commemorative mass for the victory of the Allies in World War II and for the role of the Brazilian Expeditionary Force, which fought at Monte Cassino. Important civil and military authorities attended the mass celebrated by the auxiliary bishop, Dom Edmilson da Cruz. In his sermon the bishop praised the devotion of the military to the principles of the nation and their valor in fighting for liberty and freedom in Italy. But he went on to describe the situation in Brazil and questioned whether liberty existed; whether in fact the ex-combatants defended in their own country what they had fought for in Italy.

As a citizen and not as an ecclesiastical authority, taking advantage of this propitious occasion with you military men, as one who loves our nation as much as any one, I submit the following question: In the present Brazilian situation can we speak of liberty of the press? of radio?[57]

In the middle of the sermon most of the military men rose and left the church. Noting their departure, the bishop asked them to speak out: two did, harshly and furiously. When the bishop left the church he was accosted so violently by the deputy-General Artur Carvalho that his friends had to take him away. Three days later the commander of the military in the region declared bluntly that the revolution of 1964 and the armed forces had been slandered and the Church profaned by one who had the greatest obligation to defend it.[58] The conflict was thus initiated by the bishop's comments questioning liberty in Brazil and by the reaction of military men. This reaction has to be understood in the light of the previous two years of conflicts, as the result of which a few words were enough

---

[56] *Telepax* 138, 31 May 1968. This argument was repeated by others, including the MFC directorate in *Jornal do Brasil*, 9 May 1968.

[57] *Telepax* 138, 31 May 1968. He was referring specifically to the radio incident the year before.

[58] 'The Commander of the Federal Garrison publicly spurns grave and slanderous insults against the revolution and the Armed Forces by the auxiliary bishop of São Luís: I do not want to be again saddened by any depressing, shocking, or revolting spectacle such as a Church being profaned by one who has an obligation to defend it.' *NIU* 68/72, p. 20.

to confirm what some military personnel already thought about subversion in the Church.

This conflict was worked out through statements and counterstatements. All the clergy in São Luís and hundreds of laymen backed Dom Edmilson and the position taken in his sermon.[59] The archbishop, Dom João José da Mota e Albuquerque, put the conflict into perspective when he defended his auxiliary's and the Church's mission of announcing the truth. 'The Church in Brazil today is living in greater profundity her prophetic mission of denouncing error and of announcing the truth.'[60] This mission is not negative nor against any particular individual, but is the Church's contribution in the present situation towards helping the country. The Church had the right and the duty to criticize some aspects of the government and society, and this was founded in its prophetic mission. After a week the conflict was formally resolved and the officers paid the bishop a visit, but relations remained tense between the army and the archdiocese of São Luís.

Another important conflict was initiated in June by the publication of a working paper written by Pe. José Comblin. In preparation for the Second General Assembly of the Latin American Hierarchy (CELAM) at Medellín, Colombia, which Pope Paul VI was to attend, the Council of the organization prepared a basic document for review by Latin American bishops. In Recife Dom Helder had several experts study the document in preparation for the meeting where a response would be formulated. One of the experts consulted was Pe. Comblin, a Belgian, who had been involved with social and theological questions in Latin America for ten years, first in Chile and then in Brazil. At this time he was a professor at the Institute of Theology in Recife. Pe. Comblin prepared a paper on the basic document, which he criticized as being too general and too pedestrian, and then went on to write a working paper in which he placed the Church in the historical and political context of the continent. He also related the Church to questions of the 'conquest and exercise of power' and its responsibility in the development process.[61] The working paper and the subsequent meeting with Dom Helder were intended to be restricted to a very small group of experts. However, a longtime and vociferous enemy of Dom Helder, Councilman Wanderkolk Wanderlei, somehow obtained Pe. Comblin's paper and had it published nationally as an example of the ideology emanating from the bishop's subversive 'think tank'. When sections of the paper, which were taken out of context and presented as a final document, became public, both Dom Helder and Pe. Comblin were attacked as subversives and as threats to national security; it was suggested that Pe. Comblin be invited to leave Brazil. What seemed important in the initiation of this conflict was the trouble some conservative elements went to in order to accuse Dom Helder and other sectors of the 'progressive Church'. In attacking Pe. Comblin, enemies of the Church thought they

[59] *Telepax* 138, 31 May 1968.
[60] *Ibid.*, p. 4.
[61] For the document, see *NIU* 'Documentos' 1968, No. 13; *NIU* 68/72, p. 20; and *SEDOC* 1 (September 1968), special number, pp. 451–69.

had located the mastermind behind subversive ideologies circulating in the institution. The importance given to him and his ideas is suggested in the following passage from *O Globo* of 17 June 1968: 'The Brazilian state will certainly run some risk if it is deceived into believing that the plan of operation of Père Comblin is a theology text. If it is theology, the red book of Mao is a treatise on quietism.'

Pe. Comblin was defended by elements in the Church and intellectuals in general on two main points: the document was merely a working paper and nothing more, so to publish it without approval was unjust; and, even though rough and incomplete, the document was basically accurate in its discussion of the role of the Church *vis-à-vis* political power. This could basically be reduced to a situation in which the Church was renegotiating – or redefining – its position and role (model of influence, if you prefer) in society. Pe. Comblin treated this matter thoroughly in his paper, but the statements of support were phrased in the simple terms of the Church needing to break its ties with traditional society and commitments so as to come closer to the masses. For example, 'He thinks that the Church will fight to distinguish itself from political and economic groups in order to become a popular Church. "She will lose social and political prestige in order to reinstate herself with the masses. In the meantime, there are two religions: one for the aristocracy and another for the poor."'[62] The debate over Pe. Comblin and his paper continued for about three weeks in the national news media before it was finally superseded by other issues. However, some conservative groups continued to attack Comblin for at least another six months and in early 1972 he was refused entry into Brazil. The result of the episode was to give a more coherent rationale to elements within the Church, which were growing in the face of conflicts, for a break with the traditional Church. Pe. Comblin's draft paper made the point very well and subsequent interviews with his supporters amplified it further. On the other hand, enemies of a social involvement orientation saw in Comblin and his supporters the key figures in a deliberate subversive plot to justify what was known as 'Communization of the clergy'.[63]

The next important conflict revolved around the imprisonment and subsequent expulsion of Pe. Pedro Wauthier during July and August 1968. This conflict demonstrated that a certain plateau had been reached in the process of conflict between Church and state. It showed that the immunity of the clergy had completely disappeared; that even moderate and compromised bishops like Cardinal Dom Rossi could be implicated; that the government was not willing to allow a renegotiation of the Church's role without a fight; and that such a fight, or conflict, only strengthened the resolve of the Church to redefine its role. Pe. Wauthier was born in France, but had been ordained in Brazil and was a worker priest in the Mission of Saint Peter and Paul. He was not politically active but recognized

---

[62] Interview with Msgr. Marcelo Pinto Cavalheira in *Correio da Manhã*, 16 June 1968. Same point made in interview with Frei Eliseu Lopes in *Jornal do Brasil* on the same day; more of the same in the long essay by Hélio Pellegrino in *Correio da Manhã* of 30 June 1968.
[63] *NIU* 68/72, p. 32–3.

the implications of saying mass in the factory as the management requested, and refused to do so. The workers in the factory, in Osasco, São Paulo, went on strike in mid-July over a general list of grievances. The management asked him to use his influence with the workers to call off the strike, but he refused. The day after the strike began, Pe. Wauthier and two other workers were arrested at gunpoint by one of the company executives and the police. The priest was put in prison for one month and was then allowed to go into house arrest at Cardinal Dom Rossi's residence in São Paulo.[64] On 27 August, while Cardinal Rossi was attending the CELAM meeting in Medellín, the priest was taken from the residence and deported. The conflict was thus initiated by the arrest, imprisonment and subsequent expulsion of a worker priest who was involved in a strike.[65]

The government apparently made no official statements on the priest's expulsion. He was charged with participating in the strike at Osasco, but this did not provide grounds for deportation, as there had been other strikes with other priests involved and until this time no one had been forced out of the country. A group of lawyers attempted to obtain an answer from the government on this matter, but their letter to the Minister of Justice, Gama e Silva, was not answered. After the deportation the government no longer participated in the conflict, although later reverberations did concern it, and other elements in the society engaged the Church on the issue.

Statements in support of the priest and in protest against the government's action came from every state in Brazil and from all sectors of the Church. The Clergy Council of São Paulo sent letters of protest to the Pope, the papal nuncio in Brazil, CELAM, CNBB, CAL and to the foreign clergy in general working in Latin America. The public debate over the case lasted until December 1968, and there were reverberations even to March 1969.[66] The auxiliary bishop of Pôrto Alegre, Dom Ivo Lorscheider, argued that the deportation was unjust, 'because he acted in defense of the legitimate rights of his companions in the factory'.[67] This point was elaborated in a statement from 90 priests in Rio Grande do Sul: 'It does not only signify the expulsion of a foreign priest but reflects the real attempt to remove the Church from the side of the oppressed and those suffering from injustice in Brazil.'[68] These two statements are important, because the Church in the South is traditionally the most conservative and least outspoken. The classic statement arising out of this conflict, and one which would be heard again and again in future conflicts, was made by a group of clergy and laymen in São Paulo and published on 1 September.

[64] Another priest, Pe. Antônio de Almeida Soares, was arrested on the same day and released a week later. *NIU* 68/72, p. 25.
[65] For many documents on the case see *SEDOC* 6 (December 1968), pp. 815–37. Interviews in São Paulo in June 1970 substantiated my analysis here.
[66] At the later date conservative papers such as *Estado de São Paulo* and *Jornal da Tarde* brought up the case again by saying that Pe. Wauthier was living on the French Riviera with a blonde. They played a cat and mouse game with the Cardinal on this issue for months, although he denied all the allegations concerning the priest and had proof from Switzerland to back his statements. *NIU* 3 (1969), p. 14.
[67] *Jornal do Brasil*, 31 August 1968.
[68] *Correio da Manhã*, 29 August 1968.

They accept a Church that preaches for the established order, even if unjust, and reject a Church that preaches the Gospel of conversion to justice and fraternity among men [leading to the] elimination of the serious social and economic inequalities, caused by the disorder of the present structures not by the limitations of the poor.[69]

Because of this conflict, even Cardinal Dom Rossi could no longer temporize between the role of the traditional Church and the demands of a changing political environment. And once he became involved in the conflict process, he had a difficult time extracting himself. President Costa e Silva was scheduled to visit São Paulo on 2 and 3 October and, by the traditional formula, the Church in the person of Cardinal Dom Rossi was included in the festivities. The Cardinal was to receive the Order of National Merit from the President at the headquarters of the II nd Army and then to celebrate a mass for the birthday of Costa e Silva. A group of clergy and laity in the city, as well as other bishops, requested the Cardinal not to accept the award, for they noted that he himself had signed a document in Medellín which opposed trafficking in honorary titles.[70] In addition to the Medellín statement, the group argued that the honorary title was a political scheme to smooth over Pe. Wauthier's removal from the Cardinal's residence and the ensuing conflict. The Cardinal took their suggestion seriously and in an unprecedented move wrote to the President refusing the title and left São Paulo during the period of the visit, so that he could not celebrate the birthday mass. It seems unlikely that without the Pe. Wauthier incident he would have taken these serious steps, which served to move him away from the government and traditional Church compromises. The Cardinal probably had little option in the matter, but his refusal of the title shows that by this time the process had seriously worsened relations between the two orders.

The Cardinal's action led to various reactions, which all served to create further opposition and tensions. The *Estado de São Paulo* spoke of the 'incomprehensible attitude' of the Cardinal; the *Jornal do Brasil* referred to it as 'the extraordinary attitude of disrespect for the institutions, without precedent in Brazil'; and the papers would later wage a smear compaign on the Cardinal and the priest which would involve other issues still.[71] Most important in the immediate context were the problems created between the Cardinal and the local military. Cardinal Dom Rossi was not allowed as usual to celebrate the First Communion Mass for children of the military in December. Upon his arrival at the Church he was informed that he was *persona non grata* and should leave.[72] There continued to be

---

[69] *Jornal do Brasil*, 1 September 1968.

[70] The Medellín statement included the following: 'We ask that the clergy and faithful treat us in a manner which becomes our mission as priests and pastors, thus we want to renounce the honorific titles belonging to other epochs.' Cited in *NIU* 68/72, p. 45. Interviews with two lay people in São Paulo, one of whom helped convince the Cardinal, indicated that it was not easy to persuade him to take the step. And, as will be seen later, he equivocated: on the one hand defending the institution and on the other seemingly supporting government repression. Dom Helder apparently had something to do with this affair. Cf. de Broucker, p. 12.

[71] *Estado de São Paulo*, 4 October 1968; *Jornal do Brasil*, 5 October 1968; later was 6 February 1969. See *SEDOC* 2:7 (January 1970), pp. 903–8 for other smears.

[72] *Correio da Manhã*, 11 December 1968.

considerable ill-will in São Paulo which, while related to the whole process of local and national conflicts, revolved around the Pe. Wauthier case.

Before describing the last and most serious conflict before 1969, it is useful to demonstrate just how far Church–state relations had deteriorated during the previous two years of conflict. The General Albuquerque Lima incidents and the Dom Fragoso subversion case will illustrate how unfriendly and antagonistic the relationship had become by mid-1968.

For the most part senior government officials had attempted to resolve the conflicts as quickly as possible. Thus while a colonel or a general would denounce Church subversion, those in formally civilian positions would attempt to white-wash the conflicts or resolve them. Therefore when General Albuquerque Lima, the Minister of the Interior and potential contender for the presidency, began to attack the Church in October for various and sundry reasons, it was considered a 'grave and serious warning' to the church to change its ways.[73] In a series of lectures delivered throughout the South, the General denounced the Church in explicit terms: 'The Communists, the priests and bishops of the "festive Left" must understand once and for all that the Armed Forces will never permit a return to the past.'[74] He argued that the world plan of the Communists had several phases: first, to do away with the Armed Forces, 'then with the Church, which is a strong moral force already penetrated by the Communists, and finally with morals and the family . . . Priests and nuns in the *colégios* of Rio inculcate in youths of thirteen and fourteen years problems determined to finish off the family'. He attacked the clergy and nuns for the destruction of the family and noted, 'they collaborate in the dissemination of theses intended to awaken abnormal sexual tendencies in the youth'. And on returning from a trip to the Northeast he denied that he was campaigning for the presidency and insisted that instead he was defending the revolution, 'target of the demoralizing campaign in which the Church participates'.[75] At this time in Brazil there was serious talk of another coup from the hard line, or at least a strengthening of the authoritarian element, so that criticism of this sort coming from a high government and military official was very serious. It really indicated that the Church would be directly attacked if it continued with its 'subversion'.

In late November Dom Fragoso was accused by the Secretary of Security of Guanabara of having connections with the Communist terrorist, Carlos Marighela, who was then robbing banks and making life difficult in Rio and São Paulo. The proof of the accusation was a letter from Dom Fragoso to a person somehow connected to Marighela, congratulating her on a new baby.[76] The case was obviously contrived and absurd, and was seen as another attempt to tarnish Church prestige. The Church's reaction showed that it was tired of these stupid attacks and was continuing to move away from the government which made

---

[73] *NIU* 68/72, p. 48.

[74] *Ibid*. The 'festive left' refers to those who talk revolution, but do not act; it is thus an insult. The 'past' means pre-1964.

[75] The first statement was in the Military Circle of São Paulo on 14 October the next on the 15th; and the last in Rio on 27 October. See *NIU* 67/72, pp. 48–9.

[76] Copy of letter in *NIU* 68/72, p. 29.

them. Forty bishops in the Northeast committed themselves to imprisonment with Dom Fragoso if he were arrested or even questioned. The auxiliary bishop of Rio, Dom Castro Pinto, stated, 'They attacked Dom Fragoso because he bothered many people, which gives an idea of his effect. It is very good that a bishop acts in such a way as to bother the powerful in defense of the unprotected.'[77] As the situation deteriorated the Church increasingly adopted the role for which it was being attacked. That is, it engaged in more serious thought about alternative influence models and opposition to the state.

The last big conflict before the 5th Institutional Act was by far the most serious to date. The first conflict in 1966 initiated the process; by the time of the Dom Waldir episode in late 1967 it was building up momentum, and by late 1968 the process had a tremendous dynamic. This clash would add to the dynamic, but because the 5th Institutional Act was decreed midway through the incident the manner of working it out would be different. The 5th Institutional Act tightened the dictatorship and enforced censorship, and as a result Church–state conflicts became more serious but less public.[78]

The conflict was initiated when the military in Belo Horizonte arrested three French priests and one Brazilian deacon belonging to the Congregation of the Assumption on 28 November 1968. The Assumptionist Order has been active in Brazil since 1936 and in Belo Horizonte since 1966; its primary orientation is evangelization through reflection on concrete reality and engagement in human promotion (i.e. promote the human as 'body' not only as 'spirit'). The four members were arrested mainly because of the latter role, although they fulfilled both in the professions. One was a professor at the Institute of Philosophy and Theology and another taught at the Catechism Institute. They were assistants to Juventude Operária Católica (JOC), and the Commission for Workers' Pastoral, and lived in Horto which is a slum suburb of the city. They were arrested, held incommunicado for a week and charged with various forms of subversion; they made confessions under torture, were kept in prison until 6 February 1969 and then placed under house arrest. In other words, the initiation of this conflict was much more serious than in other cases, for several priests were involved; they were subjected to torture; and they confessed to subversion.

This conflict was acted out in a way similar in form to previous cases. However, this time the statements were from broader sectors than ever, were more outspoken and left no doubt that an enormous separation had developed between Church and state. By this time the government's position on these conflicts had become standardized. The Church merited respect as an institution integral to Brazilian society, but its function was exclusively religious. When 'limited elements' within it became involved in 'subversion' the Church deserved punishment like any other group or organization. The military knew there was an enemy at large in the Church; their background and ideology told them this much; they simply had to find him and root him out.

[77] *Jornal do Brasil*, 29 November 1968.
[78] On censorship see *SEDOC* 2:1 (July 1969), p. 55; on conflict see *NIU* 68/72, pp. 57–61 and *SEDOC* 9 (March 1969), pp. 1207–57 and newspapers.

The official statement by General Alváro Cardoso, Commander of the IVth Military Region in Minas Gerais, is a succinct illustration of the government's position in the conflict.

It is known that the authorities are not against the Church and do not persecute it. They are astonished by this scene never before witnessed in history: that some clergy support the handing over of our country to one of the Church's worst enemies.
It is claimed that priests are being incarcerated because they have preached the scriptures. It is known, however, that those priests were imprisoned because they abandoned the preaching of the scriptures to devote themselves to political and ideological preaching, and to the organization of subversion, and to the armed guerrilla movements for the overthrow of the regime. What kind of scripture is this?...It forgets to preach respect and obedience to the legitimately constituted authority and forgets that, as citizens, the clergy are subject to that authority for security, order and all other acts of government. What is the meaning of so much consternation over the imprisonment of people who preach equality and fidelity to ideals of subversion? The police authorities are now obliged to repress priests who should be controlled by their hierarchical superiors.[79]

The Commander of the 1st Army, General Sizeno Sarmento, also made use of the 'specific versus institution' argument. While visiting Cardinal Dom Jaime in Rio on 5 December in order to convince him that the military was handling the case correctly, he stated, 'There was not and could not be any disrespect toward the Church. Nor [was there any] attempt to weaken her. Our training would not allow such a thing to happen.'[80] And on the 9th, 'We are not acting against the Church, but against people responsible for acts of subversion which are now being investigated.'[81] Many civil government officials made similar statements, as if to present a united front in the case. Typical is an interview with Gama e Silva, Minister of Justice: 'The protective mantle of a cassock cannot cover up a crime: and he considered legitimate the imprisonment of the priests by the military authorities. "The prison", he said, "is the fate for all those who violate the laws and make assaults against the present regime."'[82]

Since the arguments of the government all involved talk about subversion, guerrilla movements, revolution and so forth, it is worth examining the evidence, in order for the reader to be able to make his estimate of the validity of the government's case, the work of the priests and the Church's reaction to the proof. The government offered five types of proof in the case. First, books, journals, folios, etc. which were about China, Cuba or other revolutionary systems. However, none of this material dealt with programs for fomenting a Brazilian revolution, and all of it could be expected among the books of any intellectual, especially a

---

[79] *Jornal do Brasil*, 3 December 1968, quoted in *SEDOC* 9 (March 1969), pp. 1210–11.
[80] *Correio da Manhã*, 6 December 1968.
[81] *Jornal do Brasil*, 10 December 1968.
[82] *Correio da Manhã* for the interview on 8 December 1968. Also the statements of Lira Tavares of the Army; Albuquerque Lima of Interior; Jarbas Passarinho of Labor; Magalhães Pinto, the Chancellor. *NIU* 68/72 has the statements of the former ministers.

professor. Judging from the press, very few accepted this form of proof.[83] Secondly, one of the priests, Pe. Michel LeVen, was specifically accused because of a letter he had sent to his superior general in France. He had stated that the government was a dictatorship and stifled liberty. This was critical, perhaps dangerous for a foreigner to write, and maybe it was subversive, although having a strong element of truth.

> There was a profound crisis in the university and the worker milieu which was apparently calmed only by the force of the police, the army, and a totalitarian government that does not hesitate to employ any means to quieten the aspirations of the people and to put down any attempts at political organization for liberation . . . We took a position in the name of the Commission of Workers Pastoral and from then on the order of the day for the Army was that the enemy was no longer the Communist or the student, but the priest. Rumors circulated that four priests would be imprisoned. More than ever we sensed what it meant to be a priest in the midst of men and to preach the Gospel to the poor . . The combination of all these events made us live and make us live today more faithfully according to our religious vocation.[84]

The letter speaks for itself. It was very critical, but given the fact that the priest was arrested it does have the ring of truth. The personal reaction of the priest to other conflicts is significant, especially when justified in terms of adherence to the Gospel; and when opposition leads to greater consciousness in living what he considered the significance of his religious vocation.

Thirdly, the military emphasized that the four were in some way related to JOC. They attempted to discredit this organization by identifying it with Ação Popular. They argued that JOC promoted subversion, class warfare and the overthrow of the government. For example, 'Adopting the Marxist dialectic, they concentrate on the man and the masses, attempting to destroy the spiritual values that still exist in them in order to impregnate them with new leftist ideas. They rely on a false Christian doctrine and apply above all a prophetic attitude with bases in Biblical messianism.'[85] The criticism of JOC, a movement that the bishops had not eliminated after 1964, affected the organization nationally and the hierarchy which was responsible for it. Dom Lucas Moreira Neves, then National Secretary of the Lay Apostolate for the CNBB, defended JOC and effectively rebutted the charges.[86] Fourthly, Pe. LeVen's notebooks were cited as proof, and *O Globo* referred to them as 'Communist primers'. These notebooks, used in preparing lectures, were enough to convince the military of subversion. However, a priest in Belo Horizonte made a study in which he compared the precepts in the notebooks with current Church teachings on society ('Populorum Progressio', the Medellín statement and the discourses of Paul VI) and found that while the notebooks were advanced they were no more so than the current thinking of Rome and the continental hierarchies.[87] This is important, for if the

---

[83] There is a good article on this material in *SEDOC* 9 (March 1969), pp. 1216–17.

[84] *Jornal do Brasil*, 12 December 1968.

[85] *Correio da Manhã*, 6 December 1968, cited in *SEDOC* 9, pp. 1212–13.

[86] *SEDOC* 9, pp. 1213–16.

[87] Study by Pe. Pascoal Rangel in *SEDOC* 9, pp. 1217–20.

military found the priest's notebooks subversive then current Church social doctrine was subversive as well.

Finally, the strongest proof obtained by the military was the confessions of the four that they had organized subversion, carried out socialist indoctrination and prepared for guerrilla warfare.[88] There is, however, widespread doubt about these confessions. The facts admitted to were largely absurd, and the manner of obtaining the confessions was unorthodox. The priests were held incommunicado for more than a week, after which they could be visited only under close supervision, and they were apparently strongly pressured to make the confessions. The Archbishop of Belo Horizonte, Dom João Rezende Costa, prepared a homily to be read in all the churches of the archdiocese on 15 December. 'And now, brothers, with my authority as pastor of the Archdiocese of Belo Horizonte and with the unanimous approval of the clergy, I must denounce what I know through my direct and personal knowledge: The statements of the imprisoned priests and deacons cannot be accepted as an expression of truth because they were obtained through beatings and tortures.'[89] In conclusion, the four religious may well have been subversive in the eyes of the government, but in that case so was much of the Church. The books and journals were commonly sold in Brazil; the letter of Pe. LeVen was outspoken, but did not indicate a plan of subversion; JOC was an official Church organization; the notebooks were legitimate given current Church teachings; and confession under torture is certainly understandable. The conflict was initiated not because of any increase in Church subversion, but rather due to the expansion of the government's definition of what was subversive. With the definition of principles by each side, a clear opposition between them was obvious and the conflict was merely a manifestation of it.

The statements of support generated by the conflict for the four religious and their position were unprecedented in the history of the Brazilian Church. Four main positions were taken in the statements of defense. All of these had been expressed and defined previously, but never so candidly or aggressively.

The first position asserted that the Church now identified with the people because of conflict; this was desirable as the problems of the masses became those of the Church. This was lucidly expressed in a homily prepared by the auxiliary bishop, Dom Serafim Fernandes, and the Priests' Council, which was read in the churches the First Sunday of Advent.

[Due to the conflict]...the clergy is even happy for it begins to live the life of those that suffer, of the people who are also imprisoned. Don't they arrest students and workers? Why should we be different?...We do not want privileges just because we are priests. [The closer to the people, the easier it is to appreciate their problems.] How can we not see the situation of the people if we are not blind, how can we not hear their outcry if we are not deaf, how can we keep secret their problems if we are not dumb? Furthermore,

[88] See *Jornal do Brasil*, 10 December 1968, regarding Pe. Xavier's confessions. He admitted to having 40,000 guerrillas prepared in Pernambuco.
[89] *NIU* 68/72, p. 58, which also includes a direct reference by Dom Helder to torture. For the entire case see argument for a Habeas Corpus in *SEDOC* 9, pp. 1225–35. The homily was read in 95% of the churches.

the light that illuminates us, the voice that speaks to us is the voice of Christ crying out in the midst of this tense situation.[90]

Thus if the Church was close to the people, as Christ was, it could speak for them and denounce the injustice that plagued them. And it is for this reason that the priests were called subversives. The archdiocesan paper, *O Diário*, in the context of the conflict and in reference also to Dom Fragoso's problems with the government noted:

We are not surprised that it is now the turn of the clergy – of priests who, because they are fulfilling their mission of clamoring against social injustice, are sometimes also given the vulgar nickname of 'subversive' and seen as dangerous for the country's social and political stability. Indeed, it is good to emphasize that the Church, persecuted or not, will continue bringing the scriptures to the people and, by the same token, will clamor against any and all injustice which may impede the fundamental rights of man.[91]

In short, as the Church moved closer to the people, it was easier for it to understand them and their problems and to denounce injustice, which was a duty arising from the Gospel.

The second position was that a social mission was completely legitimate for the Church. The homily read in the churches of Belo Horizonte on the First Sunday of Advent pointed out that the priests were arrested for this social mission and not because of the Church's political motives.

We want to be imprisoned for our fidelity to the Gospel of Christ, and from this comes the obligation which we feel of removing it [the Gospel] from any political sentiment or ideological line. Those who suffer for their political ideas suffer for their motives, and those who are faithful to the Gospel suffer for the Gospel of Christ. . . What we think in political, social and economic matters is very clear. We believe what the Constitution 'Gaudium et Spes' states, what 'Populorum Progressio' states, and the document of Medellín states.[92]

The combination of the Church's social doctrine and the denunciation of injustice became, in this conflict, the 'mission of the Church', which had to be fulfilled despite opposition and persecution. Many of the statements illustrated this point, including the formal appeal to habeas corpus for the release of the four. Cardinal Dom Jaime of Rio and his clergy published a letter to this effect, which was read in the churches of the archdiocese.

The Church of Christ, here in Brazil, cannot stop being faithful to her mission specially when misunderstanding and foolishness impede her. . .Presently in our nation, the Church is undergoing tensions which include suspicions and accusations against various ministers. . .We cannot allow them to deny us the liberty of preaching and to silence the preachers of the Gospel by calling them Communists. . .Christ himself (and with this we are consoled and stimulated). . .the same God Jesus was punished for subversion which was the principal 'proof' in his process with the Roman attorney. . .We

---

[90] *Jornal do Brasil*, 1 December 1968, cited in *SEDOC* 9, pp. 1207–8.
[91] *Correio da Manhã*, 1 December 1968, cited from *O Diário* of 30 November.
[92] *SEDOC* 9, pp. 1027–8.

reaffirm, defend, and assert the right of the Church to organize and choose her methods of evangelization.[93]

Therefore, if the Church's mission was to preach a Gospel of social content, it was not just a few elements which were subversive.

If the Church was acting legitimately in carrying out this mission, then the question arose as to who was acting subversively. This was the third position: the Church is not subversive, but those who harass and persecute it are. This argument had been used before by the archbishop of Fortaleza (in the Maranhão radio conflict), so it is not surprising that the statement from his archdiocese made the point again.

The Church is not subversive. Subversives are those who criminally deprive the majority of Brazilians of bread, basic education and participation in the benefits of technological progress.[94]

This argument came into common use, although it did not always place specific blame on the government. For example, the archdiocesan paper of São Paulo, *O São Paulo*, referred to the Pe. Wauthier case and to the present conflict.

Basically the Gospel proclaims the success of those who suffer for truth and justice. Those who really subvert are not imprisoned...Subversion is to defend the peasant who has been left outside the law without the benefits of education, health and civilization. Subversion is to aim at a university reform which may enable us to turn out the technicians we need for our development, instead of whole classes trained according to European patterns. Subversion is to pretend that the Church should become God's People, the Church of the Poor, as John XXIII used to say.[95]

In the light of the three previous positions, a fourth is suggested. The Church must be independent. If it now identified with the people, proclaimed a mission which conflicted with the government, and considered its enemies to be the subversives, then a certain amount of independence, or autonomy was indicated. Several statements support this point. The initial homily of Belo Horizonte stated, 'We have not made a compromise with anyone. And if it appears as though we have then it is because we still lack total and complete fidelity to the Gospel of Christ. We want to be independent and free in order to serve God and man.'[96] Independence, in this context, was put into perspective in the editorial of *O Diário* on 2 December.

The imprisonment was only the occasion that led us to become conscious of the reality: the dominant power supports the Church, respects the Church, even uses the Church while she serves its interests. It tolerates her opposition, her annoying presence up to the point where she does not seriously threaten the system of injustice. There is freedom to preach the Gospel if it does not demand a profound change. Otherwise, any preacher,

[93] *O Globo*, 14 December 1968.
[94] *NIU* 68/72, p. 60.
[95] *Correio da Manhã*, 12 December 1968.
[96] *SEDOC 9*, p. 1208.

like Christ himself, will be accused of 'subverting': they will say today as they said then, that he caused the masses to rebel.[97]

The statement of Cardinal Dom Jaime and his clergy also demanded the right to define what was properly religious, for at this time the government, many news-papers and individuals were all ready to tell the Church what was correct doctrine and what were its implications. In this conflict the CNBB had occasion to defend and define the autonomy of the Church in preaching and carrying out its mission. The Secretary General, Dom Aloísio Lorscheider, published an official note defending the social mission which read in part, 'the judgment concerning whether preaching is authentic or not is for the exclusive competence of the ecclesiastical authority.'[98] Dom Aloísio was obliged to make a second and then a third official statement on the independence and competence of the Church in interpreting its doctrine because of continuing external attacks on this competence. In this conflict, then, many sectors of the Church, including some which had been con-servative and unaware before, found it necessary to define their autonomy, for they were surrounded by people who claimed this competence for their own ends.

This conflict demonstrates the difficulty of resolving a situation which cannot be covered over or ignored. It is similar to the Pe. Wauthier conflict, or that of Dom Waldir, in which the process of conflict led to such opposition between Church and the government that there was little possibility of resolution. Costa e Silva was to visit Belo Horizonte on 12 December and the traditional Church–state festivities were planned. However, the archbishop and auxiliary bishop made it clear that the Church would not celebrate anything in conjunction with the government while the four religious were kept imprisoned. Apparently they kept their word, for in 1970 the priests were out of jail and the bishops were only then beginning to resume contacts with the government.[99]

The process so far outlined was given a jolt by the 5th Institutional Act and what followed. As noted earlier in the chapter, institutional acts were promul-gated, all of which further tightened the system; censorship was enforced, Costa e Silva died and was replaced by General Médici; torture became prevalent; and there has also been an economic 'miracle'. The process of conflict has not been halted by these events, and in fact is more serious, but the 'open period' of 1968 when the press was relatively free and the Church could easily speak out is gone.

The process of conflict since the coup within a coup

Since the decree of the 5th Institution Act, the conflicts appear to have decreased slightly in frequency while increasing in gravity and scope. I use the term 'appear' advisedly, because it is very possible that there has been no decrease in frequency; since the news media are censored one cannot know for sure, but from all indica-tions there were many more conflicts than one might have realized. By the end of

---

[97] *Jornal do Brasil*, 3 December 1968.
[98] *Correio da Manhã*, 5 December 1968, cited in *SEDOC* 9, p. 1221.
[99] Interview with pastoral coordinator on 30 June 1970.

1968 the conflicts followed a predictable pattern and this pattern was not modified by the Act but only increased in intensity. Rather than describe the dozen or so conflicts catalogued for the period since late 1968, a discussion in depth of four of them will show the continuation of the pattern, its increasing severity and the present apparently polarized situation between Church and state. The four are illustrative, in that they concern all levels of the Church, take place in all parts of the country and ultimately involve high levels of the government. The four conflicts are: one involving two priests who were imprisoned in São Luís do Maranhão in late 1970; another involving Dom Helder in a national smear campaign from roughly mid-1970 until at least mid-1971; that concerning a priest and his assistant who were imprisoned in São Paulo in early 1971; and a continuation of the Dom Waldir incident, which became more serious and continued until at least mid-1971. Three of these four concern cases of torture and those dealing with the bishops might be seen as continuations of the conflicts begun in 1966 and 1967.[100]

Pes. José Antônio Monteiro and Xavier de Maupeau, the latter a Frenchman, worked on the formation of basic religious communities in the village of Urbano Santos, about 100 miles from São Luís. As part of their mission, and with the knowledge and support of the bishop, they encouraged participation and *conscientização* among the faithful. This type of work did not endear them to the local political elites, who denounced them as communists and complained to the police about their actions. In late July 1970, while the priests were at a meeting in São Luís, the police broke into their house in Urbano Santos and removed a great deal of 'communistic material'. When Pe. José Antônio returned to his parish to find out what had happened, he was put under arrest by the Federal Police and taken back to São Luís. Pe. Xavier de Maupeau, following a request of the police to the archbishop, presented himself for arrest on 4 August, thereby joining his colleague. Pe. José Antônio was interrogated for several hours, tortured at length, and finally signed a confession implicating himself and the other priest in communist activities. They were both held incommunicado for a week; then the Federal Police accused them of subversion and arranged a trial early in September. In late August the local newspapers published accounts claiming that the priests were indeed subversive and should be imprisoned as any communist would be, and the Federal Police promoted a television program which condemned them and noted that all subversives would be eliminated.

The trial began on 2 September, a month after the priests had originally been imprisoned, and the efforts of the bishops were successful in having it removed from the Federal Police to the Army Court of Justice. During two days of evidence,

---

[100] As printed sources are scarce I must rely heavily on interviews. Because of the delicate political situation the informants cannot be identified. I have excluded the following conflicts: the case of eight Dominicans imprisoned in São Paulo in 1969; the incident over the bishops' new catechism, which was attacked by the Minister of Education on television in early 1970; the imprisonment and torture of JOC personnel in Rio in late 1970; the raid on a Jesuit development institute and subsequent questioning of Dom Aloísio Lorscheider, of the CNBB, for five hours; and several incidents involving torture of priests, nuns and laymen on which material is sparse.

demonstrations of the marks of torture and perjury, the priests came to be recognized as victims of injustice. Two statements by witnesses for the prosecution were repudiated and the 'witnesses' indicated that the police had forced them to accuse the priests. Another prosecution witness stuck to his story, although he did not know what the word subversive meant, never saw any of their documents and indicated that his evidence for their subversion was based on the statement 'Love one another, as I have loved you'. After a few more incidents of this sort the Court found the priests innocent and released them.

There is a lot of material on the São Luís incident, which not only gives the details of testimonies and accusations but also demonstrates the feelings and actions taking place within the Church.[101] The activities within the Church were *de rigeur* according to the pattern established before 1969. The archbishop, Dom João José Mota, wrote an article defending the priests, in which he defined the nature of their activities and noted that their persecution was due to partisan political concerns of local power groups and that another priest had been imprisoned only the week before. This article was published in a local paper and that evening the auxiliary bishop, Dom Edmilson, read it over the Archdiocesan radio station. Immediately afterwards the Federal Police arrived and prohibited further communication regarding the case. The archbishop travelled to Recife, Fortaleza and Brasília in order to clarify the issue nationally and to try to arrange a more impartial court for the trial. Later in the month, after the torture was made public, the bishops of Ceará, Maranhão and Piauí published a document in which they described the incidents relating to the imprisonment and located them within a political context. They noted that the Church worked to make the people aware and encouraged them to participate. Yet these actions were denounced by the landowners and politicians and at times the police were called in as well. In the face of this series of events, the bishops reaffirmed their commitment to change and noted that those who denied it were in fact the subversives. To the imprisoned priests and to the many others in similar circumstances they gave their encouragement, support and blessings and noted from the gospel: 'Happy are those who suffer persecution for the sake of Justice.' (Matthew 5:10).

Throughout the whole month of the priests' imprisonment the local clergy, religious and laity met often, discussed the case and generally became involved on behalf of the priests. They prepared public statements of support and described in some detail the types of tortures used by the police. What comes through most significantly is the high level of awareness that emerged from discussing and agonizing over the incident. The drama brought about region-wide mobilization, a close following of political and police tactics and a real evaluation of whether the two priests were indeed acting subversively or whether they were simply being persecuted for religious actions. In essence the case persuaded many Brazilians to concede a larger mission for the Church and made them realize the opposition this Church might have to face. An eyewitness wrote at the conclusion of the

[101] This material was collected by one of my informants, whose name cannot be used here. The material includes private letters, priests' statements from jail, the public documents of the bishops and analyses by on-the-spot observers.

trial: 'This chapter is over. Another is in the writing, I suppose. A new Church, a living Church, a united Church, the Church of Maranhão, is ready to live those chapters of a book entitled "Gospel Lived Today in Maranhão".' Conflict, in short, brought about both unity and awareness. The primary impact of this conflict was on the local or regional level, however, as the news media did not carry information on the trial at the national level.

On the other hand, there has been a great deal of publicity concerning Dom Helder Câmara and it is uniformly bad. Dom Helder is not particularly popular with the elements that came to power in 1964 and has been involved in numerous incidents since 1966. The last chapter showed his sphere of action in Recife to be severely limited, but nothing was said about his national and international role as spokesman for the progressive group within the Church. When it became clear that Dom Helder would not be intimidated, the public campaign of calumny began. (He went so far as to denounce Brazilian tortures while abroad in Paris in May 1970.) Many newspapers, including the *Estado de São Paulo*, magazines like *O Cruzeiro* and radio and television programs unleashed a vicious and scurrilous attack, which did not diminish until it became known that he was not going to receive the Nobel Peace Prize, for which he had been nominated.[102] Most important about the attacks was the apparent acquiescence of the government, as though it were an official program, and the denial to Dom Helder of means to defend himself in public. As noted previously, there is more about Dom Helder in foreign news media than in Brazil, except for the attacks on his person and orientation. He is attacked for his past affiliation with the *Integralistas*, for being a 'red, Communist, Cuban sympathizer, enemy of Christ, traitor of the Church'; the Governor of São Paulo called him 'a Fidel Castro in a cassock'; and his name and face have been associated in the media with pornographic pictures and immorality.[103]

The reactions within, and even outside, the Church have been more than the government probably anticipated. The Central Commission, at their meeting in October 1970, referred to the defamation and calumnies directed against pastors, but much more pointed documents of support were published by individual bishops and regional groups. The outlawed UNE published privately a very outspoken defense, as did some workers' groups. The various reactions boiled down to the realization that Dom Helder was critical, not to say prophetic, that he indeed wanted to see changes in society and that those who attacked him (and this certainly included the government) simply wanted to support the status quo and could not tolerate people of his ilk criticizing them. These onslaughts are evidence of the fact that Dom Helder is the most well-known progressive; the media's irresponsible and degrading attacks indicate that they are afraid of his message and influence among the people. Because of this the clergy and laity

---

[102] For a good analysis of this series of attacks see Joe Page in the *New York Times*; the interview Dom Helder gave to *L'Express* is found in *SEDOC* 27 (August 1970), as is his letter of reply to the attacks in *Estado de São Paulo*, pp. 219–38.

[103] See *O Cruzeiro*, 22 September 1970 and 6 October 1970 for a series by David Nasser on low personal attacks.

closed ranks and became more aware of the problems involved, but they simply could not publish much in his defense.

Conflict has varying effects on individuals at the various levels of the Church. While Cardinals Rossi, Jaime Câmara and Vicente Scherer signed documents denouncing torture and defended other members of the hierarchy and clergy, one had the feeling that their hearts were not really in it and that they reacted as much for institutional unity as for humanitarian considerations. Cardinal Rossi equivocated in the process of conflict, as he did on all political and religious issues. He did not meet with Costa e Silva, he did refuse the decoration, but then he turned around and cooperated with the government afterwards and made a statement which was not clearly in defense of the clergy and Dom Helder. Without too much trouble, then, the government could emphasize his warm support, the papers featured his statements, and the others in the Church and society who were being tortured and denounced could be more easily isolated.[104] Even though Dom Eugênio was promoted over Dom Helder, lauded nationally and internationally and praised by the Pope, the Vatican has followed a different path and replaced Cardinal Rossi with Dom Evaristo Arns. After many statements by international bodies, on-the-spot research by important international Churchmen and action by the Pontifical Commission for Justice and Peace, the Pope on 22 October 1970 condemned torture in no uncertain terms. While not specifically mentioning Brazil, the combination of factors leads one to believe that he was referring to incidents there.[105] The day after the Pope's statement on torture Cardinal Rossi was promoted and moved out of Brazil; his best auxiliary replaced him. The coincidence seems too great; the action removed the most centrally located conservative element and equivocator, head of the biggest archdiocese and President of the CNBB, from the process. His removal opened the way for a rather more serious and unequivocal stance by his successor, Dom Evaristo Arns, in the face of another conflict.

In late January 1971 the São Paulo police raided the office of a priest who was active in the working-class areas around the capital. There they found a stencil dealing with a union movement for better wages which was supported by the archdiocese. The police confiscated material and money and imprisoned the priest, Pe. Giulio Vicini, an Italian, and his social assistant, Iara Spadini. They were taken to police headquarters and brutally tortured, although neither was

---

[104] My interviews in São Paulo in June 1970 indicated that Cardinal Rossi went out of his way to improve relations with the government after his little conflict. One of my informants pointed out that he watched color television with the Governor, the one who said Dom Helder was 'a Fidel Castro in a cassock', during the World Cup Soccer Games in June 1970. On his equivocations on the question of torture, see the *LADOC* reprint of *Mensaje* of July 1970, in I, 18 August 1970. See his long interview with the *Estado de São Paulo* on 7 June 1970.

[105] *The New York Times* states this directly on 23 October 1970; statements on torture are reprinted in *National Catholic Reporter* of 30 October 1970; and the background to the Pope's statement and other actions by groups are well analyzed in Ralph della Cava's piece in *Commonweal* of 24 April 1970.

told what they were charged with.[106] When the archbishop discovered that the two were in prison he attempted to communicate with them and verified that they had been tortured. He went to see the Governor about the matter and was informed that he should take doctors with him to obtain proof of the tortures. When Dom Evaristo returned to the jail with the doctors, he was confronted by the police and was not able to see the prisoners. Thereupon the archbishop responded rapidly and broadcast information about the tortures. He promoted local meetings, similar to those in São Luís, in which the incidents were discussed and statements formulated which asked for proof of the subversion. An important distinction was made between preaching or acting for justice and political subversion. If the issue was not clarified by the government, and this was specifically requested, more conflicts could be anticipated. It was further noted that priests were judged guilty of subversion and tortured accordingly without even being tried. The arch-diocesan journal, *O São Paulo*, published ample material on the case and defended the two prisoners. Notices were read in the churches and posted in public places. A Church research organization carried out minor studies and published their analysis of the relations between the Church and state since the coup, which raised very serious questions about the two institutions' continued cooperation. Dom Evaristo collected material on the tortures and presented it to the XIIth General Assembly of the CNBB, then meeting in Belo Horizonte. As Joseph Novitski of the *New York Times* noted on 12 Febrary 1971, 'The Archbishop's statement was the strongest, baldest assertion that prisoners had been tortured yet made by a prelate of the church in Brazil.' The bishops at the assembly in Belo Horizonte sent a statement of support to the archbishop, in which they noted the fact of tortures and spoke strongly for respect of human dignity. Beyond this the incidents were publicized throughout Brazil by Church facilities, which made it evident that the two had been tortured and that the government was not acting to find out who was guilty in the incident. At roughly the same time (early February 1971) General Humberto Melo, Commander of the IInd Army in São Paulo, stated that some priests and two archbishops were acting in opposition to national security.[107] As the archdiocese was already mobilized over the case of the two prisoners, they simply incorporated this matter, turned the tables around and requested that the general clarify his remarks and bring charges.

Information is lacking on whether the two prisoners were ever brought to trial and if their torturers were ever made known. However, it is obvious that Dom Evaristo Arns responded more quickly and effectively than Cardinal Rossi had done in previous incidents. He immediately verified for himself that the two had been tortured, made it known everywhere in the country, informed other bishops, and took advantage of the case to get his priests and the laity to reflect on the situation and its implications for the Church. Some very worthwhile studies and documents came out of the conflict, which showed an increased commitment to preaching and action for social justice, as well as a critical analysis of the relations

---

[106] For descriptions of torture which came out in the press see *Jornal do Brasil*, 13 February 1971.
[107] On this case see *Jornal do Brasil*, 6 March 1971.

between Church and state. The leadership found lacking in Cardinal Rossi was clear in Dom Evaristo Arns and the logical implications of conflict in forcing Church and state apart (and framing a social mission) were eloquently stated by the archbishop in many public speeches, which were sometimes reprinted in the archdiocesan papers and even in the national news media.

In Volta Redonda Dom Waldir initially became involved in conflict with the military in late 1967 and until 1972 was still involved, although more seriously.[108] The initial conflict involved a Colonel Armênio Pereira, Commander of the 1st Infantry Battalion near Volta Redonda. After the 5th Institutional Act the colonel imprisoned many people for subversion, including two Catholic labor organizers associated with the bishop. He let it be known that he had imprisoned them because of their association with the bishop, who he thought was a Communist and a subversive, and in meetings with Catholic leaders the colonel supposedly provided proof that the bishop was highly suspect. In short, he was attempting to isolate Dom Waldir as Dom Helder had been isolated through intimidation and suspicion. The bishop heard about what was going on and decided to put an end to it by presenting himself for arrest. Thus on 14 January 1970, Dom Waldir showed up at headquarters and spent the day trying to get the colonel to face up to the situation while the latter introduced him to the other officers, gave him lunch, showed him around and generally evaded the issue. Finally after twelve hours he got the colonel to admit that he had arrested the Catholics because of their association with him and that he thought the bishop was dangerous. Dom Waldir then refused to leave and asked to be placed under arrest, for it was not right for a dangerous man like himself to be free while his mere accomplices were in prison. The colonel said that he could not put the bishop in prison and became very unnerved; he eventually called in the press, the radio and local authorities to show that the bishop was either crazy or dangerous. Dom Waldir took the opportunity to explain why he was there, made his point well to the detriment of the colonel and finally left that evening with the two prisoners. The bishop acted very intelligently as well as courageously in this incident and further demonstrated his mettle by writing a pamphlet on the incident and distributing it widely; in it he recounted the subversive 'proof' with which the colonel had confronted him. This however, was not the end of the conflict.

In May 1969 Dom Waldir heard about the torture and imprisonment of a worker with seven children. The bishop visited the man in the hospital to verify the torture and, along with eleven of his priests, wrote to the Commander of the Army in Rio to complain. The Commander sent a colonel to verify the facts and interview the prisoner, the military and the priests, but he found that the bishop's charges were not correct, that they were in fact an attack on national security, and began a criminal process against the bishop and some thirty priests. There began a Military Police Investigation (IPM), which lasted three months and in

---

[108] I interviewed Dom Waldir in Volta Redonda on 19 June 1970 and am relying mainly on this information, as well as mimeographed pamphlets which were distributed in the diocese, for the following discussion up to mid-1970. For the period until mid-1971 I am relying on his documents sent to the bishops, assembly in Belo Horizonte in February 1971.

January 1970 concluded that the bishop and sixteen priests were guilty of breaking some parts of the Law of National Security. The case pended until early 1971, while the military decided what to do. According to the bishop many in the military investigation team realized that the Church was innocent, but the Commander, General Sizeno, wanted to make an example of them. Throughout the whole case, Dom Waldir sent information to all the other bishops to keep them in touch. He noted that the Central Commission of the CNBB sent him a strong note of support, which helped him along and infuriated the military. The colonel even went so far as to say that all those who signed the statement of support were also guilty of crimes against the national security.[109]

Even while Dom Waldir was being tried early in 1971 he became involved in more incidents of torture in his diocese. In late 1970 the military made a raid on JOC in Rio, imprisoning many and torturing some. The same sort of thing took place in Volta Redonda, where thirty priests and laymen were put in prison for various periods of time. Of the thirty, six remained in jail until Christmas, including a Pe. Natanael Campos; they were all tortured. Even in late January 1971 two were still in prison, including the priest. The tortures were horrible and the bishop assembled a dossier of information on them and sent it to the other bishops. The bishops assembled in Belo Horizonte sent Dom Waldir a very strong note, in which they declared their solidarity with him and with his denunciation of the tortures and those who performed them. What emerges from this series of incidents is the fact that the military is willing to go to any lengths not only with laymen and priests, but even with bishops.

There are other incidents of conflict since February 1971, but these should suffice. After a while torture, inhumanity and oppression cease to be meaningful and the above incidents are enough to convey the relations currently existing between the Church and state in Brazil. Quite clearly the present Brazilian regime is different from previous governments and it is still relying on severe oppression and torture to maintain order and discourage opposition. The Church, as the only institution in Brazil that can still be vocal and independent, is obviously a target for attack if it does not at all times agree with the military's view of the world and 'development'.

[109] For the statement see *SEDOC* 2:5 (November 1969), p. 644.

10. Consequences of conflict:
autonomy and the prophetic mission

The conflict process promises to activate an institutional revolution in the Church. In certain respects the process is similar to the experience of 1874, as the goals of Church and state have apparently already diverged and thus the conflict simply makes this fact manifest, but at the same time the conflicts do more than define the divergence – they give it impetus. As the goals are differentiated and shown to be opposing, the conflicts also encourage the clergy to support these goals. Thus there is not an easily visualized two-stage process of changed autonomy relationship and then adoption of a new model – but rather a more complicated one in which already modified goals accelerate a process of conflict, which leads both to a different relationship and a new model of influence. The conflict between Church and state is now a 'social fact', and no longer a simple process; there is a strong commitment to a new influence model.

There is a need to clarify briefly the facts of the conflict process itself to emphasize its dynamic character as sectors within the Church, all responsible government officials and the news media have consistently stated that there is no conflict but just a few 'misunderstandings'.

Number of conflicts
In 1966 there was one important incident; in 1967 one important conflict and four which were not so important; in 1968 three important conflicts and five less so; in 1969 at least three important conflicts and because of censorship nobody knows how many less important. One of these concerned the imprisonment of Dominican priests implicated in the death of Carlos Marighela and another was associated with the death of Pe. Henrique Neto. In 1970 at least five important conflicts took place; up to the middle of 1971 there were two important conflicts. There was thus a general increase in the number of conflicts and most certainly an increase in the important ones.

Geographical distribution
Originally the conflicts occurred in the Northeast, but with the Dom Waldir incident of late 1967 the process spread to the South. Of the four described in some detail at the end of Chapter 9, two took place in the Northeast and two in the South. Several others took place in Rio, São Paulo and Belo Horizonte. Therefore, while the Northeast probably has a disproportionate number of conflicts, the process is well established in most areas of the country.

Individuals
Originally the conflicts were not only located in the Northeast, but revolved around the personalities who were active in the pre-1964 CNBB. From the time of the Dom Waldir incident, however, the process has involved members of the

hierarchy such as Dom Aloísio Lorscheider, Dom Evaristo Arns and Dom João Rezende Costa, who had never previously been involved in social matters and are not known for their radical orientation. A study of the priests active in the process would probably show a very broad geographical distribution, but with particular focus on the younger ones and especially on foreigners. The former characteristic is to be expected, for younger priests are more likely to be involved in areas which might not be construed as purely 'religious', such as pastoral work with students, assistance to Catholic Action, 'experiments in parishes' and so forth. The focus on foreigners is not due to their greater radicalization, but rather to the ease with which the government can direct public opinion against them and deport them.

Manner of enactment
Initially the conflicts were worked out through statements and counterstatements and while this still continues other more serious means are now used; torture began with the Belo Horizonte conflict and most certainly persists; deportation of foreigners started with Pe. Wauthier in 1968 and by late 1969 eleven foreign priests had been removed; to the best of my knowledge there has been at least one murder, in 1969, and cases of attempted suicide have been reported but censorship makes it impossible to learn for sure what has happened. Even without comments on the increasing gravity and seriousness of the conflicts and simply relying on the facts of numbers, individuals and geographical distribution, there can be no doubt that the process of conflict is dynamic and has achieved a momentum of its own.

Despite these facts, many in society and the Church deny that any dissension exists between Church and state. Cardinal Rossi was cited innumerable times by the *Estado de São Paulo* as arguing that there was no conflict between Church and state, despite the fact that he was centrally involved in at least one incident. Dom Vicente Scherer was also quoted by the same paper as making essentially the same point; during an interview he emphasized the good relations between the two institutions.[1] Dom Eugênio Sales has often made the same point in public and his orientation at the national level was manifested when he acted as Papal representative to the Brazilian government on the occasion of the VIIIth National Eucharistic Congress in May 1970. On this occasion, as on many before and after, Dom Eugênio emphasized the cooperation and understanding between Church and state. The government has left no doubt at all that it is on the friendliest terms with the Church. The Presidents and other top officials in both civil and military capacities have never ceased declaring their Catholic beliefs and commitments and their fervor in accepting the Papal documents. On the occasion of the above-mentioned Eucharistic Congress the government of President Médici took every opportunity to demonstrate the warm and cordial relations: The President met Dom Eugênio at the airport; all the bishops were invited to a government reception; two colonels visited the bishops in many of their sessions;

---

[1] For Cardinal Rossi see the long interview in *Estado de São Paulo*, 7 June 1970; interview with Cardinal Scherer in Pôrto Alegre on 26 June 1970.

the Minister of Justice appeared at one session; and *Veja*, on the basis of the public view, reported that the meeting of the two sides on the occasion of the Congress represented 'a new type of relationship between the Catholic Church and the Brazilian government'.[2] In reporting the Dom Waldir incident of 1967, the *Jornal do Brasil* distorted the bishops' reactions to the conflict and a key point dealt with the meaning of the event: misunderstanding or conflict. Since that time, and particularly since the 5th Institutional Act, the reporting has deteriorated. The *Estado de São Paulo* cannot be expected to report accurately on Church–state relations and indeed it does not. The *Jornal do Brasil* is better, for at least it often publishes the original Church documents, but the emphasis tends to be on conciliation and cooperation. *Veja* relative to other periodicals is mildly progressive. However, a content analysis of a few months' issues on Church topics shows that its reporting is also distorted. The discrepancy between facts and reporting is obvious in its analysis of the Congress in May 1970, where it argued that there was a 'new relationship between . . .'. On reading the original documents from the meeting and then interviewing a half dozen bishops, priests and laymen who were present, it became clear that no new relationship was in the offing; if anything the situation was more strained than ever before. At the formal level, Dom Eugênio and the President enjoyed close cooperation and understanding, but such was not the case with a large proportion of the bishops.[3] The *Veja* reporting on the CNBB elections in February 1971 is similar. The progressives won this election, Dom Evaristo Arns reported on the imprisonment and torture of the priest and lay assistant, three letters of support were sent out (to Dom Waldir, Dom Evaristo Arns, and the Provincial of the imprisoned Dominicans), and yet the news-magazine emphasized cooperation and moderation. The title of the article was 'Agreeable Masters of Moderation: The Church that Stays United, Stays,' in it they quoted an extremely reactionary bishop, Dom Proença Sigaud, in such a way as to give the impression that he represented a significant number of his colleagues.

There is an abundance of documents and statements which demonstrate that no conflict exists between Church and state. Yet there are undeniably some 'problems' at times between members of the Church who are 'acting not as Churchmen but as subversives' and the police or military. The incidents are always put into individual categories; they represent personal cases and must be dealt with by particular criminal processes. The news media (even if the publishers do not believe this because of their own orientations) must adhere to a government line because of censorship. The bishops (such as Cardinals Rossi and Scherer) are of the mentality attributed to Dom Eugênio: neo-Christendom requires power and thus the Church must cooperate with the state for resources and support. The government desires Church support for purposes of legitimacy. If it can create the impression that the institution is close to the government, then it is not difficult to isolate a few subversive individuals, such as Dom Helder and Dom

[2] *Veja*, 27 May 1970; see also the description of events at this Congress.
[3] For critical laymen's comments on this meeting and extensive citations from the press which show how the bishops 'sold out', see *LADOC* 1:47b (December 1970).

Waldir or young and foreign priests and deal with them as criminals. There are, therefore, powerful forces making for cooperation. Most of the older bishops want it, the government most certainly does and the news media work on it as a main line of propaganda. Nonetheless, the previous chapter has demonstrated that the conflict process is dynamic and becoming more serious; from these instances and interviews in Brazil I am relatively secure in asserting that the conflict between Church and state is a social fact and thus more than a process.

The divergent goals of Church and state

In the Introduction I noted that a relationship of conflict is one in which the actors hold mutually exclusive or antagonistic goals and operate through distinct structures. Formally the Church is concerned with religious goals and the government with secular ones. However the Church has always been involved with the secular and has not hesitated to enter the temporal sphere. The goals now being defined appear to be antagonistic. The antagonism is best described under four headings.

The social mission of the Church

Since the mid 1950s, supported by Rome and never formally repudiated by the hierarchy, the social mission has become an integral part of a new influence model. Initially it was sponsored by only a few bishops and priests, but with the strategies of change and opposition from the government it has become cemented into the self-image. In the present circumstances the social role does not amount to much more than a compromise to involve the Church in society and work for its betterment. However, in spite of this token involvement, the government's unhesitating acceptance of the Pope's encyclical and even Dom Eugênio's comments on the 'Social Action of the Church' or other abstract guidelines, when some elements in the Church (or in general society for that matter) attempt to implement the role, they are called 'subversives' and persecuted. The government seemingly finds it impossible to distinguish between legitimate social action by the Church and subversion. A brief recollection of the conflicts described in Chapter 9 will indicate that the majority dealt with a layman, priest or bishop acting in accordance with his social mission and being attacked for it. Therefore, while in abstract terms Church and state are identical in their approach to social improvement, when there is action or even specific discussion of this mission, it is obvious that there is an exclusive element here between Church and state. Some form of social role for the Church is necessary, although in theory it does not have to conflict with the state. It is worthwhile citing some statements by the bishops on their social role, for they were signed by the most important prelates and published shortly after the 5th Institutional Act. They demonstrate that even at this level of the institution the social mission is accepted.

We strive in our efforts to live by the Christian social doctrine in preaching the Gospel, which demands reforms that the Government itself has reaffirmed and is now able to carry out with speed because of the exceptional powers it possesses. These are reforms which do not subvert the existing order, but rather change the archaic structures that constitute obstacles to our development.

In November 1967, we wrote: 'Although the Church's teaching, based on the message revealed by Jesus Christ, refers essentially to the truths defining man's eternal destiny, it also includes a defence of human values which are the foundations of transcendental existence. We reject the Marxist thesis that religion dispossesses man, consoling him with a perspective of future happiness to compensate for the unfailing earthly frustration. To state that the religious mission of the bishops must not go beyond the limits of the so-called "spiritual life" is virtually to accept the Marxist concept of religion. To proclaim the protection of Christian civilization while imposing restrictions on the teaching mission of the Church as she defends human values is to bolster paganism in disguise.'

Even though it may create many problems and personal difficulties, we have decided to implement the principles of the Second Vatican Ecumenical Council, of the social encyclicals, and now of the Second General Conference of Latin-American Bishops, held in Medellín. This is our response to the Holy Father's request, to the needs of our people, and to the demands of civilization.[4]

In a more recent statement of the Central Commission the general commitment to the social mission was reaffirmed.

Christianity supercedes and transcends systems of government and political regimes. Its mission, however, cannot be indifferent to the concrete situation of the people. If it is not within the role of the Church to conduct officially or exclusively the transformation of temporal structures, its role is, however, to present principles and norms that, in the light of the Gospel, can promote models and projects of social life.[5]

Later documents have more or less reiterated these commitments to a social mission for the Church. It may be argued that these are empty words and are not implemented by the bishops, but some bishops and priests have been attacked for saying no more and under the protection of the legitimacy provided by such statements other elements in the Church might well act.

Antagonism generated by institutional defense
For whatever reason, some sections in the military have gone out of their way to attack 'subversives in the Church' and the government has apparently been a party to the smear attacks on Dom Helder Câmara. The bishops (not to mention priests and laymen) have banded together in support of the attacked figures more than expected and issued statements of solidarity. This was obvious in all the conflicts involving Dom Helder, and the bishops' statements in early 1971 aligned them with Dom Waldir, Dom Evaristo Arns and the Provincial of the Dominicans. The unity is not perfect, as I noted with regard to Cardinal Rossi, but it is enough to oppose the Church to those who are responsible for extreme forms of attack on groups within the institution. The hypothesis of Lewis Coser is relevant here:

---

[4] The statement appeared in *Fôlha de São Paulo*, 25 February 1969 and *SEDOC* 1:10 (April 1969), pp. 39–59; *NIU* 69/10; *Visão*, 14 March 1969; its repercussions are discussed in *Vozes* April 1969.
[5] *SEDOC* 2:5 (November 1969), p. 640 from statement of September 1969.

'conflict sets boundaries between groups within a social system by strengthening group consciousness and awareness of separateness, thus establishing the identity of groups within the system'.[6]

Government approach to development

The present military regime differs from those in the past in that it is preoccupied with development and, in the economic realm at least, is successful. However, this development is being paid for in large part by the lower classes and 'development' per se means nothing more than economic growth. The human element is missing in the present regime's definition of development, despite the fact that President Médici is constantly making claims to the contrary. Even though the Church has traditionally been a bulwark for the existing order, neither internationally nor nationally is the institution specifically committed to a particular economic system. Recent Papal encyclicals have pointed out the distinction between economic growth and development, as have the statements of the Northeastern bishops during the 1950s. If a good example of unbridled capitalism exists today it is in Brazil; in the General Assembly of May 1971 the bishops referred to the success of the Brazilian government with development – in the economic and financial side – but asked for a reconsideration of the process along the lines of 'integral development' in which the human being is given a value.[7]

But the antagonism between the goals of Church and state on development is not simply a matter of an emphasis by the latter on economic matters and by the former on human. The regime wants economic growth so that Brazil will become a great country and fulfill the destiny which it feels is her due. Probably the most accurate short analysis of the present regime would emphasize its concern with national security. The government wants economic growth: steel plants, manufacturing and energy to ensure the survival of the country in a world divided by two ideologies. They came into power because of the fear of Communist takeovers and the humiliation of being a third-rate country; since 1964 they have faced what they apparently perceive to be both indigenous and international threats from subversive elements. The country today is certainly turned toward development, but this orientation is infused with large elements of nationalism and security considerations. The combination of the various strands adds up to what might be called 'an ideology of national security'. The ideology has been analyzed and categorized by Dom Cândido Padim in an excellent article which goes far beyond the document of Pe. José Comblin.[8] In some of the bishops' meetings Dom Padim had talked about the ideology of national security and as other bishops did not know precisely what he meant he formulated an internal document on it. The document, like so many others, became public and he

---

[6] Lewis Coser, *The Functions of Social Conflict* (New York: The Free Press of Glencoe, 1956), p. 34.

[7] This part of their statement is reprinted in *LADOC* 1:13 (June 1970).

[8] Apparently his document had some effect, as the first Central Commission statement after the 5th Institutional Act warned the government about the danger of abuse and cited a long section from the Encyclical 'Mit brennender Sorge' which was directed to the Nazis in Germany. For Dom Padim's document, see *SEDOC*, September 1968.

finally published the whole thing. His analysis, which he assured me in 1970 was appreciated by 80% of the bishops, shows that the ideology of the present regime is not far from a totalitarianism of the German or Russian variety. He then goes on to formulate what could be called a Church ideology on social matters and demonstrates the exclusive character of the two approaches to development.

The political situation

This category is closely related to the previous one, although it is more strictly political. The Church originally supported the military because it seemed a viable alternative to the Goulart government and because it was in power. In the meantime, however, the government has become increasingly arbitrary, authoritarian and closed to all outside criticism. In superseding the Constitution of 1967 the military have allowed flagrant violations of human rights to take place, even if they do not condone torture *per se*. Many of the later conflicts discussed in the last chapter centered on questions of torture. This matter, as well as the decree of the death penalty in 1968, failure to return to a democratic system and the general closing of all channels, has brought the Church into opposition with the government. In the first statement after the 5th Institutional Act the Central Commission requested an immediate return to democratic forms.[9] And in the bishops' statement of May 1970, while the government was denying that torture existed in Brazil and on the day after the Minister of Justice personally affirmed this, they published a document supported by 159 votes to 20, which very clearly denounced torture and criticized the government on other points. Given the context of the time and the personal efforts by the President and other high government officials, it is a very strong statement indeed.

It would be an evasion of our duty as shepherds responsible for bringing the gospel to the people if we failed to voice our views regarding certain basic aspects of our present situation as they affect the human person.

We mention first of all the administration of justice, which is indeed regulated and protected by our laws, but which we sincerely feel is frequently ignored. It is ignored in the case of trials conducted in an illegal and dangerous manner, of arrests based only on suspicion or baseless accusations, of investigations which drag on for months, of jailing men incommunicado, and of the total lack, in many instances, of the basic right of defense.

Again it is a well-known fact, in spite of all denials, that there exists among our own people, as well as among other peoples throughout the world, the firm conviction that there are repeated cases of torture in Brazil.

One of the basic tasks, which calls for a common effort by everyone in building this nation, is to contribute constructively to the social, civic and moral growth of our people, so that more and more Brazilians can participate maturely and practically in the country's political, economic and social life, thus giving to private initiative its proper role.

---

[9] See document in *SEDOC* 1:10 (April 1969). I was told by one bishop that when Cardinal Dom Jaime and Dom Aloísio Lorscheider presented this document to Costa e Silva he became infuriated and asked them to leave.

Such an effort presupposes a constructive and truthful expression of opinion, including the opinion of those who disagree with present official policies so that they can achieve the status of a serious opposition, as befits a nation that claims it has reached maturity.

It is of capital importance for us to make a distinction between the kind of opposition that aims at undermining peace and social life through a systematic use of violence, and the kind of opposition that is based on differing viewpoints and principles. The latter is an indispensable factor of the criticism all human institutions need in order to strive for perfection.[10]

More recent statements have emphasized essentially the same points; the need to return to democracy, the necessity to end torture and repression, a more human approach to development and the requirement for a political program which emphasizes social development.[11]

These four categories could be elaborated, but this is sufficient to show that the goals of Church and state are mutually exclusive. Not all the clergy are aware of this fact. However, the Bishops' statements are the most conservative and really most important. The goals of the two institutions are in conflict, but most of the bishops continue to believe in the good faith (*boa fé*) of the government. However this good faith is rapidly dwindling, as torture continues while the government persists in denying its existence. Clergy and laity have indicated that they know for certain that the goals of the Church and state were in opposition. Even while the supply of good faith is diminishing through the conflict process, it appears as though not only are the goals mutually exclusive but even the structures are becoming distinctive.

Autonomy and the definition of separate structures

Coser points to a central process in his proposition that conflict sets boundaries between groups and thus establishes the identity of groups within a system.[12] In the discussion of the Christendom and neo-Christendom models I noted that integration of Church and state was desired, and as power was required for the exercise of influence, autonomy was not an issue. Because of conflict, the Church is being forced to develop an identity for itself separate from, and in opposition to, the state, as it becomes aware that others in society are claiming control over the orientation of the institution. Conflict is making parts of the Church aware of the traditional autonomy relationship and forcing them, even at times against their wills, to define their independence.

The definition of autonomy slowly entered the debate as the process of conflict developed momentum. In the 1966 incident it was not really an issue, although three of the defenders of Dom Helder (Alceu Amoroso Lima, Edgar Mata Machado and Dom Waldir for the bishops of Rio) argued that the conflict was due to a change in the Church's role in society without a corresponding change in

[10] Translation taken from *LADOC* 1:13 (June 1970).
[11] See for instance the statement of the Central Commission of October 1970.
[12] Coser, p. 34.

the government's. To these three the Church could not be seen as an institution unto itself, but only in relation to others. This observation presently led to recognition that other interests, and even private groups, wanted to control the Church. Following the series of conflicts culminating in the Dom Waldir case of late 1967, the Central Commission found it necessary to define Church autonomy in the face of outsiders' claims. In their 'Mission of the Hierarchy in Today's World' the elite clearly stated their autonomy as well as the institution's. In meetings after this the question of autonomy was a common point of emphasis.

The homily of the bishop and clergy in Belo Horizonte noted their independence from temporal powers; the archdiocesan paper observed that their independence tended to disappear as the Church threatened the regime; the homily of Cardinal Dom Jaime in Rio demanded independence for the Church; and three times in as many statements the CNBB pointed out that it was up to the Church to judge its own actions. By this time awareness had become a common theme, but still the government and papers would not admit that they did not have the right (or even duty) to direct the Church.

Despite the reporting in the media of the May 1970 General Assembly, the documents support (as do those who attended) a further definition of independence from the state. The government made very serious efforts to get the bishops to support its position unequivocally and to cease agitating about torture. Nonetheless they spoke out on torture and made a very deliberate statement of their independence from the government. If 'on the one hand, the Church in Brazil recognizes obvious achievements, on the other, it judges with dignity and loyalty that it can diverge from orientations or positions of the government'. The more progressive bishops wanted a more forceful statement, but the fact that it was approved by the vast majority of the bishops was a positive sign. At the Central Commission meeting in October 1970 the bishops once again stated their independence: 'In the judgment of what is really meant by the Gospel and its application, the bishops of Brazil do not allow the transfer of responsibilities which are theirs by divine command.'[13] In short, because of the conflict process the bishops have been forced to define their independence from the state and groups in society. The statements themselves are not especially dramatic, but if one remembers that the Church has been committed since 1889 to re-integrate itself with the state, and even up until the mid-1960s still desired this integration, they are significant.

In the context of identity and autonomy, the CNBB meeting in February 1971 was important. The main purpose of the meeting was to elect a President, General Secretary and other officials, after Cardinal Rossi had been transferred to Rome. The two recognized contenders for the post of President were Cardinal Scherer of Pôrto Alegre and Dom Aloísio Lorscheider, General Secretary of the CNBB. Cardinal Scherer is strong, authoritarian, conservative in political and social matters, believes in Church–state cooperation and is known to be a good friend of President Médici. Dom Aloísio has developed with his role in the CNBB, become

[13] Published in *Jornal do Brasil*, 17 October 1970.

more progressive, stood up to the government and just four months earlier had been detained by the military in Rio for five hours and questioned in the case concerning Instituto Brasileiro de Desenvolvimento (IBRADES). Dom Aloísio was elected President and another progressive, Dom Ivo Lorscheider, his cousin, was elected General Secretary.[14] The results of the elections are significant, as they showed that the bishops would not elect a candidate known for his intimate relations with the present regime, even though he was older and more powerful, but rather one who had already had problems with its police apparatus. Further, with the combination of the two Lorscheiders there is some possibility that the CNBB will become more of a viable entity than it has been at any time since 1964.

The parting of the ways in terms of structure is a mutual process. On the one hand the Church is defining its autonomy and identity in opposition to the regime. On the other the government is less in need of the Church's support. In fact the government goes out of its way to gain the favor of the Church and is eager to demonstrate that relations are in the best possible state. But there are several points which need to be clarified to show that the regime can be expected to ignore the Church or wage an all-out war on it. So far the government has defended its actions in the conflicts by suggesting that there are a few individuals and groups in the institution who act as Communists, subversives or anti-Christs. But it is becoming increasingly difficult for the government to insist that only a few infiltrators are causing problems. When they attempted to isolate Dom Helder the other bishops united around him; when they investigated Dom Waldir the same thing happened; when they imprisoned and tortured clergy in Belo Horizonte, Maranhão and São Paulo, other clergy and bishops declared their solidarity with them. And now the archbishop of São Paulo has confronted the government over torture. Only through self-deception and propaganda can the regime claim that a few subversives are causing all the problems. If the cause is the social mission and the government's subsequent definition of this as subversion, then more problems can be expected. As the regime comes to realize this it will cease attempts at cooperation and understanding; it will treat the Church as it would any political opposition group.[15]

There are several sectors of the Church that are happy to cooperate with the regime, even as the larger institution seems to draw away from its orientation. A well-established movement, the Tradição, Família e Propriedade (TFP), was founded in 1960 by Plinio Corrêa de Oliveira, a lawyer and retired professor of

[14] For the elections see *Veja* 17 February 1971; on his personality see the poor interview in *Veja* 3 March 1971. I interviewed Dom Ivo in Pôrto Alegre in 1967 and found him extremely aware.

[15] A number of my informants noted in 1970 that the government had a section in the Defense Ministry conducting research on the Church, its social ideology and personalities. I have not seen any reference to this research, but it seems logical enough when we recall that even the U.S. State Department has commissioned such a study of the Church throughout Latin America. If the Church concerns the State Department, how much more concerned should the Brazilian Government be to learn about an institution which is causing them many internal and international problems? See Luigi Einaudi *et al.*, *Latin American Institutional Development: The Changing Catholic Church* (Prepared for Office of External Research, Department of State) (Santa Monica, California: The Rand Corporation, 1969).

history. The core of the organization is provided by an 'integralist' ideology, which supports an active militancy in defense of traditional Catholicism. The TFP is in favor of extreme moralism, against divorce, against Communism and against change. It has by and large ignored the Second Vatican Council and some of its important members have criticized Popes John XXIII and Paul VI for their leftist leanings.[16] The organization has the complete support of a handful of bishops and about a dozen have a more or less defined sympathy for the goals of the organization, if not its methods. There are at least 1,500 male militants in the organization; it publishes a weekly paper, *O Católicismo,* and it is extremely active in pursuit of its goals. The TFP is a live organization and extremely influential among certain sections in the government and upper middle-class society.

From its inception the TFP diverged from the mainstream of the Church, which was at that time defined by the CNBB. Thus when the Central Commission and various regional groups of bishops came out in favor of agrarian reform and other structural changes, the TFP denounced such moves as Communism. In fact, it published a book entitled *Reforma Agrária: Questão de Consciência,* in which agrarian reform as supported by the CNBB was condemned.[17] After the coup and subsequent elimination of the CNBB the importance of the TFP grew. At times the military commanders conducting the purges of Church militants stated clearly that theirs was the Church of Dom Sigaud and not of Dom Helder. Their activities took on such importance that in June 1966 the Central Commission was obliged to point out that the organization was a civic entity and thereby lacked competence in the religious sphere. In the atmosphere of the post-coup era many had apparently thought that the TFP was the Church.

From the beginning of the conflict process the TFP and its members in the hierarchy have sided with the government in opposition to Church sectors. In the 1966 conflict in the Northeast Dom Castro Mayer was critical of the bishops' statements. During the CNBB General Assembly in July 1968 the bishops sympathetic to the TFP wrote to Costa e Silva and denounced what amounted to a new Church identity. Dom Sigaud referred to the support given by bishops and clergy to Pe. Comblin's paper as 'full and irrefutable proof of the fact that Communism has penetrated our ranks'.[18] During July and August 1968 the TFP promoted a petition to present to the Pope in Medellín, which denounced the 'Communization of the clergy in Brazil'. Dom Sigaud attacked the beliefs and personalities of Dom Helder and Dom José Maria Pires. While Dom Padim presented his study on the Doctrine of National Security and showed its incompatibility with Church doctrine, Dom Sigaud defended the Council of National

---

[16] See *SEDOC* 1:7 (January 1969), pp. 991–6 for two articles on TFP; Sanders, 'A Typology of Catholic Elites', Field Letter (TGS-10) to Richard H. Nolte, Institute of Current World Affairs, New York, 21 February 1968, deals with TFP comparatively; see *Jornal do Brasil* 27 October 1968, for numbers, description etc.; Frei Hubert Lepargneur 'Lógica do Integrismo', in *Convergência* 1:3 (April 1968).
[17] Dom Antônio Castro Mayer *et al., Reforma Agrária: Questão de Consciência* (São Paulo: Editôra Vera Cruz, 1961).
[18] *SEDOC* 7 (January 1969), p. 995.

Security.[19] In the middle of the Belo Horizonte conflict, when broad sectors of the Church denounced the military, Dom Sigaud exalted the action of the armed forces and literally blessed their arms.[20] In short, while a large part of the institution was defining its independence from the state and becoming committed to a new social mission, the TFP remained firmly entrenched in an archaic but nonetheless aggressive form of religion. Following considerable criticism from within the Church of the statements and behavior of the TFP in October 1968, the Central Commission appointed a commission to investigate it.

However, while the TFP moved further and further away from the mainstream of the Church, it moved ever closer to the government. It is worth noting the reaction of the *Estado de São Paulo* to the Central Commission investigation. In reference to the fact that the TFP was under investigation it noted, 'And, as was inevitable, all those inside the Church that courageously raise their voices, attempting to reestablish the truth and call the process of subversion by its name are the target of a systematic campaign of defamation and discredit.'[21] TFP members were acclaimed several times by high military officials; one of them met with the President on political matters; and another received the 'Great Cross of Order of Military Merit' from the Minister of the Army. If the government does not want to refer to the somewhat archaic TFP in showing that a true Church still exists in Brazil, it has a few other similar groups which support it while attacking parts of the larger institution. The group around the journal *Permanência* represents a line not far from that of the TFP, but somewhat more modern; they are closest to that line associated with the *Estado de São Paulo* in its attacks on the progressives. A good deal more significant is a group around *Hora Presente*, for they are much closer to the present government's orientation on more than just opposition to Church subversives. They follow the approach of nationalism, economic development, Brazil as great power and so forth, all the while attacking sections of the Church and justifying their actions in terms of both religion and the national interest. Therefore the regime does have alternatives to fall back on for religious support, if the larger institution should fail it.

However, if the regime does break with the Church it will not really need to rely on a part of the institution. It appears as though the regime has moved from a weak polity of low mobilization and ideological orientation to something closer to Ataturk's system in Turkey, or in some respects even to Nazi Germany. The military have completely monopolized politics; technocrats make the economic policies; an ideology is formulated at the top and is now being disseminated through the school system; organized labor is highly controlled; political opposition and discontent are handled by an amazingly efficient police and military network; and so far the masses have been given an Amazon highway and a World Cup in soccer.[22] This regime, if it continues to evolve along the present path,

---

[19] *Jornal do Brasil*, 24 July 1968.
[20] *Estado de São Paulo*, 3 December 1968.
[21] *Estado de São Paulo*, 3 October 1968.
[22] See Thomas Sanders, 'Institutionalizing Brazil's Conservative Revolution', AUFS Reports, 14:5 (December 1970).

simply will not need the Church for legitimacy. It legitimizes itself through the Institutional Acts and its ideology and educates the children in its tenets.

The conclusion to be drawn from this discussion of the goals of the Church and state, and of the definition of autonomy and distinctiveness on both sides, is clearly that the process of conflict has led to a relationship of conflict. The goals are antagonistic and the structures are becoming distinct. However, the Church is still bound up in the neo-Christendom model of influence, which relies on power for influence, on state supports and resources for Church goals, and thus finds itself in a bad position. The government has been cutting down on resources for Church activities and as the regime becomes more 'modern' it is likely to take over more of the Church's traditional functions.[23] It seems as though the paring process, the elimination of extensive Church functions that O'Dea cited in his work on the post-Vatican II Church, is becoming a fact in Brazil. But the process of transition, which is not easy anywhere under normal conditions, is even more difficult in Brazil because of the conflicts and tensions involved.[24] The transition is happening very quickly in Brazil – so fast that it may not even be realized by most of the hierarchy – and the options in the present situation are severely limited. There is a new influence model coming to the fore, as conflict leads to change in the relationship and in the commitment to a social mission, but in the present circumstances it is almost impossible to implement it. Its general outlines include: the promotion of socio-political change as the main organizational principle; a break locally and nationally with social and political elites; a focus on marginal groups; and a confusion concerning the instruments or mechanisms for exercising influence. The social mission is clearly the main orientation today, but the present system severely limits its implementation. Mobilization of the layman is becoming a necessity obvious to bishops and clergy, but with political repression it is almost impossible. A break from the elite and the middle classes is suggested, but any connection with the masses in viable programs and movements leads to charges of subversion. In this context of change in the Church, adoption of a new influence model, conflict and a repressive regime, the prophetic mission seems at the moment to be the basic denominator of transformation.

Adoption of the prophetic mission

A prophet is one who receives the word of God and makes clear its meaning and significance in concrete situations. A prophet is first of all a spokesman and moreover he is compelled to speak. He has no choice in the matter, as his mission from God is to carry His message and draw out its applications in the world.

[23] Interviews in 1970 indicated that the government was reviewing the tax benefits of Church affiliated institutes, schools, etc. and in some cases the taxes have already been greatly increased. For example, the taxes of the Benedictine Monastery in Salvador have increased 500% in the past three years. The Catholic University in Recife has been receiving less government money each year and the story is similar elsewhere in Brazil.

[24] For a discussion of the difficulties caused by these changes see Thomas O'Dea, *The Catholic Crisis* (Boston: Beacon Press, 1968).

Frequently prophecy assumes a political connotation, and a revolutionary one at that, as the prophets call for a break in the established order. They are not necessarily successful as insurgents and may well be persecuted without ever attaining their goals, for their mission is viewed as a threat. For Max Weber the essential criterion in defining prophecy was whether or not it called for a break with the established order; for him the prophet was the prototype of charismatic leadership. The prophet was the agent of a breakthrough to a higher cultural order, particularly at the level of religious ethics, but these ethics presupposed direct significance for all other orders as well.[25] Sectors of the Brazilian Church are assuming a prophetic mission; it is essentially revolutionary and they are persecuted for it.

By April 1968 the prophetic mission was being discussed, advocated by some and criticized by others. The letter from the 300 priests of 1967 contained an extensive section on prophecy, one part of which states, 'We believe that it is our duty today to enforce frequently our role as prophets. We must grow in our consciousness and action as prophets.' The analytical and prescriptive book by Michel Schooyans, *O Desafio da Secularização* (The Challenge of Secularization), in which he discusses problems confronting the Church and possible alternatives, continually returns to the prophetic mission and argues that the Church can and must exercise it. A group of priests has distributed several documents advocating the adopting of the prophetic mission. Some titles should illustrate their orientations: 'Prophetic Mission of the Priest in the Brazilian Social Process'. 'Importance of Recapturing the Prophetic Aspect of the Priest', 'Reflections on Propheticism', and with a different title but the same general line, 'Evangelization and Testimony'.

However, promoting the adoption of the prophetic mission has not been confined to priests alone. Dom Fragoso has for a long time been an advocate of the role, as has Dom José Maria Pires. In several of Dom Fragoso's statements are found sections such as the following:

It is dangerous to be a prophet in the world today. Yet all the people of God are prophets. Do we have the courage to assume our prophetic mission?

But in the matter of Church–state relations in Brazil, I do not think we use our prophetic role vigorously enough.[26]

In an interview shortly after the first conflict Dom Waldir pointed out the responsibility of the Brazilian Church to speak out in public, and he put this in terms of a prophetic mission. It will be noticed, however, that at this stage the mission was directed to the elites and not the masses.

The Church must always exercise the prophetic mission, and this it will do. It is to shout, speak, insist; that is, to make those who are responsible for politics...conscious of

---

[25] Talcott Parsons' *Introduction* to Max Weber, *The Sociology of Religion*, trans. Ephraim Fischoff (Boston: Beacon Press, 1963).

[26] The first is from a speech given in Belo Horizonte on 22 January 1968 and translated in the *National Catholic Reporter* of 8 January 1969. The second comes from an article on the Church and state which was printed in *Razon y Fé*, Madrid (May 1970) and reprinted in *LADOC* 1:37 (October 1970). Statement by Dom José Maria Pires in *Jornal do Brasil*, 21 July 1968.

the truth in order that they decide in favor of a stategy of indispensable transformation, which is necessary and urgent for establishing a more human and fraternal society.[27]

The 1967 statement by the Central Commission of the CNBB noted, 'The teaching mission [of bishops] also includes the aspect of prophetic announcement.' In October 1968 the Central Commission commended the members of the hierarchy for acting to promote social change in society 'as an expression of their prophetic munus [mission]'. In the Belo Horizonte conflict the initial homily touched upon it; the Archbishop discussed its applications; and even the homily of Cardinal Dom Jaime included a reference. Since then most of the public statements have included some reference to this mission. Significantly, the military have recognized the prophetic mission and do not like it. The statement prepared by the military in the Belo Horizonte conflict talks about the JOC mobilizing the masses and how it impregnates them with new leftist ideas, that are based 'on a false Christian doctrine and apply above all a prophetic attitude, including bases in Biblical messianism'.[28]

At first sight, this prophetic mission, like other issues such as mobilization of the layman and reform of the Church's structures, appeared to be discussed but not really implemented. However, upon a review of the literature of ancient Judaism and prophecy, and the statements as well as actions of large sectors through the conflict process, I find that even the Brazilian bishops, like Monsieur Jourdain in Molière's play, have been 'talking prose' for some time.[29] Certain similarities between the ancient prophets and the Brazilian Church are obvious.

The prophets held that society must be properly ordered so that the religious imperatives of God could be implemented. The same idea is behind pre-influence: the Church had to take a role in changing society, because society was so unjust and oppressive that a purely religious message was unrealistic. The Church has not retreated during the past few years from this focus on the religious within the larger social context, and in most of the public statements particular emphasis is given to social questions. For example, in one of their most moderate statements the bishops in a General Assembly noted, 'We proclaim as a requirement of the Gospel itself the imperatives of development. Our life in Faith, our participation in the mystery of Christ, the Spirit that animates us, all of these bring us to pledge ourselves to the promotion of all Brazilians.'[30] The link is made between the Gospel message, particularly as updated by Papal social encyclicals and regional (CELAM) statements, and the social situation in the country. This of course is what all the early conflicts were about. A continuing regard for the social situation,

---

[27] Interview December 1967, in *NIU* 68/01, p. 3.
[28] *SEDOC* 9 (March 1969), p. 1213.
[29] The literature on prophecy is vast. See for example, Max Weber, *Ancient Judaism*, trans. by H. H. Gerth and D. Martindale (Glencoe, Ill.: The Free Press, 1952); Abraham J. Heschel, *The Prophets* (New York: Harper and Row, 1962); Jacob Hoschander, *The Priests and Prophets* (New York: The Jewish Theological Seminary of America, 1938); R. B. Y. Scott, *The Relevance of the Prophets* (New York: MacMillan and Co., 1944); Max Weber, *Sociology of Religion.*
[30] *Correio da Manhã*, 21 July 1968.

which is not separate from religious concerns, motivates the clergy to make the statements.

Therefore, while subjectively not political partisans, the prophets were objectively acting in a political manner. The Church and its individual members have always been political agents but in an accepted context in support of the established regime. A movement away from this traditional role has led to attacks by critics claiming that the Church is 'acting politically'. The vast majority of the conflicts have involved some aspect of this question and there is really no way to resolve it. On the one hand any change in the Church, particularly if the change includes a social role, must be political simply because the institution has always been a legitimizing force for the system and because it has relied upon power to define and exercise its influence. On the other hand the priests and bishops who are most active in promoting change are the least likely to be involved in political parties. Dom Helder, for example, refused to have anything to do with the MDB or the embryonic *Frente Ampla*, but he is denounced as a political priest. There is really a dilemma here: almost anything worth doing in Brazil today can be seen in a political light and those involved will probably be denounced for betraying 'their true mission'. But this does not mean that the individuals concerned are acting for political reasons, or are even deceiving themselves, for they find their directions in their reading of the Gospel. To illustrate this it is worth quoting from a statement by Dom Fragoso.

In this respect, there is a serious test for us as priests in the prophetic vocation. We are tempted to become involved – be it sympathetically with or against radical groups – and we can easily forget that our mission is to bring together all those who make these [political] options, to reflect with them and to help them see farther and more clearly, but without ourselves becoming involved in a political group.[31]

For the prophets, religious content was more important than the forms of external manifestations. Religious and ethical behavior were identical. In many of the conflicts the government and social elite asserted their commitment to the faith and justified their actions in defense of 'our Christian traditions and Western civilization'. They are referring to the forms of Christianity, civilization and the faith, with a minimum concern for the content. Acceptance of 'Populorum Progressio' with much fanfare but no action reflects the same 'form versus content' dichotomy. As change has taken place, the clergy and bishops have often left old forms behind and adopted a mission which has more of an ethical content and few of the traditional forms. When this is recognized, they have been attacked 'for

[31] From an undated and unsigned mimeographed statement of five pages sent to me by a friend of Dom Fragoso's. I disagree with the statement in the Rand report: 'Indeed, the attractiveness of the prophetic mission is precisely that it enables Catholics to surmount the divisive impact of partisan politican participation.' Luigi Einaudi *et al.*, 'Latin American Institutional Development: The Changing Catholic Church', p. 48. In theory this is correct, but when this mission is actually acted upon those concerned are enticed by various radical political groups and attacked by conservative elements. They seem to have all the liabilities of political participation without any of the benefits.

abandoning Christian traditions while they should be the first to ensure their continuation' and external elements have been only too ready to interpret theology and give courses on Canon Law.[32] Clergy and bishops consider the state's reliance upon traditional forms, with little content, to be cynical and self-serving. As one priest observed in commenting on just this, 'our "Christian traditions" signify a Church whose principal function is to be a guardian of the museum of Western civilization'.[33]

The prophets voiced the needs of the oppressed and economically exploited masses. They were thus charged as subversives by the elite, who feared the eruption of discontent among the lower classes. In Brazil the masses have no spokesmen. Political parties are hollow shells with no connection with the bases; unions are impotent bureaucratic toys under elite control; rural unions, like all other groups that had some contact with the people, are illegal. Given the background of apathy, primitive religiosity, respect for authority and an effective police apparatus, the masses are not especially discontented and are unlikely to revolt. The Church has slowly been discovering the masses and is being attacked for it. A number of statements make the same point as did the Central Commission of 1967, when the bishops promised to pay special attention to the 'poor and humble, for whose evangelization Christ sent us'. When an individual such as Dom Helder or Dom Waldir tries to apply these precepts he is attacked as subversive, for the elite are apparently afraid of mass mobilization. This was clearly the issue in the case of the two priests in São Luís do Maranhão, Belo Horizonte and São Paulo in 1971. Most simply, as the Church discovers the poor and speaks out for them, elements in the society attack it for subversion. There has been a particular vehemence in these attacks, for an impression apparently exists that the Church possesses a great deal of prestige and influence among the lower classes. The elite seem to believe, and they may even be correct, that if the Church so desires it can mobilize the masses against the government.

In sum, the conflict process has engendered a situation in which large sections of the Church have been acting as did the prophets in Ancient Israel. Within it, however, can be distinguished individual actors and different ways of acting out the prophetic mission. A Dominican superior, well informed about the Church and politically sensitive, stated in 1970 that the prophetic mission used to be a flag (*bandeira*) but is now a fact. Precisely what is the prophetic mission? It is distinguished from a purely political role by the scope of its mission; it is oriented to the City of God and not that of man and is not affected by time as is an ideology.

There are scores of examples to show that today in Brazil bishops, clergy and laymen are acting out a prophetic mission, and in many cases suffering because of it. I do not want to enshrine any particular individual in Brazil, especially when the military might also be interested, but I will pick people who have already had problems and are therefore already known to the regime. Dom Helder is attacked

---

[32] For example of this attitude, see Carlos Studart Filho, *Temas Sociais* (Fortateza, Ce.: Imprensa Universitária, 1969).
[33] Frei Mateus Rocha, 'A Igreja e a Revolução de Abril', in *Correio da Manhã*, 17 December 1967.

mainly because he has shown great concern for the masses and has always advocated a more enlightened social policy, and on account of his national and international denunciations of torture. As Scott says of the prophets:

The prophets' quarrel with their social order was that it did not enshrine and sustain the human and social values integral to Yahweh, but on the contrary destroyed them...The foundations upon which the economic and political structure must be reared are ethical and religious – a 'rightness' of human relationships by Yahweh's standards, and the dependable 'justice' which maintains this norm in social life.[34]

Dom Waldir was tried under the National Security Act for 'subversion' because of his role in defending the masses, denouncing torture, helping laymen organize labor groups and occasionally speaking out against the government's policies. He has probably been focused upon because his diocese includes the large proletarian section around the Volta Redonda steel mill and he lives in a humble house alongside the workers. Hoschander notes that the authorities tried to stop the prophets:

In a country where moral corruption prevailed, and this was the case in both Israel and Judah where the nobles and rich were powerful and the poor were oppressed, the activity of the true prophets who publicly in the name of Jahveh condemned these social abuses was exceedingly dangerous to the ruling classes, as it might have led to civil war. The poor who constituted the overwhelming majority of the population would have been encouraged by the prophetic activity to rise against their masters and attempt to change these conditions. This was a sufficient reason for the government to look upon these prophets as demagogues and suppress their activity.[35]

The Brazilian priest imprisoned and tortured in São Luís, Pe. José Antônio Monteiro, wrote a document while in jail in which he discussed the work in the parish and talked about the educational aspect.

This [conscientização] aggravated some people, since it meant that the poor would no longer be easily manipulated for votes at election time. However, voting and elections were not topics which we discussed with our people.

Hate grew among those who preferred that the 'status quo' enslave the poor, and it became so intense that they finally denounced us to the police, saying we were communists. A local congressman took this as his 'duty', denouncing us publicly.[36]

And as Scott notes on polarization of feelings over the prophets:

They risked their reputations and their lives with utterances which searched the moral foundations of settled conditions, and of hoary taboos and practices. Their words threatened the prerogatives of those who held power, ecclesiastical, political, and economic.[37]

---

[34] Scott, p. 167. See Brady Tyson, 'Dom Helder as a Symbolic Man', reprinted in *International Documentation on the Contemporary Church (IDOC)* 22, 27 March 1971.
[35] Hoschander, p. 158.
[36] From mimeographed statement printed 15 August 1970.
[37] Scott, p. 99.

Most of those priests and laymen who have been in jail and at times are still there, who have been tortured and who have been denounced, are victimized because they were acting out the prophetic mission of denouncing injustice, teaching the masses and taking stands. The question arises, of course, as to why the prophetic mission seems to have suddenly caught on in Brazil, when it was not so significant in 1968.[38]

Initially the new idea had been promoted and discussed only since around 1967, and 1968 was simply too early for it to be adopted widely. In 1970, after three years of promotion, most people in the Church had at least been exposed to the mission, could refer to it in their statements and defenses and might even act upon it. Then, too, the literature on prophecy and evangelization has increased in the past few years and seminarians were exposed to this as they had never been in the past. Therefore the intellectual formulation of the concept of the prophetic mission merely helped individuals to realize that they were 'speaking prose' all along; now they simply possessed better intellectual tools with which to work.[39]

There is much more to this than the discovery of an idea or a concept for self-realization. Some explanation is needed of why the clergy have advocated the mission after some thousands of years in which it has lain passive and, more important, why it is being adopted. In the present case, the best explanation is found in the perceived similarity of social and political situations in present-day Brazil and ancient Israel. A review of the literature reveals that Israel experienced serious political problems, social tensions, blatant exploitation – and the largest part of the religious institution was compromised by this shameful situation. The prophets, of course, are like Moses or even Christ, and the institution is represented by the priests with the Golden Calf. In Brazil today large sectors are very much aware of the serious social and political situation and want to improve it. However, they are largely prevented from acting. The institution, taken in the broadest sense of the term to include all the features of the neo-Christendom model (schools, hospitals, internal structures, past compromises and images), which seems only to exclude personnel and ideas, is compromised by the existence of the status quo. Even if the institution were not compromised, given the strict laws and penalties against social change, the pre-1964 form of socially progressive neo-Christendom– the exercise of social change as a means of influence – is impossible. So even if the clergy merely wanted to form rural unions, sponsor basic education and undertake other such structural programs, they could not. What then are the options? Because of increasing awareness, general changes in the Universal Church and the

---

[38] I should note that a greater awareness of the mission and its significance is demonstrated by Thomas Sanders, writing in August 1968. This could be because four months made a big difference in the formulation of the mission, because Sanders is more perceptive or because his familiarity with Chile made him more attuned to nuances than I was in Brazil. Personally I feel it is due to a combination of the first and third reasons. Thomas Sanders, 'Religion and Modernization: Some Reflections', Field Letter (TGS-14) to Richard H. Nolte, Institute of Current World Affairs, New York, 4 August 1968.

[39] For an excellent formulation of the mission, which deals generally with prophecy in the Old Testament, but has unmistakable relevance to Brazil, see Carlos Mesters, *Palavra de Deus na História dos Homens* (Belo Horizonte: Livraria-Editôra 'O Lutador', 1969).

stimulus of conflict, large sectors of the Church want to play a socially progressive role. They cannot do so in the present situation through the existing structures; all that remains is the role of speaking out, of denouncing, of preaching the truth. The explanation is, therefore, the combination of the idea or concept of prophecy with a socio-political situation which seems to encourage this mission. If the society was unconstrained, if channels of social mobility were open, politics democratic and the situation of the masses improving, it is not likely that the prophetic mission would be assumed. However, this is not the case. The statements of Dons Helder, Fragoso, Waldir, etc., of priests in São Luís and São Paulo, and of the imprisoned Dominicans make it evident that the social situation is horrible and injustice seems to rule.

Because prophecy focuses on the social and political as well as the spiritual, it bears a revolutionary potential. The literature on prophecy makes this point and people in Brazil also realize the possibility. The Brazilian government seems also to recognize this potential and therefore might possibly be accurate in attacking elements in the Church as subversive. Again, the individuals and groups following the prophetic mission are not intentionally political activists, but given the nature of society and their religious message they are objectively political. Prophets have always been persecuted and Brazil provides no exception. The conflict process indicates that the levels of persecution have increased from year to year, but as in ancient times those adopting the prophetic mission have not decreased. If anything, the process of conflict seems to encourage more adherents and I would say that if the regime continues its social, political and religious policies as it has in the past few years, much of the Church will adopt the mission. If, on the other hand, the regime changes its policies, prophecy will either diminish or turn into straight-forward ethical criticism with little political content.[40]

[40] A good illustration of how this mission is formulated in experience is the case of Frei Beto (Carlos Alberto Libanio Cristo), a Dominican studying at the major seminary in Rio Grande do Sul. In order to put together his ideas on persecution and the mission of the Church he was writing a paper entitled Church and Persecution (*Igreja e Perseguição*). Before finishing the paper he left the seminary for a break, was apprehended for alleged involvement with a terrorist group and when I last heard was still in prison and had been tortured.

Conclusion

In the Introduction, I outlined three tasks to be undertaken in this book. Before dealing with the last, which concerns the political implications of current trends in the Church, it is useful to review briefly some of the findings on the other two. This work is primarily a study of change in one Latin American Catholic Church, although it has obvious implications for the other national Churches. There are several rather distinct stages which the Brazilian Church has gone through in the past few hundred years and the relevance of my analysis to the other countries seems to depend upon whether or not these stages can be recognized. It comes as no surprise that there has been change in the Brazilian Church. There has been no change in the primary goal of the Church, which is to influence man and societies to find their salvation through the direction of Christ's teachings. But in a broader and more concrete perspective considerable change is obvious. If the categories I have utilized throughout this work are briefly considered, it can be seen that the organizational principle, or the orientation of the Church to society, has changed from one of territorial coverage to a legitimization of social change through religious justification; the groups or strata focused upon are still in theory comprehensive, but in fact today particular emphasis is placed upon the poor and marginal strata; the Church–society relationship at the national level is claimed to be all-inclusive, but now it is in favor of change and at the local levels is experiencing a breaking away; the old mechanisms of the cult, sacraments and reliance upon social structures are being modified, as the Church extracts itself from total coverage and searches for other mechanisms. That is, the past mechanisms are no longer deemed sufficient and are in some cases rejected, but so far a new assortment has not been agreed upon.

What is unique about Brazil and complicates a direct comparison with other countries is the fact that little change at all took place before the second half of this century. Until 1889 the Church remained bound to an archaic pattern of influence and was, for that matter, extremely weak. Changes began in the 1890s; although the mechanisms of influence became stronger, the nature of the model returned to the archaic form during the Vargas era. A key to this regression was the restoration of the power of the state to exercise influence, so that innovation virtually came to a standstill. However, in the face of tremendous social and political threats after World War II, there was innovation and a new pattern of influence was created. The essential novelty of this model was its promotion of social change through both legitimation and programs, so that evangelization would be more realistic. This pattern still relied upon power and sought influence by two stages (pre-influence and evangelization). It closely resembled the experiments with Social Christianity in Chile and to a lesser extent in Colombia and Uruguay. The approach to influence being currently adopted by the Brazilian Church has much in common with that before 1964, although for a few years it looked as though the clergy would regress, as occurred during the Vargas era. Its outlines indicate clearly that the main thrust is for the promotion of social change; old commitments and compromises are being broken, but the details are still indistinct. The main reason for lack of clarity lies in the impossibility of implementing the new approach to influence. The statements of the Brazilian Church suggest that it has changed tremendously during the past two decades and this change affects most of the hierarchy and clergy, but since action is now impossible it is difficult to determine how far the Church would go if it were totally unrestrained. My impression, gained from interviews and close observation, is that the institution has adopted the new model although there are certain important exceptions at the elite level.

The title of this book was chosen with a purpose. It seems appropriate because the working proposition, that change comes about as the autonomy relationships are modified, seems to be accurate. The Brazilian, like other Latin American Churches, was founded on a model which provided state power for the maintenance and generation of influence and thus there was no real need to create autonomous bases of religious influence. Once this model was established, given the weak Rome – Latin America links over three centuries, the Churches relied almost exclusively on the state for orientation and support. I have studied three instances when the influence model changed as the autonomy relationships were modified: 1889, which began a period of innovation; 1934, which saw a return to the previous model; and the 1950s, when the CNBB established new relationships and created a social change orientation towards influence. Goals and implementation of influence are determined by the Church, in interaction with the state and the Holy See. In terms of social concerns, as compared with 'purely religious' ones, the state's relationship is the more important. The approach to influence changed with the relationships; in the case studies of four dioceses it was seen that the crucial problem of change today lies precisely in changing the relationship even more. Because of the six-year period of conflict, the relationship with the state is changing and a change in the influence model follows from this. There are problems today, however, as the changed relationship presupposes a cut in state resources for the Church and the Church's goals are now considered subversive. The current period for the Brazilian Church is indeed one of crisis, because it is confronting the crucial dimension of change, which is political, while all along it has relied upon and sought this political dimension. Today the Church must make a choice between, on the one hand, power and the subsequent neglect of the new approach to influence, and, on the other, adherence to the new goals and no power, which also means, in the Church's view, no influence.

At least since Weber one of the main interests in the study of religion has been its role in promoting or discouraging socio-political change. Most recently a number of sociologists interested in religious institutions and beliefs have formulated a concept which concerns the 'transformative capacity' of religion. Included in this group are individuals like Ivan Vallier, Robert Bellah and S. N. Eisenstadt. They examine questions of autonomy, conflict and new principles of legitimation, whereby society is changed through pluralism, structural differentiation, autonomous legitimation and so forth. The literature referred to in the Introduction suggests that Brazil has institutionally been a very stable country and the present regime is committed to maintaining the social and political (though not economic) status quo, which highlights the significance of change in the Church. Insofar as the above-mentioned sociologists are accurate in their analysis of the role of religions in socio-political change, the present experience in Brazil promises interesting and important lessons. However, the situation is developed further by the fact that the heat of conflict, persecution, the adoption of new social goals and general awareness have caused many in the Church to adopt the prophetic mission. All those who have studied prophecy, or prophetic movements since Ancient Israel point out that it involves a revolutionary orientation and activity. Weber used the prophets as a prototype of charismatic leadership and stated that they were agents of breakthrough. Dawson traces a link between prophetic movements and revolutionary movements throughout history. O'Dea states that the prophetic function is often a source of social protest against established forms and conditions. That is, not only is the Church changing so as to be able to act in a 'transformative capacity' but it is also assuming a function that can only be termed revolutionary.

Adoption of a revolutionary mission, however, does not necessarily mean that a revolution can be expected momentarily, as there is more involved. The government is obviously so strong economically and militarily that it could not only halt revolutionary movements but also discourages their inception. The lower classes in Brazil are renowned for their passivity and apathy and a first stage must be their mobilization through education along the lines of *conscientização*. There are international considerations as well, and it goes without saying that the Catholic Church is primarily concerned with the spiritual, and with the social and political spheres only as they relate to the spiritual. However, the types of changes taking place in the Brazilian Church suggest that it will force significant modifications in society and there is no guarantee that they will be nonviolent.

As change occurs in the Church the institution is rapidly diminishing in size. It has traditionally included not only personnel but all the schools, hospitals, structures at the local level and commitments at the national level, which involved the institution with all the other sections and interests in society. Through conflict and the policies of government, and to a certain degree by the express intent of some Church elites, the institution is being forced down into a sort of core. Quite possibly, as it diminishes in size and abandons its old compromises and images, the layman may become a part of the Church. Institutional disintegration is the *sine qua non* of lay participation in the Brazilian Church. And, while all the data indicate that the Church has lacked and still lacks much religious influence, the return to a small group of conscious and mobilized individuals might just create the conditions for a higher level of religious influence: a breakthrough at the level of religious ethics. It is clear now that religious influence, in the old sense of mass attendance and 94% of the population declared in the faith, is no longer relevant and new means of understanding and evaluation are being adopted. It seems broadly accepted today in Brazil that for the Church to 'save' anyone, it must help them find social and political liberation.

The crucial question today, as always, in relation to the direction and nature of Church change and the continuation of the prophetic mission is political. Will the regime continue, as it has for the past several years, with repression and persecution and will the Church continue to confront it? Or will the regime change, and even if it does not, will the Church accommodate itself? The process of conflict is critical to further change at this point and if either the regime relents or the bishops back down this change will assume a different orientation. It is clear that most of the bishops, as represented by men like Dom Eugênio Sales, want to cooperate. They are still inspired by images from the past and want state power for religious influence. On the other hand, after seven years of conflict a sizeable proportion of the bishops, most of the clergy and what mobilized laity exists (excluding the rightist groups) are aware and pushing the Church ahead. The political dimension is critically important. On it depends the continuation of the conflict process, the availability of power for the definition of influence and the resources that might serve to co-opt the Church. In Brazil Church transformation comes about through political forces and the nature of influence is determined by the availability of power. Given the opposition of the state and the absence of power, the Brazilian Church may well become revolutionary.

Appendix

TABLE 6   *Increase in ecclesiastical units in Brazil in relation to population*

Period	Number of units	Population	Population unit
1600	2	30,000	15,000
1655	3	57,000	19,000
1700	4	557,000	139,250
1750	9	1,400,000	155,555
1800	9	3,400,000	377,777
1825	9	4,600,000	511,111
1850	10	7,063,000	706,300
1875	12	10,717,523	893,127
1900	17	17,218,556	1,018,738
1910	30	23,151,669	771,722
1920	58	30,635,605	528,200
1930	88	37,625,436	427,562
1940	100	41,114,000	411,140
1950	113	51,976,000	459,965
1960	145	70,799,000	488,269
1964	178	78,319,500	439,997
1967	190[a]	86,616,800	458,094

[a] Composed of 31 archdioceses, 118 dioceses, 40 prelatures and 1 abadia 'nullius'.

Source: Winfredo Plagge, *A Igreja no Brasil* (CERIS, 1965), 108 until 1964; *PMV*, 33 for 1967.

TABLE 7   *Founding of secular and religious seminaries*

Period	Secular major	Secular minor	Religious major	Religious minor
1890	8	11	1	2
1900	10	13	2	4
1910	10	18	6	5
1920	12	24	8	6
1930	15	32	15	17
1940	15	40	33	44
1950	15	52	50	66
1960	15	72	67	123
1961	15	76	70	126

Source: Gustavo Pérez *et al.*, *O Problema Sacerdotal no Brasil* (Rio de Janeiro: CERIS, 1965), 174–94.

TABLE 8   *Profession, occupation and status of seminarians' fathers in Brazil, 1960*

	Salaried		Independent		No response		Total	
	No.	%	No.	%	No.	%	No.	%
Liberal profession	74	10.5	69	4.3	5	0.7	148	4.9
Executives	19	2.7	58	3.6	4	0.6	81	2.7
Public and private employees	186	26.5	14	0.8	1	0.1	201	6.7
Businessmen	60	8.6	279	17.2	10	1.4	349	11.7
Farmers and ranchers	62	8.8	969	59.6	19	2.8	1,050	35.0
Miners	11	1.6	2	0.1	0	0	13	0.5
Transport	23	3.2	28	1.7	0	0	51	1.7
Workers and artisans	104	14.8	113	6.9	6	0.9	223	7.4
Services	74	10.5	17	1.1	1	0.1	92	3.1
Rents or retired	79	11.2	28	1.7	70	10.7	177	5.9
Unclassified	11	1.6	48	3.0	554	82.7	613	20.4
Total	703	100.0	1,625	100.0	670	100.0	2,998	100.0

Ibid., p. 105.

TABLE 9 *Family size of Brazilian seminarians, 1960*

	1 child No.	%	2 to 3 No.	%	4 to 6 No.	%	7 to 9 No.	%	10 or more No.	%	Total No.	%
I. Secular clergy by region												
Northeast	1	0.5	6	3.0	31	15.5	44	22.0	118	59.0	200	100
West	2	0.7	19	6.3	66	21.8	70	23.2	145	48.0	302	100
South	6	1.2	37	7.6	110	22.5	132	27.0	204	41.7	489	100
Pio Brasileiro in Rome	1	1.3	4	5.3	16	21.3	19	25.4	35	46.7	75	100
Total secular	10	0.9	66	6.2	223	20.9	265	24.9	502	47.1	1,066	100
II. Regular clergy												
Total regular	13	0.7	108	5.6	352	18.2	497	25.7	962	49.8	1,932	100
Overall total	23	0.8	174	5.8	575	19.2	762	25.4	1,464	48.8	2,998	100

Ibid., p. 87.

TABLE 10 *Urban, semi-urban or rural origins of seminarians, 1960*

	City of 500,000 or more No.	%	City of 50,000 to 500,000 No.	%	City of 10,000 to 50,000 No.	%	City of less than 10,000 No.	%	Foreign No.	%	No reply No.	%	Total No.	%
I. Secular clergy by region														
Northeast	0	0	19	9.5	33	16.5	144	72.0	4	2.0	0	0	200	100
West	18	5.9	18	5.9	60	19.9	202	66.9	4	1.4	0	0	302	100
South	19	3.9	31	6.3	82	16.8	327	66.9	27	5.5	3	0.6	489	100
Pio Brasileiro in Rome	10	13.3	11	14.7	47	62.7	5	6.7	2	2.6	0	0	75	100
Total secular	47	4.4	79	7.4	222	20.8	678	63.6	37	3.5	3	0.3	1,066	100
II. Regular clergy														
Total regular	69	3.6	139	7.2	478	24.7	1,028	53.2	204	10.6	14	0.7	1,932	100
Overall total	116	3.9	218	7.2	700	23.4	1,706	56.9	241	8.1	17	0.5	2,998	100

Ibid., p. 80.

TABLE 11   *Growth of parishes by region*

Year	Total parishes in Brazil	Parishes per Geographical regions				
		North	Northeast	East	South	Central west
1933	2,441	111	393	1,103	746	88
1943	2,848	91	433	1,220	1,003	101
1953	3,378	136	528	1,356	1,241	117
1954	3,460	136	534	1,382	1,286	122
1955	3,543	139	541	1,405	1,325	133
1956	3,749	151	557	1,438	1,458	145
1957	3,805	152	569	1,444	1,489	151
1958	3,902	155	581	1,459	1,547	160
1959	3,981	156	585	1,489	1,577	174
1960	4,115	159	602	1,519	1,649	186
1961	4,201	159	614	1,542	1,692	194
1962	4,327	164	623	1,561	1,778	201
1963	4,558	175	635	1,652	1,887	219
1964	4,600	175	641	1,662	1,903	219
1965	4,764	177	674	1,706	1,975	232
1966	4,947	184	746	1,698	2,080	239

Source: CERIS, 1969.

TABLE 12   *Inhabitants per parish in Brazil.*

Year	Population (estimated)	Parishes	Inhabitants per parish
1963	76,409,000	4,555[a]	16,775
1964	78,809,000	4,597	17,144
1965	81,301,000	4,764	17,066
1966	83,890,000	4,947	16,958
1967	86,580,000	5,069	17,080
1968	89,376,000	5,289	16,898

[a] The data differ from the previous table because they were collected at a different date.

Source: CERIS, 1969.

TABLE 13 *Comparative data for parishes in other countries (late 1960s).*

Countries	Catholic population	Total population	% of Catholics per total population	Parishes	Catholics per parish
West Germany	24,786,100	56,172,000	44.12	11,734	2,112
Brazil	72,937,110	78,427,000	93.00	4,600	17,049
Spain	30,000,000	30,559,000	98.17	19,662	1,525
USA	40,000,000	187,069,000	21.38	18,000	2,222
France	38,000,000	46,209,000	82.23	38,212	994
Portugal	8,000,000	9,167,000	87.26	4,142	1,931

Source: CERIS, 1969.

TABLE 14 *Priests in Brazil: Brazilian and foreign, 1964*

Country of origin		Country of origin	
Brazil	7,263	Ireland	34
Italy	1,409	Switzerland	26
Germany	990	Lithuania	20
Holland	967	Hungary	19
Spain	562	Yugoslavia	17
USA	271	Japan	17
Poland	157	Malta	16
France	112	Lebanon	12
Belgium	89	Czechoslovakia	12
Portugal	87	Ukraine	11
Canada	63	Others	63
Austria	50	Undeclared	241

Total number of priests: 12,589
Total Brazilian priests: 7,263
Total foreign priests: 5,326

Source: CERIS, 1969.

TABLE 15   *Age of the clergy in Brazil, 1964*

Age	Priests			Brazilian		Foreign	
	Total	Sec.	Rel.	Sec.	Rel.	Sec.	Rel.
under 30	806	234	572	183	357	51	215
30–34	1,820	592	1,228	493	748	99	480
35–39	2,043	710	1,333	640	770	70	563
40–44	1,612	561	1,051	500	523	61	528
45–49	1,434	549	885	460	368	89	517
50–54	1,509	541	968	438	296	103	672
55–59	977	392	585	295	132	97	453
60–64	623	292	331	225	80	67	251
65–69	390	180	210	145	62	35	148
70–74	251	115	136	95	29	20	107
above 75	403	201	202	152	27	49	175
undeclared	721	462	259	162	83	300	176
Total	12,589	4,829	7,760	3,788	3,475	1,041	4,285

Sec. = Secular   Rel. = Religious.
Source: CERIS, 1969.

TABLE 16   *Growth in total number of nuns entering and leaving orders, 1958–68*

Year	In	Yearly rate of growth		Out	Yearly rate of departures	
		Absol.	%		Absol.	%
1958	31,111	1,513	4.86	–	–	–[a]
1959	32,624	1,486	4.55	–	–	–
1960	34,110	929	2.72	–	–	–
1961	35,039	1,565	4.46	270	7	2.59
1962	36,604	1,143	3.12	277	33	11.91
1963	37,747	1,886	4.94	310	85	27.41
1964	39,613	900	2.27	395	32	8.10
1965	40,513	758	1.87	427	82	19.20
1966	41,271	622	1.50	509	158	31.64
1967	41,893	−33	−0.07	667	197	29.53
1968	41,860			864		

[a] No information available on departures for 1958–60.
Source: CERIS, 1969.

TABLE 17   *Average number of inhabitants per priest and per nun, by geographical region, 1966*

Region	Inhabitants per priest	Inhabitants per nun
Maranhão	29,656	9,616
Bahia	15,346	6,534
Piauí	14,393	6,390
Alagoas	13,623	2,716
Paraíba	11,440	3,704
Rio Grande do Norte	11,066	4,100
Sergipe	9,480	5,220
Rio de Janeiro	9,416	3,300
Goiás	9,160	3,500
Pernambuco	8,923	2,704
Espírito Santo	7,970	4,251
Ceará	7,818	2,472
Acre	7,584	3,511
Pará	7,239	2,509
Paraná	7,120	2,178
Minas Gerais	5,772	2,163
São Paulo	5,599	1,554
Rondônia	5,588	3,245
Mato Grosso	5,572	2,262
Amapá	5,522	5,244
Guanabara	5,359	1,382
Amazonas	5,332	2,546
Rio Grande do Sul	4,150	837
Santa Catarina	4,145	963
Rorâima	2,907	1,643
Distrito Federal	2,426	650

Source: CERIS, 1969.

TABLE 18   *Selected indices of organizational life*

Education

Universities: total number, 1964	37
Secular universities	25
Catholic universities	12
Faculties: total number both independent and those linked to universities	564
Secular faculties	418
Catholic faculties	146
Total students in universities	142,386
% of students in Catholic universities	22.5%
Secondary schools: total number, 1962	7,254
Public secondary school	2,215
Total private secondary schools	5,039
Catholic secondary schools	2,074
Secular secondary schools	2,965
Total students in secondary schools	1,464,361
Total in public secondary schools	528,160
Total in private secondary schools	936,201
Catholic private secondary schools	230,029
Secular private secondary schools	698,972
Primary Schools: total number, 1962	105,525
Public primary schools	96,418
Total private primary schools	9,107
Catholic primary schools	2,184
Secular primary schools	6,923
Total students in primary schools	8,535,823
Total in public primary schools	7,541,794
Total in private primary schools	994,029
Catholic primary schools	413,963
Secular primary schools	580,066

Health and welfare projects (staffed by religious) in 1963

General hospitals	865
Number of beds	62,485
Specialized hospitals	79
Number of beds	21,692
Number of patients attended in 1963	855,852
Number of Nursing Sisters	895
Auxiliary Nursing Sisters	1,118
Practical Nursing Sisters	1,247

Social works (staffed by religious) in 1965   2,334

Welfare	69
Homes (for the aged, orphanages, etc.)	1,432
Re-education projects	47
Economics and finance	313
Religious and Social	390
Social service agencies	26
Social centers	16
Undifferentiated	41

Source: CERIS, 1966.

TABLE 19 *Relative importance of minifúndios (I), of family plots (II), of medium size plots (III) and of latifúndios (IV), by state and territory, 1950 and 1960*

	Proportion of establishments								Proportion of land							
	I		II		III		IV		I		II		III		IV	
	1950	1960	1950	1960	1950	1960	1950	1960	1950	1960	1950	1960	1950	1960	1950	1960
Amazonas	41	65	31	28	22	6	6	1	*	2	2	4	16	7	82	87
Pará	27	34	56	51	16	14	1	1	*	1	10	15	22	32	68	52
Estados do Norte	30	45	51	43	17	11	2	1	*	2	6	9	19	19	75	70
Maranhão	72	81	14	12	12	6	2	1	2	5	2	5	35	41	61	49
Piauí	13	36	38	34	45	28	4	2	*	1	4	6	43	51	53	42
Ceará	12	16	48	51	38	32	2	1	*	*	9	11	58	57	33	32
Rio Grande do Norte	20	27	29	31	41	35	10	7	*	1	3	4	25	26	72	69
Paraíba	32	45	35	31	28	21	5	3	2	3	7	8	31	33	60	56
Pernambuco	55	64	27	22	15	12	3	2	5	6	9	9	30	30	56	55
Alagoas	55	51	17	18	23	26	5	5	4	4	4	4	23	24	69	68
Estados do Nordeste	44	55	29	25	24	18	3	2	1	2	5	8	40	43	54	47
Sergipe	53	59	38	33	7	6	2	2	4	5	23	24	26	24	47	47
Bahia	27	34	32	30	39	35	2	1	1	2	6	7	49	55	44	36
Minas Gerais	10	14	25	29	52	47	13	10	*	*	2	3	27	29	71	68
Espírito Santo	2	4	21	25	73	68	4	3	*	*	4	6	67	67	29	27
Rio de Janeiro	21	24	33	37	38	33	8	6	1	1	5	8	31	35	63	56
(Guanabara)[a]	62	65	20	20	17	15	1	*	14	17	17	20	41	41	28	22
Estados do Leste	20	26	29	30	44	39	7	5	1	1	4	5	34	38	61	56
São Paulo	15	27	33	36	45	32	7	5	1	2	4	6	31	30	64	62
Paraná	7	18	29	40	58	39	6	3	*	2	4	11	38	44	58	43
Santa Catarina	9	17	73	70	15	11	3	2	*	1	30	36	25	25	45	38

Rio Grande do Sul	6	11	75	75	18	14	1	*	1	*	20	23	54	52	26	24
Estados do Sul	9	18	56	55	31	25	4	2	1	*	14	17	40	40	46	42
Mato Grosso	9	28	30	43	45	21	17	7	*	*	1	2	15	18	84	80
Goiás	12	14	42	49	43	35	3	2	*	*	5	9	52	56	43	35
Estados do Centro-Oeste	11	19	39	46	44	31	6	4	*	*	3	5	32	36	65	59
Acre	23	21	35	50	21	16	21	13	*	*	*	*	1	1	99	99
Rio Branco	8	15	1	14	58	42	33	29	*	*	*	*	22	18	78	82
Amapá	2	19	6	28	48	42	44	11	*	*	*	*	14	8	86	91
Rondônia	22	11	26	54	41	33	11	2	*	*	*	*	7	17	93	78
Territórios	18	18	25	43	33	26	24	13	*	1	*	5	4	2	96	98
Brasil	23	32	38	38	34	27	5	3	1	1	6	8	35	38	58	53

Source: Censo Agrícola de 1950 e Censo Agrícola Preliminar de 1960.
a City of Rio de Janeiro. * Less than 0.5%.
Source: CIDA Study, p. 96.

Selected bibliography

Books

Abbott, Walter M., SJ., and Gallagher, Msgr. Joseph, eds. *The Documents of Vatican II.* New York: Guild Press, 1966.

Alonso, P.A., SJ. *Universidades Católicas a Serviço do Desenvolvimento.* Rio de Janeiro: AEC, 1963.

Amorim, Carlos. *A Influência do Clero na Constituição de 1934.* Rio de Janeiro: Editôra Moderna, 1935.

Amoroso Lima, Alceu. *Indicações Políticas: Da Revolução à Constituição.* Rio de Janeiro: Civilização Brasileira, 1936.

João XXIII. Rio de Janeiro: Livraria José Olympio Editôra, 1966.

O Bom Combate. Belo Horizonte: Imprensa Official, 1929.

O Cardeal Leme: Um Depoimento. Rio de Janeiro: Livraria José Olympio Editôra, 1943.

Pela Cristianização da Idade Nova. Rio de Janeiro: Agir, 1946.

Anderson, Charles W. *Politics and Economic Change in Latin America.* New York: Van Nostrand Reinhold Co., 1967.

Andrade, Juracy. *A Igreja na Cidade.* Rio de Janeiro: Tempo Brasileiro, 1965.

Antoine, Charles. *L'Eglise et le Pouvoir au Brésil.* Paris: Desclée de Brouwer, 1971.

Audrin, Frei José M., O.P. *Os Sertanejos que Eu Conheci.* Rio de Janeiro: Livraria José Olympio Editôra, 1963.

Baer, Werner. *Industrialization and Economic Development in Brazil.* Homewood, Ill.: Richard D. Irwin, Inc., 1965.

Barbosa, Pe. Manoel. *A Igreja no Brasil.* Rio de Janeiro: Editôra e Obras Gráficas A Noite, 1945.

Barbosa, Rui. *Obras Completas de Rui Barbosa.* Volume 17. Rio de Janeiro: Ministério de Educação e Saúde, 1946.

Barnard, Chester. *The Functions of the Executive.* Cambridge: Harvard University Press, 1938.

Beaulieu, G., Charbonneau, P. E., and Martins, L. Arrobas. *Educação Brasileira e Colégios de Padres.* São Paulo: Editôra Herder, 1966.

Becker, Dom João. *A Religião e a Pátria em Face das Ideologias Modernas.* Pôrto Alegre: Typographia do Centro, 1939.

Bendix, Reinhard. *Nation-Building and Citizenship.* New York: John Wiley and Sons, 1964.

Blau, Peter, and Scott, Richard. *Formal Organizations.* San Francisco: Chandler Publishing Co., 1962.

Bosworth, William. *Catholicism and Crisis in Modern France.* Princeton: Princeton University Press, 1962.

Boxer, C. R. *The Golden Age of Brazil: 1695–1750.* Berkeley: University of California Press, 1964.

Buarque de Hollanda, Sérgio. *Raízes do Brasil.* Rio de Janeiro: Livraria José Olympio Editôra, 1936.

Callado, Antonio. *Tempo de Arraes: Padres e Comunistas na Revolução Sem Violência.* Rio de Janeiro: José Alvaro Editôra, 1965.

Callahan, Daniel. *The Mind of the Catholic Layman.* New York: Scribner's, 1963.

Câmara, Dom Helder, *et al. Novas Estruturas na Igreja.* Lisbon: Livraria Morais Editôra, 1966.
Revolução Dentro da Paz. Rio de Janeiro: Editôra Sabiá, 1968.
Camargo, Procópio. *O Movimento de Natal.* Brussels: Centre de Documentation sur L'Action des Eglises dans le Monde, 1966.
Camilo de Oliveira Tôrres, João. *Estratificação Social no Brasil.* São Paulo: Difusão Européia do Livro, 1965.
História das Idéias Religiosas no Brasil. São Paulo: Editorial Grijalbo, 1968.
Caramuru de Barros, Pe. Raimundo. *Bens Temporais numa Igreja Pobre.* Petrópolis, R.J.: Editôra Vozes, 1968.
Brasil: Uma Igreja em Renovação. Petrópolis, R.J.: Editôra Vozes, 1967.
Comunidade Eclesial de Base: Uma Opção Pastoral Decisiva. Petrópolis, R.J.: Editôra Vozes, 1967.
Carneiro, J. Fernando. *Catolicismo, Revolução e Reação.* Rio de Janeiro: Livraria Agir Editôra, 1947.
Centro de Estatística Religiosa e Investigações Socias (CERIS). *Anuário Católico do Brasil. III Edition.* Rio de Janeiro: CERIS, 1965.
César, Waldo A. *et al. Protestantismo e Imperialismo na América Latina.* Petrópolis, R.J.: Editôra Vozes, 1968.
Coleman, William J. *The First Apostolic Delegation in Rio de Janeiro and its Influence in Spanish America.* Washington, D.C.: The Catholic University of America Press, 1950.
Congar, Yves, O.P. *Lay People in the Church.* Translated by Donald Attwater. Rev. ed. Westminster, Md.: The Newman Press, 1965.
Priest and Layman. Translated by P. J. Hepburne-Scott. London: Darton, Longman and Todd, 1967.
Conselho Episcopal Latino Americano (CELAM). *A Igreja na Atual Transformação da América Latina à Luz do Concílio: Conclusões de Medellín.* Petrópolis, R.J.: Editôra Vozes, 1969.
Correia de Andrade, Manoel. *A Terra e o Homem no Nordeste.* São Paulo: Editôra Brasiliense, 1963.
Coser, Lewis. *The Functions of Social Conflict.* New York: The Free Press of Glencoe, 1956.
Costa, Esdras B. *Religião e Desenvolvimento Económico no Nordeste do Brasil.* Brussels: Centre de Documentation sur l'Action des Eglises dans le Monde, 1966.
Cross, Robert. *The Emergence of Liberal Catholicism in America.* Cambridge: Harvard University Press, 1958.
Crozier, Michel. *The Bureaucratic Phenomenon.* Chicago: University of Chicago Press, 1963.
Cruz Costa, João. *A History of Ideas in Brazil.* Translated by Suzette Macedo. Berkeley: University of California Press, 1964.
da Cruz, Mariano. *Vinte Anos a Serviço da Educação.* Rio de Janeiro: AEC, 1966.
Dahrendorf, Ralf. *Class and Class Conflict in Industrial Society.* Stanford: Stanford University Press, 1959.
Dale, Frei Romeu, O.P. *et al. Pastoral do Conjunto.* Petrópolis, R.J.: Editôra Vozes, 1968.
Davenport, Frances, ed. *European Treaties Bearing on the History of the United States and its Dependencies to 1648.* Washington, D.C.: The Carnegie Institution, 1917.
Dawson, Christopher. *Religion and Culture.* New York: Meridian Books, 1959.
de Azevedo, Thales. *O Catolicismo no Brasil.* Rio de Janeiro: Government of Brasil, Ministério de Educação e Cultura, 1955.

de Broucker, José. *Dom Helder Câmara: The Violence of a Peacemaker.* Translated by Herma Briffault. Maryknoll, N.Y.: Orbis Press, 1970.

de Carnaxide, Visconde. *O Brasil na Administração Pombalina.* São Paulo: Companhia Editôra Nacional, 1940.

de Kadt, Emanuel. *Catholic Radicals in Brazil.* London: Oxford University Press, 1970.

Deelen, Godofredo J., SS.C.C. *A Sociologia a Serviço da Pastoral.* Volumes 4 and 5. Petrópolis, R.J.: Editôra Vozes, 1966.

della Cava, Ralph. *Miracle at Joaseiro.* New York: Columbia University Press, 1970.

de Macedo Costa, Dom Antônio. *A Questão Religiosa do Brasil Perante a Santa Sé.* Lisbon: Llemant Frères, 1886.

de Magalhães, Basílio. *Estudos de História do Brasil.* Rio de Janeiro: Companhia Editôra Nacional, 1940.

de Oliveira, Dom Oscar. *Os Dízimos Eclesiásticos do Brasil: Nos Períodos da Colônia e do Império.* Belo Horizonte: Universidade de Minas Gerais, 1964.

de Oliveira, Dom Vital Maria Gonçalves. *O Bispo de Olinda e os seos accusadores no Tribunal do Bom Sento.* Recife: Typographica Classica de J.F. dos Santos, 1873.

de Oliveira Vianna, Francisco. *Instituições Políticas Brasileiras.* Rio de Janeiro: Livraria José Olympio Editôra, 1955.

O Idealismo da Constituição. São Paulo: Companhia Editôra Nacional, 1939.

O Ocaso do Império. Rio de Janeiro: Livraria José Olympio Editôra, 1959.

Populações Meridionais do Brasil. Volumes 1 and 2. Rio de Janeiro: Livraria José Olympio Editôra, 1938.

Deschand, Pe. Desiderio. *A Situação Actual da Religião no Brasil.* Rio de Janeiro: H. Garnier, 1910.

de Tarso, Paulo. *Os Cristãos e a Revolução Social.* Rio de Janeiro: Zahar Editôras, 1963.

Dornas Filho, João. *O Padroado e a Igreja Brasileira.* Rio de Janeiro: Companhia Editôra Nacional, 1937.

Duarte, Nestor. *Ordem Privada e a Organização Política Nacional.* São Paulo: Companhia Editôra Nacional, 1966.

Eisenstadt, S. N., ed. *The Protestant Ethic and Modernization.* New York: Basic Books, 1968.

Faoro, Raymundo. *Os Donos do Poder.* Rio de Janeiro: Editôra Globo, 1958.

Fernandes, Florestan. *Educação e Sociedade no Bras l.* São Paulo: Dominus Editôra, 1966.

Ferrari, Alceu. *Igreja e Desenvolvimento: O Movimento de Natal.* Natal, R.N.: Fundação José Augusto, 1968.

Florêncio da Silveira Camargo, Msgr. Paulo. *História Eclesiástica do Brasil.* Petrópolis, R.J.: Editôra Vozes, 1955.

Fragoso Batista, Estanislau. *A Revolução de um Padre.* Salvador: Editôra Mensageiro da Fé, 1966.

Freire, Paulo. *Educação Como Prática da Liberdade.* Rio de Janeiro: Paz e Terra, 1967.

Freyre, Gilberto. *The Masters and the Slaves.* Translated by Samuel Putnam. New York: Knopf and Co., 1946.

Nação e Exército. Rio de Janeiro: Livraria José Olympio Editôra, 1949.

Furtado, Celso. *Diagnosis of the Brazilian Crisis.* Translated by Suzette Macedo. Berkeley: University of California Press, 1965.

Galilea, Segundo et al. *Pastoral de Grandes Cidades.* Petrópolis, R.J.: Editôra Vozes, 1967.

Gentil, Alcides. *As Idéias do Presidente Getúlio Vargas.* Rio de Janeiro: Livraria José Olympio Editôra, 1939.

Gomes de Souza, Luís Alberto, ed. *Cristianismo Hoje*. Rio de Janeiro: Editôra Universitária, 1962.

O Cristão e o Mundo. Petrópolis, R.J.: Editôra Vozes, 1966.

Govêrno do Brazil. *II Encontro dos Bispos do Nordeste*. Rio de Janeiro: Presidência da República, 1959.

II Encontro dos Bispos do Nordeste. Convênios. Rio de Janeiro: Ministério da Agricultura, 1960.

Resultados dos Encontros dos Bispos do Nordeste. Rio de Janeiro: Ministério da Agricultura, 1962.

Gregory, Pe. Affonso, ed. *A Paróquia Ontem, Hoje e Amanhã*. Petrópolis, R.J.: Editôra Vozes, 1967.

Guerra, Pe. Aloísio. *A Igreja Está com o Povo?* Rio de Janeiro: Editôra Civilização Brasileira, 1963.

Hales, E. E. Y. *Pio Nono*. Garden City, N.Y.: Image Books, 1954.

Haring, C. H. *Empire in Brazil*. Cambridge: Harvard University Press, 1958.

Henriques, Affonso. *Ascenção e Queda de Getúlio Vargas*. Volume 1. São Paulo: Distribuidora Record (n.d.).

Heschel, Abraham J. *The Prophets*. New York: Harper and Row, 1962.

Hildebrando, Pe. *Visões e Resonâncias: Algums Aspetos Socias do Catolicismo no Brasil*. Campinas, S.P.: Typographica Livro Azul, 1917.

Hirschman, Albert O. *Journeys Toward Progress*. Garden City, N.Y.: Doubleday and Co., 1965.

Honório Rodrigues, José. *Conciliação e Reforma no Brasil*. Rio de Janeiro: Editôra Civilizaçao Brasileira, 1965.

Hoschander, Jacob. *The Priests and Prophets*. New York: The Jewish Theological Seminary of America, 1938.

Houtart, François, and Pin, Emile. *The Church and the Latin American Revolution*. New York: Sheed and Ward, 1965.

Instituto Brasileiro de Estatística. *Anuário Estatístico do Brasil—1967*. Rio de Janeiro: Fundação IBGE, 1967.

James, Herman. *The Constitutional System of Brazil*. Washington, D.C.: The Carnegie Institution, 1923.

Josaphat, Frei Carlos. *Evangelho e Revolução Social*. São Paulo: Livraria Duas Cidades, 1963.

Kalverkamp, Frei Desidério, O.F.M., and Kloppenburg, Frei Boaventura, O.F.M. *Ação Pastoral Perante o Espiritismo*. Petrópolis, R.J.: Editôra Vozes, 1961.

Katz, Daniel, and Kahn, Robert. *The Social Psychology of Organizations*. New York: John Wiley and Sons, 1966.

Kennedy, John J. *Catholicism, Nationalism and Democracy in Argentina*. South Bend, Indiana: University of Notre Dame Press, 1958.

Kiemen, Mathias C., O.F.M. *The Indian Policy of Portugal in the Amazon Region 1614–1693*. Washington, D.C.: The Catholic University of America Press, 1954.

Kloppenburg, Frei Boaventura, O.F.M., and Baraúna, Frei Guilherme, O.F.M. *As Grandes Tensões na Igreja Pós-Conciliar*. Petrópolis, R.J.: Editôra Vozes, 1956.

Leers, Frei Bernardino, O.F.M. *Religiosidade Rural*. Petrópolis, R.J.: Editôra Vozes, 1967.

Leite, Serafim, SJ. *Summa Histórica da Companhia de Jesus no Brasil 1549–1760*. Lisbon: Junta de Investigações do Ultramar, 1965.

Leme, Dom Sebastião. *Carta Pastoral a Olinda*. Petrópolis, R.J.: Editôra Vozes, 1916.

Lindberg, Leon. *The Political Dynamics of European Economic Integration*. Stanford: Stanford University Press, 1963.

Lipset, Seymour Martin and Solari, Aldo. *Elites in Latin America*. London: Oxford University Press, 1967.

Lowenstein, Karl. *Brazil Under Vargas*. New York: MacMillan, 1942.

Maria, Pe. Júlio. *Apóstrophes*. Nicteroy, R. J.: Escola Typographica Salesiana, 1898.

O Catolicismo no Brasil. Rio de Janeiro: Livraria Agir Editôra, 1950.

Marins, Pe. José. *Cravinhos*. Petrópolis, R.J.: Editôra Vozes, 1965.

Presbítero Hoje. São Paulo: Editôra Ave Maria, 1966.

São Paulo de Potengi. Petrópolis, R.J. Editôra Vozes, 1965.

Mayer, Dom Antônio de Castro *et al*. *Reforma Agrária: Questão de Consciência*. São Paulo: Editôra Vera Cruz, 1961.

McKenzie, John L. *The Roman Catholic Church*. Garden City, N.Y.: Doubleday, 1969.

Mecham, J. Lloyd. *Church and State in Latin America*. Rev. ed. Chapel Hill, N.C.: University of North Carolina Press, 1966.

Melo, Father Antonio. *The Coming Revolution in Brazil*. Translated and introduction by Robert Menzel. Jericho, N.Y.: Exposition Press, 1970.

Mendes, Cândido. *Memento dos Vivos: A Esquerda Católica no Brasil*. Rio de Janeiro: Tempo Brasileiro, 1966.

Metz, René. *What is Canon Law?* Translated by Michael Derrick. New York: Hawthorne Books, 1960.

Moberg, David. *The Church as a Social Institution*. Englewood Cliffs, N.J.: Prentice Hall, 1962.

Moreira Alves, Márcio. *O Cristo do Povo*. Rio de Janeiro: Editôra Sabiá, 1968.

Mutchler, David. *The Church as a Political Factor in Latin America: With Particular Reference to Colombia and Chile*. New York: Praeger, 1971.

Nabuco, Joaquim. *Um Estadista do Império: Nabuco de Araujo*. Volume 1 and 2. São Paulo: Editôra Nacional, 1936.

Nonato Pinheiro, Pe. R. *Dom João da Mata*. Petrópolis, R.J.: Editôra Vozes, 1956.

Noronha, Dom Marcos. *A Igreja que Nasce Hoje*. Petrópolis, R.J.: Editôra Vozes, 1970.

Nunes Leal, Victor, *Coronelismo, Enxada e Voto*. Rio de Janeiro: (n.p.), 1948.

O'Neil, Sister M. Ancilla. *Tristão de Athayde and the Catholic Social Movement in Brazil*. Washington, D.C.: The Catholic University of America Press, 1939.

Pan American Union. *Posse e Uso da Terra e Desenvolvimento Sócio-Econômico do Setor Agrícola: Brasil*. Washington, D.C.: Comitê Inter-americano de Desenvolvimento Agrícola, 1966.

Pérez, Gustavo, Gregory, Affonso, and Lepargneur, François. *O Problema Sacerdotal no Brasil*. Rio de Janeiro: CERIS, 1965.

Pin, Emile, SJ. *Elementos Para Uma Sociologia do Catolicismo Latino-Americano*. Translated by Rose Marie Muraro. Petrópolis, R.J.: Editôra Vozes, 1966.

Plagge, Winfredo. *A Igreja no Brasil*. Rio de Janeiro: CERIS, 1965.

Poggi, Gianfranco. *Catholic Action in Italy. The Sociology of a Sponsored Organization*. Stanford: Stanford University Press, 1967.

Prado, Caio, Jr. *The Colonial Background of Modern Brazil*. Translated by Suzette Macedo. Berkeley: University of California Press, 1967.

Prado, Paulo. *Retrato do Brasil*. São Paulo: Editôra Brasiliense, 1944.

Regina do Santo Rosário, Irmã Maria, O.C.D. (Laurita Pessôa Raja Gabaglia.) *O Cardeal Leme*. (*1882-1942*). Rio de Janeiro: Livraria José Olympio Editôra, 1962.

Rodrigues, Leôncio. *Conflito Industrial e Sindicalismo no Brasil*. São Paulo: Difusão Européia do Livro, 1966.

Rubens Brandão Lopes, Juarez. *Crise do Brasil Arcaico*. São Paulo: Difusão Européia do Livro, 1967.

Desenvolvimento e Mundança Social. São Paulo: Companhia Editôra Nacional, 1968.

Sociedade Industrial no Brasil. São Paulo: Difusão Européia do Livro, 1964.

Saldanha Marinho, Joaquim (Ganganelli). *O Brazil Mystificado na Questão Religiosa.* Rio de Janeiro: Typographica da Reforma, 1875.

Schneider, Ronald. *The Political System of Brazil.* New York: Columbia University 1971.

Schooyans, Michel. *O Comunismo e o Futuro da Igreja no Brasil.* São Paulo: Editôra Herder, 1963.

O Desafio da Secularização. São Paulo: Editôra Herder, 1968.

Scott, R. B. Y. *The Relevance of the Prophets.* New York: MacMillan Co., 1944.

Selznick, Phillip. *Leadership in Administration.* Evanston, Ill.: Rowe, Peterson and Co., 1957.

Shaull, Richard. *As Transformações Profundas à Luz de uma Teologia Evangélica.* Petrópolis, R.J.: Editôra Vozes, 1966.

Shiels, W. Eugene, SJ. *King and Church: The Rise and Fall of the Patronato Real.* Chicago: Loyola University Press, 1961.

Silvert, Kalman H., ed. *Churches and States: The Religious Institution and Modernization.* New York: American Universities Field Staff, Inc., 1967.

Skidmore, Thomas, *Politics in Brazil, 1930–1964.* New York: Oxford University Press, 1967.

Smith, Donald Eugene. *Religion and Political Development.* Boston: Little, Brown and Company, 1970.

Spencer Maciel de Barros, Roque. *A Illustração Brasileira e a Idéia de Universidade.* São Paulo: Universidade de São Paulo, 1959.

ed. *Diretrizes e Bases da Educação Nacional.* São Paulo: Livraria Pioneira Editôra, 1960.

Tavard, George H. *The Church Tomorrow.* New York: Herder and Herder, 1965.

Telfer, W. *The Office of a Bishop.* London: Darton, Longman and Todd, 1962.

Texeira de Souza, Aníbal. *Os Bispos do Nordeste e As Migrações Internas.* Rio de Janeiro: Instituto Nacional de Imigração e Colonização, 1961.

Thompson, James, ed. *Approaches to Organizational Design.* Pittsburgh: University of Pittsburgh Press, 1966.

Organizations in Action. New York: McGraw Hill, 1967.

Thornton, Sister Mary Crescentia. *The Church and Freemasonry in Brazil 1872–1875: A Study in Regalism.* Washington, D.C.: The Catholic University of America Press, 1948.

Troeltsch, Ernst. *The Social Teaching of the Christian Churches.* Translated by Olive Wyon. 2 volumes. New York: Harper Torchbooks, 1931, repr. 1960.

Turner, Frederick. *Catholicism and Political Development in Latin America.* Chapel Hill, N.C.: University of North Carolina Press, 1971.

Vallier, Ivan. *Catholicism, Social Control and Modernization in Latin America.* Englewood Cliffs, N.J.: Prentice Hall, 1970.

Veliz, Claudio, ed. *Obstacles to Change in Latin America.* London: Oxford University Press, 1965.

von Pastor, Ludwig Freiherr. *The History of the Popes.* Translated by E. F. Peeler. Volume 7. St. Louis, Mo.: Herder and Herder, 1898, repr. 1953.

von Ranke, Leopold. *The History of the Popes During the Last Four Centuries.* Translated by George R. Dennis. London: G. Bell and Sons, Ltd., 1913.

Weber, Max. *Ancient Judaism.* Translated by H. H. Gerth and D. Martindale. Glencoe, Ill.: The Free Press, 1952.

Weber, Max. *On Charisma and Institution Building*. Edited and with an introduction by S. N. Eisenstadt. Chicago: University of Chicago Press, 1968.
  Sociology of Religion. Translated by Ephraim Fischoff and with an introduction by Talcott Parsons. New York: Beacon Press, 1963.
  The Protestant Ethic and the Spirit of Capitalism. Translated by Talcott Parsons. New York: Charles Scribner's Sons, 1958.
Willems, Emilio. *Followers of the New Faith*. Nashville, Tenn.: Vanderbilt University Press, 1967.
  Uma Vila Brasileira. São Paulo: Difusão Européia do Livro, 1961.
Yinger, J. Milton. *Religion in the Struggle for Power*. Durham, N.C.: Duke University Press, 1964.

Articles

'A Presença da Igreja no Brasil de Hoje'. *Paz e Terra* 6 (April 1968), 149–281.
Assman, Hugo. 'Tarefas e Limitações de uma Teologia do Desenvolvimento'. *Revista de Vozes* 62 (January 1968), 13–22.
Bastide, Roger. 'Religion and the Church in Brazil', in Smith, T. Lynn, and Marchant, A. *Brazil: Portrait of Half a Continent*. New York: Dryden Press, 1951.
Bellah, Robert. 'Religious Evolution'. *American Sociological Review* 29 (June 1964), 358–74.
Boehrer, George. 'The Church and the Overthrow of the Brazilian Monarchy.' *Hispanic American Historical Review* 48 (August 1968), 380–401.
  'The Church in the Second Reign, 1840–1889' in Keith, Henry & Edwards, S. *Conflict and Continuity in Brazilian Society*. Columbia, S.C.: University of South Carolina Press, 1969.
Bonilla, Frank. 'Brazil' in Coleman, James, ed. *Education and Political Development*. Princeton: Princeton University Press, 1965.
  'A National Ideology for Development' in Silvert, Kalman. *Expectant Peoples*. New York: Random House, 1963.
Camargo, Procópio. 'Essai Typologie du Catholicisme Brésilien'. *Social Compass* 14 (May–June 1967), 399–423.
Cardozo, Manoel. 'Azeredo Coutinho and the Intellectual Ferment of his Times' in Keith, Henry & Edwards, S. *Conflict and Continuity in Brazilian Society*. Columbia, S.C.: University of South Carolina Press, 1969.
  'The Brazilian Church and the New Left'. *Journal of Inter American Studies* 6 (July 1964), 313–23.
  'The Holy See and the Question of the Bishop-Elect of Rio, 1833–1839'. *The Americas* 10 (July 1953), 3–75.
  'The Lay Brotherhoods of Colonial Bahia'. *Catholic Historical Review* 33 (April 1947), 12–31.
Cloin, Pe. Tiago. 'The "Natal Movement" in Brazil'. *Christ to the World* 7 (1963), 117–28.
Comblin, Pe. José. 'Para Uma Tipologia do Catolicismo no Brasil'. *Revista Eclesiástica Brasileira* 28 (March 1968), 46–74.
  'Situação Histórica do Catolicismo no Brasil'. *Revista Eclesiástica Brasileira* 26 (September 1966), 574–601.
Crespo, Pe. Paulo. 'O Problema Camponês no Nordeste Brasileiro'. *Síntese* 5 (January 1963).
de Azevedo, Thales. 'Catolicismo no Brasil?' *Revista de Vozes* 63 (February 1969), 117–24.

Deelen, Pe. Godofredo. 'O Episcopado Brasileiro'. *Revista Eclesiástica Brasileira* 27 (June 1967), 310–32.
de Kadt, Emanuel. 'Paternalism and Populism: Catholicism in Latin America'. *Journal of Contemporary History* 2, No. 4 (October 1967), 89–107.
'Religion, the Church, and Social Change in Brazil' in Veliz, Claudio, ed. *The Politics of Conformity in Latin America*. London: Oxford University Press, 1967.
della Cava, Ralph, 'Brazilian Messianism and National Institutions: A Reappraisal of Canudos and Joaseiro'. *Hispanic American Historical Review* 48 (August 1968), 402–20.
Dill, William. 'The Impact of Environment on Organizational Development'. In Mailick, S., and Van Ness, E. *Concepts and Issues in Administrative Behavior*. Englewood Cliffs, N.J.: Prentice Hall, 1962.
Eisenstadt, S. N. 'Transformation of Social, Political and Cultural Orders in Modernization'. *American Sociological Review* 30 (October 1965), 659–74.
Fernandes, P. Geraldo. 'A Religião nas Constituições Republicanas do Brasil'. *Revista Eclesiástica Brasileira* 8 (December 1948), 830–58.
Hall, Clarence W. 'The Country that Saved Itself'. *Reader's Digest* (November 1964), 135–58.
Hammond, Phillip. 'Religion and the "Informing" of Culture'. *Journal for the Scientific Study of Religion* 2 (October 1963), 97–107.
Hewitt, Cynthia. 'Brazil: The Peasant Movement of Pernambuco, 1961–64' in Landsberger, Henry, ed. *Latin American Peasant Movements*. Ithaca, N.Y.: Cornell University Press, 1969.
Huntington, Samuel. 'Political Development and Political Decay'. *World Politics* 17 (1965), 386–430.
Hutchison, Bertram. 'The Patron-Dependent Relationship in Brazil: A Preliminary Examination'. *Sociologia Ruralis* 6 (1966), 3–30.
'The Social Grading of Occupations in Brazil'. *The British Journal of Sociology* (June 1957), 176–89.
Iglesias, Francisco. 'Estudo sôbre o Pensamento Reacionário (Jackson de Figueiredo)'. *Revista Brasileira de Ciências Socias* 2 (July 1962), 3–53.
Kosinski Cavalcanti, José. 'A Revolução da Juventude'. *Paz e Terra* 3 (April 1967), 83–99.
Lacombe, Americo Jacobina. 'Brasil'. In Pattee, Richard, ed. *El Catolicismo Contemporáneo en Hispano-America*. Buenos Aires: Editora Fides, 1951.
Leavitt, Harold S. 'Applied Organizational Change in Industry: Structural, Technological, and Humanistic Approaches' in James G. March, ed. *Handbook of Organizations*. Chicago: Rand McNally, 1965.
Leeds, Anthony. 'Brazilian Careers and Social Structure: An Evolutionary Model and Case History'. *American Anthropologist* 66 (December 1964), 1,321–48.
Lepargneur, Hubert. 'Lógica do Integrismo' in *Convergência* 1, No. 3 (April 1968).
Linz, Juan J. 'An Authoritarian Regime: The Case of Spain' in Allardt, Erik, and Littunen, Yrjo, eds. *Cleavages, Ideologies and Party Systems*. Helsinki: Transactions of the Westermarck Society, 1964.
Moraes, Clodomir. 'Peasant Leagues in Brazil' in Rodolfo Stavenhagen, ed. *Agrarian Problems and Peasant Movements in Latin America*. N.Y.: Garden City, Doubleday and Co., 1970
Moreira, J. Roberto. 'Sociologia Política de Lei de Diretrizes e Bases da Educação Nacional'. *Revista Brasileira de Estudos Políticos* 9 (July 1960), 177–213.
Mutchler, David. 'Adaptations of the Roman Catholic Church to Latin American Development: The Meaning of Internal Church Conflict'. *Social Research* 36, No. 2 (Summer 1969), 231–52.

'Nova Questão Religiosa?' Paz e Terra, No. 2 (September 1966), 240–88.
O'Dea, Thomas. 'The Institutionalization of Religion'. *Social Compass* 7 (1960), 61–9.
Polsby, Nelson. 'The Institutionalization of the U.S. House of Representatives'. *American Political Science Review* 62 (March 1968), 144–69.
Pompéia, Theresa Maria. 'Presença da Igreja no Desenvolvimento Nacional'. *Texto e Contexto* (September 1967), 42–53.
Ricard, Robert. 'Comparison of Evangelization in Portuguese and Spanish America'. *The Americas* 14 (April 1958), 444–54.
Rolim, Frei Francisco. 'Católicos e o Catolicismo'. *Revista Eclesiástica Brasileira* 30 (July 1970), 325–48.
'Catolicismo no Brasil'. *Limiar* 26 (April 1970), 93–154.
'En Tôrno da Religiosidade no Brasil'. *Revista Eclesiástica Brasileira* 25 (March 1965), 11–28.
'Quelques Aspects de la Pratique Dominicale au Brésil'. *Social Compass* 14 (May–June 1967), 457–68.
Rubert, Pe. Arlindo. 'Os Bispos do Brasil no Concílio Vaticano I (1864–1870), *Revista Eclesiástica Brasileira* 29 (March 1969), 103–20.
Sanders, Thomas. 'Catholicism and Development: The Catholic Left in Brazil' in Silvert, Kalman, ed. *Churches and States, The Religious Institution and Modernization*. New York: AUFS, 1967.
'The Church in Latin America'. *Foreign Affairs* 48 (January 1970), 285–300.
Selznick, Philip. 'Foundations of the Theory of Organizations'. *American Sociological Review* 13 (1948), 25–35.
'Institutional Vulnerability in Mass Society'. *American Journal of Sociology* 56 (January 1951), 320–31.
Shils, Edward. 'Charisma, Order and Status'. *American Sociological Review* (April 1965), 199–213.
Tavares Cavalcanti, Manoel. 'Relações Entre o Estado e a Igreja'. *Annães do Congresso Internacional de História da América* 6 (September 1922), entire issue.
Terreberry, Shirley. 'The Evolution of Organizational Environments'. *Administrative Science Quarterly* 12 (March 1968), 590–613.
Thompson, James, and McEwen, William. 'Organizational Goals and Environment'. *American Sociological Review* 23 (February 1958), 23–31.
Vallier, Ivan. 'Church "Development" in Latin America: A Five-Country Comparison'. *Journal of Developing Areas* 1 (July 1967), 461–76.
'Comparative Studies of Roman Catholicism: Dioceses as Strategic Units'. *Social Compass* 16 (1969), 147–84.
'Extraction, Insulation and Re-Entry: Towards a Theory of Religious Change' in Landsberger, Henry, ed. *The Church and Social Change in Latin America*. South Bend, Indiana: University of Notre Dame Press, 1970.
'Religious Elites: Differentiations and Developments in Roman Catholicism' in Lipset, Seymour Martin, and Solari, Aldo. *Elites in Latin America*. New York: Oxford University Press, 1967.
Vaz, Pe. Henrique. 'Igreja-Reflexo versus Igreja-Fonte'. *Cadernos Brasileiros* 46 (March 1968), 17–24.
Vilhena de Morães, Eugênio. 'O Patriotismo e o Clero no Brasil'. *Revista do Instituto Histórico e Geográfico Brasileiro* 99 (1926), 113–68.
Wiarda, Ieda and Wiarda, Howard. 'The Churches and Rapid Social Change: Observations on the Differences and Similarities Between Protestants and Catholics in Brazil'. *Journal of Church and State* 12, No. 1 (Winter 1970).

Willems, Emilio. 'Religious Mass Movements and Social Change in Brazil'. In Baklanoff, Eric, ed. *New Perspectives of Brazil*. Nashville, Tenn.: Vanderbilt University Press, 1966.

Unpublished material

Ação Popular. *Documento da Base*. Position paper for the organization. Goiânia, Centro de Cultura Popular. January 1963.

'A Hora de Opção'. Notícias da Igreja Universal 68/72 (January and February 1969, respectively). Special issue. São Paulo.

Bandeira, Marina. 'MEB—"Movimento de Educação de Base"'. Paper given to the Catholic Inter-American Cooperation Program (CICOP) Chicago. 23 January, 1964.

Câmara, Pe. Miguel. 'Comportamento Religioso do Nosso Povo'. Unpublished paper. Fortaleza, 1967.

Conferência Nacional dos Bispos do Brasil (CNBB). *Plano de Emergência*. Rio de Janeiro: Livraria Dom Bosco Editôra, 1962.

da Costa Souza, Mauro Roberto. 'Igreja e Desenvolvimento'. Unpublished research report No. 1.18 of PPC of CNBB. Rio de Janeiro: CERIS, 1968.

de Assis Ribeiro de Oliveira, Pedro. 'Catolicismo Popular no Brasil'. Unpublished research report No. 9. Rio de Janeiro: CERIS, 1970.

'Pesquisa sôbre o Clero—Sumário'. Unpublished research statement of CERIS. Rio de Janeiro, 1968.

Deelen, Pe. Godofredo. 'A Pessoa do Bispo nas Cartas Pastorais' and 'O Bispo e o Clero'. Chapters 3 and 4 of unpublished manuscript. Rio de Janeiro. July 1967.

'Diocese de Caravelas: Bahia'. Unpublished research report in two volumes. Rio de Janeiro: CERIS, 1966.

Donida, Pe. Domingos Armando. 'Estudo Interpretativo das Organizações Sociais Católicas da Cidade de Salvador'. Unpublished research report, prepared for Ação Misereor. Rio de Janeiro: CERIS, 1967.

Einaudi, Luigi *et al.* 'Latin American Institutional Development: The Changing Catholic Church.' Memorandum RM-6136-DOS. The Rand Corporation. Santa Monica, California. October 1969.

Engel, Otto. 'Dom Helder: O Profeta da Revolução'. Unpublished manuscript. Rio de Janeiro. 1967.

Foland, Frances M. 'Brazil: The Political Mood'. Field Letter (FMF-20) to Richard H. Nolte, Institute of Current World Affairs, New York. 9 November 1968.

'Northeast Brazil: The Archbishop of Recife and Olinda'. Field Letter (FMF-8) to Richard H. Nolte, Institute of Current World Affairs, New York. 4 October 1967.

'Northeast Brazil: Violence'. Field Letter (FMF-21) to Richard H. Nolte, Institute of Current World Affairs, New York. 14 November, 1968.

Kloppenburg, Frei Boaventura. 'Spiritism in Latin America: A Growing Threat'. Paper given to the Catholic Inter-American Cooperation Program (CICOP). Chicago. 19–21 January 1966.

MEB. 'MEB Em Cinco Anos: 1961–1966'. A report in two volumes (mimeographed). Rio de Janeiro. 1966.

'O Conjunto Didático "Viver e Lutar"'. A report (mimeographed). Rio de Janeiro. July 1964.

Mutchler, David E. 'Roman Catholicism in Brazil'. Studies in Comparative International Development. St Louis, Mo.: Washington University 1965. 1, No. 8, 104–17.

Pinto Cavalheira, Msgr. Marcelo. 'O Tipo do Padre Que a Igreja Espera após o Concílio Vaticano II". Unpublished mimeographed report. Serviço de Apostilas No. 5. Recife: CNBB NE 2. 1967.

Pro Mundi Vita. 'Brazil: The Church in Process of Renewal'. Bulletin No. 24 (1968). Brussels.

Rodrigues Villa Lobos, João Eduardo. 'Diretrizes e Bases da Educação: Ensino e Liberdade'. Unpublished thesis, University of São Paulo, 1966.

Rolim, Frei Francisco. 'Cidade de Tupi Paulista: Aspectos Sócio-Religiosos'. Unpublished research. Rio de Janeiro: SPESE, 1966.

'Estrutura da Igreja no Brasil'. Unpublished research report No. 1.2 of PPC of CNBB. Rio de Janeiro: CERIS, 1968.

et al. 'Diocese de Oeiras, Piauí'. Unpublished research. Rio de Janeiro: SPESE, 1966.

'Diocese de Santos: Levantamento Sócio-Religioso'. Unpublished research. Rio de Janeiro: SPESE, 1966.

SAGMACS. 'Paróquias do Rio de Janeiro'. Unpublished research report. Rio de Janeiro. 1958-9.

Sanders, Thomas G. 'A Typology of Catholic Elites'. Field Letter (TGS–10) to Richard H. Nolte, Institute of Current World Affairs, New York. 21 February 1968.

'The Paulo Freire Method: Literacy Training and Conscientizacion'. Field Letter TGS–12) to Richard H. Nolte, Institute of Current World Affairs, New York. 6 June 1968.

'The Regional Seminary of the Northeast'. Field Letter (TGS–3) to Richard H. Nolte, Institute of Current World Affairs, New York. 5 August 1967.

'Religion and Modernization: Some Reflections'. Field Letter (TGS–14) to Richard H. Nolte, Institute of Current World Affairs, New York. 4 August 1968.

'Institutionalizing Brazil's Conservative Revolution'. Fieldstaff Reports. AUFS, 1970.

Senna, Pe. Luís. 'Por um Pastoral no Nordeste'. Unpublished paper. Recife. 1965.

Serviço de Orientação Rural de Pernambuco (SORPE). 'Pequeno Resumo do Movimento Sindical Rural em Pernambuco'. Unpublished mimeographed bulletin. 31 May, 1966.

Shaull, Richard, 'O Desenvolvimento numa Perspectiva Teológica'. Unpublished paper. Curitiba, Paraná: Centro Ecumênico, 1965.

Studart Filho, General Carlos. 'Temas Sociais'. Fortaleza, Ceará: Imprensa Universitária, 1969.

Teixeira, Anísio. 'Brazilian Education Between 1914 and 1960'. Unpublished paper. Rio de Janeiro. 1967.

Thornton, Sister Mary Crescentia. 'The Church in the Old Republic'. Unpublished manuscript. 1968.

'Uma Nova Questão Religiosa?' Notícias da Igreja Universal 46/47, 1 and 15 February 1968, respectively. Special issue. São Paulo.

Wiarda, Howard J. 'The Brazilian Catholic Labor Movement'. University of Massachusetts, Labor Relations and Research Center, 1969.

Periodicals consulted on a regular basis

Newspapers

Estado de São Paulo, 1967–71
Correio da Manhã (Rio), 1967–9
Jornal do Brasil (Rio), 1967–71
Última Hora (Rio), 1967–8

O Globo (Rio), 1967–9
Veja (S.P.) (magazine), 1970–1
Visão (S.P.) (magazine), 1967–9

Church publications

A Ordem (Centro Dom Vital), 1922–60
Boletim Informativo of CERIS, 1966–72
Comunicado Mensal (CNBB), 1957–65
Convergência (CRB), 1967–9
Nacionais Informam (CNBB), 1966–70
Notícias da Igreja Universal (*NIU*), 1968–9
Paz e Terra, 1966–8
Revista Eclesiástica Brasileira, 1955–70
Serviço de Documentação (*SEDOC*), 1968–71
Telepax (CNBB), 1966–8

Index